Drinking Water

Principles and Practices

Drinking Water

Principles and Practices

P. J. de Moel
TU Delft, The Netherlands

J. Q. J. C. Verberk
TU Delft, The Netherlands

J. C. van Dijk
TU Delft, The Netherlands &
Kiwa Water Research, The Netherlands

 **World Scientific**

NEW JERSEY · LONDON · SINGAPORE · BEIJING · SHANGHAI · HONG KONG · TAIPEI · CHENNAI

Published by

World Scientific Publishing Co. Pte. Ltd.

5 Toh Tuck Link, Singapore 596224

USA office: 27 Warren Street, Suite 401-402, Hackensack, NJ 07601

UK office: 57 Shelton Street, Covent Garden, London WC2H 9HE

British Library Cataloguing-in-Publication Data
A catalogue record for this book is available from the British Library.

English translation and editing: Adele Sanders, Delft EdiTS
Design and layout: Eefje Ooms, Delft University of Technology

First published 2006
Reprinted 2007

DRINKING WATER
Principles and Practices

ISBN 981-256-836-0

Editor: Tjan Kwang Wei

Printed by FuIsland Offset Printing (S) Pte Ltd, Singapore

Preface

Drinking water: the miracle from the tap

For many people drinking water is something we usually do not think about and don't know much about either. We open the tap and clean and fresh drinking water pours out. We take it for granted. We know the water quality is excellent and that it is actually not necessary to buy bottled water. Nevertheless, we sometimes read in the newspaper alarming articles about the pollution of our drinking water sources. How does that happen? How do the drinking water companies actually purify our drinking water, and will they continue in the future? Similarly, there are several other questions people sometimes ask about our drinking water:

- Why do we flush our toilet with clear and costly drinking water?
- Is our water "hard" and should we believe the commercials about water softeners?
- Which elements does water actually contain?
- Is drinking water healthy?
- Can you purify water with your own filters?
- Is it safe to drink rainwater?
- How is the quality of our drinking water being safeguarded?
- Is groundwater abstraction responsible for the deterioration of national parks?
- What is the function of a water tower?
- What do the drinking water companies do in restricted areas and in national parks?

Students who follow courses in drinking water at Delft University of Technology also have these questions.

For whom is this book meant?
This book contains the course material about drinking water for students in the Bachelor of Science program (BSc) of Civil Engineering at Delft University of Technology.
In these courses the students acquire a broad view of the drinking water service. Not just the theoretical principles, but also the practical operation of drinking water companies. Not just the techniques, but also the historical background, the judicial arrangements, the financial aspects, the global situation, etc.
The course material should give all Civil Engineering students a vast and sound base, which can be used in their future profession. For students who will specialize in the Master of Science program (MSc), the course material will provide a basis for specialist courses like "Drinking water production" and "Drinking water distribution."
The course material follows a modular structure and emphasizes independent learning. That makes this course material also very suitable for many others: from students seeking a higher professional education, to people who are involved in one way or another in the drinking water service, to the drinking water consumers who would like to know more about "the miracle from the tap."

How is the book structured?
The modern student is an independent learner, meaning that time and planning are much more determined by the student himself than by the course schedule. Modern course materials are adapted to this.
This book consists of ten independent modules. All modules follow a uniform design. First, there is a page of information about the module under the headings of "Framework," "Contents," and "Study goals." Next,

the actual learning material (contents) is presented. Following that is a list of recommended literature and websites. Because of the broad character of the course material, a list of references is not included. Finally, questions and answers are presented. The questions challenge the students' recall of the material read, the applications ask students to put their understanding to use.

Courses from this book

Because of the module structure, this book can be used as teaching and learning material for different courses in drinking water supply. Each module can be used independently, but also in courses dealing with specific focus points. Examples of such courses can be given as:

Module / Course	Sanitary Engineering	Amsterdam water	Drinking water companies	Planning and design	Finances	Water consumption	Water quality	Groundwater	Surface water	Distribution
Basic short course	●	●	●							
Design			●	●	●					
Water treatment			●				●	●	●	
Water distribution			●			●				●

ir. P.J. (Peter) de Moel
dr. ir. J.Q.J.C. (Jasper) Verberk
prof. ir. J.C. (Hans) van Dijk

Delft, April 2006

Contents

Detailed contents (per module)

Public water

Sanitary engineering   11

Water companies

Amsterdam water   41

Drinking water companies   89

PUBLIC WATER

Sanitary engineering

percentage not connected and number of deceased due to typhoid

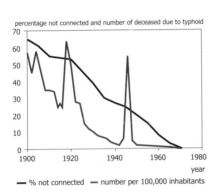

— % not connected — number per 100,000 inhabitants

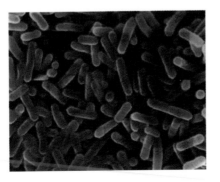

Framework

This module represents an introduction to sanitary engineering for students at the level of Bachelor of Science in Civil Engineering. Sanitary engineering comprises the infrastructural works of the "urban water cycle", namely drinking water supply, sewerage and wastewater treatment.

Contents

This module has the following contents:

1. Introduction
2. What is sanitary engineering?
   - 2.1 Why sanitary engineering?
   - 2.2 Sanitary engineering in and around the house
   - 2.3 What does a sanitary engineer do?
3. History of sanitary engineering
   - 3.1 The Romans
   - 3.2 The Middle Ages
   - 3.3 Modern infrastructure
4. Public health
5. Sanitary engineering worldwide

   Further reading
   Questions and applications
   Answers

Study goals

After having studied this module, you will be able to:
- identify which disciplines and subjects are of importance within sanitary engineering
- identify how our present sanitary systems came into being
- explain what influence sanitary engineering has had on public health
- describe and explain the differences in sanitary engineering in the world

1. Introduction

The term "sanitary engineering" does not have only one meaning. It can be defined as "technology for hygiene," under which concept a diverse number of medical techniques would fall.

However, it typically refers to civil sanitary engineering or public health engineering and is divided into three specializations:
- drinking water supply
- wastewater collection and urban drainage
- wastewater treatment

Related specializations such as waste disposal and water treatment in swimming pools can also be included in sanitary engineering.

However, in this module, we will restrict ourselves to the infrastructural works of the urban water cycle.

The term "sanitary engineering" is used throughout Anglo-Saxon countries. The word "sanitary" is a general word used for bathrooms, washbasins, toilets, etc. The term primarily refers to personal hygiene. Good personal hygiene plays an important role in the health of the general population. The significance of this role is easily seen in countries where there is no safe drinking water supply, and/or no disposal of human excrements (toilets and latrines).

Drinking water supply and sewerage are municipal services for general and public use and are provided in addition to electricity, gas, telephone and cable television.

Drinking water supply is the responsibility of drinking water companies. Quite often, these companies originated as a municipal service, which, through the years, evolved into an independent professional entity, usually with the municipality as owner or major shareholder.

In general, sewerage is the responsibility of the municipality. Their responsibility not only encompasses household sewage but also the drainage of rainwater runoff from roofs, streets and other paved urban areas. Collected wastewater can no longer be discharged before it is treated.

Wastewater treatment is the job of water quality boards, formerly part of the different water boards. The water boards in the Netherlands are primarily responsible for maintaining the water level and its quality.

A few typical characteristics of the urban water cycle are:
- large scale, specialized infrastructure
- great importance for public health and environment
- clearly formulated goals
- implemented by well-organized organizations or companies

In this module, sanitary engineering is dealt with in its entirety, with an emphasis on its historic development and related issues. In the conclusion, a general description of the worldwide differences in water development is given.

2. What is sanitary engineering?

It is obvious that knowledge about, and continuous maintenance of, good water quality for man and the environment are the most important areas of interest in this field. Because of the large-scale nature of sanitary engineering, a combination of process knowledge and hydraulics is involved.

The most important areas of knowledge for sanitary engineering are, therefore:
- water quality
- water treatment processes
- hydraulics

Specific areas of interest are water abstraction, water treatment and water transport, as well as the supporting disciplines of water-related chemistry and microbiology.

Additionally, the sanitary engineer makes use of knowledge about hydrology, structural design, computer science, project realization and management.

Sanitary engineering takes place typically within the urban or small water cycle (Figure 1), which is itself, again, part of the greater hydrological cycle.

Urban cycle in brief

Drinking water is obtained from groundwater or surface water. The water is treated and subsequently transported to the users (i.e., households and industries), by way of an extensive distribution network.

After use, the wastewater is collected, often together with the drainage water, again via an extensive sewage system. Subsequently, the wastewater is transported to the wastewater treatment plant, where it is relieved of unwanted pollutants.

After this treatment the water is discharged into open surface water, after which it finds its way back into the natural hydrologic cycle.

2.1 Why sanitary engineering?

The main reasons for building sanitary engineering works are:

- public health
- public comfort
- environmental protection

Drinking water supply

A good water supply is an essential part of human society - not only as drinking water, but especially for personal and domestic hygiene, such as bathing and washing. Good personal and domestic hygiene is a primary condition for good public health.

However, a water supply can also present a great danger as a vehicle through which contagious diseases can easily spread. Through a large-scale water supply, a large group of people come in contact with water from the same single source. Infections can, therefore, strike vast numbers of

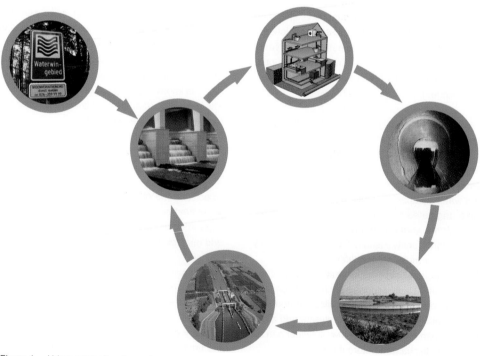

Figure 1 - Urban or small water cycle

people in a very short time. History has taught us that this danger is a real one.

The spreading of pathogenic (disease-generating) microorganisms that may cause cholera, typhoid and diarrhea constitutes the most important danger in this case.

In the case of a central water supply, also the health risks of life-long exposure to the distributed water, have to be considered. It is here, especially, that one has to take into account the weaker members of society, such as babies, sick people, and senior citizens. The major goal for a proper water supply system is to have distributed water that can be drunk safely, without the user having to use extra treatment devices, such as filters, or without having to do anything extra at all.

Sewerage
The subject of water supply cannot be dealt with separately from the wastewater problem. Water does not simply disappear after being used, but is, to a greater or lesser degree, now polluted. This polluted water has to be transported out of urban areas to avoid the accumulation of pollutants, which can then lead to disease and other problems.

It is a very attractive solution to transport human excrement alone with the polluted water. Transport of this excrement via the sewage system has a great advantage, in that no temporary storage of the excrement is necessary in the urban areas, eliminating all the dangers that such a storage would have on public hygiene. Sewerage is, therefore, important for the health of the general public.

Wastewater treatment
Polluted wastewater will eventually be transported back into the environment. In the ideal water cycle, this water would be returned to its collection point and to its original quality.
Because of its transport in the natural water cycle, it makes no sense to return the water to its point of origin. And likewise, treatment does not have to bring the water back to its original quality. In the natural water cycle, water changes its quality

anyways, and we can even speak of the "self-purifying" quality of nature. However, discharged wastewater must not put an unacceptable load on a natural system. For this reason, it is necessary that wastewater go through an intensive treatment before the water is brought back into the natural water cycle again.

2.2 Sanitary engineering in and around the house

In daily life almost everybody comes into contact with water, typically in the form of drinking water. We drink water because our body needs it to grow, and we also use it in the house to do the washing, to take a shower or bath, to flush the toilet, to prepare the food, to water the garden, etcetera. In the Netherlands, we use 130 liters of drinking water per person per day.

Besides this, we are confronted with water in the form of precipitation. The Netherlands is often depicted as a rainy country, although in a normal year an average of 125 days pass without a drop of rain having fallen. During the rest of the year there is an average of about 775 millimeters (mm) of rainfall in 570 hours. Normally, most rainfall takes

water supply
water drainage

Figure 2   - Water in and around the house

place in the summer months. In general these showers are short, but of high intensity.

The water flow that we come into contact with in the home is depicted in Figure 2. It can be seen that the input of water in the form of rain and drinking water has to be discharged in some way. For this input of drinking water and the output of wastewater and rain, an infrastructure is needed. Civil sanitary engineering deals with this infrastructure.

2.3 What does a sanitary engineer do?

The sanitary engineer occupies a unique and responsible position in the urban water cycle. He/She is the person responsible for research, design, and realization of these infrastructural systems for drinking water and wastewater. In cooperation with chemical engineers, microbiologists, ecologists, mechanical engineers, electrical engineers, architects and others, the sanitary engineer remains the classical design engineer who can translate process goals into actual buildings and installations.

The sanitary engineer has the following concrete tasks:

- research
- studies
- design
- start up
- operation
- management

These activities are executed by drinking water companies, municipalities, water quality boards, water boards and other related professionals such as consulting engineers, research organizations, contractors and equipment suppliers.

Master of Science thesis projects for Sanitary Engineering are predominantly carried out in collaboration with, and quite often at, these organizations, which typically produce interesting and informative results.

3. History of sanitary engineering

Since the beginning of time, people have established themselves at places where fresh surface water was available. Cities generally developed along rivers or in the immediate vicinity of water resources. The importance of a good drinking water supply was highly regarded, as can be seen from the statement made by Archimedes: "one should assess the city council board by means of the care they give to the drinking water supply."

In periods during which the ancient civilizations flourished (e.g., the Mesopotamians, Greeks and Romans), the population in the cities increased rapidly. When the drinking water supply became inadequate, people were compelled to transport water to the city from elsewhere, often over large distances. Also, from the moment in time that people started living in cities, they made use of sewers in order to transport rainwater and wastewater beyond the city borders.

As a result, some ingenious water systems were developed (Archimede's screw, aqueducts (Figures 3 and 4), Cloaca Maxima), which we still make use of today. These systems were based mainly on experience, and that is one reason so much went wrong. However, time and circumstances have destroyed most of the evidence of these.

Figure 3 - Roman aqueduct

Figure 4   - Pont du Gard near Nîmes (France)

Much has been written about the history of sanitary engineering, and describing it in great detail goes beyond the scope of this section. Only the water system of Rome will be explained further.

3.1   The Romans

The Romans regarded personal hygiene as very important. In the Roman cities there were many bath houses and public toilets, some provided with running water. Feces were transported by means of a sewage system (the Cloaca Maxima) to a discharge point outside the city, and the rainwater was also discharged. In order to achieve such a level of personal hygiene, the Romans elevated the building of water distribution systems to a true art form. This is all the more astonishing when recognizing that the Romans had no formal knowledge of hydrology or hydraulics.

Drinking water supply

The excavations in Herculaneum and Pompeii demonstrated that the inhabitants initially provided for their need of water by withdrawing it from streams. In addition to this, groundwater and rainwater were used. After the building of an aqueduct, the situation changed drastically and large quantities of water were made available. As early as 100 A.D., the city of Rome (roughly 1 million inhabitants) was provided with drinking water by an ingenious system of 11 large aqueducts. The water was abstracted in the mountains ten kilometers from the city of Rome and, after having passed through a sedimentation basin, flowed via gravity through an aqueduct to the city.

The Romans' water transport system ended in central flow splitters in the city (Figure 5). From this point the water flowed by gravity to different areas in the city. Besides the central distribution flow splitter, their drinking water system often had secondary flow splitters. By way of these flow split-

Figure 5   - Roman flow splitter

ters, the water was transported to private users and also public establishments, such as bathing houses and public toilets. The water was led to a distribution tower where it passed into an open basin. From there it was transported to homes by means of lead pipes. Those people who could not pay for a private connection to the water system collected their water from public fountains.

The simultaneous existence of different types of water supply was probably designed to compensate for dry periods and varying capacities of the aqueduct. What we know for sure is that the aqueduct was to be cleaned at specific times, which stopped the water supply entirely. Reservoirs that could bridge these maintenance periods were most probably not built. The city of Ostia, the harbor city of Rome that came into decline in the third century A.D., had storage basements (cisterns) that probably provided a buffer for periods of low water supply.

The rainwater that fell on roofs was collected in an "impluvium" that was located at the bottom of an atrium. From there the water was transported to a cistern. Calculations show that the collected quantities of water were enough to supply the drinking water needs of 5 to 6 people for one year. Only the houses of the rich were fitted with an "impluvium," and they usually also had a well from which groundwater was collected.

The knowledge that the Romans had about the basic design of water transport systems has been

passed on to us in the form of a book written by Sextus Julius Frontinus. Frontinus wrote the book after Caesar Nerva named him the "curator aquarium" (the director of the Roman water company) in 97 A.D. From his writings we can deduce that the Romans did not know how to calculate the flow through a pipe. They did have an understanding of the influence of the slope of a pipeline, and also that resistance played a role in that flow. However, what the relationships were, they did not know.

As a result of our better knowledge of the laws of mechanics, we now know, for example, that a pipeline can burst as a result of thrust-forces that can occur in the bend of a pipeline. If the bend is not anchored, the pipeline cannot cope with these forces. The Romans could not rationally explain why their pipelines collapsed. They assumed, therefore, that it was due to the spirits. By building an aqueduct where a lead pipeline changed directions, they assumed that the spirits disappeared out of the water through the free water surface.

A striking phenomenon in aqueduct design is that the secondary and tertiary pipelines had standardized dimensions. After the fall of the Roman Empire, it is not until about 1900 A.D. that we see a re-introduction of the standardization of pipe dimensions in Europe and the United States. The fact that the construction of aqueducts relied on experience can be seen from the well-known dimensions of the aqueducts, and height differences. Calculations show that the slope was between 5 and 33 m/km. The water velocity in the pipelines was between 0.6 and 1 m/s. If we were to build similar aqueducts today, we would derive approximately the same design with very similar results. We can now conclude that a velocity in a pipeline of 0.8 to 1.2 m/s generally leads to the most economical design.

Sewage system

Almost every house in the Roman cities had a toilet; not only on the ground floor but also on the floors above. Some houses had more than one toilet, while bigger houses sometimes had multiple toilets in one area (Figure 6). Feces were collected in cesspools. Houses that were connected to the public water system also had their toilets

Figure 6   - Roman public toilet

connected by pipes to the system. The water that was transported to the toilets also flushed out the toilets, thereby ensuring good personal hygiene. The collected feces and urine had market value. Feces were used as fertilizers, while urine was involved in the production of leather and wool.

Beneath almost every street there was a sewer that primarily served to discharge wastewater from toilets and kitchens, as well as from the overflow of "impluviums" and springs. Rainwater was discharged both above the ground, via the street, and under the ground. The transport of rainwater via the street was a highly practical and economical solution.

Often, when referring to antique sewer systems, the Cloaca Maxima is mentioned. This is a sewer, of which a section still exists, that was built in Ancient Rome in order to discharge wastewater and rainwater into the Tiber River. In technical literature, the durability of this structure is often emphasized. The Cloaca Maxima is also an indication of the Romans' knowledge and skill in the area of design and construction of large hydraulic structures.

Wastewater treatment

As far as we know, the Romans did not give much attention to the treatment of wastewater. This was considered neither important nor a necessity, unlike today. On the one hand, except for Rome, city populations were quite small. On the other hand, wastewater discharge, at least in Rome, went directly into the Tiber River. The Tiber is a large river that could probably handle the waste-

water without too many problems. From preserved manuscripts, it seems that these discharges did not produce problems.

Operation and Management

Operation of the public water supply and sewage system, as well as the sanitary facilities that were situated on public ground, was in the hands of the city council. Citizens were responsible for the operation of those facilities that were situated on private property. The operation was formidably organized.

The transport of drinking water to private homes had to be paid for. In the same way as today, payment was made according to the amount of water that was used. The Romans assumed that the amount of water that was transported to a particular house was proportional to the area of the pipe that transported it there. Sometimes the lengths of the pipes from the flow splitter to the different house sites were equal, in which case the assumption was correct, but this was not always the case, and, not surprisingly, many disputes arose. Users who lived far away from the flow splitter complained that they received less water than the people who lived close to it.

Suppose a certain pipeline is twice as long as another. A calculation made using simple hydraulic formulas shows that the discharge through the longer pipe will be approximately 30% smaller than in the case of the shorter pipeline. Using simple volumetric measurements, the person who was connected to the longest pipeline could show that he received less water than his neighbor who lived closer to the flow splitter. However, the judges assumed that one of the consumers cheated with the measurements, and, if that was not the case, they assumed that it had something to do with the gods.

Cheating was a common practice. Evidence of this can be seen in the illegally enlarged openings that were sometimes made to the lead distribution pipes so a larger diameter pipe could be connected. Caesar Agrippa put an end to these irregularities by decreeing that the lead pipes were only allowed to be connected to a bronze joint that had a precisely determined cross-section and that was hard enough that it could not be re-adjusted. The Romans, then, went to the trouble of not only standardizing the pipe diameters, but also the weight of the pipe per unit of length. These regulations applied to the whole of the Roman Empire.

An analysis of excavated pipes shows that the lead used was of a high and consistent quality. It is, however, not known whether the diameter of the sewage pipes was standardized in relation to the water volume to be discharged.

Rome was not the only Roman city that was supplied with water via an aqueduct transport system. For example, Cologne (Germany) was supplied with water by an aqueduct that had a length of 80 km (Figure 7). In Heerlen, Maastricht and Nijmegen, archeological remnants have been found of the Roman bathing culture.

The Romans built and maintained waterworks that ensured a good living and working climate in the cities. The design and construction of the aqueducts and the distribution networks were prime examples of their engineering skills, which were only matched after 1850 A.D.

3.2   The Middle Ages

After the collapse of the Roman Empire, the Roman water systems were no longer maintained and they fell into decay. The Romans' acquired specialized knowledge was also not preserved. Once again people in the cities had to rely on water from wells, surface water, and rainwater collection. Feces and garbage were dumped on the street and/or thrown in the canals, and there was a lack of personal hygiene. Refreshing the urban surface water rarely took place.

As a result of the worsened conditions, the population decreased due to the Plague, contagious diarrhea sicknesses and smallpox. In about 100 A.D. Rome had about 1 million inhabitants, but by 600 A.D. this had been reduced to about 20,000! The construction and maintenance of large water systems became impossible as a result of the many wars and the limited power of the regional government. Fragmentation of the land took place and smaller feudal areas developed. In the countryside the quality of the drinking water was not so bad. Because there were no high population concentrations, pollution of the water by feces was not serious. Sometimes, however, wells were placed too close to manure heaps and that led to contamination of the well (Figure 8).

When looking at the sources of drinking water in the Netherlands since the Middle Ages, we can distinguish three natural options:
- rainwater

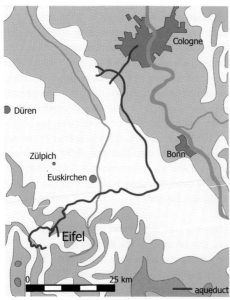

Figure 7   - Roman aqueducts from the Eifel to Cologne (Germany)

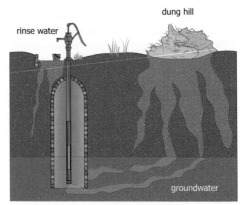

Figure 8   - Pollution of reliable groundwater by feces

- well water
- surface water

Rainwater

In areas where the groundwater was too salty or where there was peat in the ground, and in areas where there was no surface water, rainwater was used as a source of drinking water. These areas are the present provinces of Friesland and Zeeland. Rainwater from the roofs was collected in rainwater tanks. Because the needs of the people exceeded the quantity available, some municipalities built central rainwater reservoirs at churches and townhalls.

The greatest disadvantage of rainwater as a source of drinking water is that the people are dependent on the climate. In dry seasons the reserves were quickly exhausted, and the people had to resort to other water of often inferior quality.

A second disadvantage had to do with hygiene. As a result of the softness of rainwater (a quality highly appreciated for washing), it quickly becomes aggressive when it comes into contact with lead, leaching the material that was used the most in those days for gutters and pipes. Another hygiene-related disadvantage is that rainwater can easily be contaminated by excrement from birds.

Well water

In the dune areas and in the southern and eastern parts of the Netherlands, well water (i.e., groundwater) was primarily used. Originally, it was abstracted by means of open waterwheels; later closed handpumps with pistons were developed. The quality of this water was, and still is, fairly good. There were no great concentrations of inhabitants, and there was enough good quality groundwater available.

Surface water

For a long time, surface water (e.g., rivers, streams, canals) served as the people's source of drinking water in its untreated state.

As soon as the surface water became visually dirty, the people moved further upstream to collect

water. In the cities, water from canals and wells was used as drinking water. However, the quality of both water sources was not very good.

In the beginning of the 16th century, people in Amsterdam still used canal water as their drinking water. But, because the sea corridor north of Amsterdam was widening, Amsterdam's canal water became more and more salty, until it could not be drunk anymore. Inspections were not maintained and pollution from a growing city completed the contamination of the canal water.

Therefore, early in the 16th century, water was transported in water-carrying vessels from the Vecht to Amsterdam (Figure 9). As a result of the continually increasing population and the increasing water usage per person, water transport developed into a new profession, namely that of the "Verschwaterhaalders" (the "Fresh Water Fetchers"). The quality of this water was now inspected by the "Inspecteur van het Versch Water" ("Inspector of the Fresh Water").

In Europe in the Middle Ages nothing happened for quite a long time in the area of sanitary technology. From about 1600, however, theoretical knowledge of fluid mechanics and hydrology started to accelerate. Around 1700 the Industrial Revolution took place in England and France. Many people moved to the city looking for work, which resulted in an enormous increase in the population. The division of labor and specializations resulted in a significant increase in efficiency as well as in the number and kinds of activities performed. Moreover, many machines were developed during this period. The

Figure 9   - Water transport by ship

Figure 10 - The court's gardens of Versailles daily consumed five times the water available for Paris's inhabitants

The 60 companies that existed by 1900 supplied about 100 municipalities with water. Of these 60 companies, 13 used surface water, 11 abstracted water from the dunes, and the rest used groundwater. In 1898 a total of 58.7 million m^3 of water were produced. By this time, all large municipalities were supplied with drinking water through pipelines.

It was not profitable for the small municipalities in the countryside to lay pipelines. So, in 1910 a public limited liability company was established by 24 of the 25 municipalities of Zuid-Beverland (one of the islands of Zeeland) with the intention of establishing and operating a group water pipe-

increased industry mainly established itself close to cities, positively influencing employment rates there.

These advantages resulted in an even greater growth of the cities, but also a growth in the hygiene problems. An increasing number of people lived in the same small area. Human excrement infected the drinking water, and the first cholera epidemic broke out in 1830 in the area around the mouth of the Thames. Faster ships and more intensive traffic meant that bacteria from India (Bengal) could come to Europe via "living" carriers. Thousands of people died, especially the poorer class in the cities. The need for good sanitary facilities became even greater.

3.3 Modern infrastructure

Drinking water

The history of the Dutch drinking water supply starts with the construction of the first water pipeline in 1853. This pipeline transported dune water from the Haarlem dunes to Amsterdam. In contrast to the Vecht water that was transported by boat, dune water was treated by slow sand filtration before it was transported to the city. In Amsterdam the water was distributed at a price of 1 cent per bucket (about the same as €0.5 per m^3, and about half of the present price). After Amsterdam, drinking water companies were also established in other cities.

Establishment of water companies
1853 Amsterdam
1855 Den Helder
1874 The Hague, Rotterdam
1878 Leiden, Katwijk
1879 Nijmegen
1881 Groningen
1882 Dordrecht
1883 Utrecht, De Bilt, Delfshaven, Gouda
1884 Vlissingen
1885 Arnhem, Baarn, Soest, Alkmaar, Vlaardingen
1886 Schiedam, Gorinchem, Hilversum, Zaanstreek
1887 Maastricht, Den Bosch, Sliedrecht, Roosendaal
1888 Leeuwarden, Kampen, Oud-Beijerland, Nieuwer-Amstel, Delft
1889 Amsterdam Vechtleiding, Zutphen, Venlo
1890 Tiel, Amersfoort
1891 Maassluis
1892 Middelburg, Enschede, Almelo
1893 Zwolle, Deventer
1894 Breda, Apeldoorn, Meppel, Delden
1895 Tilburg
1896 Hellevoetsluis, Harderwijk, Zeist
1897 Hengelo, Assen
1898 Nijkerk, Rheden, Zwijndrecht, Haarlem
1899 Bergen op Zoom, Helmond, Roermond

line. Also, in other provinces, similar groups were established.

In order to join a group water pipeline system, the municipalities had to agree to include an obligatory connection in their building regulations, for houses that were less than 40 meters from the main pipeline. This obligatory connection provoked a lot of resistance. Why would you have to pay for something that had always been free? Hadn't grandfather, after having drunk water from the canal his whole life, become ninety years of age without ever having become sick? Nevertheless, by 1940, 712 of the 1054 Dutch municipalities had become part of a central drinking water supply.

The growth of the drinking water industry took place mainly as a result of small groundwater abstractions, which brought about a considerable shift in the resources used. In 1898 surface water comprised about half the total abstracted water, which by 1939 had dropped to 26%. The rest was abstracted groundwater, of which more than a third was dune water.

Only the less populated regions had not gone over to a central drinking water supply, because the construction costs could never be covered by the expected revenues from the water users. In order to achieve a connection percentage of almost 100%, the government took full financial responsibility for the operational deficit resulting from these unprofitable services. In this way, the few remaining areas in the Netherlands were connected to the central water supply by 1963. And, in 1968, more than 99% of the population had access to this much desired drinking water.

At present all 16 million inhabitants are connected to a drinking water system.

The number of drinking water companies significantly decreased after the Second World War (Figure 11). The reason for this is that the small water companies were incorporated into the larger ones as a result of the increase in supply areas of regional water companies. In 1940 there were 210 water companies in the Netherlands, but by 2004 the number decreased to 14.

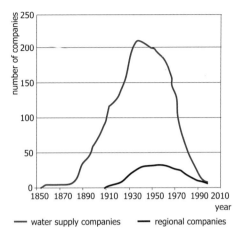

Figure 11 - Number of water companies in the Netherlands since 1853

Sewerage

In the 16th and 17th centuries, a separation was made in the disposal of wastewater between human excrement and other wastewater. Feces were collected in a cesspool, so that they could be used as fertilizer and so that they did not contaminate the surface water.

By the beginning of the 18th century, however, the inspection process deteriorated, and cesspools were often built with a spillway that spilled excess water into the surface water, to avoid frequent emptying. This water became both a source of drinking water and a dumping place for human excrement, wastewater, rubbish and other waste. Fortunately, the dumped waste was sometimes dredged. Surface water, though, fulfilled an important function for transport, city defense and drainage.

Around 1850 the urban population started to increase, which resulted in a denser population within the city walls. At this time, hygienists proved a correlation exists between bad living conditions and bad public health. As a result of this and the ever increasing stench, interest in processing solid, as well as liquid, waste increased dramatically.

Several inventors, engineers and hygienists sought a solution to what was called the "sewer problem." Besides improving public health, an important incentive for this was the related manure problem.

There was a plea for the return of nutrients from the cities back to the countryside in order to stimulate the supply of food as well as the biological cycle.

A variety of possible solutions existed:
- The Barrel System

This was one of the simplest systems. Human solid waste was collected in barrels in order to be used directly on the farmed land. Urine was frequently drained into the sewer together with household water, which was actually disastrous for the manure value of the solid waste.

- The Cesspool System

Human solid waste was collected in a cesspool. Other wastewater was drained via trenches or sewers directly into the surface water, preferably via a sedimentation tank so that the solid parts could sink. Household waste was put in a separate watertight sink. In both the barrel and the cesspool systems, transportation of the barrels and the emptying of the cesspools were seen as very unpleasant activities.

- The Liernur System

This is the predecessor of the vacuum sewer system and was based on conservation of the manure value of feces and urine by mixing them into the ground within one day, using an injection apparatus that was specially developed for this purpose. Collected feces could also be processed into compost or fine powder. Two disadvantages of this system were that it was not a well-known technique and the system's construction activities had to be carried out within the houses.

- The Flushing System

The design of this system required the discharge of wastewater, as soon as possible, into a river where the feces and solid waste were washed away by flushing water. Sometimes, rainwater was also allowed through this system. If the sewers were level (not sloped), then a large quantity of flushing water was needed. Moreover, the flushing system caused pollution of the surface water that could not always be flushed away. That is why there was a call to treat the wastewater before discharging it.

Around 1870 the Dutch government could no longer hide behind the fact that there was a lack of insight in wastewater technologies, and it had to choose a new system. Both the barrel and the Liernur systems had positive influences on public health, and provided a solution to the manure problem. The liberal attitude of the government ensured that the solution to the sewer problem would need to at least cover all its costs, and would likely generate some profit. In the largest part of the Netherlands a choice was made, therefore, for the barrel system (Figure 12).

However, in 1900 the situation was again totally different, as a result of changes in scientific and social insights. For example, by this time it had been discovered that bacteria could spawn sicknesses. The close relationship between diseases such as cholera, on the one hand, and the quality of drinking water, on the other hand, could be proven. Also, the need for human excrement as manure had strongly diminished. The government slowly started taking responsibility to improve the situation and, as a result of increasing support from the population, it became possible for the private construction of drinking water pipelines. Slowly, it became known and understood that the profit that could be achieved by a sound and reliable system of public hygiene could not be directly realized financially within the system.

The barrel and Liernur systems were not able to meet the high expectations of profit. The reason

Figure 12 - Girls waiting for barrels to be picked up

for this was that Liernur's complete design was not carried out. Although the feces would be separately collected in undiluted form, more and more flushing toilets were connected to the system, which caused the processing of collected feces to be much more expensive. In practice, the barrel system had problems with stench, as well as wastewater spillage when the overly full barrels were emptied. Therefore, municipalities had to make a choice, once again, as to which system they would choose to solve the sewage problem.

Because criteria such as the preservation of the manure value and profitability no longer played a role, the flushing system was the best option. However, implementation of the flushing system in existing situations went very slowly. By 1940 only 49% of the municipalities had a sewage system, while 12% of the municipalities still used the barrel system, and in 45% of the municipalities cesspools were still used.

Wastewater treatment

After World War II the pollution of surface water became a serious problem. The self-purifying capacity of the water was no longer satisfactory, so a decision was made to start treating wastewater at wastewater treatment plants. Since then, the amount of wastewater has only increased. In addition to this, there has been an increase in industrial waste, which is often very difficult to break down.

The Netherlands today

At this time, almost every household is connected to the drinking water network (99.8%). Via this network, hygienically safe, clear and colorless water with a good taste is being provided. About 2/3 of the drinking water is abstracted from groundwater. As a result of the large service area, there is little relationship to the local geo-hydrological situation.

It must be remembered that the price of drinking water is determined largely by the water transport costs but also by the treatment costs. Therefore, the price that is paid for drinking water varies. In 2001, the people of the province of Utrecht paid €0.82 for 1 m^3 of drinking water, while inhabitants

of The Hague paid €1.71 for 1 m^3 (price includes house connection). The reason for this price difference is, among other things, the use of different water sources. For example, the treatment of surface water is more expensive than that of groundwater. And, construction of an infrastructure to distribute water is very expensive. In the case of The Hague, water has to be transported over 60 km from the Meuse River.

During the last few decades, water use has increased considerably. In 1850 about 10 liters of water per person per day were used, whereas, in the year 2000, water usage increased to 126 liters pp/d. Because the general population could make use more and more of good quality drinking water, people started using water for other purposes than drinking. In the last few years, there have been experiments with the distribution of a second, inferior quality water for non-drinking water applications because of the expected environmental profit. Over the last 10 years, water usage has stabilized as a result of public awareness campaigns about saving water.

As of now about 98% of the households are connected to the sewer system for the transport of wastewater. The remaining 2% discharges directly into either the surface water or groundwater, or is directly connected to the local treatment system. About 93% of the collected wastewater is treated in wastewater treatment plants. This treatment is initially directed at the removal of settleable solids and materials that consume oxygen. Nowadays, also the removal of the nutrients nitrogen and phosphorous is included.

At times of especially high precipitation, overflows in mixed systems have a detrimental effect on surface water. The damage that is caused to the environment by this is dependent on the amount of overflow water, its composition, and the sensitivity of the local environment.

4.   Public health

For hundreds of thousands of years, our ancestors lived in small groups off the gains from hunting, fishing, and gathering. They were at the mercy of the elements: their food supply was uncertain, they were constantly confronted with the weather and wild animals, and natural disasters such as floods, large fires and drought took their toll. Looking from the point of view of diseases, there were, however, advantages. Infectious diseases, which do not originate from local flora, but that need large populations to be transmitted, had a very small chance of spreading. Also, waste products created no large problem. Nevertheless, the life expectancy of our nomadic ancestors was low: the average age at death (the age at which 50% of a generation died) was less than 25.

About 8000 B.C., the Neolithic Revolution started. This took place first in southern Turkey and later spread across the globe. In the new Stone Age, man attempted to reduce his dependency on nature. Animals were kept and intentionally bred, food crops were cultivated, and places of residence became permanent: they developed from tent camps to settlements to villages to cities. As a result of specializations, improvements in primary production were made possible by irrigation channels, reservoirs, water storage, and reliable time calculations. But, disadvantages also came as a result of the concentration of the population: epidemics, stench and noise pollution, polluted water resulting from waste products, etc. Therefore, measures were needed for water supplies and waste disposal. Because cities and their surroundings were still frequently small islands without much interaction with the rest of the world, the advantages had the upper hand and, in this way, the primary needs of the people were effectively addressed.

During the Bronze and Iron Ages, as a result of more complex technologies, distant trade routes for tin, copper, lead and iron developed. Also, production surpluses of grains, salt, animal skins, silk and earthenware were exchanged between different areas. Germs traveled across these great distances as well, causing this period to become well-known for the plagues that developed into epidemics and spread, especially in the region around the Indian Ocean, which was then the center of world traffic routes. Each time that the

border of the known world was extended, the "virginal" population fell prey to epidemics such as smallpox, cholera, the Bubonic plague, and typhoid fever.

From the Bronze and Iron Ages onwards, a gradual expansion of the known world was visible, chipping away at its surroundings of loose entities. At first this merging, as already has been said, resulted in high fatalities among the new people. After some time, however, a gradual recovery took place among them.

Many infectious diseases continued to pose great threats to the people of large European cities that were expanding during the second half of the Middle Ages. The situation was so dramatic that the average age of death was between 5 and 10 years, a figure which lays far below that in the successful Neolithic cities.

The Modern Time, from about 1500, marks the actual involvement of the whole world. An unprecedented exchange of people, animals and plants from several continents took place. This also means that germs and/or their diseases from still unknown regions reached the New World. For example, smallpox literally decimated the population of Mexico and Peru in the first half of the 16th century. And even in the 19th century, 90% of the population of the Fiji Islands died in a short span of time after the introduction of measles there.

When the Industrial Revolution attracted large numbers of people to the cities, social hardships and advancements in the sciences, such as biomedical science, resulted.

Then, around 1800, the study of demography and speculation concerning the future possibilities for humanity were dominated by the concept of Thomas Malthus.

Malthus did research into the population development in Great Britain and reached the conclusion that a population always tends to grow exponentially. In reality this happens seldomly, or perhaps only for a short while. Epidemics, armed conflicts, famine and natural disasters regulate this growth; these factors work individually or sometimes together. If, for example, the circumstances are

Cholera

It is presumed that the catchment area of the Ganges and the Brahmapoetra is the birthplace of this acute intestinal disease. The disease was brought to Western Europe by infected seamen. Cholera has an incubation period of 10 hours to some days and is characterized by watery diarrhea and vomiting. The loss of many liters of fluid and valuable minerals often cannot be compensated by drinking and leads to a fast death. Up until recently it was thought that mankind was the only infection reservoir and that any case could eventually be traced back to a human patient. Recently, Rita Colwell showed, however, that cholera bacteria can also survive in plankton in the oceans. The disease is usually transmitted through drinking water containing cholera bacteria or through food that has been prepared with this water.
The fact that cholera epidemics occur in waves is related to the community within a population, and also to weather phenomena such as El Niño (change in ocean currents can lead to polluted water flowing inland). Immunity is high after an epidemic but reduces afterwards until sufficient contagious individuals emerge. Cholera is a disease that can flourish only under poor sanitary conditions. All energy must be directed towards the supply of reliable drinking water and food in the community.

 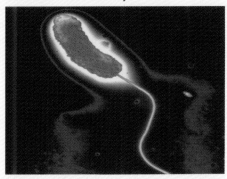

favorable, population growth can be so explosive that food and water will be insufficient for everyone's needs. As a result, famine will end this growth, unless someone finds a solution in the form of reclamation and innovation of agricultural methods.

Malthus did not particularly want to predict disaster, but rather prevent it. He knew that it was precisely the poorer people who tended to reproduce themselves uncontrollably. "But," he said, "the large table of nature has not been laid for everyone." According to Malthus, aid to the poor was absolutely wrong, and whoever could not help himself had to perish. Contraceptives were also taboo. However, he did recommend that the poor and uneducated marry at a later age and practice restraint in order to keep their birth rates under control.

In 1850 the Epidemiological Society was established in London. There they studied, among other things, the distribution patterns of all kinds of diseases and wanted to find out whether certain diseases were contagious. Doctor John Snow published his findings in 1854 about a London cholera epidemic; in ten days there were more than 500 fatal cases. He found that nearly all of the cholera patients around Broad Street used water from the same pump (Figure 13). The water had to have contained a pollutant, he theorized. Based on his findings, the epidemiologist was able to have the handle of the pump removed. Thirty years later his pollutant theory was confirmed by microbiologist Robert Koch, who had travelled to Egypt and India to find a disease breeder.

Other microbiological discoveries were made by Doctor Ignaz Semmelweis and chemist Louis Pasteur. Doctors realized, sometimes without even knowing the exact causes of contagious diseases,

27

Typhoid

Another disease that played havoc among the Dutch population in the previous century and caused thousands of deaths was typhoid. The disease-causing bacteria live exclusively in humans but can also survive in water for some time. After an incubation period of 2 weeks, a series of symptoms emerges, characterized by high fever, weakness, dizziness and diarrhea. Futhermore, a slow pulse is noteworthy. Without treatment, about 15% of the patients die, depending on their resistance. Modern medicine has reduced the mortality to 3%. These days, the typical patient is someone who comes back from vacation healthy and then develops the disease.

Unlike cholera, a relatively small amount of typhoid bacteria is capable of infecting a patient. The infection is fecal-oral and can take place through drinking water, but also through hands, fleas or the soil. Up until the beginning of the 20th century, infections occurred regularly through milk in the Netherlands. Farmers flushed their milk cans thoroughly, but did this often in ditches that were also used for the drainage of sewers. Sanitary engineering is the answer to the typhoid problem, because it is essential to separate the removal of feces from the drinking water and food supplies in order to avoid disease carriers from spreading. The construction of water supply systems in the Netherlands (percentage not connected to water supply) has run parallel to the decrease in the mortality rate from typhoid.

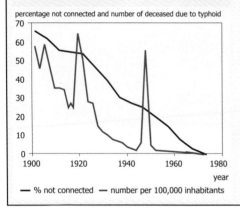

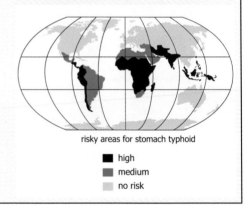

Figure 13 - Broad Street pump

that hygiene, with regard to provision and attitude, favorably influences the health of individuals and groups. Basic provisions that were made for the whole population in the second half of the 19th century form the basis of the good public health we have today.

These days we can say that the world has become one, because, strictly speaking, there are no longer any large regions that are completely isolated. Spores of some diseases have already been introduced almost everywhere in the world and can no longer cause a surprise attack. The fact that cities around the globe form a worldwide network, where people, animals and plants can travel relatively

Legionellosis (Legionnaire's disease)

The most important microbiological discovery of recent years has been the cause of Legionnaire's disease. In the summer of 1976 some 4400 war veterans gathered in a hotel in Philadelphia. In total 149 persons became ill with symptoms that could not be traced to any known disease. The primary feature was severe pneumonia. In 1977 the cause was found: a bacterial infection from Gram-negative, rod-shaped bacteria which can multiply in water and air-conditioning systems. The organism, which was unknown until then, was named *Legionella pneumophila*.

The Netherlands was also frightened by an outbreak of Legionella in February 1999 in Bovenkarspel. A total of 242 people were infected through two jaccuzis at a flower exhibition, 32 people died. This outbreak led to a plan of action by the Ministry to prevent future epidemics. One part of the plan of action deals with informing medical doctors and health services, and also saunas, swimming pools, campsites, hotels, and the public at large. Next to this, technical measures, such as flushing pipelines, have been devised to limit the infection risks in hot water. These measures have to be carried out at those high-risk facilities (saunas, swimming pools, jaccuzis, etc.). The actual infection from the bacteria occurs through the lungs by means of aerosols (airborne bacteria).

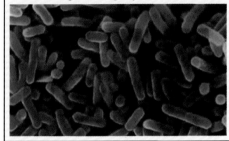 

quickly, however, poses a great danger. As a result of the enormous increase in contact possibilities and the minimization of the travelling time, there have been cases in the past of for example, lassa hemorraghic fever and ebola fever observed outside of the tropics, their natural region. Also, as a result of the continuing mega-urbanization, there is a greater chance of the occurrence of sicknesses which coincide with crowding, such as diarrhea sicknesses and meningitis.

In the coming 30 years, health care services, scientists and politicians will have their hands full with infectious diseases and microorganisms. In general, there will be a decrease in disease and mortality figures, which will be seen from the steadily increasing life expectancies. Nevertheless, old spores will emerge again and again in new surroundings and among other population groups. Also, the resistance of microorganisms will cause

problems in the treatment of patients. Moreover, new germs will be discovered, like the recently discovered one responsible for Legionnaire's disease. Nevertheless, experience tells us that we will be able to react adequately.

5.   Sanitary engineering worldwide

Water plays an extremely important role in the world. Some even call it the gold of the 21st century, in the same way as oil was seen in the 20th century. The available water supply is becoming relatively smaller, however, because of human consumption and the many types of water pollution. Moreover, in the future, the water demand will only increase. It is, therefore, very important that a balance be found between the economic needs of a rapidly growing population and the need for a clean environment.

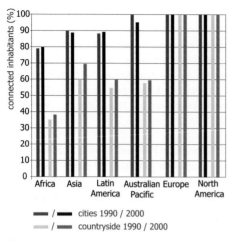

Figure 14 - The development of water supply in the world between 1990 and 2000

Legend:
━ / ━ cities 1990 / 2000
▬ / ▬ countryside 1990 / 2000

In this section a number of cases will be discussed. Practical examples will illustrate the importance of sanitary engineering by means of the broad differences in development worldwide. For less developed regions, there are also large differences between the cities and the countryside (Figures 14 and 15). In many cases we see that finding solutions for problems, such as water pollution and the shortage of drinking water, is technically very simple, but that the actual implementation is anything but simple.

Table 1 - Differences in the area of wastewater treatment in Europe (1990)

	Treated domestic wastewater
The Netherlands	93%
Germany / Great Britain	87%
France	68%
Belgium	29%

Belgium

In contrast to the Netherlands, Belgium's untreated wastewater was discharged, untreated, into the surface water. Very little was invested in sewer systems or water treatment plants because the Belgian authorities were not very concerned about the pollution of surface water. This apathy was supported by the fact that the population in Belgium is more evenly spread out than in the Netherlands, which would lead to rather high costs for the construction of public works. The figures from 1990 (Table 1) show that in Belgium less than 30% of the domestic wastewater was treated.

With the unification of Europe, however, Belgium has had to satisfy European directives. For this reason, since 1990, everything has been put into place to catch up with the rest of the European countries in the field of sewerage and wastewater treatment (Table 2). Since then, the number of sewage treatment plants has almost doubled and the length of sewer pipes in kilometers has tripled.

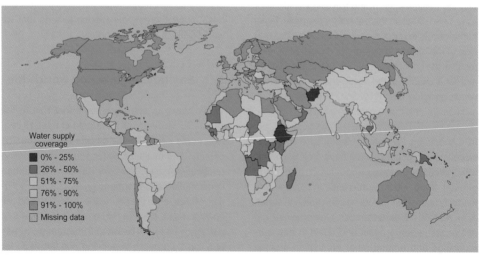

Figure 15 - Water supply coverage in the world (2000)

Table 2 - Development of wastewater infrastructure in Belgium from 1990 to 2000

	1990	2000
Number of STPs	106	176
Number of pumping stations	226	642
Length of pipes in km	1,124	3,339

Though still not truly adequate, now approximately 50% of household wastewater is treated before being discharged into the surface water.

Los Angeles

Los Angeles is a city that grew enormously within a short period of time. In 1900, the city had 100,000 inhabitants, and in 1994 9,000,000. At the beginning of the 20th century, the water supply consisted of rainwater catchment and a rapidly diminishing groundwater supply. That is why plans were made by the Los Angeles Department of Water (LADWP) to try to cope with the increasing demand. The Los Angeles Aqueduct was built (Figure 16), which provided Los Angeles with water from Owens Lake. The water had to be transported over a distance of 370 km. This was, however, not a problem, because Owens Lake lay 1,300 meters above Los Angeles.

The farmers who lived in the Owens Valley had to give up their water rights, under pressure from the central government, because the continuous growth of the city of Los Angeles was deemed more important. The farmers opposed the intake of water from the lake. The once so fertile agricultural land dried up as a result of the extensive abstrac-

Figure 17 - Los Angeles Aqueduct

tion of water from the lake. Between the farmers and the LADWP, a couple of armed conflicts took place, with casualties on both sides. These conflicts were called the "water wars."

By 1924 Owens Lake had totally dried up and the ecosystem around the lake was destroyed. The LADWP went in search of a new water source and, in 1941, the existing aqueduct was extended to Mono Lake. In 1978 the inhabitants around Mono Lake realized that it was also drying up. A committee was established and lawsuits were filed in order to save the lake.

For the city of Los Angeles, this situation meant that a large investment had to be made into saving water and water recycling. Over the last 60 years people have changed their way of thinking about water. In 1920 it was important that the city of Los Angeles continue expanding at the expense of everything else. Since 1980, not only are economic considerations deemed important, but environmental issues play just as important a role.

South Africa - Lesotho

South Africa is a dry country (Table 3) with a wide range in rainfall, both in time and place. The

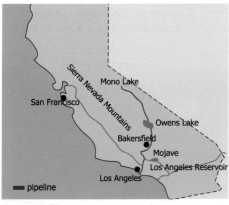

Figure 16 - Los Angeles water supply

Table 3 - Worldwide differences in the water balance

Area	Rainfall (mm)	Evapo-transpiration (mm)	Useful rainfall (mm)
World	750	545	205
Europe	734	425	319
Africa	686	547	139
South Africa	475	410	65
Namibia	280	265	15

southeastern part of South Africa has the greatest rainfall by far, and the relatively short rivers carry this water almost directly into the Indian Ocean. The large metropolis of Johannesburg is situated near the gold mines. It lies on a plateau (1,500 m above sea level) in a dry part of the country and the water supply for this area is, therefore, problematic. In the past, several rivers in Kwazulu-Natal were redirected towards Johannesburg.

Quite a distance to the south of Johannesburg lies the wet mountain kingdom of Lesotho. The lowlands of Lesotho lie in the western part of that region, the highlands in the east, and the Drakenberg Mountains lie on the border between South Africa and Lesotho. This topography results in very influential rainfall amounts. In the western part 800 mm of rain falls per year, while in the eastern part 1,200 mm falls. The water is transported by the Orange River to the southeast and flows into the Atlantic Ocean. This is too far away to be used by Johannesburg as a water resource.

South Africa's interest in water from Lesotho led to two feasibility studies about water export in the "50s and "60s. No decision was made. A new study followed in 1979 which proposed the export of 70 m³/s to South Africa and the building of a dam so that Lesotho could produce its own electricity, instead of having to import it. In 1983 the final report concluded that there were no unresolvable environmental, socio-economic or legal problems. In this report the amount of water to be exported and the design of the dam, tunnels and hydroelec-

tric facilities were stipulated, and an estimation of the cost was included.

The agreement was signed in 1986 and South Africa paid for the entire water export project and its maintenance and gave Lesotho 60 million Rand in water royalties per year. Lesotho borrowed money from the World Bank and started building a dam. The water can be transported from the dam through a tunnel bored through the mountains and carried by gravity to Johannesburg.

This is the only way for Lesotho to increase their own electricity production and end their dependence on South Africa for 90% of their electricity. Eventually, this project benefited both parties. South Africa has water for the increasing need in Johannesburg and Lesotho sells water and produces its own electricity. By 2020 four dams will have been built and a network of pipelines and tunnels will supply 82 m³/s of water to South Africa.

In 1994, there were more than 12 million people in South Africa who did not have sufficient drinking water. Since then, the new government has done a lot to improve the drinking water supply for the underprivileged. For example, the percentage of people who are not connected to a drinking water supply has been halved. Unfortunately, not much attention has been given to the sanitary situation in the last couple of years, and problems there are still tangible. For example, in the period between 1999 and 2001, approximately 900,000 people were diagnosed with cholera. As a result, the incidence of cholera (i.e., the number of new cases in a given time period) came to about 30,000 per

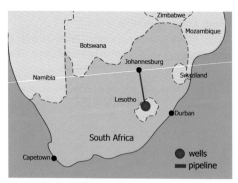

Figure 18 - South Africa and Lesotho

Figure 19 - Dam in Lesotho

year. Because of adequate steps taken by the health care services, the number of patient casualties remained low, at only 0.5%.

Organizationally speaking, there are also some inherited problems. For example, before 1994 the African National Congress (ANC) called upon the people not to pay their accounts for public services, as a way of protest. Even today, it is difficult to convince the people that they have to pay for these services. Because of this, a lot water continues to be wasted. There are households in the suburbs of Johannesburg that use more than 25 m³ per month without paying for it. For this reason, before the elections, the ANC promised that 6 m³ of water per month per household would be distributed free of charge.

This promise was made in order to appease the poor. Now that the ANC won the elections, this measure has to be implemented, and it is no easy task. For example, how do you define who is poor and entitled to a free quota? And, how do you measure the quantities used if there is no water meter? As a result of these questions and their uncertain answers, some water supply companies face serious problems, both operationally and financially.

Namibia

The capital city of the neighboring country of Namibia contends with similar problems. The capital, Windhoek, lies about 1,000 m above sea level, far from any river. And, just like in many parts of South Africa, there is very little groundwater available. Since 1968, Windhoek has treated household wastewater, as well as surface water. Windhoek was, in fact, the first city in the world that reused treated wastewater for drinking water purposes (Figure 20). As a result of the increasing water demand, the amount of reused wastewater has been increased from 2 to 7 million m³ per year. This is, however, not sufficient to satisfy the future water demand there.

For this reason, there are studies being conducted to find alternative water resources. The use of sea water is not yet an option, because Windhoek lies too far from the sea and too high above sea level,

Figure 20 - Treatment plant in Windhoek where wastewater is reused for consumption

and desalination is a very expensive procedure. For these reasons, engineers are now looking at permanently flowing rivers in the Namibian territory. There are only three: one on the southern border and two on the northern border of the country. The most logical option is to use the water from the Okavango River, a large, permanently flowing river that begins in Angola and ends in Botswana. In Botswana, the river flows into a depression, the Okavango Delta, and evaporates. The Okavango Delta is ideal for birds and animals and is thus a very important tourist attraction (revenues: US$ 250 million/year). Botswana is now worried that this nature reserve will be adversely affected if Namibia withdraws water from the Okavango River, despite the fact that Namibia only needs a relatively small amount (0.17% of the average river discharge and 3% to 10% of the river's minimum discharge). Because of these issues, negotiations have been going on for many years. These negotiations, however, have been anything but smooth because of a border conflict between the two nations over a small island in the Zambezi River, which is an entirely different matter.

Mali

Djenné is one of the oldest cities in West Africa and is especially well-known for its mosque, the largest loam construction in the world. The houses also have a very unique architecture: they have been built in the traditional manner using wood and loam, resulting in the whole town, and especially its architecture, being declared a national cultural heritage site. Conservation of the city and its unique architecture is, however, being threatened by (among other things) the wastewater problems that have arisen during the construction of drinking water pipelines.

In Djenné each house has been built around a central courtyard with at least one toilet situated on the roof (Figure 21). Up until 1982, surface water was the most important source of water for drinking and cleaning. The direct availability and untreated usage of it naturally had serious consequences for public health, which could be seen, for example, in the high infant mortality rate. Nowadays, surface water is still used for washing clothes and pots and pans, and a part of the population still drinks this water. With the help of Canadian development aid, a drinking water supply plant was built in 1982, which initially provided the people with 52 public water fountains. At present 286 of the 2,300 houses have a drinking water connection, and the number is still increasing.

The total drinking water usage has increased since the construction of these resources. This results from a decrease in the availability of surface water (the closest perennial river - carrying water in the dry periods - lies 4 km from Djenné) and a change in people's habits. These changed habits include an increase in activities such as showering and washing, as well as where these activities take

place. In general, women are now washing themselves at home. Likewise, the washing of pots, pans and clothing also takes place in the home.

The increased amount of wastewater cannot be processed properly with currently available resources. At present, wastewater is sometimes discharged directly onto the street, and then evaporates or seeps into the ground, but inadequate facilities lead to its accumulation and stagnation there (Figure 22). Together with poor solid-waste collection, what results is an increased hazard for public health, a stench, and the reduced accessibility of the roads. Moreover, in a number of cases, the wastewater has eroded the loam walls, resulting in the stability of the houses being undermined.

Studies have been conducted in order to solve the wastewater problem in Djenné, with a combination of technological, social, and organizational measures. These solutions only have a chance of success if they are supported by the local population and if it is practical to implement them.

Figure 21 - Toilets on the roof in Mali

Figure 22 - Accumulation and stagnation of wastewater on the street

Implementing infiltration measures seems to be the best option. This solution is simple and the local population understands and supports it. For this reason a pilot project has been started that teaches the residents the technique of infiltration and gives them a chance to gain experience in the construction and maintenance of such resources.

Bangladesh

In the past, a large part of the population of Bangladesh used surface water as a source of drinking water. This caused many diarrhea-related diseases which led to a high mortality rate, especially among small children. Development aid from organizations such as UNICEF provided the people with tube wells (hand pumps), which made it possible for them to use groundwater as drinking water. This was such a huge success that the population started saving money themselves in order to build more pumps. Now 97% of all water used by the population is groundwater.

In 1990, another problem arose. Water that was pumped up with the shallow tube wells turned out to be badly polluted with arsenic. A problem with arsenic is that it dissolves in water and cannot be tasted, seen or smelled. It is initially very difficult, therefore, to know if the water is toxic. The long-term effect of drinking water that is polluted with arsenic is skin discoloration, blisters on the hands and feet, and internal tumors (blackfoot disease). Any vitamin deficiency (particularly vitamin A) worsens these effects, which eventually can be fatal. This could mean that, in the future, 1 out of every 10 people will die from arsenic poisoning. It is not easy to find a direct link between polluted water and occurring diseases because they often only show up many years or even decades later.

A majority of the population does not know that the water is poisonous, because the government is scared that panic will break out. These days, some water pumps are painted red as a warning.

The red paint, however, has had little effect, particularly because there are no other safe pumps in the area. In Western countries there are many ways of treating the groundwater or surface water, but many

Figure 23 - In Bangladesh 50% of all 10 million hand pumps have an arsenic problem (red spout)

solutions do not work in Bangladesh. Because specific circumstances vary in each village, such as the concentrations of arsenic and minerals, it is difficult to tell which solution is best.

Israel

Israel has an extreme shortage of water. The country has a semi-arid climate, where a majority of the rain (80%) falls in the northern border region with Lebanon, Syria and Jordan. The only river of any importance is the Jordan, which flows into the Sea of Galilee. Because most of the population lives in central Israel (where Tel Aviv and Jerusalem are also situated), and the availability of irrigation water is a necessity for agriculture in the desert areas, the government decided, after the establishment of the state of Israel, to build the National Water Carrier (NWC), a water transport pipeline from the Sea of Galilee, via central Israel, to the Negev Desert.

The water in the Sea of Galilee lies 200 meters below sea level and is pumped to a height of 150 meters above sea level. This amounts to about 8% of the national electricity usage! The pipeline is made of concrete with a steel core and has a diameter of 2.8 meters. Other sections are constructed as a canal. The total capacity of the Jordan River and some smaller rivers which flow into the Sea of Galilee amounts to approximately 800 million m³/year. Evaporation, as a result of the long time that water stays in the lake, amounts to approximately

35

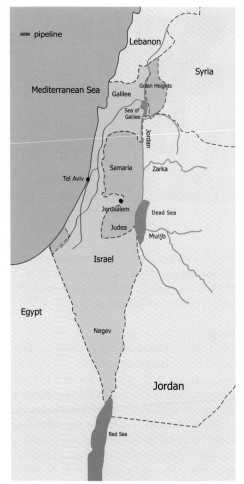

Figure 25 - Reservoir in the National Water Carrier

also used. Wastewater is an important resource in Israel, and in the very near future 100% of it will be reused.

As a result of this transport system, Israel has enough water, for the time being. Armed conflicts with Jordan concerning water rights have not yet occurred, although Jordan also needs water from the Jordan River. However, because of the growing need for water in this region, the future is uncertain.

Moreover, there is a large water shortage in the adjacent Palestinian areas. The Palestinians only get per person 1/10th of the amount of water the Israelis use. While Israeli gardens are green, the Palestinian areas have insufficient water to provide for a family. The problem of dividing the water plays an important part in the negotiations between Israel and the Palestinians concerning the return of occupied Palestinian areas. Israel considers water abstraction in the Palestinian areas vital for itself and wants to keep the drinking water supplies in these areas under its control.

Colorado River

The Colorado River originates in the middle of the United States, flows via the Grand Canyon to Mexico and into the Gulf of Mexico. In 1944 a treaty was made between the USA and Mexico in which Mexico was guaranteed a certain amount of water.

The water from the Colorado River was used, among other things, for irrigation. The drainage water from the irrigation has a high salinity, which means that the Colorado River water could be no

Figure 24 - The National Water Carrier in Israel

300 million m³/year. Most of the remaining water is pumped into the NWC, which is the life source of Israel. The remaining flow in the Jordan River decreased as a result of the project.

The main transport pipeline is coupled, at dozens of places, to local water supply systems and provides water to municipalities, kibbutzes and the agricultural sector. In the winter, when water use is low, water is filtered into the dunes, for example, at Tel Aviv. In many places water from local groundwater abstractions is also pumped into the main pipeline and transported to other regions. In the past and for some years, treated wastewater was

Figure 26 - Desalination plant for the Colorado River

longer used by the farmers in Mexico for agriculture. In 1961, Mexico submitted an official protest against the US concerning water quality, because agricultural production in the Mexicali Valley was adversely affected.

In 1972, a solution was found for the problem. In addition to the treaty of 1944 concerning the quantity of water in the Colorado River, an agreement was now made concerning the water quality of the river. The US built the world's largest desalination plant in Arizona. This factory treats 390,000 m³ of salt river water per day (Figure 25). Using a membrane filtration installation (reverse osmosis) the salt is concentrated into a concentrate stream, and desalinated water (an amount of 275,000 m³ per day) flows into the river. The concentrate stream, which consists of water with a high concentration of salts, is discharged directly, by means of a pipeline, into the Gulf of Mexico.

Libya

At the moment, a large project to transport groundwater to densely populated coastal areas in Libya is being undertaken. In the south of Libya 4 large groundwater reservoirs containing 35 billion m³ of fossil water exist. From these reservoirs large transport pipelines run to the coast (Figure 27). The pipelines are made of pre-stressed concrete with a length of 1,900 kilometers and a diameter varying from 1.6 up to 4.0 meters. The pipes are buried in gutters seven meters deep.

The project has been subdivided into a number of phases. When all phases have been carried out, the capacity of the completed system must be 3 million m³/day. This is approximately equal to the total drinking water production of the Netherlands.

The project has the following advantages for Libya:
- the agricultural sector is no longer dependent on fresh water resources and the resulting salt intrusion
- development of large fertile agricultural areas

- possibilities for light industry in the cities
- growth of cities and villages as a result of the end of the water shortage

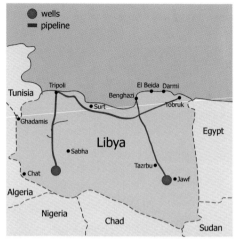

Figure 27 - The transport of water in Libya (Great man-made river project)

Further reading

- Global water supply and sanitation assessment, WHO/Unicef (2000)
- World water development report, UNESCO (2003/2006)
- Review of world water resources by country, FAO (2003)
- World atlas of epidemic diseases, A. Cliff / P. Haggett / M. Smallman-Raynor, Arnold (2004)
- Die Wasserversorgung antiker Staedte, Verlag Philipp von Zabern (1998)
- Water om te drinken, S. Wijmer, VEWIN (1992)

- www.unesco.org/water
- www.fao.org
- www.europa.eu.int
- www.who.int
- www.wateraid.org
- www.waterland.net
- www.nwp.nl
- www.irc.nl
- www.waterhistory.org
- www.wssinfo.org

Questions and applications

What is sanitary engineering?

1. What are the three specializations of sanitary engineering? Give, also, their main goals.

2. What is the primary motive to construct a central drinking water supply and what is the potential risk?

History of sanitary engineering

1. Give the most important characteristics of sanitary engineering in the period of:
   - the Roman Empire
   - the Middle Ages
   - the modern age

2. Give some solutions to the sewer problem together with their primary benefits.

Public health

1. Give the three most important diseases that are transmitted through water systems.

2. Give the difference between infection from cholera and from Legionella.

Answers

What is sanitary engineering?

1. Specializations of sanitary engineering:
   - Drinking water supply (public health, comfort)
   - Sewage (public health, comfort)
   - Wastewater treatment (the environment, public health)

2. The primary motive is the supply of sufficient water for personal hygiene (drinking, bathing and washing) through well-organized companies. The main risk is a rapid outbreak of diseases when the water is not safe.

History of sanitary engineering

1. Roman Empire: well-organized central drinking water supply and sewage disposal, no wastewater treatment

   Middle Ages: no central facilities

   Modern age: well-organized central facilities for drinking water supply, sewage and wastewater treatment

2. Solution to the sewer problem (benefit):
   - barrels (reuse of manure)
   - cesspools (reuse of manure)
   - Liernur system (reuse of manure)
   - flushing system (comfort)

Public Health

1. Diseases:
   - cholera
   - typhoid
   - Legionelloses

2. Cholera bacteria multiply in the human intestine and die slowly in the environment. The infection enters through drinking water (gastro-intestinal canal).

Legionella bacteria can multiply in water pipelines provided sufficient nutrients and elevated temperatures are present. The infection does not occur through drinking, but through inhalation of aerosols in showers and jaccuzis.

WATER COMPANIES

Amsterdam water

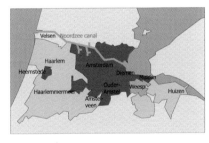

Framework
This module outlines the drinking water service of Amsterdam, as an illustration of historical developments, technical innovations and social influences on the drinking water service.

Contents
This module has the following contents:

1. Introduction
2 The Netherlands
   2.1   The Netherlands and the sea
   2.2   Water in the Netherlands
3. Amsterdam
   3.1   Inhabitants
   3.2   Means of existence
   3.3   Drinking water service without pipelines
   3.4   Drinking water service with pipelines
4. Developments in water consumption and distribution
   4.1   Distribution without pipelines
   4.2   Distribution with pipelines
   4.3   Water consumption
   4.4   Water meters
5. Developments in drinking water production
   5.1   Leiduin - historical development
   5.2   Leiduin - current setup
   5.3   Weesperkarspel - historical development
   5.4   Weesperkarspel - current setup
6. Developments as enterprise
   6.1   Private enterprise
   6.2   Municipal company
   6.3   Governmental corporation
   6.4   Organization and technique

   Further reading
   Questions and applications
   Answers

Study goals
After studying this module you will be able to:
- outline the historical developments of the drinking water service of Amsterdam
- give examples of social developments in the drinking water service
- explain the emergence of dune infiltration
- explain the developments in disinfection with chlorine and in softening
- explain the advantages and disadvantages of water meters

1.   Introduction

The modern drinking water services in cities and regions have all emerged within a period of 50 to 150 years. The current drinking water companies exist as a consequence of their history.

This history has been different for all companies: not just because the companies have started at different times or used different sources, but also because different political and business choices have been made. Because of this there are sometimes remarkable differences between companies and their services, even in similar situations. For a designing engineer, this also indicates that there are often multiple solutions to the same issues.

The following examples can be mentioned as typical differences between companies:
- ownership (municipal companies, governmental corporations, private companies)
- organizational structure (centralized vs. decentralized functional clustering)
- tariff structure (fixed asset vs. usage tariff, depressive vs. uniform)
- sources (groundwater, surface water)
- treatment (system and process choice, target quality)
- distribution (structure of areas of service, with or without water meters)

To illustrate such historical developments and their final consequences, this module presents the drinking water service of Amsterdam, the capital of the Netherlands (Figure 1).

From its foundation in 1853, the Water Company of Amsterdam has taken a remarkable and prominent position in the development of the modern drinking water service.

Typical examples of this are:
- first water company of the Netherlands
- "last" municipal company in the Netherlands
- "first" water chain company in the Netherlands (from 2005)
- initiator of large-scale application of artificial recharge of surface water in dune areas, a unique concept worldwide

- first surface water company in the world not using chlorine in water treatment or distribution
- first company in the world with large-scale softening by crystallization
- "last" company in the Netherlands to install water meters for all consumers
- example company in the world because of large international network

In this module, a brief overview will be given of the Netherlands and its water.

Then, the historical developments of the city of Amsterdam will be described globally, including the development of the drinking water service in the city.

Subsequently, the specific developments will be explained with respect to choice of source, treatment and distribution of drinking water within the Water Company of Amsterdam. With the description of these developments, the emphasis will be on the rationale for the choices that were made and the consequences of those choices.

The notion of historical developments is also important for designing engineers who assess situations where the drinking water service is still immature, which is the case in many developing countries.

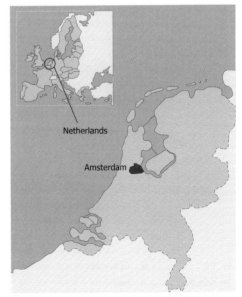

Figure 1   - Amsterdam, capital of the Netherlands

2   The Netherlands

2.1   The Netherlands and the sea

The Netherlands is the result of climate changes across Ice Ages and warming periods. Because of these, the area of Amsterdam became situated between 100 meters below sea level and 100 meters above sea level.

During the coldest Ice Age, glaciers reached from the North Pole to Amsterdam, which can be seen by the Utrechtse Heuvelrug, a glacial ridge at about 20 km southeast of Amsterdam.

The warming period after the last Ice Age raised the sea level a little more than 40 meters in 8,000 years, causing Amsterdam, once again, to be situated close to the sea.

By the rising of the sea level, clay was precipitated and vast peat areas emerged, characteristic of a swamp landscape (Figure 2).

Land losses by the sea

During the last 2,000 years the sea level only rose a few meters. However, this caused large-scale erosion of peat deposits, not only near the coast, but also inland. This crumbling away increased from the Roman Age on because of excavation in the peat-soil areas for fuel mining(Figure 3).

The rising sea level and the natural settling of drained peat-soil areas forced the inhabitants to protect their country against the sea by constructing dikes and dams, like the dam in the river Amstel.

The dunes on the west coast of the Netherlands were a naturally-shaped ally during its battle against the sea. This dune row emerged during the previous 10,000 years by sand being blown inland from the beaches.

This battle against the sea will only increase in the future because of the further rising of the sea level and the continued settling of the ground.

Gaining back the land

With help from windmills it became possible to further drain the region and even retake the lost areas from the sea. Afterwards, this drainage effort was supported by steam engines, diesel engines and finally electro-engines (Figure 4).

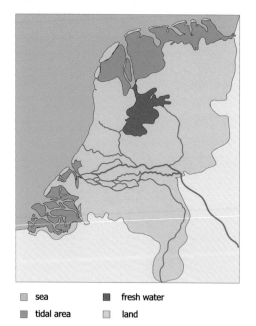

| ☐ sea | ■ fresh water |
| ■ tidal area | ☐ land |

Figure 2   - The Netherlands around the year 800 A.D.

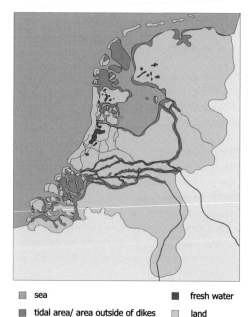

| ☐ sea | ■ fresh water |
| ■ tidal area/ area outside of dikes | ☐ land |

Figure 3   - The Netherlands around the year 1250

- sea   ▪ 1200 - 1600 A.D.
- fresh water   ▪ 1600 - 1900 A.D.
- land   ▪ 1900 - 1970 A.D.

Figure 4 - Land expansion in the Netherlands since 1200

At present, about half of the Netherlands would be flooded if there were no dikes. Habitation is only possible by an extraordinarily vast system of water control. Water boards form the organizational units for this. They are even older than municipality institutions as regulatory institutions in non-urban areas.

The underground in the Netherlands

The influence of the sea is also visible in the structure of the ground in the Netherlands (Figure 5). Typical characteristics of this are:

- ground mainly consists of poorly permeable sedimentary clay and peat-soil
- permeable sand precipitations mainly in higher areas
- groundwater in deeper layers (weakly) brackish
- sweet groundwater only in areas with infiltrating rainwater, floating on more brackish groundwater

2.2   Water in the Netherlands

Rivers

The Netherlands mainly forms the delta of the Rhine and the Meuse (Figure 6).

The catchment area of the Rhine includes almost all of Switzerland and Luxembourg, and a large part of Germany. The river is about 1,300 km long and has a mean flow of 2,300 m³/s. The Rhine is a glacier river with a relatively high minimum flow.

The catchment area of the Meuse includes a part of France and a majority of Belgium. The river is about 900 km long, and it has a mean flow of about 230 m³/s. The Meuse is a rain river with a relatively small minimum flow.

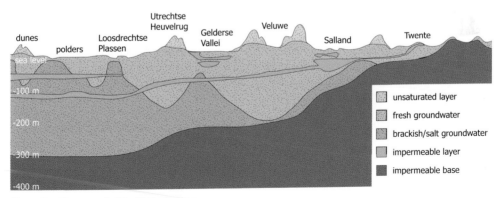

- unsaturated layer
- fresh groundwater
- brackish/salt groundwater
- impermeable layer
- impermeable base

Figure 5 - The ground of the Netherlands

45

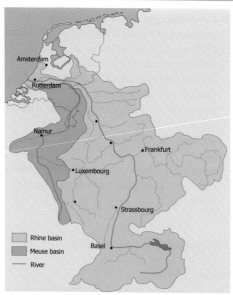

Figure 6 - The Netherlands, the delta of Rhine and Meuse rivers

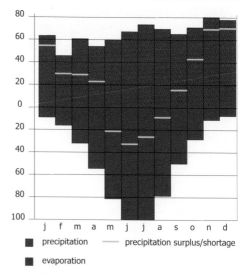

Figure 7 - Rainfall and evaporation (reference evaporation) in the Netherlands, variation over the year

Hydrology

The average rainfall in the Netherlands is 775 mm per year. This rainfall falls over about 570 hours. Around some 125 days per year are without any rain. The monthly rainfall is fairly equally distributed over the year, though most rain usually falls during the summer months. Then, the rain falls at a greater rate but the duration is shorter than in the winter.

An amount of about 10 millimeters or more falls in the Netherlands on about 20 days a year. A very large rainfall of about 30 millimeters in one full day occurs in the Netherlands, at the very most, once a year.

The mean reference evaporation in the Netherlands is about 540 mm a year. During the entire month of January this reference evaporation is about 8 mm, versus 90 mm during the entire month of July. Over the years this number has varied little; during the years from 1961 until 1990, the highest yearly sum was 629 mm, and the lowest was 497 mm.

The mean rainfall surplus for an area with reference evaporation is (775 - 540 =) 235 mm a year (Figure 7). Because of the Netherlands' flat sur-

face, almost the entire rainfall surplus ends up in the soil.

3.   Amsterdam

3.1   Inhabitants

Amsterdam has emerged as a small village near the banks of the Amstel, close to the place where this river flowed into the IJ, a sea arm of the former Zuiderzee.

Here, a dam was constructed in 1220 as protection against the tide. The place name 'Aemstelledam' was mentioned for the first time in 1275 in a document in which Count Floris V exempts the inhabitants from toll collection. In 1306 the place received city rights, and from 1317 the city officially belonged to the country of Holland.

The city is quite young compared to other, much larger Dutch cities of that time like Haarlem, Leiden, Nijmegen, Utrecht and Dordrecht.

However, halfway into the 15th century Amsterdam was growing rapidly, owing somewhat to her popularity as a pilgrimage site as a consequence of many miracles.

Because of the power of attraction of the city, the borders had to be enlarged repeatedly. In the beginning these expansions included canals and city walls for protection. The city expansion of 1612 was the largest in the world at that time: Amsterdam became one-and-a-half times as big (Figure 8).

Inspired by the Renaissance, people tried to build a perfect city. The city comprised a classy residential area, currently known as the 'Grachtengordel', and the 'Jordaan', which includes small and larger companies. The three canals (Heren-, Keizers- and Prinsengracht) were constructed as waterways for the transport of goods for the new inhabitants: the merchants, who had become rich by trading overseas. Because of a subsequent city enlargement, canal rings on the east side were developed. The characteristic crescent-shaped canal belt was thus created.

Czar Peter the Great was so impressed by the canals and bridges after a visit to the city in 1697, he used this polder model as a basis of design for his new city that had to build on swamps: St. Petersburg.

The crescent-shaped canals were intersected by a number of narrow, radial canals and streets.
The "Venice of the North," therefore, consists of about 90 islands, separated by canals, with a total length of 100 km and connected by over 200 bridges.

From 1700 until 1840 no city expansions worth mentioning took place. The city was in an economic crisis for a long time. Even a decrease in inhabitants occurred: people left for other cities in Germany and Belgium. Poverty ruled and slums emerged.
At the end of the 19th century the city council decided to backfill a number of canals, with the primary aim of easing the emerging horsecart traffic of merchants and traders. Hence, several canals were filled in. However, when the Reguliersgracht was threatened to be filled, the inhabitants' protests grew in such a way that by 1901 destruction of the canals ended.

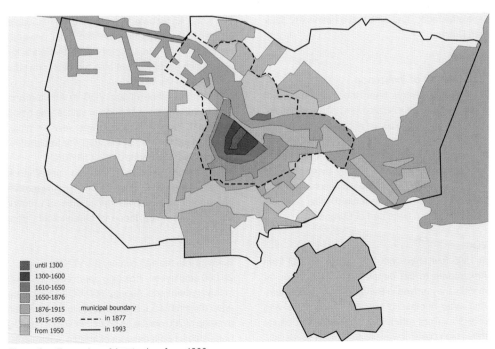

until 1300
1300-1600
1610-1650
1650-1876
1876-1915   municipal boundary
1915-1950   - - - - in 1877
from 1950   ——— in 1993

Figure 8   - Expansion of Amsterdam from 1300

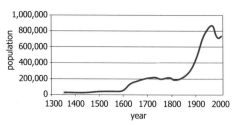

Figure 9 - Population growth of Amsterdam

In the 20th century there was a substantial increase in population (Figure 9). Together with the demand for a larger living area per person, vast uniform city quarters appeared and, subsequently, new independent "garden cities" emerged around Amsterdam.

By 1960 many inhabitants had moved from the old city center of Amsterdam to the surrounding communities, such as Purmerend, Lelystad and Almere. Then, because of urban renewal in the old center, the population increased again after 1986.

Amsterdam currently has an international population. Almost half the residents were not born in the Netherlands, and 27% has a nationality other than Dutch.

3.2   Means of existence

Trading has always been the most important source of income for Amsterdam. In the beginning, fish and beer were exported and salt was imported, the latter to preserve the fish (salting). Later on, the export of butter and cheese started, and spices and coffee were imported. Initially, these products were brought by the Portuguese sailors from Asia to Lisbon. Dutch ships distributed Asian products from Lisbon to a large part of Europe.

VOC

In 1595 four ships with 240 sailors set sail from Amsterdam to get pepper from Asia. After 14 months they arrived in Bantam, Java (Indonesia). And, after another 14 months, three ships with only 85 sailors returned to Amsterdam. Despite these high costs, it was regarded as a successful venture.

Once the route to Asia was known, eight ships embarked from Amsterdam in 1598. After only 14 months, four ships returned; the other four ships had traveled on to the Molukken Islands (Indonesia) and returned after 24 to 27 months. This expedition was a big commercial success. Because of these successes, different enterprises from other Dutch cities started equipping ships. This resulted in competition and lower revenues.

To reduce the competition, in 1602 the States-General granted sole rights for trading with and shipping to Asia to the Dutch East India Company (VOC) for a period of 21 years. The VOC represented six Dutch cities: Amsterdam, Middelburg/Veere, Hoorn, Enkhuizen, Delft and Rotterdam. The head office of the VOC was located in Amsterdam.

The VOC was owned by shareholders, and the "Heeren Zeventien" (17 men) acted as the directors. Within the VOC 1,143 Amsterdam shareholders initially owned 57% of the shares for a total of 6.4 mln guilders. Eight of the seventeen directors came from Amsterdam.

The Republic repeatedly prolonged the monopoly of the VOC. It was not only the most powerful company in the Republic of the Netherlands for almost two centuries, but also the most powerful enterprise in the world.

At the head office of the VOC in Amsterdam, almost the whole world trade in spices was being managed. Trading in spices was very lucrative. The dividend remitted by the VOC was impressive: 18% on average and in 1642 it hit 50%!

The revenues were such that the capital stock remained the same. In later years big Amsterdam shareholders took over the shares of smaller stakeholders, even those of shareholders from other cities.

Halfway into the 18th century the VOC had almost 25,000 employees, including approximately 3,000 in the Netherlands. About 2,000 VOC ships managed the almost 5,000 departures to Asia, with an average of 200 people on board per ship. The VOC had established a network of trading settlements, including South Africa, India, Sri Lanka, Indonesia,

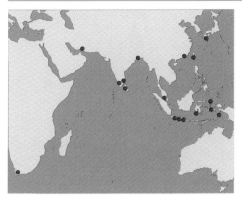

Figure 10 - Trading settlements of the VOC in 1689

China and even Japan, where they were the only European business partners (Figure 10).

The VOC was a private enterprise that operated abroad as the Dutch state. It had sovereignty over a number of areas, such as the managing of an army and a fleet, the signing of treaties, the declaration of war, and the signing of peace. At the end of the 18th century, the VOC was involved in colonial wars against England, in which they were defeated.

The VOC was dissolved officially on the 17th of March, 1798. The Dutch government (Bataafse Republiek) took over their debts and possessions.

WIC
In 1621 the Dutch West India Company (WIC) was established using the VOC as its model. With the monopoly that was given to them, they obtained a monopoly position over the west coast of Africa, the Americas and all islands in the Pacific Ocean between the Americas and the eastern point of New Guinea.

The most important regions controlled by the WIC were New Holland (including New Amsterdam, the current New York), Curaçao, Brazil and Surinam. No sovereignty rights were assigned to the WIC. Should it wish to declare war, it had to ask permission of the States-General first.

Just like the VOC, the WIC was established as a limited-liability partnership. Within the WIC, the people of Amsterdam owned 44% of the shares.

The major products that were imported to Europe by the WIC were sugar and tobacco. Unfortunately, the WIC obtained a regretable reputation due to its capturing of foreign ships and their engagement in the slave trade.

The ships usually undertook a cycle of three journeys: from the Dutch homeport with trading goods to Africa, from Africa with slaves to America and from America with sugar or tobacco back again to the homeport. The transport of slaves was their most profitable segment.

Even though the WIC was a trading company by name, it actually spent more time on political and military matters than on commercial activities. The company was dissolved in 1791.

Colonial period
After the dissolution of the VOC and WIC, the trading activities from the Netherlands, and, therefore from Amsterdam, remained of great importance.
The Netherlands owned some colonies, of which the Dutch East Indies (Indonesia) was the most important. On the one hand, Indonesia was the origin of the world trade in spices. On the other hand, plantations were established that cultivated all kinds of products like coffee, tea and sugar on a very large scale.
In the 20th century industrial activities developed in Indonesia, including oil production.

Currently, Amsterdam remains a city of trade, finances and service. Various multi-nationals have placed their European head offices in Amsterdam. Large-scale industry has been developed within limits, and it is concentrated at the port on the west side of the city.

Even though Amsterdam is the capital of the Netherlands, the Dutch government actually settled in The Hague, at a distance of about 50 km southwest of Amsterdam. This means that there are hardly any governmental services like ministries, governmental institutions or embassies in Amsterdam.

3.3 Drinking water service without pipelines

The Amstel and canals (1200-1651)

The first inhabitants of Amsterdam were dependent on the Amstel River as a source for their drinking water. The presence of this river was, after all, the main reason for the existence of the city. The fresh river water was separated from the salt seawater by a dam in the Amstel.

Other sources were hardly, or not at all, available. The peat soils, upon which Amsterdam was built, offered little opportunities for the exploration of groundwater, and the capture of rainwater would have been limited.

As a consequence of the rapidly growing population, the city struggled with pollution of the river by garbage, and human and animal excrement.

This is supported by some preserved documents from 1413, in which the city council prohibits the casting of dead animals, butcher disposal, manure and such in the Amstel, the canals or the river IJ. Unfortunately, that order was not sufficient. Therefore, the beer brewers of Amsterdam decided, in 1480, to get their water by ship from the Haarlemmermeer, and from 1514 from a stream near Kockengen, upstream of the Amstel, at a distance of 30 km from the city.

In 1505 the city council placed nine rain reservoirs in the city for common use. Richer inhabitants of Amsterdam captured their own rainwater.

In 1530 it was again decided to prohibit the throwing of garbage, urine and feces into the canals and that these wastes should be buried. This order also applied to dead cats and dogs. Besides this, the tanners and dyers were no longer allowed to discharge into the canals as well. All these measures still were not sufficient. When the mighty emperor Charles the V visited Amsterdam in 1540, he moved his residence to Haarlem, because he found the drinking water in Amsterdam unacceptable.

In 1595 new laws were written to improve the quality of the canal water. Public toilets were intro-

Figure 11 - Water from the canal near a city gate of Amsterdam (ca. 1600)

duced, and their contents were removed regularly to be buried elsewhere.
In 1620 it was prohibited to cast dead fish into the canals.

The lack of hygienic circumstances was shown by different outbreaks of the Plague. In 1622 6,000 dead were counted (5% of the population), in 1636 17,000 people died (11% of the population), and in 1664 24,000 people died (12% of the population).

In 1672 the 44-year old mathematician and physician Johan Hudde became mayor of Amsterdam. During the 31 years that he was mayor, different projects were executed to flush the water of the canals with fresh water from the Amstel.
The sanitary services were also improved, by placing cleaner drinking reservoirs near churches and public buildings and by the improvement of city toilets.

Beer brewers (1651-1786)

In 1651 ten Amsterdam beer brewers united to secure a constant supply of brewing water. The first joint activity was the purchase of an icebreaker that could secure the passage of different water vessels during winter. These water ships didn't take water only upstream of the Amstel, but also from the river Gein near Abcoude, a distance of 15 km southeast of the city. Because of quality, soon water was taken from the Vecht near Nigtevecht, about 20 km from the city. Both rivers flow parallel to the Amstel and end in the Zuiderzee (Figure 12). Barge

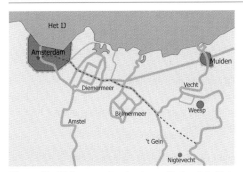

Figure 12 - Water near Amsterdam with Amstel, Gein and Vecht (1660)

canals were constructed to connect the city with both rivers. Usually, the ships in these rivers used horses to pull the vessels from the towing path.

Every morning multiple water vessels departed from the city to the different water inlet sites and returned to the city by night. The brewers sold the water from the water vessels to the inhabitants of Amsterdam and to the sea captains of the port of Amsterdam.

In 1695 a new icebreaker was purchased, this time financed by the brewers guild, which included all Amsterdam brewers.

About ten horses were needed for the operation of the icebreaker, which increased in hard winters to about 30 horses. Transporters guided these horses, while other men were busy helping the icebreaker by breaking the ice with axes and removing it from the waterway (Figure 13).

The price of water increased to 15 (guilder) cents per bucket, because of the costly operation of the icebreaker. For poor people this price was too high. These people had to melt ice from the canals, which resulted in many sick people.

In hard winters it was no longer possible to cover the costs of the operation because of the low sales and the high operation costs. Therefore, the brewers decided to cease water transport during periods requiring the use of the icebreaker.

However, the city council signed a municipal order in 1745 and again in 1769 that required the water supply to continue during winter. Of course, the brewers tried to ignore this obligation.

Versch-Water Sociëteit (1786-1853)

To break through the deadlock about the use of the icebreaker, the municipality of Amsterdam took over the icebreaker and a number of water vessels in 1786. They formed the Versch-Water

Figure 13 - Water vessel preceded by an icebreaker, pulled by horses (1740)

Sociëteit to oversee the water supply from the Vecht. This society granted concessions to water merchants for transportation and trading within the city. The brewers were only allowed to transport water for their own consumption. They had to pay a sum per water vessel to cover the costs of the icebreaker.

In 1806, 1814 and 1819 the municipality wrote ordinances for the management of the Versch-Water Sociëteit. These regulations were written for the hygienic operation, the conditions of selling, cost structure, fixed prices and so on.

For example, an empty water vessel had to be inspected for cleanliness and impermeability when leaving the city. The taking in of Vecht water was done under the supervision of a municipal inspector, who provided a certificate to the skipper. The skipper had to show the certificate when arriving at the city gate.

In 1818 King William I made a decree which stated that regional and local medical committees had to be installed who would supervise the purity of the drinking water.

The water from the vessels was transferred to some 30 water tanks in the city and another 200 smaller water boats, which were anchored at different locations throughout the city. The water was sold to the people from these tanks and boats.

The total sales of the Versch-Water Sociëteit was about 0.4 - 0.7 mln m^3 a year, which equaled about 5 to 10 liters per resident a day.

For public water facilities, rainwater from the roofs of the churches and captured in water tanks was also used. This water was less suitable for drinking water, because research in 1794 showed it had a concentration of lead that proved to be too high for safe human consumption.

Of course, the residents used their own captured rainwater as well. The inhabitants also used canal water, but mainly for the cleaning of their houses and streets.

After the introduction of dune water in 1853, the water supply of Vecht water by vessels disappeared.

The turnover of Vechtwater shippers decreased dramatically, which forced the city council to stop the operation of the icebreaker. In 1870 the last water traders from the Versch-Water Sociëteit quit their activities.

3.4 Drinking water service with pipelines

Duinwater-Maatschappij Inc. (1853 - 1896)

The Duinwater-Maatschappij was an initiative of state lawyer and popular writer Jacob van Lennep. He had been trying since 1845 to bring a modern drinking water service to his place of residence, Amsterdam, based on the technical ideas of the retired genius-engineer Christiaan Dirk Vaillant. Many enterprises had already presented plans for the water supply to Amsterdam, but all these plans were either technically or financially unfeasible.

Two years before its start-up, the Duinwater-Maatschappij Inc. began acquiring the necessary concessions and licenses, but most of all,

Figure 14 - Water boat for the distribution of Vecht water in the canals of Amsterdam

they were busy finding the funds. Only 4% of the required 0.8 million euros was financed by Dutch investors, the remainder came from British investors. The British did not share only money, but also technical knowledge and material. About 25 large cities in England had already constructed modern drinking water facilities, with pumps that were fed by steam engines and with cast-iron transport pipes. In the Netherlands a similar system had not yet been installed anywhere.

The water of the Duinwater-Maatschappij was abstracted at the Woestduin estate, owned by the family van Lennep and situated in the Kennemer dunes southwest of Haarlem.

The terrain was used for drinking water production in an ingenious way. The dune area was drained by a channel 3,500 m long, and by gravity the water flowed through a large storage reservoir to and through the sand filters in the clear water storage. The facilities within the dune still form the heart of the Leiduin production company.

From the clear water storage, the water was put under pressure by steam-driven pumps and then transported through a 23 km long pipeline, with a diameter of 12" (300 mm), to a fountain near the western gate of Amsterdam. The fountain was situated just outside the city, because neither money nor license was available for the construction of pipes within the city.

In June 1853 operation of the fountain started.

Then a decision still had to be made as to what extent the water was suitable to be sold as drinking water. The doctors thought that the water would not be reliable because it had been in the pipe for such a long time. Also, the Versch-Water Sociëteit objected because it had the exclusive license to supply water to the city.

In December 1853 the water supply of the Versch-Water Sociëteit stagnated as a consequence of a period of hard frost. Immediately, the city council gave permission for the selling of the water and, on 12 December 1853, people could buy a maximum of 2 buckets of water between 8 in the morning and 4 in the afternoon, for the price of a (guilder) cent.

As of 1854 the water was transported through pipes to standpipes in the city and finally even directly supplied to a number of households.

The new drinking water facilities were a success. The sales of water rapidly increased. In 1863 the length of the canals in the dunes already had to be more than doubled.

In 1866 there were 8,505 house connections and 56 standpipes spread over the whole city. The total supply to the city was about 2 million m^3 a year, which was 21 liters per capita per day (263,000 inhabitants).

The importance of a good drinking water service was underlined during the cholera epidemic of 1866. There were many more victims in other cities compared to Amsterdam. In the peak days of the epidemic, Amsterdam even supplied free dune water to its poorest residents.

Water consumption was growing rapidly.

In 1877 the abstraction area was expanded and a second pipeline was constructed between the dunes and Amsterdam.

Even this proved to be insufficient, mainly because of the massive growth of the city between 1870 and 1890 (408,000 inhabitants as of 1890). As a consequence of this growth, the water supply was

Figure 15 - Leiduin pumping station with slow sand filters, pump building (steam) and standpipe tower (1895)

not sufficient and the upper floors in buildings frequently didn't receive any water.

There was also criticism over the high tariffs caused by the high dividends paid to shareholders.

To increase the production of drinking water, the city council planned to build a new drinking water production plant near Driemond, about 10 km southeast of the city borders of that time. The water of the Vecht would be treated there.

However, the doctors of the Municipal Sanitation Committee declared that, despite the treatment, this water would not qualify as drinking water. It could only be used for scrubbing and scouring, and for the city to extinguish fires. Therefore, the water had to be distributed via a separate pipeline network in the city.

The Duinwater-Maatschappij was forced, within the concession, to execute this project. In 1888 the Weesperkarspel production plant was completed.

The consumption of Vecht water was very small because of its limited usage possibilities and therefore limited acceptance by the population. As a consequence the Duinwater-Maatschappij had to invest to expand the dune water system. This was unbearable for the company considering their obligations to the concession for maximum water tariffs and minimum supply to the municipality.

At last, in 1896, the municipality of Amsterdam took over the Duinwater-Maatschappij.

Municipal water company Amsterdam (1896 - present)

On May 1, 1896 the Duinwater-Maatschappij was purchased for 12 mln guilders by the municipality of Amsterdam, whereupon the company was continued as a municipal utility with the name Gemeentewaterleidingen. This now included the water company of the municipality of Nieuweramstel (currently Amstelveen), a neighboring municipality of Amsterdam, and a large area which was incorporated by Amsterdam. This water company owned a production company in Hilversum, where groundwater was treated to produce drinking water.

The problem of the drinking water shortage in Amsterdam was solved, at first, by building a distribution pumping station near the Haarlemmerweg, situated along the western border of the city at that time. This distribution pumping station contained large drinking water reservoirs and pumps to distribute the water. In this way the transport capacity of the pipelines between Leiduin and the city was expanded. On the one hand, this was because water could be transported during night hours, when there was relatively no demand. On the other hand, the pressure near the Haarlemmerweg was very low, so all available pressure could be used for the transport pipelines. In this way the available transport capacity of the pipelines almost doubled. The distribution pumping station started its operation in 1899.

In 1900 the facilities at the Leiduin production plant were completely renewed and expanded, with new slow sand filters and a pump building.

To expand the production capacity of Leiduin as well, wells were dug in 1903 in the dune area, so that it became possible to abstract deep groundwater.

To complement the rapid growth of the population and the accompanying rapid growth in water consumption per person, two extra transport pipelines were constructed between Leiduin and Amsterdam, in 1908 and 1912. In 1916 the very first transport pipeline ended its operation. After

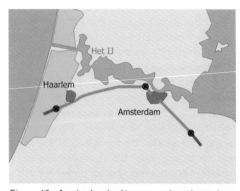

Figure 16 - Amsterdam had two separate water systems between 1888 and 1932: drinking water from the dunes and surface water from the Vecht

that the water transport between Leiduin and Amsterdam was handled by three pipelines (508, 610 and 770 mm long).

The abstraction in the dunes proved to be limited. Therefore, the local council of Amsterdam decided to produce drinking water at the Weesperkarspel production plant as well.
Therefore, the abstraction of Vecht water, as well as water from the nearby Merwedekanaal, was replaced by abstraction from the Loosdrechtse plassen (as of 1932). With this, the double distribution network became unnecessary and all distribution pipelines were used for the distribution of drinking water.

The abstraction of deep groundwater from the dunes was much greater and quicker than its natural refilling. As a consequence, deeper brackish water was pulled up. From 1957 pre-treated surface water was led into the dunes to maintain the production capacity there. This water infiltrated in the dunes and was abstracted after 100 days with the existing, as well as new, abstraction tools.
The surface water was abstracted from the Lekkanaal near Utrecht, treated and transported to Leiduin via a transport pipeline 50 km long and 1,500 mm in diameter.
In 1967 the supply and infiltration was almost doubled.

For the production plant in Weesperkarspel, a separate reservoir was created in 1957 in the Loosdrechtse plassen with the construction of a circular dike. This reservoir was fed by drainage water from the Bethune polder. This deeper polder received a lot of seepage water from the surroundings.
In 1977 the production plant of Weesperkarspel was totally reconstructed.

Until 1980, the drinking water service had been characterized mainly by a focus on providing extra capacity to cover the growth of drinking water consumption. From 1980 the primary focus shifted to improving the drinking water quality. The usage of chlorine was stopped after it was proven that undesirable and harmful by-products appeared.

Besides, the water was softened, which helped improve public health, the environment, and the comfort of the users.
Now, additional treatment processes seemed necessary to remove insecticides, like Bentazon, from the Rhine water.

In 1989 the production plant at Hilversum was closed, because of trouble with the quality of the groundwater. Renovation would be less economical because of its small scale and its production capacity could be covered very easily by the production plants in Leiduin and Weesperkarspel.
In 2003 the drinking water company got a new name: Amsterdam Water Supply. As of 2006 the water company will be merged with the Water Management and Sewerage Service of the municipality of Amsterdam into the company Waternet. With this merger, a water company will exist in which the drinking water service, sewage and wastewater treatment are all placed in one organization.

From former times, the drinking water company not only supplied drinking water to the municipality of Amsterdam, but also to a couple surrounding municipalities and to Schiphol Airport.
The current areas of supply are shown in Figure 17. The red colored area is the service area for drinking water (production and distribution) of Amsterdam Water Supply. The orange colored areas are service areas of other water supply companies, for which a substantial amount of water is produced by Amsterdam Water Supply.

Figure 17 - Service area of Amsterdam Water Supply (2005)

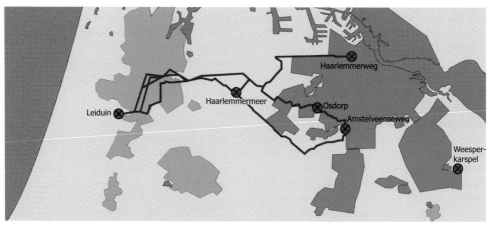

Figure 18 - Production and transport systems of Amsterdam Water Supply (2005)

The production for these areas is secured by long term contracts.

Figure 18 shows the locations of the two production plants Leiduin and Weesperkarspel and the two distribution stations Haarlemmerweg and Amstelveenseweg.
The booster station Osdorp brings water from the transport system directly into the distribution network of the city. The booster station Haarlemmermeer increases the capacity of the transport system between Leiduin and the city.

4.   Developments in water consumption and distribution

4.1   Distribution without pipelines

Rainwater and canal water
As fresh groundwater was not often available in Amsterdam, the water service during the Middle Ages was primarily based on the capture of rainwater or on canal water.

For the intake of rainwater, houses and buildings were equipped with rain barrels and rain tanks.
The available amount of rainwater was very limited. In a city of 200,000 inhabitants and a surface of 9 km^2, only 45 m^2 per person was available. Besides, not more than 20% of the surfaces were roofed. With an annual rainfall of 750 mm, there is a maximum amount of (45*0.75*0.20=) 6.7 m^3 per capita annually available, which means 18 l/p/d.

Between 1505 and 1860 10 rain reservoirs near churches were available in Amsterdam for common use. The total storage capacity of these reservoirs was 870 m^3. This is only 4 l/p for 200,000 inhabitants, providing little compensation for a dry period.

As a consequence of the limited availability of rainwater, the canal water, despite its poor quality, was important for the water service, as well as for cleaning. For this purpose about 1 - 2 buckets a day were used per capita (15 - 30 l/p/d).

Water vessels and water boats
Between 1786 and 1870, the salesmen of the Versch-Water Sociëteit sold Vecht water to companies and households.

A water vessel used for transport contained approximately 75 m^3 Vecht water. With 30 water vessels, about 5 - 10,000 transports could be made annually, which is equal to a supply of about 0.38 - 0.75 mln m^3 water annually. For a city of 200,000 inhabitants, this equals about 5 - 10 l/p/d.
Most water in the water vessels was transferred to water boats. These water boats were suitable to travel the smaller canals as well. Also, the water boats operated as sales reservoirs.

Table 1   - Capacity of the water service in 1824 (app. 200,000 inhabitants)

Part	Volume (buckets)	(buckets/p)
Transport		
30 water vessels	150,000	0.75
Transport capacity per day (0.5 - 1 freight/day)	150,000	0.37 - 0.75
Storage and distribution		
250 water boats	500,000	2.50
14 water tanks on squares & markets (not incl. 12 water tanks at brewers or 4 water tanks at hospitals & barracks)	110,500	0.55
6 water tanks being built	72,000	0.35
Total storage	682,500	3.41

1 bucket = 15 liter

Table 1 provides an overview of the facilities and the capacity of the different facets of the water service in the year 1824.

In 1837 businessmen established a company to deliver the prepared drinking water by handcars to people at home. After two years this enterprise was stopped because of insufficient revenues.
The largest share of the population preferred to get the cheaper water from the water boats in the canals.

In 1849 salesmen sold the Vecht water to small users from approximately 220 sales points spread over the city. There were about 20 fixed water reservoirs under the city squares and about 200 floating water boats in the canals. Also, there were 70 water boats to supply the businesses.
The fixed water reservoirs had a total capacity of 75 m³ and the water boats 30 m³. The water reservoirs and the water boats were equipped with a manual pump to pump the water from the storage to the customers' buckets.

If the 220 sales points would have been spread equally over the city, the distance between them would not have been larger than 200 m. Every water point could have supplied water to approximately 1,000 inhabitants (supplying 220,000 inhabitants).
The total storage capacity was enough for about 5 to 10 days' use.

4.2   Distribution with pipelines

Standpipes
In 1853 the Duinwater-Maatschappij started with a single sales point near the western city gate. On December 12, 1853, the inhabitants could get two buckets maximum for the price of one (guilder) cent per bucket between 8 am and 4 pm.
On the first day 4,450 buckets were sold and on December 17 15,000 buckets were sold (every two seconds one bucket), which equals 10% of the turnover of the Versch-Water Sociëteit.

As of 1854 the water was transported through pipelines to standpipes in the city. In November 1855, 16 standpipes existed all over the city where residents could buy water. The standpipes were equipped with multiple outlets and were checked by a salesman in recognizable uniform.

In addition, subscribers connected their houses to the pipeline network. By 1856 1,397 houses, 40 factories and 30 public institutions had subscribed to the network. The subscribers paid a tariff based on the number of rooms, toilets and baths. A house with 6 rooms (@4 guilders/room), a toilet (@5 guilders) and a bath (@10 guilders) paid annually (24+5+10=) 39 guilders. At a standpipe one could obtain almost 11 buckets or 160 liters of water daily for the same cost.

In 1866 the Duinwater-Maatschappij supplied about 2 mln m³ of water. A larger increase in sales was not possible because of the limited capacity of the transport pipes from the dunes. By this time,

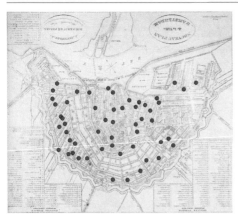

Figure 19 - The distribution of standpipes over the city (1866)

Figure 20 - Nowadays, it is still visible on some street pot covers that Amsterdam used to have two separate pipeline networks (1888-1932)

there were 8,505 subscribers and 56 standpipes. Several standpipes were leased to dealers who were allowed to deliver the water to the client at home, with the same maximum tariff of one cent per bucket.

With 56 public sales points, the distances in between were approximately 400 meters. Without home connections, every standpipe would have to supply water to 4,700 inhabitants.

The number of standpipes was not further expanded. New residential areas in Amsterdam were only supplied with water by home connections. In the older areas an increasing number of houses were connected to the network.

The last standpipe for selling water disappeared from the city sometime between 1920 and 1940.

Dual pipeline network

From 1888 there were two pipeline networks in the city: one for the dune water and one for the Vecht water. Only the dune water was considered suitable to use as drinking water.

However, distribution of non-potable water was not a success. The demand didn't meet the expectations, by far.

It was not until 1932 that the distribution of two different qualities was cancelled.

At a number of places in the inner city of Amsterdam, the remains of the double network are visible on the street pot covers which show "Vecht left" and "Dune right" (Figure 20).

The acceptance of water from the Weesperkarspel production plant as drinking water in 1932 was partly due to their use of a better water source (Loosdrechtse plassen instead of the Vecht). Greater trust in the treatment methods, the limited possibilities of expansion of dune water production, but, most of all, the very low cost of the drinking water production due to the use of existing facilities all contributed to this acceptance.

The application of a dual network was considered again in 2000 with the construction of a new residential area in IJburg. This new construction fueled a social discussion about the use of excellent quality drinking water for inferior applications such as toilet flushing and garden watering. Ultimately, the dual network wasn't operationalized because of its higher cost and the public health risk caused by incidental drinking or by cross-connections between both networks, which would undoubtedly cause deterioration of the drinking water quality.

Industrial water

From 1967 the water company supplied water to a couple of companies in the western port area of Amsterdam. The expectation was that, in this area, interest would exist for pre-treated river water, which is also used by the Leiduin production plant.

This industrial water was sold for €0.43 per m³, which was considerably lower than the price of drinking water (€1.29 per m³).

Despite the low price, the size of the supply has always been small (never over 3 mln m³ per year). Apparently, it is relatively expensive for industrial customers to have and maintain separate water systems.

Next to this, the industrial activities within the city have always been low as a result of the municipal policy of environmental protection.

The size of the existing supply is decreasing (1.8 mln m³ in 2001, 1.2 mln m³ in 2003).

Distribution reservoirs

Initially, the drinking water was pumped directly from the Leiduin production plant to the customers in the city.

After 1899 the Haarlemmerweg distribution pumping station, situated near the western city border at that time, delivered the drinking water.

The distribution pumping station contained a low reservoir with a capacity of 10,000 m³, to which drinking water was supplied during the full day. Now, with a similar pipeline, approximately twice as much water can be transported, also because the water pressure at the point of delivery is much lower. The water is put under pressure by a pump installation at the low reservoir for delivery to the customers via the distribution network.

With the expanded capacity at Leiduin, the number of low reservoirs at the Haarlemmerweg distribution pumping station also has been regularly expanded (in 1923, 1938 and 1953), together with the capacity of the distribution pumps. In 1966 the distribution pumping station was equipped with a water tower to balance the pressure changes.

Over time this distribution station was no longer situated near the center of the supply area, which expanded more and more in a southerly direction.

Therefore, in 1965 a new distribution pumping station was constructed near the Amstelveenseweg, on the south side of the city. Here, in multiple building stages, five reservoirs with a total capacity of 50,000 m³ were constructed, together with the pump facilities.

In 1994 the Haarlemmerweg distribution pumping station was totally renovated, after 100 years of expansions and reconstructions. At a neighboring area three new reservoirs were built with a total capacity of 45,000 m³, together with a new pump building.

Figure 21 - Haarlemmerweg distribution pumping station (lower left) with an important part of the corresponding area of supply

Apartment buildings were constructed at the old area, and a couple of noteworthy buildings were given a new purpose (Figure 21).

The total available storage for the production from Leiduin is 95,000 m³, which equals 65% of the plant's maximum day delivery (140,000 m³). The capacity is not only for the flattening of production and supply, but also for bridging production during reparation to one of the transport pipelines from Leiduin.

The Weesperkarspel production plant is situated much closer to the city. The drinking water produced there is pumped directly to the distribution network. Therefore, there are reservoirs present with a total capacity of 30,000 m³, which allow the production to remain constant over a full day, even with fluctuating consumption in the city. The quantity equals about 30% of the maximum daily production.

Pipeline network

Within about 150 years, the total length of the pipeline network has increased from 23 km in 1853 to 2,700 km in 2004. The technical developments during that time have been primarily determined by the pipeline material. In Table 2, the different pipeline materials in Amsterdam (excl. house connections) are compared with neighboring Amstelveen, where a substantial increase in population began appearing only after 1950.

Table 2 - Pipeline material (in km) in Amsterdam and Amstelveen (VEWIN 2001)

Pipeline material	Amsterdam[1]	Amstelveen[2]
cast iron	784	11
nodulair cast iron	388	-
steel	63	-
concrete	188	-
asbestos cement	11	55
polyvinylchloride (PVC)	538	286
polyethylene (PE)	144	19
glass fiber reinforced synthetics	3	-
various	147	-

1 incl. Heemstede, Diemen and Muiden
2 incl. Ouder-Amstel

In Amsterdam, cast iron was used until the First World War, nodulair cast iron between both world wars, and synthetic material after the Second World War. The first two materials are absent in Amstelveen, because their use has been very limited, and they have already been replaced by synthetic material.

Steel and concrete are used with diameters of 800 mm and more. Such a pipeline diameter does not exist in Amstelveen.

Remarkable is how insignificant the length of asbestos cement is, a pipeline material that has been used frequently in the Netherlands. In Amsterdam, nodulair cast iron remains in use for reasons of uniformity.

Cast-iron pipelines slowly face corrosion and can cause brown water. However, this does not jeopardize public health.

The same does not hold for lead pipelines however. Lead pipes had been used largely until 1950

for house connections and as inner pipelines in houses.

In 2000 Amsterdam Water Supply had replaced all lead service connections with synthetic pipelines. Between 1999 and 2005, houseowners could use a national subsidizing program for the replacement of lead pipelines in their houses.

4.3 Water consumption

Total consumption

The supply of drinking water was characterized by rapid growth over the years. The turnover of 15,000 buckets (225 m³) daily in 1853 equalled a total consumption of 1 l/p/d, with a population of 225,000 inhabitants.

In 1866 the total sale in the city was about 2 mln m³ a year, which is equal to about 21 l/p/d (263,000 inhabitants). More than 100 years later the total sale within that same area of delivery had increased to 65 mln m³/y. Since 1960 this consumption has stayed nearly constant. The decrease in the population between 1960 and 1985 and the increase afterwards (Figure 9) is not visible in the total water consumption figures.

In 2000 65% of the total water consumption was used in households (consumption less than 300 m³/y). The drinking water consumption in households increased between 1970 and 2000 with about 10 mln m³/y, which is equal to the decrease in business consumption (> 300 m³/y) during that period.

The total drinking water consumption per user had a nearly linear increase to 250 l/p/d in 1990 and decreased afterwards (Figure 23). The public

Figure 22 - The construction of large pipelines placed in thin bridges sometimes demands special solutions (1902)

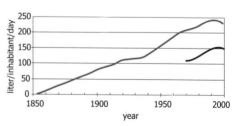

Figure 23 - Development in the drinking water consumption per user (total and domestic) in Amsterdam

campaigns in the Netherlands for water consumption reduction seem to have had an effect as also can be seen from the decrease in domestic consumption.

The increase in water consumption per person was caused by:
- greater availability (more production)
- more convenient access (no more picking up, but delivery at home)
- improvement of sanitary facilities (toilet, shower)
- increase in living comfort (more frequent showering, watering the garden, car washing)

The improved sanitary facilities have partly been enforced by the Housing Law of 1901, which demanded that every house have a toilet with reasonable ventilation, together with a sink and sewer connection.

In 1916 there were only 52,000 toilets in Amsterdam, which increased to 268,000 by 1937. The municipal order of 1932 required that a shower or bathing room be put in every newly built house. Therefore public bath houses were not built anymore in new residential areas.

Because of the introduction of sewerage systems and water closets, the service for the collection of feces also disappeared. But, until 1936 in the Amsterdam city center, these waste buckets were still emptied into pulling carts.

Fluctuations in consumption

The drinking water consumption shows a few characteristic patterns.

In the summer, consumption is higher on average. Also, a typical difference appears between low consumption during the weekend and a higher consumption during the week.

In Amsterdam the overall differences in daily consumption are not very large.

In an urban area the extensive watering of gardens is not very common, and during the weekend there are still a substantial number of activities that consume water.

Fluctuations in the daily pattern can be expressed as the relationship between an extreme consumption and the average daily consumption in a certain year.

Between 1997 and 2003, the lowest daily consumption in a year had a peak factor between 0.81 and 0.88; the highest daily consumption had a peak factor between 1.14 and 1.20. The days with low consumption were Sundays and holidays.

During the day there are also fluctuations in consumption. In Amsterdam, the hour with the highest consumption appears in the morning, and can increase to 1.6 - 1.8 times the average consumption of that day. During the night the consumption can decrease to 0.4 - 0.5 times the mean consumption.

Domestic water consumption

In Table 3 Amsterdam's household drinking water consumption is compared to the consumption in neighboring Amstelveen.

The domestic consumption in Amsterdam was higher because:
- there are a relatively higher number of one-person households and small families (i.e., fewer occupants per home)
- there are relatively more people with a non-Dutch water culture (i.e., less saving, more bathing)
- the domestic water consumption is not metered (higher consumption at no additional cost)
- some business connections might be administrated as household connections (business connected are metered and therefore more expensive)

Cost for drinking water

For domestic households without water meters, the water cost is calculated based on the number of units in the house. A calculation unit is a room of six m^2 and larger, a kitchen, a tub bath, a garage, and a garden larger than 65 m^2.

A room of over 30 m^2 is counted as two units.

A house is rated for a maximum of nine units.

In 2004 the tariff per unit was €36.19.

People living alone can call for a price reduction of 33%.

Table 3   - Domestic water consumption in Amsterdam compared to Amstelveen (VEWIN 2001)

Aspect	Amsterdam[1]	Amstelveen[2]
Water consumption		
Total consumption (mln m³/y)	65.4	5.4
Household consumption (mln m³/y)	43.3	3.2
Share household (%)	66%	59%
Number (technical) connections		
Total (households and business)	151,381	26,756
Households metered	2,413	24,694
Households not metered	130,188	803
Share households metered	2%	97%
Population		
Inhabitants	791,000	90,000
Homes	395,000	41,000
Home occupants (persons/home)	2.0	2.2
Household consumption (l/p/d)	150	97

1   incl. Heemstede, Diemen and Muiden
2   incl. Ouder-Amstel

Such a tariff structure demands extensive administration. For a municipal water company this is possible because the administration can be connected to the municipal administration and the administration for building permits.

A calculation unit can partly be considered an estimate of the number of tap locations in a house, and an estimate of the value of a house. Consequently, a tariff structure exists that is not based on water usage, but mainly on economical welfare and ownership. The owner of the house is the paying customer, not the tenant.

Tenants pay the sum as part of their rental price to the landlord who pays it to Amsterdam Water Supply. Owners receive a bill from Amsterdam Water Supply directly.

The tariff structure has not been changed for 150 years. Over time, the toilets were removed from the calculation units, and the showers were never included (the "luxurious" tub baths were). This reflects the notion that sanitary developments, as well as public health, should not be jeopardized by the pressure of economics (finances).

The ability to pay is not relevant anymore. Partly because of that, the introduction of water meters for domestic consumption began in 1999.

For a household with a water meter, a fixed tariff of € 38.88 annually is assessed for the connection. Above that, an amount of €1.28 per m³ (excluding water taxes and V.A.T.) is charged. For an aver-

age family with a water consumption of 130 m³/y, the annual drinking water costs are €205. This is equal to almost seven calculated units for a house without a meter.

The municipality of Amsterdam determines the drinking water tariffs every year. The tariffs are based on a full cost recovery.

4.4   Water meters

Social discussions

As of 1853, house connections in Amsterdam were not equipped with water meters. The motivation not to use water meters over the years, though, has changed under the influence of social development.

Initially, there were technical arguments. The largest share of the supply took place via standpipes that used buckets as water meters, and for the supply to subscribers there were no reliable water meters available.

Until the first half of the 20th century, a financial limitation on the water consumption was seen as depriving the population of sanitary living conditions, and that was unacceptable. Examples of this were found in a number of Dutch cities where the water consumption had decreased dramatically during the crisis years.

In the middle of the 20th century the economical situation was decisive. The additional costs for construction, maintenance and reading the water meters were considered more important than the possible savings as a result of reduced water consumption. Besides, it was known that water consumption in the Netherlands was (still) less than in other Western countries, and, evidently, the "water civilization" hadn't matured yet.

Water meters are equipped with a backstop, such that no (polluted) water from a house could get back into the pipeline network. Since water meters were absent in Amsterdam, between 1970 and 1980, all connections were equipped with a backstop.

By the end of the 20th century, water savings had become a social issue because of environmental considerations. It was found that the water consumption in Amsterdam was quite high compared to other Dutch cities, and that there was no incentive for the citizens to moderate their water consumption.

The water meter discussion had always been a regular issue within the city council of Amsterdam. The decision on February 4, 1998, to equip all households in Amsterdam, Muiden and Diemen with water meters can be judged as historical.

The council expected that as a consequence of the introduction of water meters, the water consumption in Amsterdam would decrease by 12%.

Introduction of water meters

From June 1999 newly built and renovated houses were metered. In January 2001 the placing of meters in every housing block started. Every year about 30,000 houses receive a water meter, so that within 10 years, 300,000 houses will have water meters.

Other houses will only be equipped with a water meter after adaptation of their water installation (Figure 24). This is probably going to take about 30 years.

A considerable number of customers have been added to the water company because of the introduction of water meters. Formerly, the house owners were taxed for their water use, based on the house composition. In apartment buildings the owners pass on these costs to their renters.

From the point of view of social integrity, one has decided that in these apartments the water consumption per separate unit will be measured as well. The placing of a single provisional water meter for the whole building will not be done.

A very gradual introduction of water meters was not only motivated by technical and logistical problems. The expected reduction in consumption after installing the water meters might influence the tariffs too drastically. Because the real costs of the water company hardly depend on consumption, the water use reduction would lead immediately

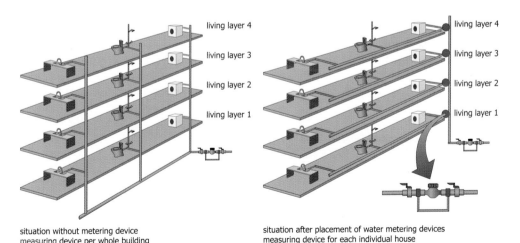

situation without metering device
measuring device per whole building

situation after placement of water metering devices
measuring device for each individual house

Figure 24 - In many houses the complete installation has to be replaced in order to install the water meter

to an increase in the water tariffs. With a gradual introduction, this effect is not as visible.

The introduction of the water meters demanded a complete renewal of the administrative process of billing. Consequently, the whole billing process is outsourced to a neighboring company, PWN Water Company Noord-Holland. This company already took care of billing its own 700,000 customers. After 2007 Amsterdam Water Supply will do its own billing.

5. Developments in drinking water production

The drinking water for Amsterdam is produced at two drinking water production plants:
- Leiduin
- Weesperkarspel

In this section the original setup of both production plants is discussed, followed by the current setup. The historical developments had the following backgrounds:
- expansion of the production capacity as a consequence of the increase in drinking water consumption
- expansion of the treatment process as a consequence of the usage of other sources, and the tightening of quality demands

Table 4 shows an overview of the produced amounts from both production companies. It shows that approximately 70% of the produced drinking water comes from Leiduin and 30% from Weesperkarspel.

The produced amount has remained nearly constant since 1995 (90 - 95 mln m³/yr) and no large changes are foreseen over the long-term. The increase in consumption, as a consequence of population growth, is expected to be covered by the water savings realized by the introduction of water meters and water efficient apparatus.

5.1 Leiduin - historical development

Capacity and space utilization
Three periods can be distinguished in the development of the drinking water production in Leiduin:
- abstraction of shallow dune water (via excavated channels)
- additional abstraction of deep dune water (via drilled wells)
- additional abstraction of infiltrated river water (via new drain pipes and existing channels)

Figure 25 shows this development in capacity and Figure 26 shows the development in space utilization.
Below, the different systems are described in more detail.

Natural situation
The Dutch dune area has emerged from thousands of years of blowing sand from the shore.
The dune area, at a height of 10 to 25 m above sea level, is a natural seawall for the land and polder areas east of the dunes.
The rainfall in this area flows via the underground to both sides of the dune area (Figure 27). The natural groundwater level, due to the flow resistance in the ground, is approximately 5 to 7 m above mean sea level.

Table 4 - *Overview of drinking water production for Amsterdam (2003)*

Destination		Leiduin	Weesperkarspel	Total
Produced for own supply area	mln m³/y	50.2	22.4	72.6
Produced for neighboring drinking water companies	mln m³/y	14.5	5.7	20.2
Total drinking water production	mln m³/y	64.7	28.1	92.8
Production capacity	mln m³/y	70.0	31.0	101.0
Utilized capacity	%	92%	91%	92%
Maximum day production (August 12)	m³/h	208,000	91,000	299,000
Minimum day production	m³/h	145,000	63,000	208,000

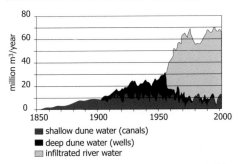

■ shallow dune water (canals)
■ deep dune water (wells)
▨ infiltrated river water

Figure 25 - Development in abstraction (capacity) of the Amsterdam Water Dunes

The dunes proved to be a very boggy environment, and the higher zones were not suitable for agriculture because of the ground structure (drift-sand). Consequently, these areas have never been fully developed for agriculture or industry.

Shallow abstraction

For the abstraction of shallow dune water, the natural terrain structure was used in an ingenious way.

The capacity of the existing stream was expanded substantially by digging a large storage reservoir measuring about 110 by 170 m, with a depth of about 6 m, near the original spring. The natural water level in this reservoir was 1 - 3 m above sea level.

This reservoir was called "Oranjewater" or "Oranje-kom," named after Crown Prince William of Orange who had set the first spade into the ground on November 11, 1851, at 11 years of age.

A channel was dug from this reservoir: 3,500 m long, 13 m wide and 3.5 m deep, in a westerly direction until about the center of the dunes. The

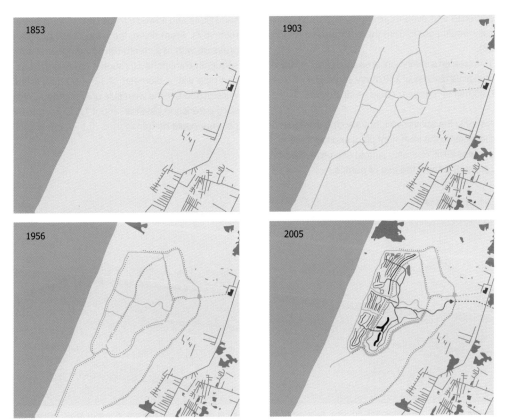

Figure 26 - Development in abstraction (space utilization) of the Amsterdam Water Dunes

A wet valley
B fresh groundwater
C salt groundwater

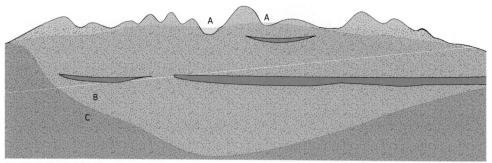

Figure 27 - Rainfall in the dunes created wet dune depressions and pushed aside the salty groundwater

rainfall excess was captured in this area via the drain channel.

In case of a decrease in the water level in the storage reservoirs, the level in the channels would decrease and even more groundwater automatically would pour in from the environment (Figure 28).

This created a catchment area of 3.4 km², in which, at a rainfall excess of 250 mm/y, some (3.4 x 0.25=) 0.85 mln m³ per year could be abstracted.

Not only the abstraction, but also the transport of the water to the treatment plant and the treatment process itself, operated almost entirely by free-fall (gravity), without the use of pumps.

The water flowed from an adjustable weir in the Oranjekom for 1.5 km through a canalized stream to the treatment plant, situated along the Leidsche Trekvaart. The water passed through three slow sand filters and flowed into the clear water storage reservoirs. From there, the water was put under pressure with two steam-driven pumps and subsequently transported through a 23 km long transport pipe with a diameter of 12" (300 mm) to the Willemspoort, at the west side of Amsterdam. With such a transport pipeline, about 1.1 to 2.2 mln m³ per year could be transported (0.5 - 1 m/s).

B fresh groundwater
C salt groundwater
D abstraction channel

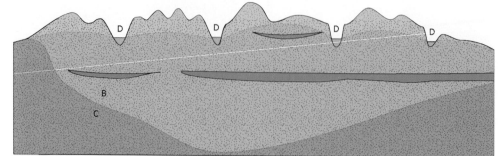

Figure 28 - The open channels not only abstracted the rainfall but also lowered the groundwater level, leaving dry dune depressions

Treatment of the shallow dune water includes two natural processes that take place in the collection system:

- natural aeration in abstraction channels, the storage reservoir and the transport channel
- natural sedimentation in the storage reservoir

The slow sand filters are the only structures specifically built for treatment. Chelsea Waterworks developed slow sand filtration in 1820 in England. It was shown that fewer sick people appeared in an area of supply that was fed by water through slow sand filtration than in surrounding areas of supply that did not use this process.

In a slow sand filter, the water flows through a 1 - 1.5 m thick mass of very fine sand that intercepts pollutants. The upper centimeters are removed after a time, because the top of the mass becomes polluted. After a few years, the sand mass is filled up again to the original mass thickness.

The new drinking water facility was a success. Water consumption rapidly increased. In 1863 the water abstraction area in the dunes had to be expanded to a total channel length of 7,620 m, which increased the catchment area to 7.9 km², about 2.3 times as large as it was.

The total abstraction in the dunes was about 10 mln m³ annually in 1885, which equals an catchment area of 40 km² at a rainfall surplus of 250 mm/y. With a total surface of the (current) Amsterdam

Water Dunes at 35 km², it is clear that there was no further expansion of the abstraction possible. Figure 26 shows that almost the entire dune area was equipped with drain channels for the abstraction of shallow dune water.

Deep abstraction

Around 1900 the delivery of non-potable water from Weesperkarpsel proved not to be a solution for the capacity problems of Leiduin. An extension of the supply power in Leiduin had to be found fast. Therefore, wells were drilled beginning in 1903 to extract deeper water from under the clay layer. The wells were drilled with a mutual distance of 100 m, along the existing abstraction channels. The pumped water was brought directly into the abstraction channels and mixed with the shallow extracted water (Figure 29).

The abstraction of deep dune water increased to 15 - 20 mln m³/y in 1930. From 1932 the further growth of drinking water consumption could be covered by the Weesperkarpsel production plant.

It was known that the deep dune water was not refilled, and that the pumping up of the water would lead, eventually, to the abstraction of salt groundwater. However, the fresh water storage was so large that pumping could be a solution for a substantial number of years.

In an area of 30 km² the abstraction of 15 mln m³/y equals a water disk of 0.5 m/y. At a porosity of 33%

B fresh groundwater
C salt groundwater
D abstraction channel
E deep well

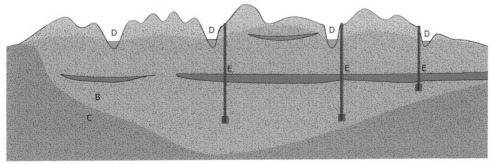

Figure 29 - The deep groundwater was abstracted by wells, but, as a consequence, the salt-water interface shifted and, at some points, salt water was also abstracted

the fresh-salt interface layer rose 1.5 m/y. With an average fresh water layer thickness of 45 m, this could last for 30 years.

In practice it proved possible to abstract deep water for approximately 50 years, because there really was a refilling from the groundwater above. Because of dehydration, evaporation was reduced, which caused an increase in the rainfall surplus.

The water level in the Oranjekom could only be lowered within limits due to the water transport between Oranjekom and the treatment area. This limited the abstractable amount of shallow dune water in dry years.

As of 1921, this limitation was removed by pumping up the water from the Oranjekom. Initially, the water was pumped up in the "oude beek" (old stream). In 1932 a larger pumping installation was built (Oranjekom 1), which transported the water via a pipeline to the treatment plant.

With a lower level in the Oranjekom, the groundwater level in the dunes also decreased. This caused a further drying of the dune area.

In contrast to the shallow dune water, the deep water contained no oxygen, but it did contain dissolved iron. With exposure to the air in the abstraction channels, this iron precipitated. From 1908 the aeration was improved by pumping part of the water up from the Oranjekom and spraying it above the water with sprinklers, allowing a quantity of the iron flocs to sink.

From 1921 the treatment process was expanded with aeration/pre-filtration by "Amsterdam" sprinklers above backwashed rapid sand filters.

Infiltration of surface water

After WW II, the production in Leiduin increased to 30 mln m³/y. However, the water from the deep wells was slowly becoming saltier, an indication that the abstraction of deep groundwater should be limited.

As a solution, a decision was made to infiltrate surface water into the dunes. Thus, the existing infrastructure with abstraction, treatment, transport and distribution could be maintained.

Experience developed with filtration of surface water in the dunes near Leiden, leading to plans for infiltration in the dunes near The Hague.

The surface water for Leiduin was abstracted from the Lekkanaal near Nieuwegein. Water flows through this channel from the Lek, one of the branches of the Rhine in the Dutch delta. This water is used for flushing the surroundings of Amsterdam, mainly for sea water intrusion control in the Noordzeekanaal.

The abstraction point is upstream of the discharge point of the treated sewage water from the city of Utrecht.

The water was pumped up from the Lekkanaal and via rapid sand filters discharged into a small storage reservoir. Then it was pumped to the dunes near Leiduin via a 50 km long transport pipeline with a diameter of 1,500 mm. From Leiduin some of the water was pumped further for dune infiltration in North Holland, and for the industrial water supply in the IJmond area.

For the infiltration, 3 - 5 infiltration ditches were excavated within an area about 1 km wide, which was surrounded by two 5 km long parallel abstraction channels (Figure 26). Horizontal drain pipes were constructed between the infiltration ditches, which drained away the collected water into the abstraction channels via a number of adjustable level-control structures (Figure 30).

Next to the infiltration area, a storage area was developed using two infiltration ditches. In this area there is hardly any water abstracted by keeping the level in the abstraction channels very high. In a period of water scarcity one can abstract extra water from here for a few weeks or months. Water scarcity can occur in a period when there is no infiltration because of pollution of the Rhine, for example.

In 1957 the infiltration was started, and the capacity was about doubled in 1968 by construction of additional facilities including a double pipeline from Nieuwegein. Nowadays, more than 80% of the abstracted water comes from infiltration.

A wet valley
B fresh groundwater
C salt groundwater
D abstraction channel
E deep well
F infiltration ditch
G storage
H drain pipe

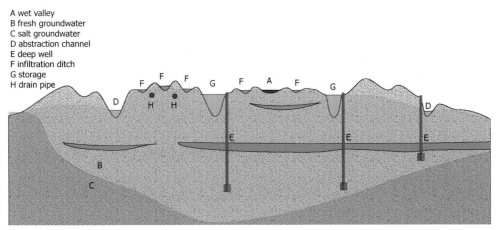

Figure 30 - Not only was the groundwater level restored by recharging with surface water, but also with the unique water storage system

In 1974 pre-treatment was expanded with coagulation, which consisted of an addition of ca. 3 mg/l iron(III)-ions, flocculation and sedimentation. This was required to enlarge the running time of the rapid sand filters and to improve the quality of the filtered water which were deteriorated by the higher suspended solids content of the raw water caused by increased ship traffic in the Lekkanaal.

Because of this coagulation process, heavy metals and phosphates were also removed. Phosphate proved to cause an unwanted disturbance of the vegetation within and around the infiltration ditches.

The better water quality also minimized the clogging of the infiltration ditches. Initially the ditches had to be cleaned a couple of times per year, by stopping the water feed after which a ditch dries up followed by natural decomposing of the bottom sludge. In the present situation the ditches have to be cleaned once in some 20 years. This is due to the low feed of suspended solids and the biological processes in the infiltration ditches.

Drinking water production and environmental policy

Appreciation for the dune area has changed considerably in 150 years. Initially, this area was seen as useless barren ground. This area was not suitable for habitation or agriculture because of the ground structure and the high groundwater level.

Through water abstraction, this area has become useful.

Through the years almost the entire dune area became the property of the municipality of Amsterdam, and then a protected water abstraction area (Figure 31). Also, because of this function, no other development such as urban build-up, road construction or hotel and camping facilities was allowed in this area in the 20th century.

In the second half of the 20th century, its environmental value was recognized. Together with that, there was strong pressure to completely free the

Figure 31 - The recharge area of the Amsterdam Water Supply shows a history of 150 years of safe drinking water supply in combination with a healthy environment policy

dune area of water abstraction, because it severely influenced the environment.

Meanwhile, the Dutch water companies have given environmental policy a prominent place in their operational activities. The drinking water abstraction also benefits from a good natural environment. These days, the Amsterdam Water Dunes welcome many thousands of visitors annually, for whom a separate visitor center has been designed.

The coming years will be dominated by the further integration of water abstraction and environmental policy. Together with that, the focus of water abstraction will be on the replacement of the open abstraction channels by closed-drain and transport pipelines equipped with different pumping systems. Thus, groundwater level management can be more adapted to the environment and contamination of the abstracted water will be prevented.

Looking at the developments of other Dutch dune water companies, one can expect that the abstraction of shallow dune water will be limited further, with a similar increase in the infiltration.

The main functions of dune infiltration within the modern drinking water supply include:

- natural filter for bacteria and viruses (100% removal)
- natural filter for organic and/or radioactive contaminants
- heat exchanger, by which an almost constant water temperature is obtained over the entire year (10 - 12 °C) in case of a closed abstraction system
- storage buffer for periods of problematic incidents (20 - 40 days)
- smoothing of the water quality by dispersal over time in the ground (60 - 120 days)

The first three functions are only feasible with an artificial recharge system, the last two functions could be realized, as well, in an open reservoir.

These five functions have proven to be so important for a safe, reliable and robust drinking water supply that the water companies now value dune infiltration to be the superior option for using surface water as a source for drinking water.

Additional treatment processes

Until 1983 a small chlorine dose prevented biological activity in the distribution network. By that time it was found that chlorination causes by-products that are harmfull for the health of the consumers. After extended research it became clear that the water from Leiduin could be distributed safely without chlorination, because of the benefits of its artificial recharge system and its treatment process including slow sand filtration.

In 1987 a new developed pellet softening process was put into operation in order to supply soft water.

In 1988 the laboratory of Amsterdam Water discovered the presence of the herbicide Bentazon in the water, not only in the Rhine water but also in the distributed water. Because of its polar molecule structure this contaminant passed the artificial recharge system as well as the treatment processes. This discovery was a result of the continuous research on more sophisticated analysis techniques to get a better view on contaminants in the Rhine water.

It was decided to extend the treatment plant with a combination of ozone oxidation and activated carbon filtration. This extension was put into operation in 1995.

5.2 Leiduin - current setup

Supply surface water

The surface water for infiltration near Leiduin is supplied by the NV Watertransportmaatschappij Rijn-Kennemerland (WRK). The WRK is a joint venture of the province of Noord-Holland and the municipality of Amsterdam. WRK produces and transports pre-treated surface water for the dune infiltration and the industry in Noord-Holland.

The WRK owns two production plants and five transport pipelines (Figure 32). The total WRK capacity is 259 million m^3/y of which 88 million m^3/y is available by contract for Amsterdam Water Supply. This amount is usually supplied by the WRK production plant near Nieuwegein. This plant has a production and transport capacity of 150

Figure 32 - Transport system for pre-treated surface water

million m³/y. Amsterdam Water Supply manages and operates this plant.

The WRK system has a sizable reliability. This is achieved by two independent inlet locations and production plants, the available reserve capacity (actual usage approx. 60%), and the five transport pipelines with flexibility of operation.
Pollution of the surface water and technical errors in production and transport can be dealt with, in most cases, by these facilities. Therefore, the storage in the dunes is almost never used.

To increase the certainty of supply, it is possible to abstract another 5,000 m³/h deep groundwater near Nieuwegein (approx. 20% of the inlet of surface water). This abstraction can only be used as an emergency facility, and may not be used longer than 25 days per year at maximum capacity (at maximum 3 million m³/y).

Pre-treated river water
From the Lekkanaal north of the Beatrix locks near Nieuwegein, the WRK takes in a maximum of 25,000 m³/h (approx. 7 m³/s) surface water, mainly from the Rhine (Figure 33-1).

The pre-treatment is designed for the removal of suspended matter, phosphates and heavy metals.
First, about three mg/l of iron ions are added together with the corresponding amount of hydroxide. By fast mixing, followed by slow stirring for 20 minutes, the flocs of $Fe(OH)_3$ emerge, and bind the contaminants that has to be removed. These flocs settle in three sedimentation basins (Figure 33-2) which have a total surface area of 36,000 m² (detention time approx. 3.5 h).
The settled sludge remains in the basins, causing them to slowly become more shallow. Every year the sludge has to be dredged away.

For the removal of the flocs that didn't settle, the water goes through 80 rapid sand filters with a total surface area of 4,320 m² (Figure 33-3). These

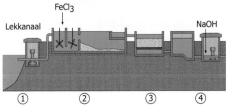

Figure 33 - Intake and pre-treatment of surface water at Nieuwegein

filters are backwashed every day by gravity flow from elevated backwash water reservoirs.

After filtration the water is captured in two filtered water reservoirs with a total capacity of 1,600 m³ (Figure 33-4). The water is transported from these reservoirs by 18 pumps and through three pipelines to the infiltration area near Leiduin.

Recharging and abstraction

The pre-treated water is transported in the dunes near Leiduin through a system of 10 km long open water channels to the 40 infiltration ditches, at a total length of 24.6 km and an average width of 35 m (Figure 34-5).

Horizontal drain pipelines at a total length of 9 km lie between the infiltration ditches which capture the infiltrated water again. The residence time in the ground is 60 days at minimum, but, because of the variation in the ground structure, residence

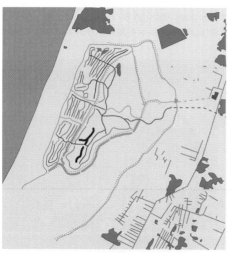

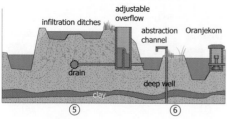

Figure 34 - Recharge and abstraction in the dunes of Leiduin

times of one year or more sometimes occur. The drain pipes expel the abstracted water via 12 adjustable overflows into the open abstraction channels.

The open abstraction channels also abstract a small amount of the infiltrated surface water and all the shallow dune water. Besides that, the deep abstracted water is collected in the abstraction channels. These channels form an abstraction, collection and transport system 33 km long, discharging into the Oranjekom collection basin (Figure 34-6).

Supply post-treatment

Four pumps with a total capacity of 20,000 m³/h take care of the transport of the water from the Oranjekom to the post-treatment installations. The maximum hydraulic capacity of the treatment installation is, according to the design specifications, 13,300 m³/h. Thus, there is always a spare pump available in case of maintenance needs or faults. In 2003 the maximum hourly production of Leiduin was 8,700 m³/h.

Aeration and rapid filtration

The water flows first over a cascade so that oxygen is absorbed by the water (Figure 35-7). Thus, iron, ammonium and manganese can be oxidized and caught in the rapid filters, together with the suspended matter from the open abstraction channels.

There are 40 rapid filters, each 40 m², and 16 rapid filters of 46 m² each, all of them with a bed thickness of 1.2 m filter sand (filtration rate 4 m/h).

After approximately three days, the filters are flushed back in the opposite direction with water and air. The backwash water is drained away for cleaning and reuse.

Ozonization

In the ozonization process, ozone-containing gas is added to the water by porous disks, with a dosage of approximately 0.8 mg O_3 per liter. The ozone is made on location from pure oxygen by ozone generators.

The ozone dissolves in the water and reacts with a large number of organic compounds, including pesticides. Thus, these compounds are broken down biologically more easily later in the process. Besides, viruses and bacteria are killed by the ozonization. Ozone also reduces the color, odor and taste.

To allow these reactions to happen, the water stays in the five ozone contact reservoirs for a minimum of 15 minutes (Figure 35-8). After that, almost all the ozone has been used.

Softening

Ozonization is followed by a crystallization process in 12 upflow hardness reductors (Figure 35-9). This process was developed by Amsterdam Water Supply. With the addition of sodium hydroxide at the bottom of the reductor, the largest amount of calcium in the water precipitates as $CaCO_3$ at the grains in the reductor. The extended grains are drained and new material is added. Because the reaction is fast, the reductors can be relatively small (contact time 2 - 4 minutes).

The total hardness is reduced to approximately 1.5 mmol/l. About 60 - 80% of the water is softened to a lower value in the reductors, followed by the mixing of the softened flow with the bypass flow. This procedure saves investment costs and the use of chemicals.

If necessary, a small amount of hydrochloric acid is added after the softening to obtain the desired pH.

The primary goal of the softening is the reduction of the copper and lead solvent capacity of the water, allowing the water to be distributed with a higher pH after the softening.

In addition, the softening has a few more advantages:

- no private softeners are needed by the drinking water consumers
- less (expensive and environment-polluting) washing detergent is necessary in washing machines
- less limestone precipitation occurs in washing machines
- consumers find it more acceptable for tea water and showering water

Activated carbon filtration

In the activated carbon filtration building (Figure 35-10), water is brought into contact for 40 minutes with activated carbon in a so-called two-trap filtration. There, the organic compounds, including pesticides and organic micropollutants, are adsorbed to the activated carbon, but also partly transformed into metabolites by the biological activity in the filters.

A small addition of oxygen could be necessary, because the biological activity consumes oxygen. If necessary, the pH is corrected as well.

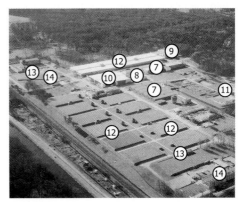

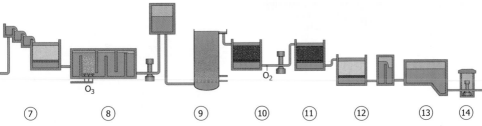

Figure 35 - Post-treatment at Leiduin

Slow sand filtration

The last treatment step is slow sand filtration. The water flows at a rate of 0.3 m/h through a filter bed of very fine sand (bed thickness 1 m). The last suspended materials in the water are captured in this bed. Also, the last remains of biologically degradable matter are removed here, together with any present bacteria. This prevents possible biological growth in the distribution network. Without the slow sand filtration, the addition of chlorine would be necessary for this, in spite of disadvantages: effect on the taste of the water and on the formation of harmful by-products.

A chlorination installation is installed but used only in case of an emergency.

Slow sand filtration requires a relatively large surface area (Figure 35-12).

Clear water storage and transport

After treatment, the water enters the drinking water reservoirs, with a total capacity of 13,400 m³ (Figure 35-13). The capacity is limited because there are large distribution reservoirs present, as well, for distribution to Amsterdam.

From the reservoirs, two drinking water pumping stations, one with nine pumps and the other with seven, pump the water to Amsterdam and to the distribution areas of other water companies (Figure 35-14).

5.3   Weesperkarspel - historical development

The development of the drinking water production plant at Weesperkarspel can be separated into five periods:
- abstraction from the Vecht (no drinking water)
- alternative abstraction from the Merwedekanaal (no drinking water)
- abstraction from the Loosdrechtse plassen
- abstraction from seepage of the Bethune polder
- abstraction from the Bethune polder, filled up by the Amsterdam-Rhine Canal

Vecht

On May 1, 1888, water production in Weesperkarspel started. The design capacity was 40,000 m³/d (10 - 14 million m³/y). The Health Committee didn't allow the treated water from the Vecht to be used as drinking water.

From the intake location in Nigtevecht, water flowed by gravity via a 5 km long, 1,220 mm wide supply pipeline, to the treatment plant in Weesperkarspel (Figure 36).

The intake location was situated at the place where, in the past, the Versch-Water Sociëteit filled the water vessels.

Consequently, the production plant would be built somewhere between the intake location and the city. The site for the production plant was chosen because of the suitable sand ground on which the buildings could be built without expensive foundations. In the vicinity of the intake site, as well as in Amsterdam, the ground mainly consists of peat

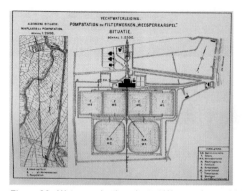

Figure 36 - Water production plant at Weesperkarspel (situation 1910-1920)

soil. In such an environment, every building has to be built on many foundation piles.

From the receiving reservoirs at Weesperkarspel, the water was pumped up by steam-fed pumps into two sedimentation basins of 8,600 m² each. From there the water flowed through four slow sand filters of 5,400 m² each. The filtrated water was captured in small clear water storage basins. From here the water was pumped up for transport to the city via two water pipelines with diameters of 610 and 680 mm.

The production plant was not provided with clear storage reservoirs for the flattening of fluctuations in demand over the full day. The whole system, including pumps and pipelines, was designed so that the desired day's production could be produced in 15 to 18 hours, taking into account the minimum or lack of demand during the nightly hours.

In the design, one sedimentation basin and one slow sand filter could be out of operation for a long time for cleaning (Figure 37). In this situation, surface loading would be 0.2 and 0.1 m/h on average, at the design capacity.

The production plant had a characteristically machine building with two chimneys (Figure 36) housing the steam boilers and two steam engines. Each steam engine, equipped with a large fly-wheel, fed a combination of a raw water pump and a clear water pump, which were connected to each other by a balance drive. The supplied water was

Figure 37 - Making the slow sand filters ice free (winter 1928/1929)

kept synchronal with the distributed water through this connection.
The steam engines of 1888 were used until 1954.

The production at Weesperkarspel was less than the original estimations because of the limited demand. Even when the large industrial customers were connected to the Vecht water, the daily use was limited to about 9,000 m³/d (slightly more than 3 million m³/y), less than 25% of the design capacity.

About 35% of the Vecht water was used by municipal services, which didn't pay anything for it. In former days, the city's rights to 12,000 m³/d free water had already been written down in the management contract of that time to the Duinwater Maatschappij.
Around 1900, production at Weesperkarspel had increased to over 6 million m³/y.

Between 1888 and 1910 a ca. 30 m high tower, with a standpipe inside, stood near the machine building. This standpipe was meant to balance the fluctuations in pressure (surge protection). In 1910 this (historic) tower was torn down.

Merwedekanaal
The water of the Vecht often contained too high a salt level, mainly because of salt seepage water originating from the Horstermeer polder. In 1896 a salt level of more than 300 mg/l was measured. Partly because of that, in 1914 an alternative intake point was made in the Merwedekanaal (the current Amsterdam-Rhine canal). The intake point was easy to construct because the supply pipeline between the Vecht and Weesperkarspel crossed this canal.
The water from the Merwedekanaal was often of very poor quality, because of discharges of sewage, and because of the higher salt levels during dry periods with very low flow through the canal.
With two available intake points, a choice was made to use the one with the least poor quality at the time of need.

In 1926 nine pre-filters were put into operation; the slow sand filters were less burdened and needed to be cleaned less often (manually). The pre-filters were backwashed every one or two days with water. From 1928 an additional air scoure was used for this activity.

In 1927/1928 disinfection by chlorine gas was also introduced, providing for bacteriologically reliable water.

In 1931 the Weesperkarspel production plant supplied about 8 million m³ of water.

Loosdrechtse plassen

In 1932 a new intake in the Loenderveense plas was build about 7 km to the south of the intake in the Vecht. The Loenderveense plas was a separate part of the Loosdrechtse plassen. The Loosdrechtse plassen had emerged between 1700 and 1900 as a consequence of the digging up of the peat soil. From this peat, people produced turf, which was used on a large scale as fuel.

Connected to the usage of this new intake was the agreement that the water company had to handle water management of the Loosdrechtse plassen and its environment.

The most important problem area for this task was the neighboring Bethune polder. This deeper polder had a good permeable underground, which caused a lot of seepage water to come up. Annually, 35 million m³ of water had to be pumped away, which is about 15 times the rainfall in this polder.

The high costs for pumping were not in accordance with the agricultural revenues. These were particularly low since the growth of the crops was limited by the low temperature of the seepage water.

The municipality of Amsterdam was allowed to use the water for its water supply on the condition that they would bare all the costs for the water management in the area. This agreement was settled in a contract "for centuries".

Without this settlement the Loenderveense plas would now be filled with municipal waste, and the Bethune polder would be under water again.

For level management of the Loosdrechtse plassen, a total of about 10 - 20 million m³ of water is needed annually. An important part of this water flows through the underground back to the Bethune polder. In this way, a net amount of 15 - 25 million m³ water can be abstracted from the whole lake district. That is mainly underground water flowing from the neighboring polders and from the Utrechtse Heuvelrug situated on the east side of the lake district.

Because of this underground flow, the quality of the water is better than the water in either the Vecht or the Merwedekanaal. As a consequence of the better water quality, and because of the improved treatment in Weesperkarspel over the years, the produced drinking water was judged suitable for drinking water.

Because of that, the production at Weesperkarspel immediately increased. In 1932 already 11 million m³ of (drinking) water was produced, an increase of almost 40% over the previous year.

Two extra slow sand filters were put into operation in 1941 to increase the production capacity. A new disinfection installation and an extra pipeline from Weesperkarspel to the city were added as well.

In 1954 a new distribution pumping station was installed, to replace the 66-year-old steam-driven pumps.

In 1956 the production plant supplied almost 25 million m³ of drinking water.

Bethune polder

In 1957 water regulation in the lake district was changed radically, on behalf of the drinking water supply.

Within the Loenderveense plas the Waterleidingplas was constructed, with a separate storage basin with a surface of 1.23 km². The Waterleidingplas was fed directly from the Bethune polder via a new 7 km long Waterleidingkanaal.

Between 1972 and 1986 several improvements were needed in and around the Waterleidingplas. Because of the increasing usage of phosphate, algae growth in the shallow basin increased, with unfavorable outcomes for water quality and drinking water production.

First, a temporary facility was made by iron dosing in the Waterleidingkanaal. This led to the precipitation and settling of ferric phosphate. This was replaced in 1983 by a separate facility with serial

Figure 38 - The cleaning of the slow sand filters (1976)

sedimentation basins. In 1976 the Waterleidingplas was significantly deepened to approx. 15 m which created a longer residence time, and further limited the algae growth.

In 1977 a whole new production plant was constructed in Weesperkarspel. This plant had a production capacity of 30 million m^3/y. After the newly built facility was in full operation, the old facility was demolished, ending its service of nearly 90 years.

The new setup of the plant was the result of years of research on improvements to drinking water quality and the optimizing of treatment processes.
A new pre-filtration was used near the Waterleidingplas, which caused the pollution in the transport pipelines to Weesperkarspel to decrease significantly.
Disinfection with chlorine was replaced by ozone disinfection, which caused no harmful haloforms to form, and which also improved the taste of the water.
The new slow sand filters were covered and equipped with a mobile cleaning machine.
However, the biggest innovation resulted from the development of a new softening process, based on crystallization in a fluidized grain bed (Figure 39). The process was included in the treatment process in 1988. The process design for this was already available when construction of the new production plant was completed, but not until 1986 were the public health authorities convinced that softening doesn't have an unfavorable influence on health.

Figure 39 - In pilot plants, processes were, and are, developed and optimized (e.g., softening 1971-1988)

Research at a test installation continues to be one of the permanent activities of a water company. Using a small-scale copy of the production company, all kinds of small setups can be tested and optimized.

Bethune polder and the Amsterdam-Rhine Canal

In 1983 an additional intake for water from the Amsterdam-Rhine Canal was constructed. Because of this extra supply possibility, the production capacity was no longer limited by the amount of seepage water from the Bethune polder.
At present, the water share from the Amsterdam-Rhine Canal is limited to 1 - 6% of the yearly production.

Because the Amsterdam-Rhine Canal is constantly flushed with about 25 m^3/s of water from the Lek (Rhine), the quality of its water is significantly better than during the period in which this canal was called the Merwedekanaal.

After the discovery of Bentazon in the water at Leiduin, it was precautionary decided also to

77

incorporate an activated carbon process in Weesperkarspel.

For this, the existing lamella sedimentation and filtration processes were converted into activated carbon filters. This was put into operation in 1992.

Future developments

With the extra intake from the Amsterdam-Rhine Canal, one expects that the capacity of the Weesperkarspel production plant could be doubled in the future.

This possibility is always kept in mind, not only in view of the needed abstraction licenses, but also in view of the required space.

For example, the Waterleidingplas can be extended by a second lake, and the location of the production plant has been prepared for a future doubling of the installations.

The water company knows that the plant's current setups can be different from the future plant's setups, under the influence of social and technical developments.

Possible options could be, for example, to execute the abstraction in the Bethune polder with horizontal drain pipes (closed abstraction) and possibly to infiltrate surface water in this area. Here, a setup would emerge according to dune infiltration. Another option is the application of membrane filtration in the treatment process.

With future developments in mind, the water company becomes an active policymaker in the development of new possibilities and techniques.

5.4 Weesperkarspel - current setup

Abstraction of surface water

At the west side of the 5.4 km^2 Bethune polder (Figure 40-1a), two large pumps in the Bethune pumping station take care of the desired water level in the polder. Because of the low location and the absence of poorly-permeable soil layers, about 35 million m^3 of water have to be pumped out (approx. 6.5 m) annually.

The water that is pumped out is transported through the Waterleidingkanaal to the pre-treatment site near the Waterleidingplas.

In the summer months the amount of pumped water is about 60,000 m^3/d, in the winter months it could reach a maximum of 110,000 m^3/d. During the summer months, water is added from the Amsterdam-Rhine Canal (Figure 40-1b), because drinking water usage is the highest during that season.

In winter the excess Bethune water is used for level control of the Loosdrechtse plassen.

The capacity of the intake facilities from the Amsterdam-Rhine Canal is built so that the intake can be used in an emergency, should the inlet from the Bethune polder be undesirable.

The Bethune polder is a protected water abstraction area.

Coagulation and sedimentation

To prevent algae growth in the Waterleidingplas, phosphate is removed from the water by dosing with iron salts (coagulation). The formed flocs are removed in two basins in series of 6,400 m^2 each (Figure 40-2).

Every year the sunken sludge is dredged from the basins.

Process reservoirs

After pre-treatment, the water ends up in the Waterleidingplas (Figure 40-3). In this reservoir, with a surface of 1.23 km^2 and a volume of 6.9 million m^3, the residence time of the water is two or three months. Natural self-purification occurs in the reservoir.

The Waterleidingplas has a very minor storage function. With an acceptable level variation of one meter, about 15 days can be bridged. The storage function can be limited because the water pumped out of the Bethune polder provides a very safe and secure supply.

The water is abstracted from the reservoir by a movable pipe, which can collect water from 1 to 13 meters deep.

Via this outlet pipe, the water flows through a shallow basin (Proefplas) with a surface of 12,000 m^2. This basin is equipped with an electric fish hold, where fish are stopped by increasing electric pulses. After this electrical fish screen, the water is pumped up to the filter building.

Capacity of the production plant

The installations after the Waterleidingplas are designed for a yearly capacity of 31 million m³ (85,000 m³/d on average, or 3,500 m³/h). Because of the higher water demand in the summer, the production plant has a maximum day production of 115,000 m³/d (peak factor 1.35). On a winter Sunday, the water demand is lower, and a daily production of 65,000 m³ will be sufficient (peak factor 0.78).

Rapid filtration

In the two filter buildings (Figures 40-4) 24 rapid filters are present in total, each with a surface of 48 m².

The filters are backwashed every day with water and air. The backwash water is captured in two sedimentation basins, where the sludge can sink.

Transport pipelines

From the filtered water tanks, the water is pumped to the production plant at Weesperkarspel through a 10 km long, double transport pipeline, both with diameters of 1,000 mm.

At the production plant, the water is captured in a raw water flow splitting device which diverts the water equally over the 4 ozon contact basins.

Ozonization

Ozone-containing gas is added to the water in the ozonization process, with doses of 1.8 - 2.2 mg O_3 per liter. The ozone is made locally from filtered fresh air.

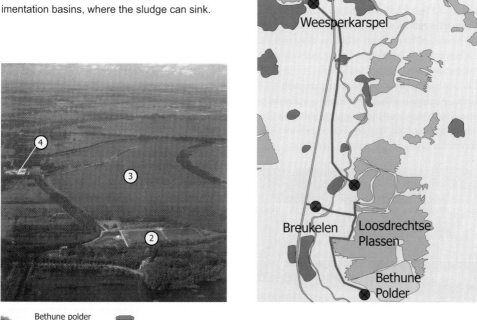

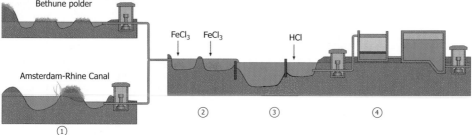

Figure 40 - Intake and pre-treatment near Loenderveen

The ozone dissolves in water and reacts with a large number of organic compounds, including pesticides. Following that, these compounds will be broken up more easily later in the process. Also, viruses and bacteria are killed by ozonization. Ozone also takes care of the conversion of color, odor and taste materials in the water. To allow these reactions to take place, the water stays a minimum of 15 minutes in the four ozone-contact basins (Figure 41-6). After that, nearly all the ozone will have been used.

Softening

The ozonization is followed by a crystallization process in 8 upflow hardness reductors (Figure 41-7). This process has been developed by Amsterdam Water Supply. By adding sodium hydroxide, a majority of the calcium precipitates a $CaCO_3$ on the grains of the reductor. The grown grains are tapped and new seeding material is added. Because the reaction is fast, the reductors can be relatively small (residence time 2 - 4 minutes).

The total hardness is reduced to approximately 1.5 mmol/l. About 60 - 80% of the water is softened to a lower level, followed by mixing the softened flow with the bypass flow. This procedure saves investment costs and also the use of chemicals.

If necessary the softening is followed by the addition of a small amount of hydrochloric acid to obtain the desired pH level.

Activated carbon filtration

In the activated carbon filtration building (Figure 41-8), the water is put into contact with activated carbon in two parallel systems for a minimum of 30 minutes. There, the organic compounds, such as pesticides and organic micropollutants, are adsorbed on to the activated carbon, but partly also degraded by the biological activity in the filters.

The biological activity uses oxygen, which requires a small, compensating addition of oxygen. If necessary, the pH is corrected as well.

Slow sand filtration

As a final treatment step, the water passes through 12 slow sand filters, each with a surface of 605 m². Slow sand filters require a relatively large ground surface (Figure 41-10).

At a rate of 0.3 - 0.6 m/h, the water flows through a filter bed of very fine sand. This stops the last floating particles in the water. Any remnants of biologically removable particles are removed, as well as any present bacteria. This prevents a possible bacteriological growth in the distribution network. Without slow sand filtration, a permanent addition of chlorine would be necessary for this and would invite all the disadvantages for the taste of the water and the forming of other harmful by-products with it.

Chlorine is dosed only in case of emergency.

Every year the slow sand filters are cleaned with a mobile cleaning installation (Figure 42).

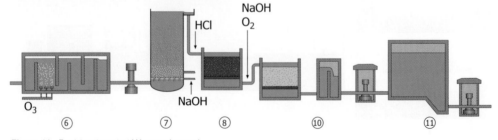

Figure 41 - Post-treatment at Weesperkarspel

Figure 42 - Slow sand filtration with mobile cleaning

Clear water storage and distribution

After the treatment, the water flows into two drinking water reservoirs with a total capacity of 30,000 m^3 (Figure 41-11). The clear water storage makes a constant production rate over a full day possible, despite a changing demand.

From the reservoirs the water is brought into Amsterdam's distribution system by six pumps, and also transported to the distribution areas of other water companies (Figure 41-12).

6.   Developments as enterprise

During the more than 150 years of history of the water company of Amsterdam, not only the engineering of the drinking water service has been changed drastically, but also the company's structure. The most remarkable characteristics are the property relationships within the company and its relationship with the government.

It is of value to study the considerations that played a role in the choices that were made.

For the water company of Amsterdam, the following entities can be distinguished:
- as a private enterprise with concession of the municipality
- as a municipal company
- as a government corporation

6.1   Private enterprise

Concessions

Until the introduction of public utility facilities such as drinking water, sewage, gas and electricity,

the municipal, provincial and national governments were rarely involved in any entrepreneurial activities. Governments had limited themselves to regulation and (securing) financing. In this situation a municipality is only involved if regulations are exceeded or there is an emergency situation.

The purchase of an icebreaker by the Versch-Water Sociëteit was an example of needed government intervention. Another example occurred when several companies had proposed plans to the municipal board in the 19th century to establish a drinking water service. The plans were very different in technical operation (location of the source, pipeline material, etc.). Finally, between 1845 and 1853 the municipality granted a concession to two companies for the construction of a drinking water system:
- Koninklijke Amsterdamse Waterleiding Maatschappij (from the Lek near Utrecht)
- Duinwater-Maatschappij (from the dunes near Haarlem)

These concessions did not include the exclusive right to supply drinking water. However, these concessions conflicted with the original exclusive concession for the supply of drinking water that was granted to the Versch-Water Sociëteit. This problem was "easily" solved by a new concession in which their exclusive right was restricted to water that was supplied via water vessels.

Release of shares

On March 4, 1851, the Duinwater-Maatschappij said that it hadn't been able to release sufficient funds, and that they had to quit their activities. On March 9, 1851, €0.82 million were invested, mainly by English financiers (Figure 43). This was judged sufficient to start the construction. With that, the infrastructure up to and including the fountain at the border of the city could be constructed.

Not until the fountain started its operation was the population of Amsterdam sufficiently convinced of its feasibility. After that, new shares could be registered, for a total sum of €0.41 million. With that, the distribution network could be constructed.

During the same period, investors could also put their money towards the purchase of ground in

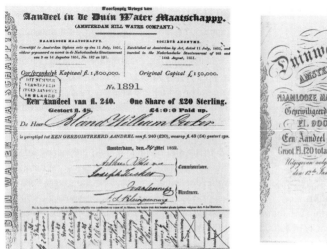

Figure 43 - Shares of the Duinwater-Maatschappij (1851 and 1856)

the Haarlemmermeer that was just pumped dry. Between 1853 and 1855 this ground was sold for €4 million. Such an investment seemed yet more attractive and, in those days, surely less risky than drinking water service.

The Duinwater-Maatschappij paid out dividends. In 1870 this was 6.3 %, increasing to 8.5% in 1874. The Duinwater-Maatschappij made a profit of €0.14 million that year.
In 1875 new shares were made available, with a total value of €0.77 million, for the construction of a second transport pipeline between Leiduin and Amsterdam. Because of the return on investment in the enterprise, it was not difficult to register these shares.

Also in 1885, shares were released for €2.72 million to extend the dune water facility and to construct the Vecht water supply system (Weesperkarspel).

6.2   Municipal company

Public influence
As a consequence of the strong growth in the population between 1870 and 1890, shortages appeared in the drinking water supply. The municipality wanted this shortage to be covered.

Negotiations about the concession in 1885 gave the municipal board the opportunity to set additional demands on the Duinwater-Maatschappij. On the one side, these were technical requirements, like the obligation to develop the new supply of Vecht water (Weesperkarspel) before November 1, 1887. Also, the Maatschappij had to guarantee that there would still be sufficient dune and Vecht water. The Vecht water, however, could not be used as drinking water and had to be distributed separately. On the other hand, it was decided that the Maatschappij should hand out a significant share of its income to the municipality.

With the small consumption of the Vecht water, the demand for dune water remained high, and the Duinwater-Maatschappij experienced serious technical and financial trouble. They were more or less obliged to sell the company to the municipality. On April 30,1896, the company was sold to the municipality for a sum of €5.4 million.

In this new property relationship, the municipality had a very direct influence on the company.
This influence was good for fast expansions, such as the construction of the Haarlemmerweg distribution pumping station and the expansion of the Leiduin production plant.

Direct influence also has a bad side. In 1916 the managing director, Pennink, was fired by the municipal board, mainly because he didn't want to expand the deep groundwater abstraction, and insisted on the use of surface water by infiltration in the dunes. In 1900 he had already presented this concept. The municipal council had the opinion that deep groundwater abstraction should be possible and moreover much cheaper. Fifty years later it appeared that the fired director had formulated the right proposals.

In later years a more balanced distance between the municipal company and the council has been established. The setup of technical designs was made within the company, the municipal council focused on judging the plans and considering the presented alternatives.

A clear example of this was the Rapport-1940 that remained in storage during the war, but was released as Rapport-1948 with limited adaptations. Here, the alternatives for dune water abstraction were presented, and the foundation was made for infiltration in the dunes. The report was the

foundation for decision-making within the municipal council.

Profit transfer

In a number of Dutch municipalities the water prices were calculated by the desired profit transfer to the municipality, as coverage for municipal expenses. From the point of view of the national government, this was seen as an undesirable way to pay taxes.

Over the last few years, the Amsterdam Water Supply transferred a profit of €0.5 million annually to the municipal government. This is about 0.4% of the turnover.

Financing

For investments, the water company borrows money from the municipality through long-term loans. The total sum of the long-term debts (approx. €300 million) is equal to the value of the fixed assets (balance-sheet value of the technical infrastructure). On these debts, an interest of about 3% is paid.

Operational costs

Because of the introduction of water meters, water consumption will decrease significantly. To prevent an increase in tariffs to offset it, the water company works to shrink its organization.

Between 2003 and 2006 the number of employees will be decreased from 710 to 610. With this reduction, the number of employees from 1980-1990 will once again be reached.

6.3   Governmental corporation

Amsterdam Water Supply is the last municipal water company in the Netherlands. The other companies all became governmental corporations, meaning their shares are owned by provincial and municipal governments.

One argument to become a governmental corporation is the influence the population has on the water company. Now, nearly 20% of the inhabitants in the distribution area don't have direct influence because they don't live within the city of

Figure 44 - Amsterdam Water Supply informs the public with its own annual report

Amsterdam (Amstelveen, Ouder-Amstel, Muiden, Heemstede and Diemen).

However, the municipal council of Amsterdam insists on keeping full control over the water company.

Water chain company

The city of Amsterdam has decided to keep the water company within the municipality. The rationale for this is the merger with the municipal department on sewerage and water management. In this a way a "water chain company" will exist within the municipality.

One expects that this merger will cause better services and a cost reduction of about 5%. This should come from the integration of repair services, purchase services, stores and the cost of tendering projects.

6.4   Organization and technique

The historical development of the Amsterdam Water Supply shows that there was a clear interaction between the organizational structure and the technical developments. This was mainly caused by the choices that were made based on considerations of the different technical alternatives. The choices were also influenced by the personal preferences of people within and around the company. Consequently, sometimes seemingly identical situations got different solutions.

Such historical choices also formed the company culture and habits.

A number of such choices were:

-   two pipeline networks between 1888 - 1930
-   the size of the current area of supply
-   introduction of technological innovations

Dual pipeline network

The choice for a dual pipeline network in the period between 1888 and 1930 was influenced by the mutual distrust between the municipal council and the private enterprise Duinwater-Maatschappij.

As a consequence, precise requirements were made for the quality of the Vecht water. Because these demands were not feasible, one had to choose a separate solution.

With a more open dialogue one would have chosen a more balanced solution. Of course, it was technically possible in those days to produce reliable drinking water from surface water. Even more, the municipal council had granted a concession 50 years before to an enterprise that transported treated Rhine water to Amsterdam. Because of the rigid attitude between 1885 and 1900, it was not really possible to change policy when the water company became the property of the municipality. Therefore, this troubling dual pipeline controversy existed until 1930.

Current size area of supply

Remarkable in the current area of supply is that, except for the municipality of Heemstede the area between Leiduin and Amsterdam doesn't belong to Amsterdam's area of supply.

Initially, the Duinwater-Maatschappij had started to supply drinking water to houses in Haarlem and Heemstede as well. However, when a shortage emerged in Amsterdam, they were not allowed to further extend this activity.

At last, the municipality of Haarlem founded its own water company in 1898. This company abstracted dune water from the dunes near Overveen, about 5 km north of Leiduin.

The municipality of Heemstede was so small that Amsterdam continued to supply Heemstede with its water.

Introduction of technological innovations

From a historical context, it appears that there was reluctance towards the introduction of technical and technological renewal. The important background of this is the desire for security, when it is applied to the drinking water service. On the other hand, this context always caused a strong drive towards improvements to the drinking water service.

In practice this attitude means that the efforts in research and development are relatively large, and new techniques are only introduced when it has been proven that they can function without complications within the company.

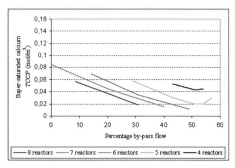

Figure 45 - Technological innovations are supported by
scientific research (PhD L.C. Rietveld)

Further reading

The Netherlands
* Water in the Netherlands, Netherlands Hydrological Society (2004)

* www.verkeerenwaterstaat.nl

VOC
* www.tanap.net
* www.voc-kenniscentrum.nl

Drinking water Amsterdam
* Een cent per emmer. Het Amsterdamse drink-
  water door de eeuwen heen, J.A. Groen jr.,
  Gemeentewaterleidingen Amsterdam (1978)
* Drinken uit de plas 1888-1998. Honderd jaar
  Amsterdamse plassenwaterleiding, H. Kosman
  Gemeentewaterleidingen Amsterdam (1988)
* Versch drinkwater voor de hoofdstad. Rapport
  over de onderscheidene middelen welke de
  Stad Amsterdam van Versch drinkwater kun-
  nen voorzien 1849, J. van Maurik / P. de Baar,
  Gemeentewaterleidingen Amsterdam (1993)
* Gemeentewaterleidingen/Waterleidingbedrijf
  Amsterdam (annual reports)

* www.wlb.amsterdam.nl

Questions and applications

The Netherlands

1. The Netherlands is quite flat and the soil consists of sedimentary deposits with deep brackish groundwater. Explain how this has emerged.

2. Much land disappeared in the Netherlands between 800 and 1250. Give the causes for this.

Amsterdam

1. Between 1960 and 1985 the number of inhabitants in Amsterdam decreased about 20%. Explain the cause of this.

2. Name the most important sources for drinking water before the introduction of piped water.

3. The drinking water of Amsterdam was a private enterprise in the 19th century. Indicate why this enterprise had a large British influence.

Developments in water usage and distribution

1. Describe the system of the water service with water vessels, as the municipal council had organized it between 1786 and 1853.

2. Amsterdam had two separate pipeline networks in the city for 44 years. Describe the background of this.

3. Indicate why the capacity of the dune water system increased with a distribution pumping station.

Developments in drinking water production

1. Describe the developments in water abstraction in the dune area.

2. Give the advantages of softened water.

Developments as enterprise

1. Give the arguments why the municipal government wanted to own the drinking water company.

Applications

1. Indicate why water meters were not used in former days, while they are now.

2. Give the advantages of dune filtration with the usage of surface water.

Answers

The Netherlands

1. The current Netherlands was part of the North Sea for millions of years. The Rhine and the Meuse transported sediment (sand and clay), which precipitated in the sea. The changes in the sea level caused spreading over a large area. After the withdrawal of the sea, the salty seawater was slowly diluted from above by fresh rainwater.

2. As a consequence of the rising sea level, the peat soil was covered with water. The pounding of the waves caused the peat soil to disappear. Also, the peat soil was dug off for the production of turf (fuel).

Amsterdam

1. The inhabitants of the old city left their small old houses. Within the municipality of Amsterdam, there was no substitute housing, but in the surrounding municipalities there was. Because of city renewal projects from 1986, substitute-housing space was built on a large scale within the existing municipal borders, and the population increased again.

2. Initially, mainly the water from the Amstel and the canals was used. Because of pollution, the capture of rainwater became more important; not only from one's own house, but also from the roofs of churches. From 1650 the supply of surface water with water vessels became more important. From 1786 this was the entrepreneurial activity of the Versch-Water Sociëteit, under the control of the municipal council.

3. The modern drinking water service developed within the Industrial Revolution, which was born in England. There, the required technical equipment was made (steam engines, pumps, cast-iron pipelines). In England several cities were already served by a drinking water system. From this background the English risked buying shares of the Duinwater-Maatschappij. The largest shareholders were the manufacturers of pumps and pipelines, who increased their turnover with the water supply system.

Developments in water usage and distribution

1. About 30 water vessels transported 75 m^3 water each from the Vecht to the city every day. There, the water vessels were unloaded into about 200 smaller water boats that were anchored in the canals. From there the population pumped their buckets full. When the waterboats were empty, they were towed to the city border to be filled again.

2. Because expansion of the dune water abstraction was not possible, a new system was realized using Vecht water. This water would be of inferior quality and was considered unsuitable for use as drinking water. Only when a better source was used and disinfection with chlorine turned out to be effective was the separate distribution abolished.

3 With a large storage the transport pipeline can operate during the full day at maximum level. Now water can be supplied during the night as well. Because the reservoir can be filled using a low pressure, there is a larger pressure difference available over the pipeline, allowing more water to flow through the pipes.

Developments in drinking water production

1. Initially the shallow water was abstracted (rainfall). When no expansion was possible anymore, deep groundwater was abstracted (old storage). When no deep groundwater was available anymore, the surface water was let into the dune area, making a considerable expansion of the shallow abstraction possible.

2. The advantages of softened water are:
   - decrease of lead and copper solvancy (saved health and the environment)
   - no softeners needed by the drinking water consumer (saved cost and the environment)
   - less usage of detergent (saved cost and the environment)
   - fewer limestone deposits in warm and hot water (saved cost)
   - more comfort for the users (better taste and feeling with soap)

Developments as enterprise

1. The municipal council thought that it didn't have sufficient insight in and influence on aspects like tariff, profit, management, reliability, and security of supply. Requirements about these could only be obtained by exhausting concession conditions, for which afterwards adaptations were not or were hardly possible.

Applications

1. Initially, there were no good and cheap water meters available. Later on one didn't want the people to save on water because that would reduce hygiene, mainly of the poor population. Nowadays, everybody is able to pay for drinking water, and non-metered usage leads to undesirable waste.

2. The advantages of dune filtration are:
   - natural filter for viruses, bacteria and contaminants
   - emergency storage
   - balanced water quality by spread of residence time
   - constant water temperature (in case of closed abstraction system)

Drinking water companies

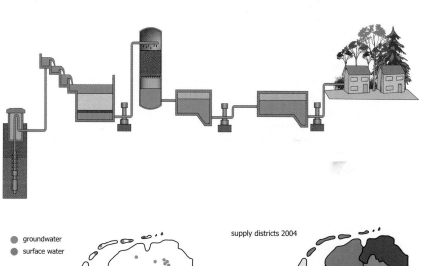

groundwater
surface water

supply districts 2004

Framework

This module will describe the technical and organizational aspects of the Dutch public drinking water sector.

Contents

This module has the following contents:

Study goals

After studying this module you will be able to:
* explain the technical parts of the public water supply
* explain the setup of production
* explain the setup of distribution
* calculate the capacity of the different parts of the public water supply (from a demand prognosis and including peak factors)
* explain the organizational scheme of the Dutch drinking water sector

1. Introduction

The public water supply played an important role in the development of our modern society. The supply of good and reliable (i.e., safe) drinking water, since about 1850, has caused public health in Western Europe and North America to drastically improve. The public drinking water supply is important for economic development as well. Because of the supply of good and inexpensive water, any economic development is less tied to the direct surroundings. Therefore industries and companies can flourish more easily.

The public drinking water supply is provided by water companies. Originally, there were municipal companies in the larger towns. Later, provincial and regional water companies were founded to supply water to the rural areas.

By 1960, almost every house and company in Western Europe was connected to a public drinking water system. The last 50 years have been characterized by an increased merging of the different water companies. For example, in the Netherlands, the number of water companies decreased from over 200 to only 14 in 2004. This trend is expected to continue over the next several years.

The public drinking water supply is regulated by national and international legislation. In the Netherlands, the Water Supply Act (WSA) applies. These laws regulate the rights and duties of water companies. According to the WSA, "The owner of any water company is obliged to safeguard the supply of sound drinking water to the users in the distribution area, in such an amount and at such a pressure that are beneficial to public health."

For water quality, there are many parameters and standards given in the WSA, and the obligation exists to adequately monitor those parameters. Regarding quantity, it is required that the water always be supplied at a minimum pressure of 200 kPa above street level. Supply interruptions should be remedied within 24 hours, and a minimum required supply capacity in case of larger calamities should be available.

This module provides the technical setup of a water company. Also, the organizational scheme of the public water sector in the Netherlands is explained.

2. Technical setup for drinking water supply

The public drinking water supply typically has a technical setup, as shown in Figure 1.

Production consists of the abstraction of raw water (either groundwater from the soil or surface water from rivers, canals and lakes) followed by treatment, in order to obtain drinking water quality. When production is located remote from the supply area, the water is first transported via transport pumps and transport pipes.

To reduce the daily variation in the water demand, distribution reservoirs are used. From these reservoirs, the drinking water is pressurized for distribution to the supply area using distribution pumps. In the supply area, there is a fine distribution network available (a system of larger and smaller pipes), transporting water to clients. In some cases, water towers are used in the distribution networks in order to lessen pressure fluctuations.

Every client typically has a home connection to the distribution network (which typically includes a water meter), that distributes drinking water to the different taps in and around the house (bath, toilet, kitchen, washing machine, garden, etc.).

In practice, there are a few variations from the setup shown in Figure 1. In some cases there is no transport system, such as when treatment, reservoirs and distribution pumps are all located at one single site. In some cases, storage is located inside the distribution network. This can be a high reservoir, functioning as a very large water tower (e.g., a large reservoir up a hill in a town), or a network reservoir. The latter is a reservoir in the

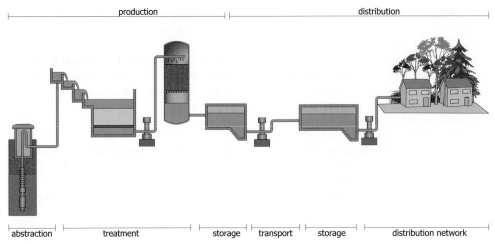

Figure 1 - Setup of the drinking water supply system

distribution area which is filled from the distribution network at night and supplies the water back through the same network during the day.

3.   Production

3.1   Drinking water resources

Fresh water
For the production of drinking water, almost exclusive use is made of water containing only a limited amount of dissolved compounds (fresh water). This choice is made in view of the high costs of removing salts from water.
Desalination of brackish water or sea water is only used in drinking water production when fresh water is scarce, like in arid areas (Saudi Arabia, Libya) and on tourist islands (like Malta, Aruba or Bermuda).

Groundwater
Groundwater can be abstracted in substantial amounts if an extensive, porous underground aquifer is available and if recharge from the surface or the surroundings is possible. The treatment of groundwater for the production of drinking water is relatively simple.

For drinking water production it is important that the aquifer be more or less isolated from the upper soil (confined aquifer). In this way contamination of the groundwater is prevented. In order to further prevent contamination, the abstraction area is marked as a water-abstraction area. A water-abstraction area is protected by strict regulations regarding land use and the use of dangerous compounds (oil, pesticides, etc.).

In areas where the aquifer has an open connection to the upper soil, the water-abstraction area is chosen considerably more carefully. In general a minimum retention time of 50 years in the underground is used to determine the size of the water-abstraction area. Because of this long retention time, groundwater is microbiologically reliable and of consistent quality. It also has a consistent temperature. These properties mean that only limited treatment is required. In some cases, no treatment at all is necessary (e.g., some sites at the Veluwe).

Groundwater abstraction influences the water level in the soil. This may cause desiccation of the surrounding area, resulting in agricultural and environmental damage. Therefore, permits are required for groundwater abstraction, in which the maximum amounts to be abstracted are regulated (yearly, monthly and daily maxima). The Dutch policy focuses on decreasing the amounts permitted and on taxation of groundwater abstraction (ecotax).

Groundwater can be abstracted adjacent to major rivers, also. This type of abstraction is called river-bank filtration.

Surface water

Surface water is commonly available in large amounts and easily abstracted (rivers and lakes). In the case of rivers having a low minimum discharge, sometimes very large storage reservoirs are constructed to cover drier periods.

Drinking water production from surface water requires an extensive treatment process. Typical are the removal of suspended solids and turbidity, the removal of bacteria and pathogens and the removal of harmful compounds and micropollutants.

Two systems for the production of drinking water from surface water are:
- storage in basins and an extensive treatment process (direct treatment)
- pre-treatment, soil aquifer recharge, abstraction and a limited post-treatment (dune infiltration)

3.2 Quality standards for drinking water

The quality of drinking water should comply with legal standards. In the Netherlands those are laid down in the Water Supply Act by the Ministry of Housing, Spatial Planning and the Environment (Dutch: Volkshuisvesting, Ruimtelijke Ordening en Milieubeheer (VROM)). The specific quality standards are elaborated in the Decree on the Water Supply.

The Dutch legislation is stricter than the general European one. Internationally, there is much reference to the directives from the World Health Organization (WHO).

Table 1 - Different groups of quality parameters in Dutch legislation

Quality parameter	Goal of standard
Public health	Healthy for drinking and breathing vapor
Operational	Prevention of quality deterioration in distribution network
Organoleptic / aesthetic	Attractive for use
Signaling	Prevention of yet unknown risks

Table 1 indicates the different categories of quality parameters in Dutch legislation.

Within the health related parameters, a distinction is made between microbiological and chemical parameters. When any one of those standards is exceeded, the water company needs to inform the VROM-inspector.

Table 2 indicates a few typical quality standards for drinking water.

The technical installations and the operation of a drinking water production plant are primarily determined by the microbiological parameters. This is because the concentration of bacteria in source waters might be some 10,000 to 1,000,000,000 times higher than the maximum acceptable value in drinking water. Therefore, even a small contamination or a small disturbance in the production process may cause the standards to be exceeded. Also, bacteria populations may develop during long retention times in installations or in pipes.

Table 2 - Typical quality standards for drinking water

Parameter	Unit	Value
E-coli	/ 100 ml	0
Colony count	/ ml	100
Pesticides (per compound)	µg/l	0.1
Bromate	µg/l	1 (5)
Iron	mg/l	0.2
Manganese	mg/l	0.05
Ammonia	mg/l	0.2
Suspended solids	FTE	1 (4)
Hardness (calcium + magnesium)	mmol	1 - 2.5
Sodium	mg/l	150
Chloride	mg/l	150
pH	-	7.0 - 9.5
Temperature	°C	< 25

3.3 Production in the Netherlands

In the Netherlands, drinking water is produced at about 220 sites. Figure 2 shows the production sites of the Dutch water companies.

The design capacity of Dutch production plants is generally between 250 and 1,500 m³/h (with extremes between 15 and 18,000 m³/h).

The plants have an occupancy use rate of 60 - 70%. This is mainly caused by fluctuations in the water demand during the year. The design capacity is sufficient for the maximum daily demand which occurs about once every ten years, an amount which is normally 1.4 - 1.6 times as high as the yearly average.

Due to the fluctuations in demand, the production capacity is more often expressed as capacity per year. The design capacity of the Dutch production plants, therefore, is between 1.5 and 10 million m³/y (with extremes between 0.1 and 110 million m³/y). From this point of view, most installations have an occupancy rate of about 90 - 100%.

Table 3 provides an overview of the size of the water abstraction by the Dutch water companies and the number of sites per type. At a few production sites, different types of water are abstracted.

Table 3 - Overview of the quantity of water abstracted by the Dutch water companies (2001)

Type of water	Abstraction (million m³/y)	Number of sites
Groundwater	758	184
Natural dune water	16	14
Bank filtration	26	12
Surface water	503	9
Total	1303	219

Surface water abstraction sites usually have a considerably larger production capacity.

Dutch water companies produced a total of 1.175 million m³ of drinking water during the year 2001 and 62 million m³ of other water. This production caused a total production loss of 61 million m³ (5%, mainly backwash water).

The supply areas for ground- and surface water in the Netherlands are indicated in Figure 3.

3.4 Groundwater

Dutch water companies produce drinking water from groundwater at about 200 sites (Figure 4). Abstraction of the groundwater is almost exclu-

Figure 2 - Sites for the production of drinking water in the Netherlands

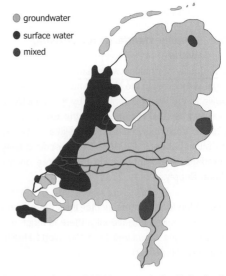

Figure 3 - Origin of drinking water in the Netherlands

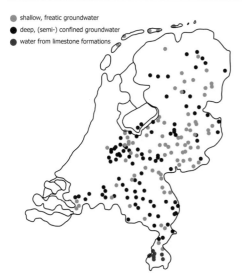

Figure 4 - Locations of the production of drinking water from groundwater

sively accomplished in a groundwater protection area.

The amounts produced per site vary between 0.05 and 25 million m³ per year.

Usually, groundwater has a long underground retention time. This causes the water to be micro-biologically stable and of an almost consistent good quality.
The chemical composition of the water, however, strongly depends on the local circumstances, which may cause wide differences.

Oxygen
The most important differences in quality are related to the oxygen content of the water (aerobic/anaerobic) or to the degree of oxygen shortage (redoxpotential).
The oxygen content actually determines the amount to which a few undesirable compounds can dissolve from the soil (iron, manganese, ammonium, methane, hydrogen sulfide).

Generally, the oxygen content can be easily predicted based on the origin of the groundwater (Figure 5). Though rainwater contains oxygen in

all cases, this oxygen can be consumed by the decay of organic compounds in the soil. This decay depends on the amount of organic compounds that are present in the soil (sand soil versus peat or clay soil). Besides, a longer retention time in the ground yields a lower oxygen concentration (water under a clay layer).

Aerobic groundwater is mostly abstracted from the freatic sand layer. It contains oxygen and typically needs only very little treatment.
Slightly anaerobic groundwater is located under a continuous clay layer in the ground. Due to this layer, no oxygen is present in the water, but ammonium, iron and manganese are. These compounds are undesirable in the water and need to be removed. However, the concentrations of these compounds are rather low.
Deep anaerobic groundwater is located below a peat layer. This water is characterized by the absence of oxygen and nitrate and by the presence of ammonium, iron, manganese, methane and hydrogen sulfide.

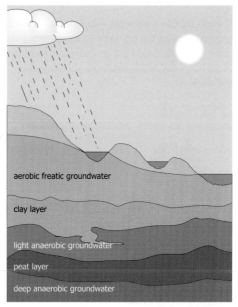

Figure 5 - Consumption of oxygen in the soil has an influence on the composition of groundwater

Figure 6 - Contamination of the soil is a threat to the quality of groundwater

pH value

A second important factor in determining the quality of groundwater is its pH value.

Rainwater always contains a small amount of carbon dioxide (CO_2), though at greater levels in industrial countries, and is often called acid rain. In acid environments undesirable metals like nickel and aluminium may also dissolve from the soil matrix.

Because of water consumption by plants (less water) and because of the oxidation of organic matter (formation of CO_2), the CO_2 concentration in the groundwater may dramatically rise.

Carbon dioxide may react with limestone in the ground, causing the pH value to increase significantly, but also causing a considerable increase in the hardness and bicarbonate concentration of the water.

Contamination from land use

A third factor determining the quality of the groundwater is related to land use.

Due to fertilizing in agriculture, the amount of nitrates in groundwater can significantly increase (Figure 6). Also, pesticides may enter the groundwater.

Of course, industrial contamination of the soil also influences the quality of the water.

Treatment setup

Because of the variety of differences in water quality prior to treatment, there is no uniform treatment setup for groundwater. In the Netherlands, almost exclusively anaerobic groundwater is abstracted, requiring aeration and rapid filtration in any treatment process (Figures 7 and 8). Aeration brings oxygen in the water and removes the dissolved gases. After this, iron, manganese and ammonium will oxidize, causing these compounds to be removed in the filter.

There have been several developments requiring the treatment process to be extended over time. For example, because of over-fertilizing an additional treatment step to remove nitrate will become necessary. By using pesticides, harmful compounds may enter the water and need to be removed.

Also, political decisions influence the groundwater treatment process. Because there is a tax levied on the amount of abstracted groundwater, the water companies reuse the backwash water from

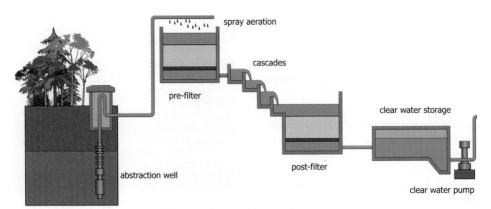

Figure 7 - Drinking water production from slightly anaerobic groundwater

*Figure 8   - Modern design of Welschap pumping station (Noord-Brabant) where anaerobic groundwater is treated to
              produce drinking water*

their rapid filters, causing the abstracted water to decrease.

In recent years, the topic of scale-up has been heavily debated. As a likely consequence of scale-up, treatment plants will become bigger, will be operated more constantly, and will help reduce local differences in water quality. This will lead to lower treatment costs.

3.5   Riverbank groundwater

At 12 sites, the Dutch water companies produce drinking water from riverbank groundwater (Figure 9). The amounts produced per site range from 1 million m³ to 12 million m³ per year. Although the share of riverbank groundwater in the total drinking water production in the Netherlands is small, the source is rather important, especially in river areas.

In some cases in the past, drinking water was derived directly from surface water, like in Alblasserdam, Dordrecht, Zwijndrecht, 's Gravendeel and Gouda. Deterioration in the quality of river water, however, caused a transition to full or partial abstracting of riverbank filtrated groundwater.

The mixing of river water with groundwater, the dampening effects because of retention time

dispersion, and the filtration capacity of the soil caused an improvement in quality.

Recently, a special form of riverbank groundwater was acquired near Roermond. Here, riverbank filtration is used near a gravel pit. This gravel pit is

● bank filtration

*Figure 9   - Locations of the production of drinking water
              from riverbank groundwater*

fed with raw Meuse water from a navigation canal next to the Meuse River.

The retention time of the water in the gravel pit is about one year. The retention time in the soil is only weeks or months. The basic setup is similar to that of soil aquifer recharge.

Two systems are recognized for water abstraction near the banks of rivers or lakes:
- riverbank groundwater
- riverbank filtration

Riverbank filtration is used chiefly in Germany. In the Netherlands, riverbank groundwater is used the most.

Riverbank groundwater
Riverbank groundwater is mainly groundwater. Therefore, it has the same properties as groundwater, so the treatment is also groundwater based (aeration and rapid filtration).

Riverbank groundwater is abstracted about 1 km from the bank of a river. The retention time of the river water in the soil is longer than one year and the flow velocity in the ground is about 0.1 m/d. Due to the long retention time and due to dispersion, the leveling effect of riverbank groundwater is high, a factor of 500 - 1,000 being common.
The capacity of riverbank groundwater wells is limited. Production amounts to circa 1 million m³ per year per kilometer of riverbank.

Riverbank filtration
In the case of riverbank filtration, the water consists mainly of river water (90%).

Abstraction wells are situated close to the river (a few meters to 100 m), causing the retention times to be shorter (about one month).
The leveling effect that can be achieved is lower as well, a factor of 50 - 100 being achievable.
The flow velocity in the soil is high; flow velocity of 1 m/d can occur, causing the capacity of riverbank filtration to be high.

Availability
In the Netherlands, riverbank groundwater is abundantly available along the 1,200 km of large rivers' banks (e.g., Rhine, Waal, Lek, IJssel and Meuse). Possible limitations are local subsidences (especially in the peaty areas in the western part of the Netherlands) and possible clogging of (shallow) wells and river bottoms.
As the bottom of a river is regularly flushed by high discharges, the danger of this latter problem is quite limited.

The availability of water is always sufficient, as the large rivers discharge large amounts of water. Therefore, additional storage is unnecessary.

Treatment setup
The abstracted riverbank groundwater is hygienically reliable because it has passed through the soil. The variations in quality (salinity, and temperature as well) are levelled off by the retention time and dispersion in the soil. The vulnerability of riverbank groundwater to calamities is small.

Riverbank groundwater treatment resembles the treatment of surface water without the production of large amounts of sludge.
When the river is contaminated, the infiltration of water into the soil cannot be stopped, because the Dutch rivers itself are of an infiltrating nature. This causes contaminations to enter the soil.
Riverbank groundwater wells may clog. This is mainly due to the mixing of anaerobic groundwater with aerobic surface water. In this case, iron

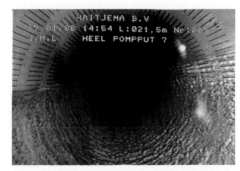

Figure 10 - Mixing of aerobic and anaerobic groundwater, which contains iron, in an abstraction well

may flocculate in the well, causing well clogging (Figure 10).

The capacity of a pumping station is related to the number of wells that can be constructed.

Generally, pumping stations are small, of a size similar to that of a groundwater plant.

The sites are usually located not far from the distribution area. Because of the short transport distances and the simple treatment setup (compared to other surface water projects), the costs are relatively low.

3.6 Surface water using direct treatment

In the Netherlands, there are 8 sites at which drinking water is produced directly from surface water (Figure 11).

Berenplaat, Kralingen, Baanhoek, Braakman (all by Evides) and Zevenbergen (by Brabant Water) obtain their water from the Meuse River (through the Biesbosch reservoirs).

Weesperkarspel (Waterleidingbedrijf Amsterdam) treats water from the Bethune polder (together with water from the Amsterdam-Rhine Canal) which passed through a shallow reservoir.

Andijk (PWN Waterleidingbedrijf Noord-Holland) treats water from the IJsselmeer and De Punt (Waterbedrijf Groningen), from the Drentse Aa.

A remark needs to be made concerning the Zevenbergen site: this was used only for industrial water production for a long time. However, currently, restarting the production of drinking water is considered again.

Every water is different, requiring different treatment setups as well. For example, at Andijk, there is a very high concentration of algae during summer, which is difficult to remove.

The Drentse Aa has a small and natural catchment area, making it relatively easy to prevent and monitor pollution. On the other hand, there is a larger variation in water quality (e.g., suspended solids). Therefore, its reservoir has mainly a dampening function.

Because the reservoir in Amsterdam is shallow, algae growth will be facilitated. Therefore, a phos-

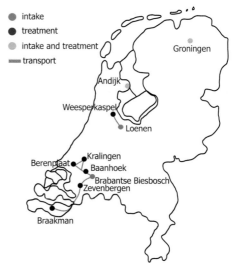

Figure 11 - Direct production of drinking water from surface water in the Netherlands

phorous removal plant was placed in front of the inlet of the reservoir.

The Biesbosch reservoirs are deep and are mixed continuously, thus limiting algae growth. Because of the long retention time, the Biesbosch water has very low turbidity. The remaining turbidity is, however, difficult to remove, and different processes (flotation, sludge blanket clarification, lamella clarification) are applied at the different sites.

Table 4 shows the total amount of abstracted surface water, the amounts of surface water used for artificial infiltration, and the water production by the Dutch water companies for the year 2001.

Table 4 - The amount of surface water at Dutch water companies (VEWIN Waterleidingstatistiek 2001)

Water balance	Amount (million m³/y)
Total amount of abstracted surface water	503
Surface water used for infiltration	213
Production loss in pre-treatment of infiltration (estimated)	10
Abstracted for direct treatment	280
Production loss in treatment (estimated)	14
Direct production of surface water	266
Supply of other water	70
Direct production of drinking water	196

General treatment setup

When abstracting river water for direct treatment to drinking water, one should consider the significantly varying water discharge as well as the variable quality. Besides, surface water is rather vulnerable to pollution (e.g., the Sandoz disaster in 1986).

For these reasons a storage reservoir is required before the treatment process itself.

The surface water that is used as a source for drinking water production is usually located at a large distance from the distribution area. For example, Rotterdam and its surroundings, and also Zeeland, are supplied with water from the Biesbosch reservoirs. This necessitates transporting the water over quite a long distance.

To prevent large flow variations in the transport pipes, distribution reservoirs are constructed in the distribution area. These reservoirs cause a rather constant flow of water to be transported, which is advantageous for the energy costs and for the operation of the treatment plants, as well.

In order to prevent sedimentation and biological growth in the transport pipes, either the total treatment process is situated at the inlet site or a pre-treatment plant is constructed there. The main treatment plant will be constructed near the distribution area in the latter case.

Reservoirs

In the Netherlands, the surface water used for drinking water production is mainly abstracted from the Rhine and Meuse rivers. These rivers are characterized by large fluctuations both in quality and in quantity. Because of these variations, water abstraction from the river is not always possible. In order to be able to supply drinking water, a storage reservoir should be available which can be used during intake interruptions (Figure 12).

Figure 12 - The three Biesbosch reservoirs for the drinking water supply in the southwestern part of the Netherlands

In most cases, a contamination is not immediately discovered. Often, the results of the analysis are only known after a week. Therefore, there is an analysis reservoir or compartment situated before the storage reservoir, in many cases.

Surface water treatment plants in the Netherlands have a rather high capacity, so the storage reservoir needs to be substantial. Therefore, use is made of large reservoirs in the case of direct production from surface water. Moreover, these reservoirs are also large to allow for a long retention time. The flow velocity in a reservoir is much slower than the flow velocity in a river. This causes many suspended particles to settle in the reservoir. A dampening of concentration peaks is also achieved.
However, because of the mere size of the reservoirs, the processes in them are not fully controllable. Weather and wind have a substantial influence on the processes.

The Biesbosch basins, for example, have a storage capacity to provide a buffer for several months. The three reservoirs range in size from 13 to 40 million m^3 (surface areas of 1.0 to 3.2 million m^2 and depths between 15 and 25 m). The storage capacity is substantially less than the size of the reservoirs, because only one reservoir is designed for a significant change in water level.
The water is transported from the reservoirs to the treatment plants through pipes having a diameter between 800 and 1,800 mm.

Suspended solids
Because of the long retention time, particles that settled will have been removed from the water. However, colloidal particles will not settle, because they are all negatively charged and, thus, repel one another.
To remove these particles, positively charged salts are added to the water (iron or aluminum salts, Figure 13). The salts reduce the negative charges of the colloidal particles, so they can collide with each other to form larger ones which can then be removed (these particles are called flocs). The use of a flocculation installation increases the probability of particle collisions.

The process of adding iron salts to the water is called coagulation; the process of neutralized colloidal particles colliding, and becoming flocs is called flocculation.
After the flocs have formed, they need to be removed from the water. This can be done in two ways. The first method is to let the flocs, which have a density slightly higher than that of water, settle to the bottom (sedimentation). The second method is to let them collide with small air bubbles, causing the density of the flocs to fall below that of water, thus making them float (flotation).

Figure 14 shows an image of flocculation and the two floc removal processes.
The flocculation/floc removal process is an important process in surface water treatment, as the flocs also contain heavy metals, organic matter, and viruses.

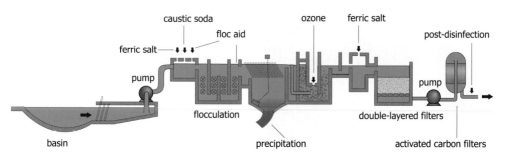

Figure 13 - The production of drinking water from surface water with direct treatment

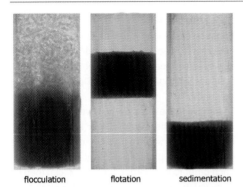

| flocculation | flotation | sedimentation |

*Figure 14 - Flocculation, with floc removal via flotation
or sedimentation*

Not all flocs are removed during sedimentation or flotation. Small flocs may remain in the water after the floc removal phase. These flocs may be removed using rapid filtration. This rapid filtration is similar to the one used for the final treatment of groundwater. However, the types of compounds that are removed are different.

A rapid filter should be backwashed on a regular basis (Figure 15). In the water after sedimentation or flotation, there are still many small flocs. These flocs clog the pores of the rapid filter rather quickly, causing the run lengths of the filters to be only 24 to 48 hours, in most cases. When the filters are used for the final treatment of groundwater, the operational periods are typically longer.

Another difference between the treatment of surface water and of groundwater using a rapid filter is that the final treatment of groundwater will

*Figure 15 - Open rapid filters are rinsed at the Katwijk
production location (Zuid-Holland)*

typically be situated in a closed system mostly, as this water is hygienically reliable. Surface water contains many pathogenic microorganisms, so rapid sand filters need not be closed from contact with outside air.

Micropollutants

In 1987 small amounts of the pesticide Bentazon was found in the drinking water of Amsterdam. This pesticide was probably present in the water for a long time, but because analytical capabilities to detect these micropollutants were not yet well-developed, this contamination could not be proven before then.

The detection of Bentazon in the drinking water started people wondering whether there were any other micropollutants in the water as well, and, if so, how they could be removed.

Organic micropollutants can be removed from the water using activated carbon filtration. Activated carbon filtration is somewhat similar to rapid filtration, but uses activated carbon grains instead of sand. Activated carbon is able to adsorb organic micropollutants. However, this adsorption is finite, meaning that after some time the activated carbon becomes saturated, so that no more micropollutants can be adsorbed. At that moment the activated carbon needs to be regenerated.

Activated carbon filtration is always used after rapid filtration. The reason for this is that any remaining flocs will be retained in the rapid filter. The activated carbon filter is therefore not loaded with those materials and, so it rarely needs to be backwashed.

Microorganisms

Surface water contains many pathogenic microorganisms. These microorganisms enter the water through sewage - in some cases treated - and the drainage of pavements.

The pathogenic microorganisms are removed by rapid filtration, but this removal is not sufficient, and an additional treatment step is required.
In the past, chlorine was applied to achieve this. However, as chlorine does have harmful side

effects, it is rarely used in the Netherlands anymore.

Other methods of disinfection include the use of ozonization and UV disinfection. Ozonization applies the strong oxidizer ozone to kill pathogenic microorganisms. Ozone is generated in an ozone generator and injected into the water in a series of contact basins. However, the use of ozone is also hindered by some harmful side effects.

UV disinfection treats the water with UV radiation having a certain wavelength, which inactivates pathogenic microorganisms. This method of disinfection is only sufficient when every drop of water is highly radiated with the UV light.

In the case of short-circuiting or deteriorating lamps, the disinfection may be insufficient.

Intake interruptions due to severe contaminations

Surface water quality may show strong fluctuations. This is mainly the case for rivers that flow through highly industrialized countries.

Because of sewage effluents, there will be temporarily higher concentrations of pathogenic microorganisms in the water, and the possibility of organic micropollutants entering the water cannot be ignored.

In periods of high discharge (melting snow in spring or substantial precipitation in the catchment area), extra contaminations may be found in the water. This is mostly caused by surface runoff and by erosion of formerly settled material.

These contaminations can hardly be prevented in practice, so their removal must be addressed during the treatment process. However, in the case of a temporary severe deterioration of the water quality, it may be wise to interrupt the intake of water.

Intake interruptions require storage facilities, in order to continue the supply to the clients.

In Table 5 the number of intake interruptions at the different Dutch water companies during a certain period is shown. Up until now the reservoir capacity has always proven sufficient, but it is evident that an increase in the number of calamities is undesirable, and measures have been designed to prevent this.

Table 5 - Number of intake interruptions due to considerable contamination of the water in the period 1985 - 1991

Water supply company	Number of intake stops	Duration per intake stop
WRK I/II (Lekkanaal)	10	3 - 11 days
WRK III (IJsselmeer)	-	-
PWN (IJsselmeer)	3	Several days
WLBA (Weesperkarspel)	-	-
WBB (Biesbosch)	20	2 - 21 days
DZH (Andelse Maas)	1	2 days
Vitens (Twentekanaal)	1	7 days

3.7 Surface water using soil aquifer recharge

In the Dutch dune areas there are many small lakes like the one shown in Figure 16. These lakes are often recharge facilities that are used by the water companies to produce drinking water. The dunes have been used for drinking water production for quite a long time already.

Originally, the dunes were only fed by rainwater and dune water was only used by the local population. After a pipe was constructed between the Zandvoort dune area and Amsterdam in 1853, Amsterdam was supplied with dune water as well. The amount of water abstracted increased further and further. As a consequence, some wells yielded salt water during the 1950s. Since that time, therefore, pre-treated surface water has been infiltrated into the dunes in order to push back the salt water and to maintain a fresh water barrier.

The infiltrated water comes from the major rivers and the IJsselmeer, in most cases. After the intake, the water is pre-treated to prevent clogging of the pipes and contamination of the infiltration area.

Figure 16 - Infiltration area in the Dutch dunes

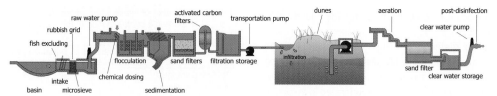

Figure 17 - Pre-treatment, infiltration and post-treatment of infiltration water

The surface water that is to be infiltrated needs to comply with the requirements of the Infiltration Regulation (Dutch: Infiltratiebesluit). Therefore, the pre-treatment of recharge water is extensive (Figure 17).

After pre-treatment, the half product is transported over distances up to 60 kilometers. For this transport, pumps are used which have substantial pressure (600 - 1000 kPa). After that, the pre-treated water is recharged to the dunes.

After the water has been re-abstracted, it is post-treated, because it has become anaerobic during the soil passage and therefore contains iron, manganese and ammonium. After treatment, the water is transported to a reservoir near the distribution area, from where it is distributed.

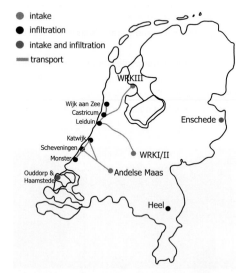

Figure 18 - Locations where infiltration water is abstracted, pre-treated, transported, infiltrated, re-abstracted and post-treated

The infiltration areas act as a storage system to cover periods in which the surface water is contaminated and to reduce quality fluctuations.

Infiltration areas are mainly situated in the dunes along the coast (Figure 18). Also, because most major Dutch towns are situated near the coast, causing the demand to be highest there. Additionally, the dunes sand is suitable for infiltration and, thus, a sufficient amount of good quality drinking water can be obtained.

Table 6 shows the total amounts of drinking water produced from surface water through soil aquifer recharge. Infiltration areas near the coast are in Ouddorp (Evides), Monster, Scheveningen and Katwijk (all of Duinwaterbedrijf Zuid-Holland), Leiduin (Waterleidingbedrijf Amsterdam) and Castricum, Bergen and Wijk aan Zee (PWN Waterleidingbedrijf Noord-Holland).
Besides in dune areas, infiltration of pre-treated surface water can also take place in other aquifers, such as in eastern Netherlands, near Enschede (Vitens).

4.   Distribution

4.1   Transport

In the setup, shown in Figure 1, there is a large distance between the production plant and the

Table 6   - Amount of infiltration at Dutch drinking water companies (VEWIN 2001)

Water balance infiltration	Amount (million m³/y)
Total infiltrated amount	213
Total abstracted amount	219
- abstracted from the dunes	181
- abstracted elsewhere	38
- change in storage volume	-6

supply area, which is bridged by a transport system. Of course, transport systems are not only pipes, but also pumping stations containing the transport pumps which provide the necessary pressure (Figure 19).

Figure 20 shows an overview of the transport system in Flevoland between the three production plants and the storage reservoirs near the towns Lelystad (1 reservoir) and Almere (2 reservoirs). Also, Amsterdam has a transport system, between the production plant in the dunes near Heemstede and the storage reservoirs in the city.

The Dutch water companies have a total of about 500 kilometers of transport pipes which have diameters between 400 and 1,000 mm. A transport system is designed based on the maximum daily use (measured once every ten years) of the supply area. The pressure in the transport system is determined by the height of the water level in the storage reservoir and by the hydraulic resistance.

4.2 Storage

The setup in Figure 1 shows that storage takes place in (drinking water) reservoirs. These reservoirs are often called "clear water tanks" in practice, as they are often dug under the ground or constructed under the treatment plant. These

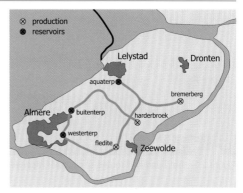

Figure 20 - Transportation system in Flevoland province

reservoirs achieve a dampening of the daily use fluctuations, so that production and transport can continue on a more or less constant level. The required contents of clear water reservoirs is roughly 25% of the daily use (or the daily production), or the production of 6 hours.

At the Dutch production sites, storage of between 1,500 and 10,000 m³ of drinking water is available. Because of supply uncertainty in the case of maintenance or defects, this storage capacity is subdivided across several distinct reservoirs or compartments. Clear water reservoirs are, of course, closed to maintain the quality of the drinking water. For the "respiration" of these reservoirs - when the water level changes, air will flow in or out - special air filters are employed.

In Figure 21 the clear water reservoirs and their relatively large size at the Berenplaat production plant of the Rotterdam water supply are clearly discernible. One needs to recognize, in this case, that a part of the storage for the Rotterdam water supply is situated within the supply area.

Water towers generally contain between 250 and 1,000 m³. These towers barely play any role in the dampening of fluctuations in use. They mainly dampen the pressure, for short periods and in case of a severely fluctuating demand.

4.3 Distribution network

From the storage reservoirs, the drinking water is pumped into the distribution network using high pressure pumps. Figure 22 shows an overview

Figure 19 - Pumps used for the transportation of drinking water

Figure 21 - The round and square clear water reservoirs at the Berenplaat production site (Zuid-Holland)

of a distribution network for a water company in a rural area. From the production site (pumping station), there are pipes going to the different villages and hamlets, where there is a water pipe in every street with houses.

In the Netherlands, there are over 100,000 km of water pipes with an external diameter over 50 mm, which amounts to about 7 m per inhabitant. The smaller branches and home connections are not included in this pipe length. Those additions will make the total pipe length per person about 10 - 13 m. In the distribution network, pipes may

have a diameter up to 1,800 mm (Rotterdam), but the majority of them have a diameter between 75 and 150 mm.

The design criterion for a distribution network is to maintain a supply pressure of 20 m above ground level (200 kPa) in the farthest branches of the network (at the home water meters). In order to achieve this, a minimum pressure of 25 m above ground level (250 kPa) in the streets is usually targeted. In rural areas with remotely situated clients, this might imply that during maximum demand there should be a pressure of 60 m above ground level at the production site. During the night, though, a pressure of slightly over 25 m will suffice, because during very low use the hydraulic resistance of the network will be very small. Near the production site, therefore, there would be large pressure differences.

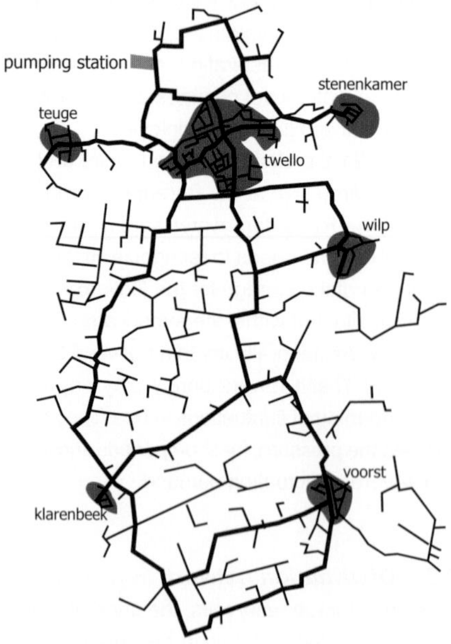

Figure 22 - A distribution network in a rural area

Figure 23 - Control room for the treatment process and the distribution network

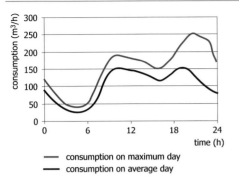

- consumption on maximum day
- consumption on average day

Figure 24 - Model for water consumption on an average day and on an extreme day

Actually, the differences will not be that great in practice, because there seldom is a "maximum day" and because the difference between the normal demand and the maximum demand is relatively high (Figure 24).

To keep the pressure in the distribution network within certain boundaries, boosters are used, in some cases. These are pumps which have been constructed in the pipe to bring the water to a higher pressure. This is only useful in a situation where there are no other pipes through which the water will flow backwards.

In an area of variable topography, one having height differences over 30 m, like in the south of Limburg, the distribution network is subdivided into different pressure zones. This prevents a high distribution pressure in the lower areas. When water is produced in the lower regions, pumping energy is also saved by this practice.

The underground distribution of drinking water is virtually invisible. And, above ground, only the water towers can be seen (Figures 25 and 26). In former days water towers were used as water hammer vessels for the distribution pumps. When the water level in the tower fell, an extra distribution pump was switched on. In this way, water towers could maintain a relatively constant pressure and could also guarantee some minutes of delivery even after a power failure at the distribution pumps.

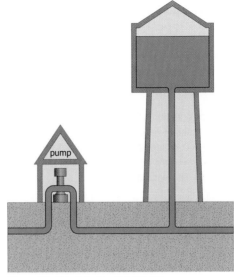

Figure 25 - Principle of a water tower

Today, water towers are no longer necessary. Speed-controlled pumps can deliver any desired amount of water on a continuous scale. Emergency power aggregates can provide power within 30 seconds and water hammer vessels at the distribution pumps have a sufficient capacity to cover this period.

Figure 26 - Water tower in Dokkum

107

Nomenclature transport pipes

In practice, transport pipes are referred to either as pressure pipes or as free-fall pipes.
This designation is only relevant when it comes to the energy supply. In the case of free-fall pipes, no external energy supply is necessary because the height difference between the start and finish allows gravity to move the water. In the case of pressure pipes, pumps supply the required transport pressure.

The designation does not indicate any information concerning the pressure in the pipe.
In the case of water power plants, there may be free-fall pipes (by gravity) having an internal pressure of 10,000 kPa (height difference of 1,000 meters).
In the pressure pipes after a polder pumping station, the pressures may be as low as 10 to 50 kPa (height difference of 1 - 5 m).

In the distribution network, there are relatively large pipes connecting the storage site to the supply area. In practice these are often called transport pipes. However, these pipes are integral parts of the distribution system. It is better to speak of the "main pipes" of the distribution network.
Those pipes are operated at the distribution pressure and are designed to meet the maximum hourly use on the maximum day.

Every dwelling is connected to the street water pipe through a home connection, which is also called a service pipe. The home connection ends at the water meter, meaning that after the water meter the client is the owner of that water.
In the Netherlands there are about 6 million technical connections to the drinking water network, of which 5.7 million are for small users. Ninety-six percent of all connections have a meter. When Amsterdam, Rotterdam and Groningen have finished their current introduction of water meters, this percentage will be 100%.

Table 7 indicates the lengths of the pipes of the Dutch water companies, per pipe material (service pipes excluded). The total length of over 100,000 km increases some 2.5% per year, mainly because of the development of new residential areas (new 3%; 0.5% removed). The low removal percentage suggests a pipe lifetime of 200 years. The technical and economical lifetime of pipes is shorter, which suggests that more pipes will need to be changed in the future.

Formerly, cast iron was used for pipes of smaller diameters. Nowadays, those pipes are mostly made of plastics (PVC, PE). Because of the sustainability and costs, asbestos cement, was often used for the middle-sized pipes. Due to the health risks of working with asbestos cement, its use is no longer permitted. The consequences of this for existing pipes are currently being discussed.

Table 7   *- Lengths and (most common) diameters of the distribution pipes of Dutch water companies, excl. pipes with an inside diameter <45 mm (VEWIN 2000)*

Piping material	Length (1000 km)	(%)	Diameter (mm)
PVC	50	46	100 - 400
Asbestos cement	35	32	250 – 600
Cast iron	12	11	50 – 200
PE	4	4	50 – 100
Steel	3	3	> 500
Nodulair cast iron	2	2	> 500
Concrete	1	1	> 800
Other	1	1	-
Total	108	100	

4.4 Drinking water installations

Before the last world war, the sanitary equipment for social housing was limited to a kitchen tap and a flushing toilet. Nowadays, a shower or a bath is also deemed necessary. More and more bedrooms are equipped with washbasins, and water closets with washbasins. The single tap in the kitchen or

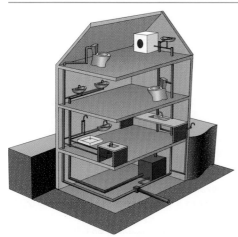

Figure 27 - Design of a drinking water installation for a single family dwelling (hot and cold water)

in the garden shed has been extended by connections for a washing machine and/or a dishwasher. The garden tap is no longer only used for watering the garden or cleaning the pavement, but for cleaning the car as well. This "water civilization" has made the sanitary installation quite a complex system of pipes and installations.

In other countries, other water-using devices may be found, like garbage disposals in America or bidets in France.

Figure 27 shows a simple hot and cold drinking water installation for a family house.

In apartment buildings it will be impossible to have sufficient pressure on the upper floors. Therefore, those dwellings are equipped with booster installations which consist of pumps and a pressure tank. The pressure tanks function as a water hammer vessel and for pressure smoothing.

5.   Capacity

5.1   Design capacity of drinking water supply

Water use by clients is decisive for the design of any drinking water production plant. Their use will fluctuate widely throughout the day. During the night, though, there is a relatively low demand.

Very high demands do occur during the early evening hours, however, on warm summer days (watering the garden).

For the drinking water installation inside a house, pipe diameters are chosen based on the maximum tap capacity of the specific taps. The home connection is determined by the maximum instantaneous use by its residents. This is less than the sum of the capacities of the different taps, because it will never happen that all taps are in use at the same time. Large industrial clients, on the other hand, sometimes have a reduced intake to obtain a lower connection price. And, they have their own storage for this end.

The distribution network has been designed for the maximum instantaneous use of all connected clients. From the end branches of the network in the direction of the production plant, the capacity will increase, because there is an increasing number of clients to be supplied. Because of the dampening of the instantaneous use by the greater number of connected clients, the fluctuations will decrease.

For the supply of a complete town or region, daily fluctuations still exist, as with individual houses. During the night the least amount of water is consumed. During the day the demand varies, with maxima around 10 a.m. and 7 p.m.

In order to limit the costs of production and transport, the storage facilities are designed for dampening the daily fluctuations.

Because of this, production plants and transport systems may be designed based on the average use on the maximum day.

Table 8 shows the general design capacities for designing the different aspects of a water supply system.

5.2   Design capacity of production

The required production capacity for a production plant is determined by:
1. the required yearly capacity
2. the demand on the maximum day

Table 8   - Rough design capacity for different aspects of a drinking water company

Part	Basic design capacity (occurrence)	Typical value (m³/h)
Tap point	Maximum capacity of the individual tap point	0.15 m³/h (toilet) 1.2 m³/h (sprinkling of garden)
House connection	Maximum use consumers	2.5 m³/h (house) 20 m³/h (large company) 200 m³/h (large industry)
Street pipe	Maximum use consumers	20 m³/h (street in residential area)
Outgoing distribution pipe	Maximum hour use (once every 10 years)	1.8 times max. day use / 24 h
Storage reservoir	Dampening maximum day use (once every 10 years)	25% of max. day use
Transport main	Maximum day use (once every 10 years)	Max. day use / 24 h
Production plant	Maximum day use (once every 10 years)	Max. day use / 24 h

Required yearly capacity

The required yearly capacity is determined from the forecast of the water demand in the supply area.

When we consider the Netherlands as a whole, the drinking water demand amounted to 1,127 million m³ in 2001, or about 70 m³ per citizen per year (193 l/citizen/d). Assuming a yearly increase in demand of 1%, the water demand in 2020 will be 122% ($1{,}01^{20}$) of the current demand, or 1,375 million m³ per year.

Considering a water loss of 15% during abstraction, treatment and distribution, in 2020 a total amount of (1,375/0.85 =) 1,620 million m³ of water needs to be abstracted.

The fluctuations due to climatological effects (e.g., extra demand during dry summers) have not been taken into account in this forecast. For the Dutch practice, this means a fluctuation between -4% to +8% of the normal yearly demand.

Demand on the maximum day

A plant's production capacity should cover all days to a probability of 99.97% (one day in every ten years, 1 - 1/3650 = 99.97%). This statistical computation is shown in Figure 28.

In this figure the daily water consumption of several years is plotted. A period of at least 5 years is required to obtain a reliable result, suitable for extrapolation.

For each year, the daily consumption figures are expressed as fraction of the average daily consumption in that year, giving figures between 70 and 140%. These figures are plotted in a cumulative occurrence graph (log probability). The observed values (blue line) are flattened by a linear (red) line for design calculations and extrapolation.

By example the figure shows that 98% of the days have a consumption factor of 1.25 (125%) or less.

The decisive peak factor at 99.97% can be read as 1.41 (141%).

The water demand on the maximum day according to the results above can be computed from:

Daily use maximum day = forecast for average day · 1.08 · 1.41

When full dampening of the demand of the maximum day is achieved by means of a sufficient storage capacity, the production capacity should at least be equal to this daily use calculation.

Required hourly capacity

The required hourly production capacity follows from a consideration of both the production capacity and the storage capacity.

Figure 29 shows that for an imaginary use pattern, no storage is necessary when production equals the maximum hourly use, and that a storage capacity of 23.3% of the average daily use is required when the production capacity equals the average use calculation.

At a higher storage volume, a multi-day dampening can be achieved with a smaller production capacity.

Figure 30 shows an elaboration of this. For an increase in the dampening period from 1 day to 7 days, slightly more than double the storage volume is required. On the other hand, the production capacity can be reduced to 84%.

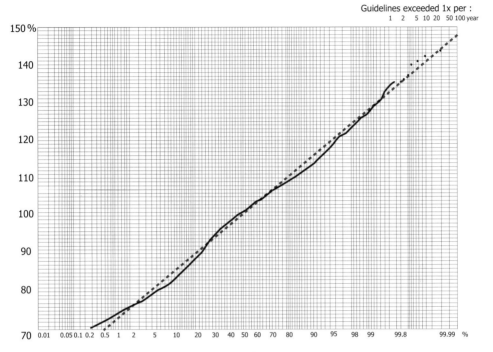

Figure 28 - Determination of decisive peak factor based on occurrence probability

For very complex and expensive production plants, the optimal capacity will be the multi-day dampening one. For production plants without treatment and with a nearby supply area, the optimal capacity will be at a dampening rate of less than one day.

Fluctuations in the production
For the operation of a production plant, not only maximum but also minimum production is relevant.

The frequency distribution of drinking water production is shown in Figure 28. The mean produc-

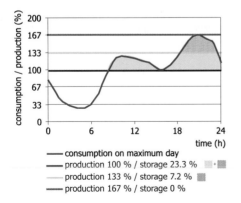

Figure 29 - Consideration of production capacity versus storage capacity

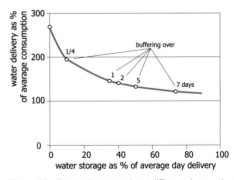

Figure 30 - Production capacity at different dampening periods

111

tion has a peak factor of 1.0. The design capacity has a peak factor of 1.41.

Once per year occurrence probabilities of 0.003 and 0.997 and peak factors of 0.6 and 1.33, respectively, are achieved, which is 43% or 94%, respectively, of the design capacity.
At 15 days per year, occurrence probabilities of 0.04 and 0.96 and peak factors of either 0.68 or 1.2, respectively, are achieved (48% or 83%, respectively, of the design capacity).

Because of these fluctuations, spare capacity is available in almost every case. This allows space for production interruptions in some parts of the plant for reasons of maintenance or repairs.

supply districts 2004

Figure 31 - Dutch water companies (VEWIN 2004)

6.   Organization

6.1   Water companies
Figure 31 shows the 14 Dutch water companies with their supply areas (mid-2004). It is expected that, because of further mergers, the number of companies will be below 10 within 10 years. Once, there were over 200 water companies in the Netherlands.

Most companies are limited liability companies, with provinces and municipalities being the major shareholders. More and more, the companies cater water to their own needs, thus reducing the frequency of supporting supplies.
Besides the 14 water companies that supply drinking water to clients, there are 2 other companies that only supply "semi-finished products" to other water companies or to industry (Water transportmaatschappij Rijn-Kennemerland and

Waterwinningbedrijf Brabantse Biesbosch). These companies account for about 65% of the total surface water abstraction.

Dutch water companies employ a total of about 7,000 people.

6.2   Turnover and capital
Table 9 shows the sales of the water companies. Through the more than 7 million (administrative) connections, 1.1 billion m³ of water is supplied, having a total sales value of €1.42 billion. Households use an average of 110 m³ per connection at an average price of €1.35 per m³ (excluding taxes, including ecotax). The cost for larger clients is lower.

Table 9   - Supply of the Dutch drinking water company, excl. export and import (VEWIN 2000)

Type	Users	Connections (1,000)	Sale (mln m³)	Value (mln euro)	Average costs (euro/m³)
Drinking water	Household use	6,741	741	997	1.35
	Small business use	297	214	251	1.17
	Large business use	4	172	170	0.99
	Total	7,042	1,127	1,418	1.26
Other water	Residential	3.6	0.08	0.05	0.61
	Other	0.2	85	39	0.46
	Total	3.8	86	39	0.46

The prices for drinking water differ significantly across water companies (between €0.78 and €1.97 per m³). This is mainly due to the differences in capital costs (old or new plants, simple or complex treatment processes). Drinking water prices are based on cost recovery, including an extra environmental tax (eco levy), which depends on the kind of water used (surface water is free of this tax).

Indirect taxes (VAT and drinking water tax) account for a price increase of €0.18 per m³ on average.

Figure 32 - Kiwa Water Research Center in Nieuwegein

The total assets of the Dutch water companies amount to €5.3 billion, of which 89% is in material assets (buildings, pipes and installations); 72% is covered by (mostly long-term) loans, and 19% is covered by the water companies' own capital.

Water companies invest €0.4 to 0.5 billion yearly, 50% for distribution processes and 40% for production processes.

6.3   Legal framework

The supply of drinking water in the Netherlands is regulated by the Water Supply Act (Dutch: Waterleidingwet, VROM). These regulations are elaborated in the Decree on the Water Supply (Dutch: Waterleidingbesluit, VROM).

The Act and the Decree determine the rights and duties of water companies. Quality standards for many parameters are laid down, as well as the obligation to monitor this quality adequately.

Supervision over the Dutch water companies is carried out by the VROM inspector.

The Decree requires home installations to comply with the "General prescriptions for drinking water installations" (Dutch: Algemene voorschriften voor leidingwaterinstallaties, AVWI 2002 - NEN1006) and with the VEWIN's worksheets on drinking water installations (Dutch: VEWIN-werkbladen Drinkwaterinstallaties, VEWIN 2004).

6.4   Organizations

Dutch water companies are organized in the Association of Dutch Water Companies (Dutch: VEWIN, Vereniging van Waterbedrijven in Nederland). This branch organization caters to, among other

things, coordination with the government and to large-scale national public relations. Also, public supervision over the management of the water companies is organized by the VEWIN by means of a national benchmark.

The testing and certifying of components which have direct contact with drinking water (like pipes and taps) are executed by Kiwa (Keuringsinstituut voor waterleidingartikelen; Testing Institute for drinking water devices), a company whose shares are held by the water companies, the VEWIN, and the Royal Dutch Waterworks Association (Dutch: Koninklijke Vereniging van Waterleidingbelangen in Nederland, KWVN). Kiwa is the main entity of the joint research program of the Dutch Water Companies. The drinking water companies together spend 0.005 euro/m³ for this research. Together, this forms a national budget of about €6 million, which is available for research investigating the fundamental questions related to public drinking water supply. Because of this joint approach,

Figure 33 - Test installation for research

Figure 34 - Drinking water installation in Bandung

Dutch research is at a high level, and Kiwa is now an internationally respected water institute.

All the institutions mentioned above have more or less originated from the KWVN. This association is more than 100 years old and includes a variety of individuals from the Dutch drinking water world.

6.5   Other countries

The Dutch drinking water supply is high quality. Throughout the years the sector has accumulated a lot of knowledge, experience and technology. It is therefore not so unusualy, then, that there is great interest coming from other countries.

First, this is true for developing countries, in which millions of children and adults die annually because of a lack of good drinking water. Of course, the Dutch water companies are glad to aid those countries with their knowledge and experience. "Aqua for all" was instituted by the Dutch water sector and supports drinking water projects in developing countries with knowledge, means and money.

Second, this is true for other countries in the Western world as well. Drinking water experts from those countries can be informed of the developments in the Netherlands at scientific conferences and during site visits. Further opportunities for the transfer of knowledge and experience are dependent upon the political situation in the relevant country, especially regarding the organization of the drinking water supply. Basically, the distinction between private and public water supply companies is important.

Europe

In Western Europe virtually all citizens are connected to a public drinking water supply. Although the technical setup is more or less equal in these countries, there remain large differences primarily in the organizational setup.

Germany (82 million inhabitants) has ca. 8,000 small, mainly municipal water companies, their size varying between a few hundred to several million connections.

In France (60 million inhabitants), 2 large companies dominate the market, Suez and Veolia. The situation is such that the municipalities own the infrastructural works, but the operation and the construction of new works is mostly delegated through long-term contracts. This results in a near-monopoly for Suez and Veolia, due to their enormous advantage regarding knowledge, experience and financial power. At the same time, these companies have been able to develop into world leaders for private drinking water projects, due to their strong home market (Figure 34). They have developed projects and currently manage installations in metropolises like Jakarta, Mumbai (Bombay), Budapest, Rio de Janeiro and Berlin.

In England and Wales (63 million inhabitants), there has been a strong concentration of companies over the past 30 years. The drinking water supply of over 80% of the connections is carried out by 10 integrated drinking and wastewater companies. These are private companies (shares not owned by the government), of which 5 are owned by foreign parties like the French Suez, German RWE and Azurix, which was part of the former American Enron group. The other 20% of the connections is supplied by 13 traditional (non-integrated) drinking water companies.

In Flanders (6 million inhabitants), there are 7 full-service water companies and 7 smaller distribution companies.

There are only small technical differences between the countries of the European Union: the requirements regarding the drinking water are the same

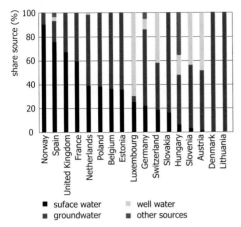

Figure 35 - Sources for drinking water supply in Europe

(EU-legislation) and the differences are mainly caused by geohydrological differences (soil condition, types of groundwater, rivers, lakes) (Figure 35).

United States of America

In the United States of America (290 million inhabitants), 85% of the population is supplied with drinking water from public companies.

There are over 160,000 drinking water systems: about 50,000 for residential areas, about 20,000 systems for buildings (schools, hospitals) and about 90,000 for campsites and petrol stations.

About 130,000 of these systems each supply less than 500 inhabitants and about 370 each cater to more than 100,000 inhabitants. Two-thirds of the American drinking water is produced from surface water.

In the American drinking water supply, there is an important role for the American Waterworks Association (AWWA). This organization has 57,000 members, both individuals and companies. In total there are 4,200 water companies associated with this organization, which together supply 180 million people with drinking water. If you compare the Dutch KWVN, which has only about 1,300 members to the AWWA in the U.S., you will find that there are 2.5 times fewer members in the Netherlands when related to the population.

There is a fundamental difference between the European and American drinking water practice, and that difference relates to the legislation regarding the water's microbiological reliability. Drinking water in the USA should have a minimum concentration of chlorine. Clients are used to the chlorine taste, which is considered proof of its microbiological reliability.

Partly because of this chlorine taste, increasing numbers of American houses are equipped with home water treatment devices (point of use filters, mainly activated carbon or membrane filters).

Further reading

- Handbook of public water systems, Wiley (2001)
- Freshwater in Europe, UNEP/DEWA/GRID (2004)
- International comparison of water and sewerage service, Ofwat ((bi-)annual report)
- Beleidsplan Drink- en Industriewatervoorziening (BDIV), VROM (1993-1996)
- Water om te drinken, S. Wijmer, VEWIN, (1992)
- Waterleidingstatistiek, VEWIN (annual reports)
- Reflections and performance 2003, Benchmarking in the Dutch drinking water industry, VEWIN (2004)

- www.vewin.nl
- www.kiwa.nl
- www.rivm.nl
- www.kvwn.nl
- www.minvrom.nl
- www.overheid.nl
- www.verswater.nl
- www.dvgw.de
- www.ofwat.gov.uk
- www.iwahq.org.uk
- www.awwa.org
- www.grid.unep.ch

Questions and applications

Technical setup of the drinking water supply system

1. Name the different parts of the drinking water supply system.

Production

1. Which three systems can be discerned when producing drinking water from surface water? Explain them.
2. Indicate which groups of parameters are discerned in Dutch water quality legislation.

Distribution

1. Why were water towers used in the distribution network and why are those towers less used today? Explain why there are still many water towers in use in France.

Capacity

1. Indicate which fluctuations exist in the different parts of a drinking water system and indicate their general magnitude.

Organization

1. How many water companies exist in the Netherlands and what is the name of their sector organization?
2. What are the most important regulations concerning public drinking water supply?

Applications

1. A water company in the eastern part of the Netherlands can choose from 2 sources to increase its capacity:
   - surface water from a large lake
   - aerobic freatic groundwater from an agricultural area

   Indicate for each aspect which of the two is preferred and give arguments for your choice:
   a hygienic reliability
   b organic compounds
   c pesticides
   d desiccation

2. The water company decides to expand its capacity by means of surface water treatment.

   Formulate a possible treatment setup in order to obtain reliable drinking water, and indicate which compounds are removed in which treatment step.

Answers

Technical setup of the drinking water supply system

1. Parts of drinking water supply system:
   - production (abstracting, treatment, storage)
   - distribution (storage, transport, storage, distribution network, use connection)

Production

1. - Dune infiltration:
     Pre-treatment, soil aquifer recharge, re-abstracting and a limited final treatment
   - Direct treatment:
     Storage in reservoirs and extensive treatment
   - Riverbank groundwater:
     Abstracting from wells near the river and post-treatment

2. - Public health parameter
   - Technical parameter
   - Organoleptic / aesthetic parameter
   - Signalling parameters

Distribution

1. Water towers are used for dampening pressures in case of fluctuating demand. Nowadays, they are less used because speed-controlled pumps can supply any amount, on a continuous scale, because emergency power aggregates can restore power within 30 seconds, and because water hammer vessels at the distribution pumps have a sufficient capacity for covering this period.
   In rural areas having large vertical differences, water towers are still more often in use to cover interruptions (reliability of supply).

Capacity

1. Fluctuations:
   - season (winter, summer)
   - week (Sunday, working day)
   - part of the day (day, night)

   Peak factors
   - daily maximum: 1.5 x daily average
   - hourly maximum: 1.8 x average daily hour

Organization

1. In the Netherlands, there are about 14 water companies. Their number is decreasing because of companies merging.
   The Dutch water companies are united in the Association of Dutch Water Companies (VEWIN - Vereniging van Waterbedrijven in Nederland).

2. Dutch drinking water supply is officially regulated by the Water Supply Act (Dutch: Waterleidingwet). More in-detail elaboration is given in the Decree on the Water Supply (Dutch: Waterleidingbesluit).

Applications

1. a Hygienic reliability: aerobic groundwater, because groundwater contains little or no microorganisms
   b Organic compounds: groundwater, due to the lower rate of organic matter, especially in sandy soil
   c Pesticides: groundwater contains few or no pesticides because of confirming layers
   d Desiccation: surface water causes no dehydration

117

2. Treatment processes and removed com-
   pounds:
   - Flocculation and floc removal: suspended
     particles, organic compounds, heavy met-
     als, microorganisms
   - Rapid filtration: ammonium, suspended
     particles, microorganisms
   - Activated carbon filtration: organic micro-
     pollutants
   - UV disinfection: microorganisms

WATER COMPANIES

Planning and design

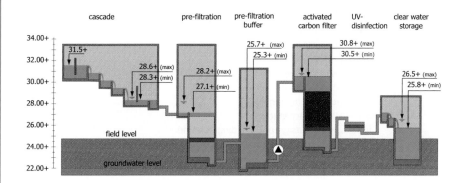

cascade   pre-filtration   pre-filtration buffer   activated carbon filter   UV-disinfection   clear water storage

31.5+

28.6+ (max)
28.3+ (min)

28.2+ (max)
27.1+ (min)

25.7+ (max)
25.3+ (min)

30.8+ (max)
30.5+ (min)

26.5+ (max)
25.8+ (min)

field level

groundwater level

34.00+
32.00+
30.00+
28.00+
26.00+
24.00+
22.00+

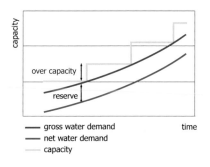

capacity

over capacity

reserve

time

— gross water demand
— net water demand
— capacity

Framework

This module focuses on the planning and design aspects for constructing the infrastructure for the public water supply. The main issue in this respect is the design of a production plant.

Introduction

This module has the following contents:

Study goals

After having studied this module, you will be able to:
* identify the different planning processes
* identify the different parts of the design process
* describe, explain and draw up the most important documents needed for the design

1. Introduction

Extensive preparations are necessary in order to build drinking water production plants. The government plays an important role in this planning process, as public health is one of the main issues concerned. However, water companies are responsible for the construction and operation of the infrastructure.

Usually, it takes many years from the time the first idea for expanding water production facilities comes up, until the completion and start-up of the new plant. During this period, a highly diverse development process is carried out, involving many different specialties. Among these are:

- mathematics (probability theory)
- treatment technology (physics, chemistry, microbiology)
- environmental science
- geohydrology (groundwater)
- hydrology (surface water)
- hydraulics (fluid mechanics)
- structural engineering (concrete, steel)
- architecture
- mechanical engineering
- electrical engineering
- process control engineering (instrumentation)
- law (property rights, user rights, contracts)
- economics (project finance, payments)

As a consequence of so many specialities being involved, expansion of the infrastructucture for drinking water production requires a multi-disciplinary approach. To have a successful project, organization is of critical importance. The complexity of the project is further increased by the fact that the existing public water supply must not be obstructed or compromised during construction of the new infrastructure.

This module will address design aspects for (re)construction of drinking water infrastructure. First, the planning process for public water supply will be presented, ranging from national long-term plans to internal management plans for drinking water companies. It will continue by focusing on the infrastructure's life cycle, paying special attention to the design aspects of drinking water production facilities. Further on, the laws, permits and standards applying mainly to drinking water supply will be described. Finally, the different parts of the design process will be examined in more detail.

2. Planning process for public water supply

2.1 Process scheme

The planning process for a public water supply is embedded in the general spatial planning process. The primary structure of and the hierarchy in this process in the Netherlands are summarized in Table 1. Of course, the planning process needs to comply with the legal framework and show mutual consistency. As a legal framework, the Water Supply Act is especially important.

Within the Water Supply Act, a Committee for drinking water supply has been formed, which has to supervise all aspects concerning the public drinking water supply. This Committee is mainly advisory, but can operate as a mediator as well.

Table 1 - Hierarchical planning process for the public drinking water supply in the Netherlands

Planning level	Name	Timeframe (years)	Organization
National policy plan	Policy plan for drinking and industrial water supply	20 – 30	Ministry VROM
National section plan	Ten-year plan	5 – 10	VEWIN
Provincial plan	Provincial policy plans	5 – 10	Province
	Provincial management plans	5 – 10	Province
Regional plan	Regional plans	5 – 10	Province
Municipal plan	Land use plans	5 – 10	Municipality
Company plan	Water supply plan	10 – 30	Company
	Multi-year investment plan	5 – 10	Company
	Business plan	5	Company

2.2 Policy plan for drinking and industrial water supply

The process of formulating the policy plan for drinking and industrial water supply is recorded in the Water Supply Act (Chapter 4 - Preparation and accomplishment of water supply works - first part).

The national policy plan for drinking and industrial water supply is a sector plan on a national level, and includes background information and preferences for the desired long-term strategic development.

The policy plan makes a long-term estimate of future water needs, typically for a period of approximately 30 years. A description is made of the available water resources from both ground- and surface water, including the advantages and disadvantages concerning public health, spatial planning, the environment, the economy, and so on. Policy choices and priority settings are made with respect to the above aspects. Finally, the plan indicates what efforts will be undertaken to safeguard the drinking and industrial water supply over the relevant 30-year period, with regard to the available water resources. Together with some policy statements, this plan forms a national spatial planning key decision.

The policy plan has a dual effect. First, it indicates land claims for spatial planning and water management. These claims should be considered when appropriating land and water on national, provincial and municipal levels. Second, the policy plan guides the water supply sector. Only in urgent situations are the water companies allowed to deviate from this plan.

The procedure for preparing a policy plan is regulated, in large part, by the Spatial Planning Act. This procedure is comparable to the process of adopting a new regulation:

- preparation of a draft plan in interdepartmental consultation
- publication of the draft plan; inviting response
- authorization by the Second and First Chambers of the Dutch Parliament

2.3 Association of Dutch Water Companies' ten-year plan

The procedure for formulating the Association of Dutch Water Companies' ten-year plan is recorded in the Water Supply Act. The plan is referred to by law as a "medium-term plan" to be drawn up by a "representative association of water companies" (Chapter 4 - Preparation and construction of water works - second part).

The ten-year plan is a medium-term plan that is prepared by the Association of Dutch Water Companies (VEWIN). When the Water Supply Act was first adopted, it was unusual to have such a national plan formulated by the involved companies and regulated in this way by law. Nowadays, the "retreating government' policy has caused this kind of regulation to be used more often.

All projects for the abstraction, storage and transportation of water that the water companies intend to undertake in the coming ten years should be recorded in this plan. Studies and research programs which will be executed over the same period should also be recorded. In this way, all water companies are closely involved in the integral planning process, because the companies themselves are expected to take the lead in proposing and preparing new projects.

The proposed ten-year plan is presented to the minister for Housing, Spatial Planning and the Environment for authorization. In deciding whether the plan will be approved, the minister needs to consider the policy plan.

The period from the 1970s to the 1990s saw the heyday of the ten-year plan, when over 100 (mainly municipal) water companies existed. Today, most water companies operate on the provincial, or even super-provincial, level. This causes the chief aim of the ten-year plan - fine-tuning the production capacity of the different water companies - to decline. Thus, the importance of the ten-year plan has decreased and part of its goal is now absorbed by policy plans of either the provinces or the individual companies.

2.4   Provincial planning

As the formulation of the ten-year plan is discussed with the provinces the provincial policy can be adapted to the plan's eventual consequences. Space for projects mentioned in the ten-year plan can be reserved in good time.

Significant provincial plans are:
- provincial groundwater management
- provincial policy plan for protection of ground-water for drinking water supply
- provincial water management plan
- provincial environmental policy plan
- provincial environmental decrees
- regional plans of the respective provinces

There is little consistency in the different ways of naming plans by the provinces, caused, in part, by the titles being adapted to the changing legal framework.

2.5   Municipal planning

All construction plans should ultimately be included in the municipal land-use plans.
In these plans specific parcels can be designated for public water supply.
The following items will be registered for the chosen parcel:
- the kind of construction allowed (reservoirs, treatment and pumping plants, workshops, company housing, etc.)
- the boundaries indicated for the buildings
- the building height allowed for the construction

A permit for (re)construction of any building is only allowed to be issued by the municipal government if the building scheme is in compliance with the land-use plan. Therefore, these activities should be coordinated in advance, even when the draft schemes for construction are not fully known.

2.6   Company planning

Of course, (re)construction plans are included in the water companies' own planning process as well. Important partial plans are:

- water supply plan
- multi-year investment plan
- business plan

Water supply plan

The water supply plan indicates the ways in which present and future water plants will meet water needs over the next 10 - 30 years.
Sometimes, regional supply plans are formulated separately, especially when a transportation infrastructure is expected to hinder supply over regional boundaries.

Multi-year investment plan

The multi-year investment plan consists of all planned investments for the next 5 - 10 years.
In addition, this plan is used for predicting future water use rates.

Water companies' business plans

Within the framework of the revision of the Water Supply Act, a proposal to have Business plans for water companies drawn up by the water companies themselves is included. These plans should supplement or replace the VEWIN ten-year plan. Every four years such an investment plan, which is coordinated with the provinces, should be made and approved by the Ministry of Environment, Planning and Housing.
This plan will provide a clear and complete overview of the investments needed for expansion or replacement to improve or maintain the quality and reliability of the water supply.

3.   Design activities in the infrastructure's life cycle

3.1   Overview of the infrastructure's life cycle

The hydrologic cycle is a well-known concept for any water company. A similar concept is that of the materials cycle and is important in designing infrastructural works (Figure 1).
During the cycle, the construction itself will generally pass through the following phases:
- planning and design
- construction

Figure 1   - The recycling of materials alongside the life cycle of buildings

- operation and use
- demolition

In practice, different sub-phases can be discerned throughout this process.

Between the different phases, no definite boundaries exist. By choosing a different way of constructing (e.g., turnkey), a different clustering will develop. However, the same elements will be present in any construction's life cycle.

Usually, the initial phase will be part of the normal business of a water company and, of course, this holds for the operation and use phase as well.
During the construction and demolition phases, most attention is paid to activities which are not part of the typical business of the water company. Because the construction phase is of a temporary nature, having a limited and well-defined time process, the building sub-phase is extremely well suited for working with a separate project organization. This organization, then, will consist of some specialists who, in their turn, will conduct a team of designers, contractors, subcontractors, etc.

Water companies' production plants feature design and use phases that are totally different from the construction phase.
The construction of any water production plant is much like the construction of any other civil work, like buildings or bridges, but the plant itself is more like a large-scale chemical industrial plant.

Table 2   - Life cycle of the infrastructural projects for the drinking water supply

Phase	Sub-phase	Typical activity
Initiative	Identification	Orientation Consideration of options Pilot plant research
	Definition	Definition of project Sketch design Building plan
Construction	Design contract	Preliminary design Final design Detailed design
	Contract	Contract documents
	Building	Management supervision Building process Ground work Main structure Process units Finishing elements Testing Delivery/take-over
Operation and use	Start up	Start-up Optimization Measurement guarantee
	Operation	Operation Adaptation Renewal of parts
Demolition		Taking out of operation Installation removal

The main part of the investment costs is relegated to construction work (e.g., reservoirs, sand filters). However, most attention is paid during design, construction, delivery, start-up and operation, to the process, including the operation and control systems.
For drinking water plants, it is a requirement that the water supply may not be obstructed, neither during construction nor during the transition from the old to the new plant.
In the following sections, each phase in the infrastructural life cycle (Table 2) will be elaborated upon separately. Aspects not directly relevant to the construction of drinking water plants will be addressed superficially. These aspects can be found in general literature on construction.

3.2   Identification

A construction project for public water supply can be initiated by different motivations. Because this project is meant to solve one or more problems, these problems need to be examined first.
Typical problems for a water supply company are:

Figure 2   - Solutions can not always be realized

- insufficient capacity due to growing demand
- decrease of production capacity due to a different source policy (i.e., reduction in groundwater abstraction)
- considerations from business economics: scaling up of plants
- technical obsolescence of current installations
- new requirements regarding the treatment process (more stringent quality levels or changing raw water quality)

All existing water supply companies have been, or will be, confronted with one of these problems. Therefore, initiating construction projects is practically part of a water company's regular business.

Preliminary studies
Within the water supply plan and the multi-year investment plan, possible solutions are drawn up and provisional decisions are made. This will be done based on feasibility studies which compare several alternatives. Technological research will lead to a general direction for the desired treatment process. Prior to the construction process, the following questions need to be answered:

- what, where, and what capacity needs to be constructed?
- when should it be completed?
- what needs to be achieved?
- what are the estimated costs?

These questions are answered in several preliminary studies, like:
- feasibility studies (technological, technical, financial, economic, environmental impact)
- location studies (possibility of land acquisition)
- literature studies
- project comparisons by site visits
- specialist research (hydraulics, (soil) mechanics, ergonomics, material science, control engineering, physics, chemistry, environmental science, social aspects, etc.)
- system design studies (comparison of different treatment methods)

Data gathering
During these preliminary studies, data which will be useful during the further process of designing and constructing will be collected. Among these are:
- data on existing plants (raw water source, process flow diagram, hydraulic scheme, drawings, operating experiences)
- data on the surrounding area (drawings, descriptions, measurements, photographs) concerning foundations, soil conditions, groundwater levels, wires, pipes, roads, working areas, property rights, obligations, utility company connections, etc.)
- data concerning necessary permits (provincial, municipal, water boards, spatial planning legislation, utility companies, public services, etc.)

3.3   Definition
The final part of the identification phase is the decision to start a new construction project. To be able to begin such a project, a few documents need to be drawn up during the definition phase:
- requirements program
- draft design
- building scheme

These documents are often formulated consecutively, but need to have good mutual coherence. This will make them suitable as basic documents for collecting employees' viewpoints and for supporting management's decisions.

Finally, these documents will, together with possible adaptations, be used for external communications as well (e.g., for permits, to consumers, etc.).

It is not wise however, to draw up the definition phase documents as contract documents. The legal wording in such documents does not lend itself to a public description of wishes, side purposes, considerations, and the like.

Requirements program

The term "requirements program" is broadly used and has many different meanings, varying from a precize contract document to a general wish list. It is also applied to the collection of documents in the construction phase.

A requirements program is, preferably, limited to the purpose and outlines of the construction project. This program considers the following aspects:

- motivation for the project
- summary of preliminary studies
- purpose of the project
- wishes and side purposes
- future developments after construction

Based on the requirements program, a draft design can be formulated.

Sketch design

In the sketch design, general options are considered, and the option finally chosen will be sketched in its technical, as well as in its spatial, outline. A sketch design can consist of the collection of relevant preliminary studies and reviews, as well as a more in-depth elaboration of the design represented by:

- treatment scheme (i.e., block diagram)
- rough hydraulic line scheme
- rough terrain arrangement
- phasing of construction
- cost estimation

A sketch design gives a good indication of the dimensions of the construction project. In it, not only is the future construction phase included, but parts planned for a later phase and terrain arrangements for future expansions are represented as well. This design is important for informing all parties involved in the project's next phases.

The building scheme can be formulated on the basis of the sketch design.

Building scheme

The building scheme is the general project plan, covering all aspects of the construction phase. It contains the full project definition and consists of:

- requirements program
- sketch design
- time schedule for design, contracting and construction
- design of the project organization (task setting between different parties involved in future studies and construction)
- estimation of investment costs (total project costs)

The building scheme is also important for internal decision making by the water company itself, including such considerations as the project mandate for organizational, technical, contractual and financial aspects.

Form of contract

During the definition phase, the project will be drawn up so that it is possible to setup the construction project (including the necessary contract documents) to be executed by a form of contract combining both design and construction, possibly even operation. Such a working method is useful if the principal does not want to bother himself with the construction process. In situations where the principal himself will be responsible for the operation of the plant after construction, such a hands-off approach is quite ineffective.

Combining the complexity of a water production plant with the great freedom during the design phase, it is difficult to formulate efficient and effective contracts. Plant operation has even more impact on product quality than the design does,

Figure 3   - A rapid sand filter as seen by a researcher, a designer and the director of the water supply company

especially when the source water has a variable quality.

Outsourcing a combination of design, construction and operation activities might be able to correct this. However, this will make it impossible to balance costs and product quality. Instead, this will lead to exhaustive discussions on causes, effects and cost sharing, instead of solving the problem. In view of the social importance of a drinking water supply, this situation is highly undesirable.

However, outside of the Netherlands, contracts that combine design, construction and even operation are widely used. This option is chosen due to limitations within the water company itself because of:
- insufficient knowledge to operate the system
- insufficient possibilities for financing new plants
- insufficient management

Thanks to increases in scale due to the merging of different companies, Dutch water companies are less affected by these issues. This very scaling up of companies was actually initiated because of the increased complexity of providing a public water supply. Complexity is mainly caused by increas-

ing distances between the source and consumers, expanding treatment processes, increasing scale of new constructions, etc.

3.4   Design

Designing a water construction plant is a creative process, influenced by several factors, which all having a different importance and typically subject to personal preferences. These differences cause people to conceive of different results. Thus, the design will need to be negotiated. The final design will, of course, be a compromise between the parties involved (e.g., managers, economists, ecologists, PR-officers, designers, builders, etc.).

During the design process, it is important that the motivation for selecting the chosen solution be made clear to third parties as well. The large number of parties involved necessitates an open planning process. In this way, different parties will have timely insight into the progress and development of the design and its associated effects on their own roles. A phased procedure, including a characteristic coarse-to-fine approach, therefore, is necessary.

At the end of every design phase, a complete image of the construction should be presented.

Figure 4   - Harderbroek production plant (Flevoland)

This will make clear not only the progress in that specific design phase, but also the way in which the design might have been modified from prior design phases. Often, besides the sketch design phase, one can discern three other design phases:

- preliminary design
- final design
- detailed design

Because it is a creative process, designing is not an easily recorded activity. Thus, it is quite difficult to define in terms of contracting to the external designer offering the lowest price. Besides, the value of an intermediate, or even of a final, result is only quantifiable during or after construction, which means this will be quite some time after the design phase. In the past, water companies attempting inexpensive design projects saw that the end-product was more in line with its price and less with its desired or necessary quality.

Changing the design

The coarse-to-fine approach is inspired by the need for changeability in the design. Passing through the construction process from identification to start-up, the project proceeds within smaller and smaller boundaries. This is expressed in:

- more precise estimations of costs
- more expensive design changes
- less freedom to change plans

In Table 3 some characteristic phases in the construction process have been quantified. The given values are indicative for a drinking water production plant.

Table 3   - Sketch of the construction process, upon completion of the different phases

Phase	Accuracy of costs	Changeability of design	Change in costs
Identification	± 50%	-	-
Sketch design	± 30%	100%	1%
Preliminary design	± 25%	40%	5%
Final design	± 15%	10%	10%
Detailed design	± 5%	2%	25%
Building	± 1%	-	100%

Design documents

During the design process, a number of documents are prepared. It is desirable that these documents remain up to date, because one would want them to be reliable images of the completed construction during later phases (not only during construction, but during actual operation as well). Figure 5 shows a diagram of the information flow during the construction's life cycle. It should be noted that most of the information related to the various stages of the design is recorded in the design documents.

Preliminary design

The preliminary design is intended to give a rough layout of the plant elements, including their mutual coherence (i.e., location and size of buildings) and a description of any large mechanical or electronic devices needed by the plant during operation.
Also during this phase, the different construction forms for the desired process will be considered,

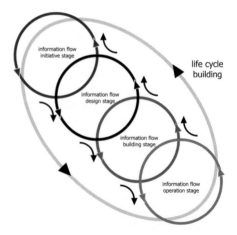

Figure 5   - Design documents provide information for the building and operation phases

possibly including a detailed preliminary design of the options to be considered. A consideration of costs, operation, flexibility, robustness, etc. makes these details necessary.

Activities for the preliminary design include:
- processing of responses to the sketch design
- discussing the design with other partners, government agencies, suppliers, third parties
- formulating process descriptions and considering alternatives
- formulating the necessary technical design drawings for the different operating conditions (minimal, maximal and normal capacity) among which are:
  - process flow diagram (PFD) (including rough balance sheets of water, energy and chemicals)
  - hydraulic line scheme
  - rough design of buildings (necessary space, building height)
- calculating rough dimensions of buildings and determining their sizes
- formulating construction drawings (floor plans, sections, views)
- specifying main components of (civil) structure (foundation, materials, architecture, spatial coding)
- specifying main components of mechanical installations (capacity, number, type, material)
- specifying main components of electrical installations, instruments and control systems
- formulating rough estimates of:
  - construction costs
  - operation costs
  - construction time
- handing out documents for approval of the results of the preliminary design

Final design
The final design follows directly from the preliminary design. This design is more detailed and contains construction drawings and the calculations of those parts which were considered "black boxes" during earlier phases. Examples of these former "unknowns" are those components not immediately involved in the treatment process, like heating, air-conditioning, pressurized air facilities,

control installations, workshops, etc. Characteristic for this phase is the check to make sure everything will fit in, not only after, but during construction as well (i.e., space for transport and assembling). Activities for the final design consist of the following elements:
- processing responses to the preliminary design
- discussing the design with other partners, government agencies, suppliers, third partners
- calculating final capacity and dimensions
- elaborating preliminary designs into final construction drawings
- formulating:
  - process flow diagrams (PFD) for mainstream and secondary flows (chemicals, energy, sludge treatment, backwash water treatment)
  - hydraulic line scheme
  - piping and instrument diagrams (P&ID)
  - control schemes based on an automatization master plan
- deciding on necessary space for auxillary facilities
- preparing requisitions for technical details and prices of necessary installations
- preparing requisitions for necessary permits including completing necessary documents
- discussing financial topics and contracts
- discussing the method of contracting
- estimating investment costs and completion time
- handing out documents for approval of the final design

Detailed design
The detailed design is chiefly aimed at the construction part of the project. For the concrete structure, this refers to reinforcement calculations and form drawings, as well as to the several finishing elements (façades, window frames, partition walls, roofing, etc.).
The mechanical part of the installation is elaborated upon with respect to the pipes (support constructions, division of pipeline parts, detailed design of vessels and appurtenances).
The electrical installation deals with cable calculations and control board design, for example.

The control system is concerned with the design of control and computer programs, and the like.

The detailed design of the structure is sometimes developed by the contractor himself.

It is important to remember that even during the detailed design phase, choices need to be made that will have a major impact on costs and quality. Therefore, it is necessary for the principal to agree with the considerations made and to be able to determine afterwards whether the construction, as it was delivered, was built as it was negotiated.

3.5   Contract

In almost every project, the actual building is done by contractors and suppliers.

This makes it important, then, that the principal be provided with the expected construction and goods of the required quality, at the agreed upon price, and at the pre-set time. Therefore, offers need to be requested that can serve as future contract documents, and later checked to determine whether the delivered item agrees with the negotiations and what the consequences will be for diverging from those plans.

Commonly, contracts are agreed upon with many bidders. This is because most bidders only can deliver within a very specific range or because they cannot guarantee quality for the entire project.

This is important, because a drinking water production plant is a factory with several specific parts, in a hygienic, quality-controlled environment.

Besides, for a water company managing the installations themselves, it is important to have direct knowledge of the products, for reasons of service, follow-up care, reparations, etc.

Though a great variety of contracts exist, both in type and in range, the following steps can always be expected:

-   formulating contract documents (specifications)
-   requesting bids
-   granting bids

Due to the large number and variety of contracts and to the necessity of monitoring all forms of progress, a separate department is charged with contract writing.

A contract is influenced by a wide variety of statutory regulations and judicial standards.

For the construction of drinking water facilities, the following should apply:

-   93/38/EEG for supplies, works and services in the utilities sectors
-   regulations for the relationship between contractor and engineering firm
-   conditions for the legal relationship between client and architect
-   uniform procurement regulations
-   general conditions for construction

In practice, several forms of contracts (turnkey, design directed building, etc.) and several forms of tendering (public, by invitation, pre-selected, with price request, etc.) are used.

Because of the special nature of water companies (construction by a third party; operation by the company itself; special requirements regarding quality), not all of those forms are suitable.

More information on those forms can be found in the extensive literature on this issue.

Specifications

The specifications consist of a detailed description and drawings of the plant. The goal is to give as accurate a picture as possible of the various parts of the plant.

The specifications should explain the different parts so clearly that contractors and subcontractors can hand in their commercial and competitive offers on a technologically equal base. The more detailed the specifications are, the better and more carefully prepared the offers can be.

Thus, the specifications have the following functions:

-   it is the chief source of information for describing the work to be conducted, so an accurate price can be set
-   it is one of the instruments for steering, controlling and supervising the building process
-   it is part of the contract, together with a description of tasks, rights and obligations of both parties

In the practice of designing, specifications are often used to further describe the design. However, it is advisable to keep the contract documents strictly separated from the design documents. The former are only relevant during construction and start-up, while the latter are important during the lifetime of the installation (if they are kept up to date).

The separation of documents is easily accomplished when using standardized specifications. For the construction of a production plant with its necessary above-ground facilities, the standard specifications for civil and utility buildings are typically used. For the construction of transport and distribution piping, similar specifications are used.

Project organization

Several project formats can be used for the construction of drinking water production plants. The most important are:

- assignment to one single main contractor
- assignment to multiple contractors (with purchase by contractors)
- assignment to multiple contractors with majority purchase by principal

When assigning the project to a single contracting company, the coordination of the construction needs to be done by the contractor who directs the subcontractors.

Because of the division of the building costs, this main contractor is, in almost every case, a civil contractor. For the building of a drinking water plant this method is less suitable, because most disputes between the water company and the contractor concern the mechanical and electrical parts of the plant. The main contractor is, in this case, the contracting party, but he is not competent in those other fields.

When assigning work to multiple contractors a direct relationship between the water company and the specific contractor must be maintained.

Wtih this organization it is possible for the water company to purchase the most important and most expensive parts directly from the manufacturer (e.g., pumps, ozone generators, emergency aggregates, valves, activated carbon, etc.) and

require the contractor to take responsibility for the assembly of those. This will create an even more direct relationship between the water company and subcontractors, which will benefit the price-to-quality relationship, as well as support with the normal operation. When assigning to multiple contractors, it is possible to have a better phased design process as well. This implies constructing the civil buildings first, after which the installation parts are assembled. Of course, this requires a sufficiently complete design at the start of construction. It is necessary that installation parts not only fit in, but that there is enough space for assembly, as well.

Construction by multiple parties

Whatever project organization will be used to complete a production plant, it will always involve more than one party. All those parties need information and they need to provide information.

For mutual information interchange, a central project database is a desirable tool (Figure 6). Some of the information in this database (detailed designs, specifications, maintenance schemes) is also necessary during normal operation, making it necessary to keep the information available after the construction process is finished.

Directive for the utility sector

In assigning construction work and services, water companies are committed to the European Directive for the Utility sector (93/98/EEC).

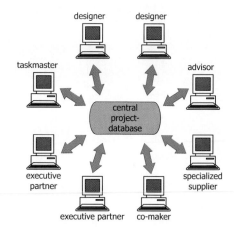

Figure 6   - Parties involved in the construction of a plant

This directive describes the manner in which contracts need to be assigned. A facility or administrative contract can consist of a preliminary study,
a preliminary design or the final design. A work
contract includes the construction of a plant. The
criterion determining whether a project needs to
be assigned by this European method is the size
of the project.

For a facility or administrative project, the criterion
is €400,000 per fiscal year and/or the full construction period. For a construction project contract,
the limiting value is €5,000,000 for the total set of
assignments for the completion of the work.
An assignment by the European rules implies that
a fully open procedure needs to be followed, from
advertising to selection, leaving everyone free to
apply. Selection needs to proceed according to
well-defined and objective criteria.

3.6   Construction

After the project has been assigned, construction
begins. Only seldom is a structure built on a location where no disturbance of the present production takes place (Figure 7).
Because of the hygienic nature of drinking water
supply, special measures to prevent contamination of the operation's production process need
to be taken.

It is always necessary to work clean during the
construction. A dirty building place will contaminate
new parts of the plant as well. At the start-up, such
contamination can be quite troublesome, making it
difficult to attain the required microbiological quality
of the drinking water being produced.

The main tasks for the water company during
construction are:
-   direction of the construction process

Figure 7   - The building area is 3-6 times larger than the building

- supervision of the construction process
- conduction of guarantee measurements and takeover

Directing

The direction on behalf of the principal consists of the following tasks:
- attending building meeting
- instructing (daily) supervisors
- supervising the building place daily, as well as the construction of smaller parts
- formulating plans and attending to, detail supervising and coordination
- controlling progress
- controlling costs
- evaluating the amount of additional or less work needed
- ordering work for the reimbursables
- advising regarding the payment terms
- executing inspections and examinations of the installations
- creating a book of measurements and calibrations

Supervision

Supervision includes a daily check on the building's construction progress. Supervision functions as the primary adjustment tool between contractor and principal. Contractual decisions will, however, not be made by the supervisor but by the principal.

Delivery and takeover

Delivery and takeover includes the verification of the completeness and correct operation of the installation. Delivery and takeover activities include:
- assisting start-up
- examining the work and verifying requested guarantees
- registering the maintenance activities
- creating or verifying the operation procedures
- starting up the process, sampling and testing
- instructing the operating personnel
- paying off the constructing sum, reimbursables, levelling costs, extra or less work, reductions, bonuses, etc.
- drawing up revision schemes
- checking third party's revision schemes

3.7   Start-up

At takeover, the water company begins handling the plant's operation. This includes the start-up of the production process.

Only after it has been proved that the plant truly produces reliable drinking water, can the water be supplied to the distribution network.

During this introductory phase, the operators need to become familiar with the installation.

At delivery, often a maintenance and warranty term (e.g., one year) between the principal and the contractor is agreed upon. The purpose is to locate possible flaws which might actually occur during normal operation. The contractor is obliged to repair the flaws or to replace the specific component.

Activities for maintenance and warranty include:
- examining the requested project warranties
- inspecting the work at the end of the maintenance term in order to check whether the contractor has successfully completed his job
- supervising reparations of flaws and failures during the warranty period
- advising on future maintenance
- advising on the final balance sheet of the work

3.8   Operation

After the start-up, the new plant will be included in the normal operation of the water company. During the production period it is not uncommon to replace whole installation components, due to technological obsolescence. Examples include the replacement of the electrical and control installations after 10 to 20 years of operation. Such extended replacements are of the same nature as a new construction project.

The main mechanical parts are seldom replaced. Rather, a whole new plant will be constructed.

3.9   Demolition

When a plant neither meets the specified requirements anymore nor can be modified to do so in

Figure 8 - Demolition has the same characteristics as a construction project

an economically feasible way, the plant will be demolished (Figure 8).

4. Laws, permits and standards

4.1 Laws and permits

Building a production plant for drinking water supply is bound to normal legal obligations. Many of those regulations are carried out by permit procedures. Those require the intended activity to be specified, including the way it will comply with the relevant legislation. After the competent authority has approved the application, the legal requirement will have been fulfilled.

Typical permits for normal construction work are:
- tree cutting permit (making the area construction ready)
- building permit (for construction)
- environmental permit (for operation)
- draining permit (for discharge of drain water)
- abstraction permit for groundwater

The specific backgrounds of these laws and permits will not be dealt with here. If interested, one should read the extensive literature on this subject.

The specific statutory aspects of and permits for drinking water facilities have partly been described above. Additional information is dealt within the chapters on water quality, groundwater, surface water, and distribution.

For building a drinking water production plant, many permits may be significant. For example, for a new surface water project including a reservoir and soil aquifer recharge, 75 permits needed to be granted. The procedures for obtaining those permits vary from long procedures via the Council of State to a simple written response to an application for a permit.

Permit procedures create a complex load on the design process. Because procedures take a long time, these permits often set the pace for the design process. Besides, these procedures require many external parties to be involved in the design process, and they all need to be informed of the background of the design for each specific permit.

Time-consuming permit applications include, for example, the Environmental Impact Assessment (EIA) permits, which are necessary in cases where more than 3 million m^3 of groundwater are abstracted, where a large reservoir is constructed, or where long and large distribution pipes are constructed.

Even simple permits can require very long processing time when a challenge to the permit is made.

The number of permits required gives the permit planning phase quite an important role in the design process. Because of this, at the start of the design phase, a complete list of the necessary permits should be formulated. One can supervise the permit process by way of a timetable, which enables supervisors to obtain a reliable impression of the progress of the procedures.

4.2 Standards

Many permit procedures require the design to comply with specific standards. These standards make up a rather complex system of technical directives and obligations.

Even when the permit does not necessitate it, testing the design against the standards is desirable in almost any case. On the one hand, this is because standards define several quality levels for the construction and, on the other hand, the standards create a more uniform design process. This will improve the quality of the design and the efficiency of the design process.

Standards are important in regulating responsibility for the design. They also play an important role in fostering good communication between the different parties involved in a construction project, as standards define the meaning of specific concepts as well.

General standards

There exist several systems of standards, which are valid for different specialties.

Within the Netherlands, the national standards are managed by the Netherlands Normalization Institute and published as NEN-standards.

European standards are managed by the CEN and published as EN-standards. Global standards are defined by the International Organization for Standardization (ISO-standards), an organization encompassing over 146 national standardization institutes. The Netherlands translates some of those ISO-standards in order to publish them as NEN-standards.

Both the CEN and the ISO revalue many national standards to European or worldwide standards as well. Important are the German Industrial Standards (Deutsche Industrie Normen (DIN)),

Figure 9 - The ISO standards become even more important once incorporated into national standardization

which, taken together, form a thorough system of standards.

Besides standards, the organizations define practical directives as well. These are elaborations and applications of certain standards for specific specialties.

In designing a drinking water production plant, for example, the "Directives for the application and drawing of process flow diagrams' (NPR 2196) is important. This directive has been replaced by the standard ISO/NEN 10628:2001 "Flow diagrams for process plants - General rules."

Also the publications on labor conditions, specifically the labor policy rules, are important for the design of drinking water production plants. These policy rules are especially aimed at the safety of operating personnel.

For international projects the British Standards, the standards of the American National Standards Institute (ANSI-standards) and the standards of the American Society for Testing and Materials (ASTM-standards) can apply.

Standards for drinking water supply

There are some standards specifically related to drinking water supply. They are not always included in the systems of standards described above. Generally, they supplement those standards.

For the Dutch drinking water supply, NEN-standard 1006 (General prescriptions for drinking water installations, AVWI 2002) is important. These prescriptions include requirements for mainly indoor installations, but it should be clear that the requirements for the production of drinking water must also abide by this standard. In addition, the Association of Dutch Water Companies (VEWIN) publishes the so-called VEWIN sheets. Table 4 gives an overview of these sheets insofar as they are concerned with the design of production plants.

In the Netherlands, the directives and recommendations of the following institutions are significant:

Table 4 - VEWIN sheets relevant to drinking water production plants

Sheet	Description
2.3	Execution of pressure tests
2.4	Flushing and disinfection of drinking water installations
3.3	Construction of drinking water installations; isolation and drain possibilities
3.4	Construction of drinking water installations; pipes in buildings
3.8	Security of appliances
4.1	Reservoirs to feed drinking water installations
4.2	Storage tanks and break pressure tanks; not intended for drinking water
4.3	Installations to increase the pressure
4.5	Installation for firefighting

- Ministry of Housing, Spatial Planning and the Environment (VROM)
- Association of Dutch Water Companies (VEWIN)
- Kiwa

In other countries similar directives of government or branch associations apply. The following institutions are highly respected worldwide:
- American Water Works Association (AWWA)
- German Technical and Scientific Association for Gas and Water (DVGW).

Some of the directives that apply to the design of drinking water production plants will be investigated in more detail in the following subsections.

Ministry of Housing, Spatial Planning and the Environment (VROM) protection plan

Required specifications can also be part of statutory regulations. For example, the "Directive for the protection plan of water companies' (VROM March 1991) does state several technical design requirements for the protection of drinking water production plants during war or in case of sabotage. The protection plans, which need to be formulated by the water companies themselves, are supervised by the VROM inspector.

A protection plan describes all relevant procedures, measures and technical facilities, as well as the design of the protection organization; and, it specifies responsibilities.

In case the public drinking water supply is no longer available, it is necessary to shift to the use of an emergency water supply.

A distinction is made between technical requirements and operational matters. Technical requirements are prescribed for the necessary level of protection against:
- emission of dangerous materials
- shock waves caused by an explosion
- sabotage

Operational matters are important for the rooms housing the plant's vital functions during unusual circumstances and include:
- connections
- electricity, including emergency supplies
- operations and residence rooms
- storerooms
- kitchen facilities, sanitary facilities, dormitories

In the technical field, some concrete examples are described so that a protection level as high as possible against external influences can be attained. Many of these measures are desirable so as to guarantee a stable operation under normal circumstances, such as:
- segmenting the infrastructure (treatment trains)
- linking transport and distribution networks to adjacent production areas
- making temporary connections with hygienic, reliable, non-public water facilities, like those at factories, large institutions, etc.
- purifying the air for aeration, backwash air for the filters, air for clean water reservoirs, etc.
- providing for the storage of chemicals, disinfectants, fuel, lubricants, etc. for at least a ten-days' supply, and guaranteeing a continuous 50% filling of storage tanks
- having a mobile or permanent disinfection installation available for disinfecting outgoing water
- installing burglary protection and alarm systems
- providing for the manual operation of process components, without using control systems
- putting lightning rods on the plants

- providing an independent energy supply by means of a ready-to-use emergency power aggregate, diesel-driven pumps, etc.
- having spare parts available
- having a crisis coordination center available
- creating emergency exits in relevant buildings
- creating special, fragment-free and bomb-resistant shelters

Association of Dutch Water Companies' policy recommendations

Until recently, the Association of Dutch Water Companies (VEWIN) published the "VEWIN recommendations for technical and hygienic policy." These recommendations are normative, because the public water companies associated in the VEWIN declare publicly what they deem are the best technical and hygienic policies.

Regarding quality the Association of Dutch Water Companies' recommendations have stricter guidelines than the Water Supply Act. The reasons for this are indicated in the publication.

Effective pressure needs to amount to at least 100 kPa at all taps, until a height of ten meters above ground level. This corresponds to a minimum pressure of 200 kPa above ground level everywhere. In the main network the pressure needs to be at least 250 kPa.

Uncomfortable pressure fluctuations should be prevented (Art. b.1.1). This might require the use of surge tanks or speed controlled pumps.

The water company needs to be organized in such a way as to be able to supply the necessary water in the supply area during the "design day." The "design day" means that the water demand has a 0.1 probability to be exceeded during a year (this means it should be exceeded less than once every ten years) (Art. c.1.2).

VEWIN

Vereniging van Waterbedrijven in Nederland

Figure 10 - The VEWIN coordinates the Dutch directives on drinking water

Provisions need to be made so that it is possible for the company to satisfy the requirement of an undisturbed water supply in case of a failure (Art. c.1.3). This is only attainable if there is a sufficient number of connections between adjacent supply areas, or if there are measures taken in order to continue production in case of failure somewhere in the system.

There should be a way to decrease or stop the direct input of surface water without unfavorable effects to the drinking water supply (Art. c.2.2). This means, in practice, that any surface water plant is required to have a protected reservoir containing storage for at least a few days, in order to let poisonous waves flow past. Also underground storage of treated water is possible.

To check on changes in the hydrological and qualitative aspects of the water, sufficient permanent measurement facilities need to be present (Art. c.5.5). Therefore, every well needs to be supplied with sampling taps, and every abstraction area needs to have sufficient monitoring wells.

It is preferable that the treatment system be tested in a pilot plant on a semi-technical scale (Art. c.6.1).

When aeration/degasification is applied, the necessary air should be filtered. Installations for aeration/degasification need to be accessible for inspections and cleaning (Art. c.6.2). It should be possible to disinfect all water to be supplied (Art. c.6.5). A connection for emergency chlorination needs to be available.

When the failure of a main distribution pipe is unacceptable for the drinking water supply in a certain area, the water company needs to make provisions for reducing the effect to acceptable levels.
The criteria are:
- the duration of the failure
- the spare supply capacity in the area
- the size of the respective area (Art. c.9.2)

In the main distribution network there should be as few pipes as possible having only a minimum flow through them (Art. c.9.3). Measurements need to be taken in order to prevent disadvantageous water hammer effects. Disadvantageous effects include:

- low pressure causing contaminated groundwater to be sucked into the network
- low pressure causing cavities, which cause pressure waves and possible pipe failure

When preparing sufficient, ready-to-use spare energy installations, pressure in the distribution network should not fall in case of an energy failure (Art. c.8.1).

Clean water tanks and accompanying installations need to be built, arranged and maintained in such a way as to prevent the contamination of drinking water. Entrances, overflow pipes and ventilation openings especially need to be attended to (Art. c.7.1). Clean water tanks need to be above groundwater level (Art. c.7.2). The tanks should not have a common wall with any buildings for non-hygienic water (Art. c.7.3).

Kiwa quality declaration

Kiwa was originally founded as an examination institute for drinking water appliances. It examined the different products to be used in the public water supply.
It has expanded to an institute not only examining products, but also standardizing water practices and certifying quality. Basically, it has grown into a research institute for the joint Dutch water companies.
Within the certifying activities of Kiwa are its declarations or recommendations of quality. Some of those activities are described below.

The "Toxological Aspects Certificate" (TAC) indicates that a specified product does not add components to the drinking water that would be damaging to public health. Standardization for the TACs is done by a committee on health aspects of chemicals and materials for the water supply, which falls under the general directorate for environmental hygiene.
TACs have been formulated for all chemicals which are allowed in drinking water production.
A Kiwa-certificate concerns the installing, monitoring, cleaning up and cathodic protection of stor-

age tanks, underground tanks and accompanying pipelines. These are tanks for storage of fluid petrol products and liquified petrol gases, as well as for fuel oil.

An examination report describes the results of a sample examination, which is formulated by Kiwa for the principal, and as a service to the water companies. The requirements for a sample examination, the sample requirements, are usually formulated by the principal himself and are dependent on the desired application. So, the requirements may differ for different sample examinations. Generally, Kiwa's experience is used by the principal to formulate an accurate set of sample requirements.

The quality system certificate applies to all activities that are involved in the production of a product, process or service. It encompasses the organizational structure, responsibilities, authorities, procedures, processes and facilities establishing quality control within the whole company. Certification is done on the basis of international quality standards from the NEN/ISO 9001 series.

The product certificate indicates proof of product quality. It guarantees to the customers that the product meets agreed upon quality standards. That certainty is supported by the fact that the certificate may only be issued to producers who control their production process in such a way as to have only flawless products leave the factory.

The declaration of water supply technical safety indicates that an installation is certified for water supply technical safety aspects. Installations include all devices that can be connected to the drinking water network.
This certification is meant to uncover possible contamination of the drinking water by dangerous devices. These devices carry with them the risk of putting contaminated installation water back into the water distribution network.

5.   The practice of designing

In the previous sections the basic elements of the design process have been explained. In the following, the design process will be further elaborated on using a single concrete project: the construction of a new drinking water production plant in Heel for the Limburg Water Company.

Not only are the design product and the background of the design choices important here, but attention is closely paid to the process of designing and the growth of the design.

The design process will be dealt with by describing the different design documents, which will be defined according to the NEN/ISO 10628 "Flow diagrams for process plants." The design will be discussed to conform to the phases given previously, accompanied by the documents which were also previously discussed.

The following items will be elucidated:
- preliminary studies
- sketch design and building scheme
- preliminary design
- final design and detailed design
- construction and start-up

5.1   Preliminary studies

Historical developments

The water supply in Limburg fully relied on groundwater. Already in the 1972 "Drinking and industrial water supply structure scheme," it was noticed that for further expansion the use of surface water would be necessary. This scheme included a reservoir from a future gravel extraction site near Heel.

Though the growth in water use that was predicted never really happened, this did lead to a spatial claim on the gravel pit. Of course, many studies have been performed since then concerning this production site and the related specific limitations and opportunities.

In 1980, when dessication became a political issue, a decrease in groundwater abstraction in Limburg was proposed. This was possible if the above project was completed.

Several investigations on decreasing dessication suggested that the best solution would be to reduce all groundwater abstraction sites in central and north Limburg by 50% of the allowed maximum - a maximum which was always used or even surpassed.

In 1993 a specific project organization was instituted, which started the practical implementation. In 1995, the provincial government of Limburg and the Limburg Water Company agreed upon a covenant to construct the project, in combination with a decrease in groundwater abstraction. The construction started in 1998 and the plant started production in 2002.

Dealing with the decreased capacity

Introducing surface water to decrease production of the existing groundwater plants could be done in a threefold way, in principle:
- all together
- groundwater separated from surface water
- surface water added to groundwater locally

In the first case all the groundwater would be transported to Heel, mixed there with the new plant's production, and afterwards distributed over all north and central Limburg. An advantage of this is a uniform scheme and a constant water quality over the entire province (i.e., no local differences).

In the second case, the groundwater plants would supply the boundary locations of the distribution area, while the centrally located Heel site would supply the immediate surroundings. An advantage of this solution is that ground- and surface water systems would remain separated.

In the third case, the water produced in Heel would be transported to the different groundwater sites and mixed with the locally produced water there.

These alternatives have been thoroughly compared. In order to do this, several studies were undertaken to investigate the consequences for the water quality, distribution infrastructure, possibility for phasing the project, costs, reliability, etc. Of course, this needed several design activities. All three possible solutions would require extensive, extra distribution infrastructures (Figure 11).

Without describing the decision process in detail, the final decision was made to have the surface water added to the groundwater (Figure 12).

Water supply plan

In most cases the production capacity is not reduced drastically. Usually, the increase in the water demand needs to be met by one or more new production plants or by expanding the capacity of current plants.

Figure 13 shows how such a demand coverage can be monitored. The net demand is shown, based on one of the different situations (minimum, maximum and most probable). From those figures and a reserve, a gross demand can be calculated.

New capacity will be realized stepwise, causing a repeating spare capacity to be available. In a water supply plan, the calculations are based on yearly capacities. Based on the expected maxi-

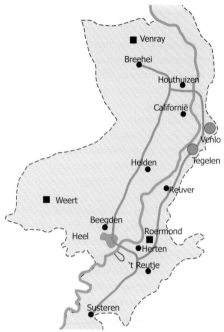

Figure 12 - Surface water treatment in Heel supplies drinking water to the province of Limburg in addition to the existing groundwater plants

Figure 11 - For all alternatives, a considerable pipeline infrastructure was needed

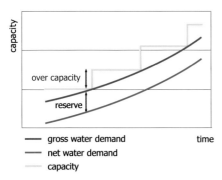

- gross water demand   time
- net water demand
- capacity

Figure 13 - Growth and coverage of water demand

mum peak factor, the maximum daily production can be determined.

In the water supply plan, a description is provided regarding which production plants need to be functional and when to increase a plant's production capacity. The uncertainty in the predictions is mainly dealt with by shifting the moment at which the additional capacity will be realized.

To estimate the time when an extra facility to handle additional capacity will be required, one can calculate backwards to determine the last possible moment to start preparations for building the new plant.

5.2   Sketch design and building scheme

Treatment process
Besides the required capacity, the treatment process needs to be decided upon as well. The following research methods are used to come to this decision:
- evaluation of current experience
- investigation of new treatment techniques
- pilot research (semi-technical scale)
- full-scale research (temporary production plant)

Time and means do not always allow the use of all those methods. This increases the uncertainty of the process design and of the entire operation. In the plant this can be compensated for by increasing flexibility and safety in the design (larger build-

ings or increased possibilities for expansion) and in the operation (increased control options, increased doses). Either of these will increase the investment costs and complicate the operation. The start-up will take longer as well, because operators might not be familiar, or are less familiar, with the chosen treatment process.

In the Heel case, all investigation methods named above have been employed. Important research inquiries included, among others:
- the necessity of either a disinfection (UV) after the active carbon filtration or of an additional disinfectant (ozone)
- the effect of a combined abstraction of both aerobic recharge water and anaerobic groundwater
- the backwash water treatment with vertical ultra filtration and air flushing

Block diagram (treatment scheme)
The design in this phase will represent the treatment process as a block diagram (ISO 10628).

A block diagram represents a treatment process, or a treatment plant or other units by rectangular blocks, which are named and connected to each other by way of streamlines. A block diagram, at the very least, consists of the following parts:

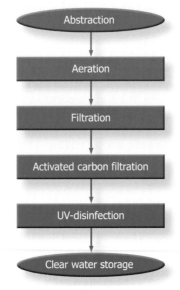

Figure 14 - Global setup of the treatment scheme

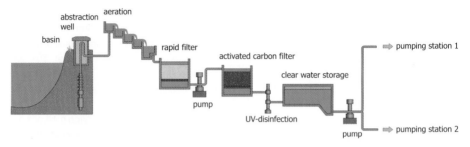

Figure 15 - Visual presentation of the treatment process

- names of the blocks
- names of in- and out-flowing mass and energy flows (for the block diagram as a whole)
- directions of the main streams between the blocks

Also, a block diagram may contain additional information, like the names of the flows between the blocks, the amounts of in- and out-flowing mass and energy flows, the amounts of the most important flows between the blocks, and the typical process conditions. A limited block diagram is shown in Figure 14.

As an addition to the block diagram, a more visual representation of the treatment process can be drawn. Mostly, this is a rough section of the process, including the most important pumping phases. Figure 15 shows an example.

Site layout plan
When the capacity and the treatment processes are roughly known, a provisional site layout plan can be drawn. This plan is especially aimed at the zoning of the plant area and at the related orientation of the buildings. Site layout plans are usually drawn at a scale of either 1:500 or 1:1000.

Typical zones within a site layout plan are:
- clean water reservoirs with high pressure pumping station
- treatment plant
- sludge and backwash water treatment units
- energy supply (including emergency power)
- additional services (e.g., workshops)
- main roads and transport routes
- space for future expansion

When formulating the site layout plan, the building boundaries are either not important or not yet known. Generally, the spatial demand per process part can be determined. In this determination, it holds that the spatial demand of most processes (i.e., filtration, flocculation, sedimentation, etc.) is about 2 to 3 times as much as the actual area necessary for the process. This is because of necessary pipe galleries and control rooms. Besides, one needs to keep in mind that during construction a large space around the building is required.

Finally, it is desirable to calculate for future developments and for future replacements. For a replacement, the new construction should be finished before an old construction is demolished, to maintain continuity in the supply of drinking water. Figure 16 gives an artistic impression of the Heel production site.

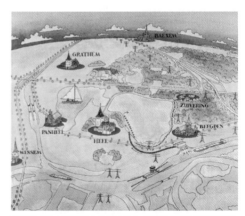

Figure 16 - Artistic impression of the Heel production site

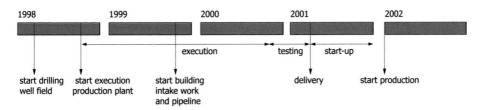

Figure 17 - Actual timeframe for construction of Heel production plant

Sketch design

In addition to the documents named above, formulating some very rough design drawings to present the intended construction to third parties may be desirable. Usually, a single floor plan and one or two sections will suffice.

Building scheme

The sketch design names the projected structures and gives their projected dimensions. The building scheme is formulated based on this design, including plans for the construction work (Figure 17). One should keep in mind that this kind of planning tends to fail, for example, because of lagging permit procedures.

During preparation for the Heel production plant, it became clear that the gravel suppliers needed an extra year to develop the gravel pit and the adjacent shores. Partly because of this extra preparation time, it was possible to raise the operational level of the reservoir, which increased the groundwater level in the area and, thereby, reduced the environmental impact. The environmental impact

was quantified as a part of the Environmental Impact Assessment procedure (EIA).

5.3 Preliminary design

The most important design documents in the preliminary design phase are the

- hydraulic line scheme
- process flow diagram
- design drawings

These documents will be explained below.

Hydraulic line scheme

The hydraulic line scheme is a design document that is typical for water treatment plants. Because of using open tanks, canals, processes with a free water surface (i.e., cascades), the water level in the processes becomes quite important, especially when an energy and cost-saving design is desired. There are no national standards for the hydraulic line scheme.

Basically, the hydraulic line scheme is a vertical section of the building, presenting the building elements schematically, but presenting relevant

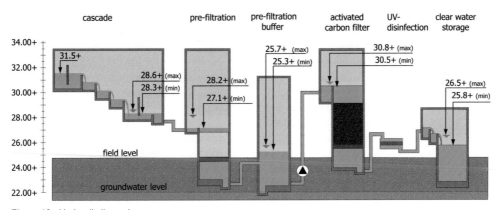

Figure 18 - Hydraulic line scheme

143

heights on an exact scale (Figure 18). In addition, other relevant data, like ground level, roof height, passage height, are indicated.

During the design process, this scheme will be further refined and other levels (e.g., emergency overflow) will be indicated.

Hydraulics plays a very important role in the design of a drinking water production plant. One reason for this is that the water will be divided over several parallel units more than once. Basically, a hydraulic division is used here, because of the robustness of hydraulic control compared to mechanical or electrical control systems (Figure 19). A hydraulic control system is often used to compensate for the increased filter resistance during the process.

Process flow diagram (PFD)

A further elaboration of the treatment process can be represented as a process flow diagram (PFD) (ISO 10628).

A PFD indicates installations, by means of standardized symbols, and the flow of mass and energy between them. At a minimum, it consists of the following blocks:

- type of equipment necessary for the process
- coding of the installation
- direction and route of in- and outflowing mass and energy
- labeling and quantifying of in- and outflowing masses
- labeling and quantifying of in- and outflowing energy flows
- typical process conditions

A process flow diagram may contain additional information, like the magnitudes of flows and amounts between process steps, major valves, functional indication of instrument and control systems in a specified position, additional process conditions, names of characteristic installation data, names and characteristic data of propulsion systems, and the elevation levels of terraces and installations.

For the design of a drinking water production plant, it is only useful to formulate a PFD in addition to the hydraulic line scheme when all parallel process parts are presented separately. This makes

division flow over streets

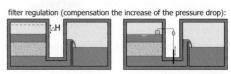

filter regulation (compensation the increase of the pressure drop):

Figure 19 - Hydraulic solutions are easier and more robust

the diagram correspond to the much used main water flow diagram (Figure 20).

This specification is desirable so that the PFD can be used to determine the different hydraulic loads of units and piping, both in normal and in special circumstances. For normal conditions one can describe the different process conditions with the diagram (e.g., filter during backwash, etc.). The extraordinary conditions determine the dimensions of the parts. In this way, the PFD is the basis for the detailed hydraulic calculations and the functional description of the control and operating system.

Design drawings

Design drawings represent the physical reality.

During the preliminary design phase, especially the dimensions of the process units and the different rooms will be decided.

More and more, these drawings are made by 3D design systems. In these designs the designer indicates the 3D elements, after which the system generates the different drawings (floor plans and sections) and some 3D representations (Figures 21 and 22). These later drawings are especially useful during the preliminary design phase, and they are comprehensible to the general public, who will benefit the design process through their feedback.

Structural aspects

During the preliminary design phase, the dimensions of the structural elements cannot be determined accurately yet. This is because the loads are only approximated. Nevertheless, it has proven feasible to make some realistic assumptions instead.

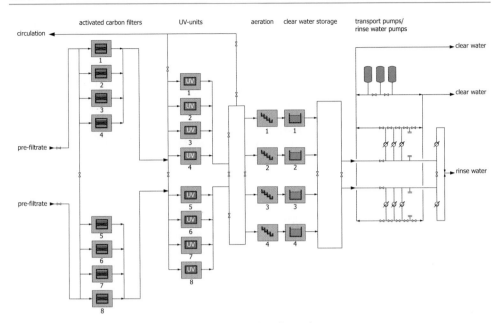

Figure 20 - A part of the process flow diagram (Main water flow diagram)

For concrete constructions, the floor and wall sizes are mostly estimated at 0.4-0.6 m. When, in a later phase, these dimensions need to be changed, typically only the inside dimensions are adjusted while the outside building size remains the same.

During the preliminary design phase it is important to examine both the foundation and the division of the building using dilatation seams in closer detail.

Architecture

In the rough design drawings, technical choices with regard to the design have been decided.

Adjustment of the design because of architectural considerations may be desirable. Therefore, it is useful to indicate the functional relationships between the different components. This will give a better indication to the architect of the degrees of freedom and of the consequences of breaking them (Figures 23 and 24).

Architectural drawings from the preliminary design phase are necessary in order to apply for a building permit.

Figure 21 - Design of building

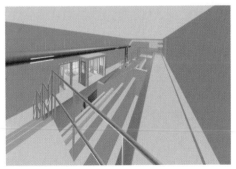

Figure 22 - Design cascade aeration

145

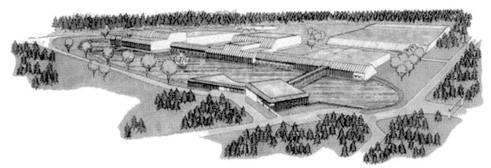

Figure 23 - Architectural design drawings

5.4   Final design and detailed design

During the final design and detailed design phases, many more design documents are still formulated. This section will only deal with the piping and instrument diagram.

Piping and instrument diagram (P&ID)

The piping and instrument diagram (P&ID) (ISO 10628) indicates the technical construction of a process by means of standardized symbols for installations, pipes, instruments and control systems.

The minimum information in a piping and instrument diagram includes the following:

- function or type of apparatus, including drives and installed spare parts
- identification number of apparatus including drives and installed spare parts
- characteristic data of apparatus (on a separate list)
- identification of nominal diameter, pressure class, piping material and classification
- details of installations, pipes, gauges and junctions

Figure 24 - An architect's scale model

Figure 25 - Heel production plant and reservoir

- process measurement installations and control systems with identification
- characteristic data of drivers

A piping and instrument diagram may also contain several additional details. The piping and instrument diagram is the central document for detailed engineering, for the mechanical parts (pumps, pipes, installations, gauges), the electrical parts (power supply), and for the control parts (measurement and control systems, operating systems).

5.5   Construction and start-up

Even during the construction phase, several design activities are performed. These may include a further detailed elaboration of the design (i.e., form and reinforcement drawings) or temporary constructions (dam walls, concrete molds).

After the construction phase, and during the start-up phase, the designer's efforts will either be proven succesfull or not (Figures 25, 26, 27).

Figure 26 - Heel reservoir

Figure 27 - Production plant at Heel

Further reading

- Water treatment plant design, AWWA/McGraw-Hill (2004)
- Aanbevelingen voor het bedrijfsbeleid in technisch-hygiënisch opzicht, VEWIN (1985)
- Beschermingsplan waterleidingbedrijven, VROM (1991)

- www. overheid.nl/wetten
- www.nni.nl
- www.cenorm.be
- www.iso.org
- www.vewin.nl
- www.kiwa.nl
- www.dvgw.de
- www.awwa.org

Questions and applications

Planning process for public water supply

1. Indicate the different plans that deal with public water supply, the plan period and the organization formulating the plan.

2. The national policy plan has two functions. What are they?

3. The Association of Dutch Water Companies' ten-year plan has become less significant during the past few years. What is the most important reason for its declining importance?

Design activities in the infrastructure's life cycle

1. Roughly indicate the phases and sub-phases during a construction project.

2. Which components make up a project definition?

3. Why are special measures necessary during the construction of a drinking water supply plant?

Laws, permits and standards

1. Indicate some characteristic permits necessary for a typical construction project.

2. Indicate a reason for using a system of standards.

Designing in practice

1. What is "formulating a site layout," and what does this mean to a water supply production plant?

Answers

Planning process for public water supply

1.

Name	Timeframe (years)	Organization
Policy plan for drinking and industrial water supply	20 - 30	Ministry VROM
Ten-year plan	5 - 10	VEWIN
Provincial policy plans	5 - 10	Province
Provincial management plans	5 - 10	Province
Regional plans	5 - 10	Province
Land use plans	5 - 10	Municipality
Water supply plan	10 - 30	Company
Multi-year investment plan	5 - 10	Company
Business plan	5	Company

2. First, it indicates the concerns for water management that need to be considered in spatial planning decisions on the national, provincial and municipal levels. Second, the policy plan is indicative for the public water supply section; only in emergencies are the water companies allowed to diverge from the plan.

3. More and more the water companies operate on a provincial or super-provincial level. This requires less mutual adjustment between the different water companies. Part of the purpose of the ten-year plan is now covered by the water companies' plans.

Design activities in the infrastructure's life cycle

1. The different phases are:
   - Initiative: identification, definition
   - Construction: design, contracting, construction
   - Operation: start-up, operation
   - Demolition: demolition and removal

2. A project definition consists of a:
   - requirements program
   - sketch design
   - building scheme

3. Because of the hygienic nature of the public water supply, special measures are necessary in order to prevent contamination. Besides, during construction clean work is necessary, because a dirty construction site will contaminate new plant units. At the start-up such contamination can be highly problematic, because it will be difficult or even impossible to achieve the required microbiological quality of the drinking water.

Laws, permits, standards

1. Some characteristic permits include:
   - tree cutting permit (making the area construction ready)
   - building permit (for construction)
   - environmental permit (for operation)
   - draining permit (for discharge of waste water)

2. For several permit procedures, the design is required to comply with specific standards. Standards are a complex system of mainly technical directives and prescriptions. Also, standards play an important role in the reproducibility and the responsibility of the design. Because standards uniquely define concepts, they are helpful in the communication between the different parties involved in a construction project.

Designing in practice

1. A site layout plan is mainly aimed at the zoning of the plant area and the related orientation of the buildings. Site layout plans are usually drawn at a scale of 1:500 or 1:1000.
   Typical zones within a site layout plan include:
   - clear water reservoirs and high pressure pumping station
   - treatment plant
   - sludge and backwash water treatment
   - energy supply, including emergency power
   - additional services (workshops, etc.)
   - main roads and transport routes
   - space for future expansions

Finances

WATER COMPANIES

PWN jaarverslag 2001

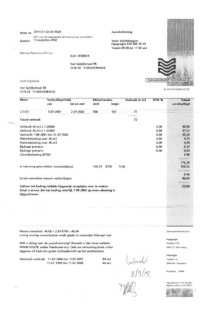

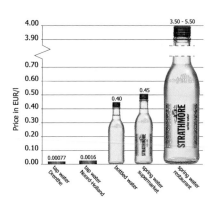

Framework

This module is about the financial aspects of the public drinking water supply. On a company level, the balance sheet of a water company and the water tarifs are discussed. Specific details will be presented on the investment and operational costs, as well as cost comparisons for alternatives.

Introduction

This module has the following contents:

Study goals

After having studied this module, you will be able to:
- identify the terms balance sheet, profit and loss account, investment costs, capital costs, and operational costs
- calculate tariffs for a cost-covering drinking water supply
- prepare an estimate of the investment costs
- prepare an estimate of the operational costs
- prepare a cost comparison of alternatives

1. Introduction

A water company is not only a technical company, but also a concern. Therefore, many different facets play a part, for example, the social aspects (e.g., staff, clients) and the financial aspects (e.g., economy).

The financial aspects have a lot in common with the technical aspects. A water company invests in a new infrastructure (i.e., production plants and distribution network), spends money on its operation (staff, energy and chemicals), and has to make sure that the expenses are covered by its income (standing charges and consumption rates).

This module looks at the financial aspects of a water company.

First, the water company is presented as a concern. Specific attention is given to the fact that a water company is a legal monopoly. Therefore, the main objective of the concern is not making a profit, but covering costs.

The financial strength and conditions of a company become clearer after reading the (financial) annual report. Understanding the report will make rate fixing clearer and a comparison across different companies possible.

Investments and operational issues are important aspects within a water supply company. These aspects will, therefore, be specifically dealt with and elaborated upon. Finally, items playing a role in comparing the costs for various alternatives will be presented.

2. Water company as an enterprise

2.1 Drinking water supply as a monopoly

Enterprises typically operate in a free market, where other suppliers are active as well. The company exists as long as clients are willing to buy the product for a price at which the company can make a profit. In such a situation, the company is forced, by the market, to balance price and quality.

Competition makes sure that the company reaches a high level of efficiency, and the company will pursue maximum profits and, therefore, cost reductions.

The company is, in this way, controlled by the market. The government mainly oversees that the different suppliers in the market do not make inadmissible market deals, that the supplied products are acceptable with relation to health and safety, and that the production and transportation of used products take place in an environmentally and technically sound way.

Monopoly

Having described how typical private companies are run, it can now be shown how a water company actually differs greatly from this.

First of all, a water company is a monopoly within the distribution area assigned by the government. The most important arguments for an assigned monopoly are that:

- the distribution of water determines the price to such an extent that it is never economically attractive to have more suppliers
- the quality and availability of drinking water is of such social importance that it should not be pressured by economic considerations of companies
- the drinking water supply does not qualify for operation by different companies, because this will make quality responsibilities and delivery guarantees very unclear. This is the reason why the government pursues the guarantee of quality (always clean and healthy) and quantity (always in the needed quantities under sufficient pressure) as an integral responsibility of one single company from source to tap

Figure 1 - Money and water: aqueduct on €5 note

Government supervision

Because of a lack of control by the market, control of a water company by the government is necessary. This is included in the Water Supply Act, where several supervisors are assigned (responsibility/authority of the cabinet minister, quality control by the ministry, supervision by public boards (in municipalities and provinces).

Next to this, the water companies in the Netherlands have created extra possibilities for a public mutual comparison of companies (VEWIN benchmark).

The government's supervision of the water company is relatively simple, because all Dutch water companies are government-owned limited liability companies, or municipal services (Amsterdam).

In a government-owned limited liability company, the company's stocks are owned by the provinces and municipalities. The owners are the democratically chosen representatives of the consumers, in as far as the stocks are proportionally divided. With this, a balanced and controllable consideration is possible between quality, reliability, nature conservation, and costs. The stocks usually represent only a symbolic value in which the owners have a minimal capital contribution (and, therefore, no expectations of capital return).

Profit

A water company does not strive to make a profit, but looks after the public interest, at cost.

An important basic principle is that consumers pay for the actual costs, and not for future expenses. Moreover they might count on a high cost efficiency within the water company.

However, making a profit is allowed under the following circumstances:
- profit can be obtained strategically, when it is used for building up company capital, thereby gaining a better position on the capital market, which can be of importance in securing loans at acceptable interest rates
- profit can be obtained strategically to avoid sudden large increases in rates. For that reason, the decision can be made for gradual, step-by-step increases and, through this, a capital reserve is built up

- profit (and also losses) can be obtained non-strategically, if the sales and the costs differ from what was estimated when the rates were being determined

A special form of company profit is the dividend paid to local authorities.

This could be a significant sum, as water rates sometimes included hidden municipal taxes. Nowadays this practice is forbidden by law.

2.2 Financial annual report

Because of their social position water companies feel more or less obligated to maintain an open communication with their consumers.

An important instrument for this communication is the company's annual report (Figure 2). An annual report gives a clear summary of the financial management of a water company. In their annual report, most water companies give consumers information about their technical and organizational developments.

A financial annual report consists of a balance sheet (list of possessions and debts at the end of the financial year) and a profit and loss account (list of incomes and expenses in the financial year).

Balance sheet

Table 1 shows an example of a water company's balance sheet.

This table shows that more than 95% of the possessions of this water company are tangible fixed assets (e.g., buildings, installations and pipes).

Figure 2 - Front page of an annual report of a water company

Table 1   - Balance sheet of a water company (PWN 2001, 100% = €784.5 mln)

Assets	(%)	Liabilities	(%)
Tangible fixed assets:		Equity capital:	
- Buildings and land	20.0	- Issued shares	0.9
- Machinery and installations	16.3	- Realized revaluation reserve	16.6
- Pipelines	52.2	- General reserves	3.6
- Other fixed company equipment	2.4	Contribution for new connections (egalization)	8.0
- Fixed capital assets under construction	4.7	Provisions	4.3
Financial fixed assets	0.4	Long-term debts	53.0
Inventories	0.2	Short-term debts:	
Receivables:		- Loans to be amortized next year	5.6
- Debtors	3.0	- Cash loans	0.9
- Other receivables	0.1	- Loans due banks	0.1
- Accrued income	0.4	- Advance payments for water	1.3
Liquid assets	0.2	- Taxes and pensions	0.0
		- Debts due suppliers	2.7
		- Accrued expenses	3.0
Total	100.0		100.0

The distribution network has the largest share of those fixed assets.

Part of the capital is fixed in installations which are not yet in active operation (under construction).

The amount of the tangible fixed assets is the sum of the book value of all company assets. The book value is the purchase value minus the accumulated depreciations.

Almost 60% of the liabilities are fixed in long-term loans (incl. loans to be amortized next year). These long-term loans consist of a very large number of loans with different terms and different interest rates. The average term of the loans in this company is about 10 years, with an average interest rate of 5.8% (range 3 - 10%). The broad range in interest rates is caused by large fluctuations in time and the continuing closure and pay-off of loans.

Due to their low investment risk, water companies can borrow money relatively inexpensively, through financial institutions for the government (e.g., Bank of Dutch Municipalities, Bank of Dutch Waterboards, etc.). An average term of 10 years means that every year 10% of the loans has to be paid off. Partially new loans will be taken for this, because the depreciation period of the company assets has an average of about 35 years, and, therefore, the loaned amount will be earned back over a longer period.

About 21% of the liabilities of this company are established in equity capital. This mainly involves the realized revaluation reserve. The revaluation reserve is built up by obtained profits because this company depreciates based on the present value, instead of the purchase value. The background for using present value is that investments they made in the past would have cost more money based on today's prices due to inflation. In this way, consumers pay in part, for future investments.

The book value of the active assets is, for this company, around 60% of the (historical) purchase value (almost 40% is depreciated). The present purchase value is its value if it were built today, which is also often used as the insurance value. The present purchase value of the company's assets is 1.58 times the historical purchase value. This valuing corresponds to an average inflation rate of 3% over 15 years (1.03^{15}).

The remainder of the equity capital consists of the accumulated profit (general reserve), and the paid-up capital of the issued shares.

About 8% of the liabilities are built up from the onetime paid charges for new or modified connection to the distribution network (new connection charge). These contributions are depreciated over the same period as the corresponding material fixed assets.

About 4% of the liabilities consist of provisions. These are mainly reserves for staff who resigned early and provisions for the planned development of the organization. Also, demolishing costs for the company facilities that will be taken out of service are part of these liabilities.

Investments and depreciations

Through depreciations a one-time expense for an asset is earned back from annual allowances. The time it takes to earn it back corresponds to the depreciation period.

The depreciation periods for water companies are relatively long. On one hand, the technical facilities last a long time (buildings and pipes); on the other hand, there is a great certainty that during the entire depreciation period, incomes from water sales will be realized.

The depreciation period preferably equals the expected actual technical lifetime of the asset. In this way, the consumers pay as evenly as possible for the investments from which they also receive "pleasure" (the consumer pays for its "own" facility).

Table 2 shows the depreciation periods maintained by the water company described above.

As in nearly all concerns, including water companies, the investment costs are straight-line depreciated. Therefore, the annual depreciation for a certain company resource is constant during the total depreciation period. However, with this method, the interest expenses of an asset are high in the beginning and decrease to zero at the end of the depreciation period. The capital expenses (interest and depreciation) for this asset are, therefore, not equal over the depreciation period.

Because a water company of considerable size has many assets that have to be expanded or

replaced at different times, the capital expenses, therefore, seemingly level off.

For companies with only a limited number of expensive components that also have to be acquired simultaneously, another depreciation method could be used.

Such a situation occurs, for example, at a large-scale surface water treatment plant. For this plant an annuity depreciation can be applied (interest plus depreciation are equal during the depreciation period), or a unitary depreciation can be used (interest and depreciation are such that the water rate is stable over the depreciation period, taking into account the anticipated development of the sales).

For every asset it is precisely registered how large the original investment was and how much is depreciated (earned back). The paid interest for this asset will not be separately listed.

The loans for all assets together equal the total loan amount. Loans are not related to the original investment works. This is because of new loans are obtained for both new investments as for the repayment of old loans.

Because of inflation, investments made in the distant past are relatively inexpensive. Through depreciation the users pay with today's money for the less expensive investments of the past.

Table 3 shows an overview of the purchase value of the assets, compared to the book value, and compared to the investments and depreciations in the given financial year.

This table also shows the large share of the distribution network in the financial balance of a water company.

An investment level equal to the depreciation shows that it is mainly a matter of maintaining the infrastructure (renewal and replacement).

A total investment level of 4% of the total purchase value equals an average replacement period of 25 years. For the pipes (see Table 3) a replacement period of 30 years (54.8/1.8) is realistic. However, this includes extensions because of the construction needed for new pipes in new resi-

Table 2 - Depreciation periods of a water company's assets (PWN 2001)

Types of company assets	Depreciation period (years)
Water abstraction facilities	25
Buildings of treatment plants	30
Filter units	25
Machinery and installations	10
Distribution network	40
Water meters	20
Office buildings	40
Inventories	5

Table 3   - Investments and depreciation of a water company (PWN 2001, 100% = €1,183 mln)

Assets	Purchase value	Book value (purchase)	Investments	Depreciation (purchase)
	(%)	(%)	(%)	(%)
Buildings and land	17.9	13.2	0.2	0.5
Machinery and installations	24.1	10.8	1.4	1.3
Pipelines	54.8	34.6	1.8	1.3
Other fixed assets	3.2	1.6	0.7	1.1
Total	100.0	60.3	4.1	4.2

dential areas. The total sales and production of this company did not increase (population growth compensated by water savings), but the number of clients did (population growth and decrease in average household size).

Profit and loss account
Table 4 provides an example of a profit and loss account of a water company.

The incomes of this water company are represented by more than 90% from the sale of water, by levies for the standing charge, and by payment for the delivered amounts of water (consumer rate). A very small share of the water revenues consists of a standing charge for fire hydrants, paid for by local governments.

The revenues for nature conservation and recreation mainly originate from admissions to the nature reserves and visitors' centers, and from camp fees.
The revenues from capitalized production mainly concern staff costs that are attributed to the investment work and which reappear in the tangible fixed assets.
The remaining revenues are derived from the execution of activities for third parties (renovation

of streets when constructing the pipes, laboratory research) and by the sales of company assets.

Capital expenses are the largest expenditure of a water company. Depreciations, additions to the revaluation reserve and interest costs are almost 45% of the total costs.

The total costs at this company include 36% for staff costs. These costs involve its own staff or hired staff for contracted work, and extraordinary costs for organizational development. The work which is contracted out mainly consists of activities in the distribution network by third parties.

Expenses for materials are non-capitalized materials. Other external costs are largely consumer goods like energy and chemicals.
This company also buys a considerable amount of drinking water from a neighboring water company.

The realized profit will be added to the general reserves of the company. The increase in the company's equity capital consists of both this profit and the addition of the revaluation reserve.
Water companies are lawfully excused from the levies of corporate taxation.

Table 4   - Profit and loss account of a water company (PWN 2001, 100% = €188.8 mln)

Revenues	(%)	Expenses	(%)
Net sales water:		Purchase of drinking water	5.1
- Small use (households)	75.7	Staff	22.9
- Mid use	4.7	Third-party work	11.0
- Large use	10.1	Extraordinary costs	2.6
- Standing charge fire hydrants	0.3	Material	5.5
Nature conservation and recreation	2.8	Other external costs	8.7
Capitalized production	2.8	Depreciation (excluding revaluation)	25.8
Other revenues	3.7	Revaluation reserves (addition)	3.6
		Interest	14.3
		Profit (result)	0.6
Total	100.0		100.0

2.3 Rate determination

In order to avoid profits or losses, it is necessary for a water supply company to charge a cost-covering rate. This rate is usually determined annually based on the budget for the coming fiscal year. In this budget, the expected expenses and incomes are noted.

For a reliable estimation of the capital costs for the coming year, it is necessary to formulate an investment budget for that year (new constructions and replacement investments), as well as an expectation of the assets which will be removed. These estimations should include assets like treatment plants and distribution network. Based on these estimations, the development of the balance sheet value over the year can be established and, with this, the capital needs (loans).

The interest costs can be reliably estimated because the largest share of the capital is loaned through long-term loans. For new loans an estimation of the interests from the coming year will have to be made.

All remaining expenses are generally reliable estimations based on the expenses of the last year. Apart from the purchase costs for (drinking) water and operational costs (energy and chemicals), these costs are hardly related to the true production and sales in the coming year.

The total expenses should be covered by the total income. The non-water income can often be estimated from historical information. The remaining part has to come from water revenues. The water revenues depends on the estimated water use within the different consumption categories and the tarif policy of the company. The tarif policy includes:
- chosen ratio between fixed rate (standing charge) and the volume rate per consumption category (small use versus large use)
- chosen ratio of cost-covering by the different consumption categories

Fixed rate versus volume rate

The water company of Table 4 uses the following rates for small use (2003):

- fixed rate (standing charge)
  €43.00 per year (6% VAT incl.)
- volume rate
  €1.34 per m³ (6% VAT incl.)

With an average consumption of 117 m³ per year per household, the annual cost for drinking water per household is €199.78 per year (43.00 + 117 · 1.34).
This means that 21% of the revenues from households consist of fixed charges and 79% of volume charges.

These cost percentages differ greatly from the water company's expenses which are mainly fixed costs for capital and staff.
A rate ratio of 90% for fixed charges and 10% for volume charges would better correspond to the actual cost relationship. In principle such a rate ratio could be adopted. However, from a political point of view, this would be considered less advisable, because there is no stimulus for the individual citizen to use drinking water economically. The ratio between the fixed and volume charges is based almost entirely on social and political arguments.

A result of the above-mentioned cost relationship is that less water consumption (due to water savings) results in an increase in the volume rate to avoid losses to the company.

The large share of fixed costs and relatively high costs to measure the delivered water (meters with an annual meter recording) are the reasons that, in some areas, an unmetered delivery is found.
The choice for metering or not is mainly a social consideration. However, from an economical point of view, the unmeasured delivery of drinking water is usually cheaper in total, as long as large spills are avoided.

The costs for delivery to and consumption by the consumer are calculated per calendar year. For large users consumption is based on the meter reading at the end of a calendar year. For small users the meters are recorded during the year

Figure 3   - Water meter

(Figure 3) after which balancing takes place with the earlier estimated annual consumption (Figure 4).

New connection charge

The connections to houses are relatively expensive, when considered as part of the total costs of the drinking water supply because of the many small pipes. Therefore, one-time entry rates are usually charged when making or changing the connection.

The water company in the sample uses the following one-time entry rates for small-scale consumers (2003):
- direct definitive entry €360.52 (6% BTW incl.)
- entry with a preliminary construction connection €882.80 (6% BTW incl.).

The received entry charges are for administrative reasons not deducted from the investment costs for these connections. The received charges are listed on the balance sheet as capital reserve. To this reserve, depreciation will be applied.

Volume rates for small and large use

Usually large users pay less for drinking water than small users. This is motivated by the relatively high costs for the small pipes in the distribution network needed for small users. In other words, large users are connected to main pipes and, therefore, do not use these small pipes. Also, large users typically use water more equally, which means that for the same annual sales smaller pipes can be used.

Table 5 shows an example of the rates for small, mid- and large users.
In this example the average rate per m³ for large users is around 75% of the average rate for small users. Moreover, the share of the fixed rate in the total costs is smaller for the large users (10% of the annual costs).

There are also companies in which there is no separate large user volume rate. This is motivated by a policy choice which states that it should be equally attractive for everyone to save water.
The relationship between the rates for large and small users is, in this way, more or less determined on political grounds. However, on technical grounds it is defensible to establish lower rates for large users.

2.4   Benchmark comparison of water companies

Because water companies are monopolies, there is no control by the market on the delivered product regarding quality, efficiency or costs. To overcome this lack of control, the Dutch water companies

Table 5   - Example of rates for small and large water users for a water company (PWN 2003, excluded 6% VAT)

Annual use	Connection		Rates		Costs	
	Maximum consumption	Peak factor	Fixed	Volume		
(m³)	(m³/h)	(-)	(€ / y)	(€ / m³)	(€ / y)	(€ / m³)
117	1.5	110	40.57	1.26	187.99	1.61
5,000	6	10	575.00	1.24	6,775.00	1.36
200,000	70	3	24,250.00	1.07	238,500.00	1.19

Nota nr. 2931121-02-07-0024

Wilt u bij correspondentie dit notanummer vermelden?

Datum 13 augustus 2002

Meneer/Mevrouw/Firma

JQJC VERBEEK

Van Speijkstraat 98
2518 GE 'S-GRAVENHAGE

Jaarafrekening

Voor inlichtingen
Haagregio 070 384 39 39
Tussen 08.00 en 17.00 uur

Duinwaterbedrijf Zuid-Holland

▶ **Verkoopbedrijf**

Leveringsadres

Van Speijkstraat 98
2518 GE 'S-GRAVENHAGE

Meter	Verbruiksperiode		Meterstanden		Verbruik in m3	BTW %	Totaal
	van	tot en met	eind	begin			verschuldigd
211351	5-07-2001	2-07-2002	398	326	72		

Totaal verbruik					72		
Verbruik 36 m3 x 1,36000						6,00	48,96
Verbruik 36 m3 x 1,32000						6,00	47,52
Vastrecht 1-08-2001 t/m 31-07-2002						6,00	45,20
Waterbelasting over 36 m3						6,00	4,75
Waterbelasting over 36 m3						6,00	4,90
Bijdrage precario						6,00	6,32
Bijdrage precario						6,00	8,64
Omzetbelasting (BTW)							9,99

							176,28
In rekening gebracht(e) voorschot(ten)			159,74	BTW	9,58		169,32

							6,96
Eerste voorschot nieuwe verbruiksjaar							46,64

							53,60

Gelieve het bedrag middels bijgaande acceptgiro over te maken.
Zorgt u ervoor dat het bedrag uiterlijk 3-09-2002 op onze rekening is
bijgeschreven.

Nieuw voorschot: 44,00 + 2,64 BTW = 46,64
Inning overige voorschotten vindt plaats in november februari mei

Wilt u uitleg over de jaarafrekening? Bezoekt u dan onze website
WWW.DZH.NL onder klantenservice. Ook uw verhuizing kunt u hier
opgeven of haal een gratis verhuisbericht op het postkantoor.

Historisch verbruik	11-07-2000 t/m 5-07-2001	64 m3
	15-07-1999 t/m 11-07-2000	64 m3

betaald

8/9/02

Correspondentieadres

Haagregio
Postbus 710
2501 CS Den Haag

Vlietregio
Postbus 12
2640 AA Pijnacker

Postbank 11600

*Ingeschreven in het Handels-
register onder nr. 27122974*

Figure 4 - Invoice for drinking water

Table 6   - Examples of statistical indicators for a water company (PWN 2001)

Quantity	Unit	Value
Sales in distribution area	mln m³ / y	104.2
Number of connections	-	692,340
Sales in own distribution area	m³ / y / connection	150
Percentage small users	m³ / m³	77%
	connection/connection	99.4%
Length of main distribution network	m / connection	13.6
Land	m² / connection	103
Staff	FTE/ 1000 connections	1.14
Equity capital	€ / connection	239
Tangible fixed assets	€ / connection	1,088
Revaluated purchase costs for active assets	€ / connection	2,711
Net sales water	€ / y / connection	247

regularly conduct company comparisons voluntarily. This is called the VEWIN Benchmark. In this company comparison, the water quality of the delivered water, consumer satisfaction regarding the service, the environmental aspects, and the economic efficiency are all involved.

Indicators for company comparison
Water companies in the Netherlands vary widely in size, technical infrastructures and financial positions. To compare water companies the information is usually expressed in amounts per connection. Within the number of connections, households are by far the largest group. Figures per connection, therefore, are characteristically for an average family.

Table 6 shows a couple of statistical indicators for the sample company. In this table both the technical and financial aspects are included. These are closely related because of the nature of water companies.

Comparison of costs per household
Table 7 shows the annual costs for an average household for different distribution areas for some Dutch water companies.

From this table one sees that surface water companies are considerably more expensive than groundwater companies, mainly because more complex treatment at a greater distance from consumers means a more expensive infrastructure.
Furthermore, from the VEWIN Benchmark, it becomes clear that within the same company there are remarkable differences between various distribution areas. This is caused by political agreements made by management when companies merge.
The rate differences can be explained by differences in:
-   age of the infrastructures (lower capital costs for older installations)
-   its performance on the capital market (realized average interest)
-   equity capital (capital needs by loans)
-   the size of the supply area (population or consumption density)
-   utilization of the infrastructure (capacity reserve)
-   productivity of the staff (company and outside employees, salary levels, social situation of former staff)
-   rate policy (mutations in equity capital, rate differences between large and small use)

Table 7   - Yearly costs for an average family with a water consumption of 130 m³/y (VEWIN 2000)

Company	Company – supply area	Yearly costs family (€ / y)
Surface water companies		
- Most expensive supply area	PWN – Region Haarlem	248
- Cheapest supply area	Water supply company Amsterdam	166
Groundwater companies		
- Most expensive supply area	Vitens – Friesland	166
- Cheapest supply area	Groningen – Province (excluded city)	101

The differences in rates will get smaller in the coming years because of company mergers and because of the rate normalization within a company.

3.   Investment costs

3.1 Definition of investment costs

The investment costs represent the total costs of developing a project or plant. These costs are paid during the preparation and construction of the project through to the moment that the project (e.g., treatment plant) is taken into operation. From that moment on, the installation generates revenues and the costs afterwards are considered to be operational costs. Usually this timing corresponds to the date the completed construction is taken over by the principal (water company).

Investment costs can also appear during the operation period of the asset. Examples include expansion of the plant and replacement of major parts.

The investment costs, both of newly built constructions and the expansion and replacement of major parts, are the basis of the capital costs of an asset.

The preparation costs are also part of the investment costs of an asset. Especially in the initial stage of a project, it is not always clear which costs really have to be ascribed to the investment costs of a future asset or to the general operational costs of a (water) company. Two examples of this are the costs for the feasibility study and the preliminary technical study (pilot plant).

For a clear picture of the costs of a water company, it is important that costs are ascribed to the investment costs of the asset in an early stage, even if the final completion of the asset is uncertain. This is one way to avoid losing the initial costs to the general costs of a company. This will also make the investment loss clear when a new construction project is cancelled.

3.2 Uniform structure of investment costs

To estimate, secure and justify investment costs, a uniform and unambiguous concept definition is necessary.

Table 8   - Overview of investment costs (according to NEN 2631)

Part		Sub part	
1	Land cost	1	Acquisition costs
		2	Costs for infrastructural facilities
		3	Site preparation costs
2	Construction costs	1a	Buildings: Structural works
		1b	Buildings: Installations (mechanical and electrical)
		1c	Buildings: Fixed furnishing
		2a	Ground: Structural works
		2b	Ground: Installations (mechanical and electrical)
		2c	Ground: Fixed equipment
3	Equipment costs	1a	Buildings: Water supply installations
		1b	Buildings: Loose installations
		1c	Buildings: Work for installations
		2a	Ground: Water supply installations
		2b	Ground: Loose installations
		2c	Ground: Work for installations
4	Additional costs	a	Preparation and supervision costs
		b	Levies
		c	Insurance
		d	Start-up costs
		e	Financing costs
		f	Risk balancing
		g	Unforeseen expenses
		h	Maintenance costs of the acquired land
		i	Sales tax

For construction in the Netherlands, presentation of the investment costs has to satisfy NEN 2631: "Investment costs of buildings - Terminology and classification." This classification is depicted in Table 8.

The definitions, according to this norm, also play a part in establishing levies like building fees. Building fees usually amount to a percentage of the construction costs, according to NEN 2631.

Land costs

Acquisition costs represent the purchase sum of the site with all its additional costs.
The costs for infrastructural facilities include the costs of construction outside the site to make it suitable for use.

The site preparation costs include, among other things, the demolition of buildings, the removal of old pipes, as well as providing accessibility for construction traffic.

The land costs vary noticeably per project. When expanding an existing installation, the terrain might already be owned by the client. When building on new locations, there are often negotiations to be made regarding the price.
Acquisition costs are usually not depreciated, assuming that the land itself has a stable value.
The land costs for water treatment plants are usually only a small part of the total investment costs (less than 1 - 2%).

Construction costs

Water installations are not a part of the construction costs. According to the norm, these belong to the installation costs.
A drinking water production plants consists, in large part, of a variety of installations. To these belong installations like filter units, clear water reservoirs, pumps and pipes, etc.
The advantage of this interpretation is that the construction fees for a new drinking water production plant will be limited. The levies are not charged on installation costs in compliance with the jurisprudence.

Included in the construction costs are, among other things, office facilities for the staff and sanitary facilities. Construction costs are separated into costs for buildings and costs for the ground.
The construction costs (in conformance with the above-mentioned interpretation) are usually a small part of the investment costs (less than 2 - 5%) in drinking water production plants.

Installation costs

The water treatment and supply installations are included in the installation costs according to NEN 2631 and are the most expensive part of constructing a drinking water production plant.

To make an initial estimation of the costs of the treatment and pumping units, cost-functions are often used, which are based on previously completed projects. In such functions, often the design capacity is typically included as a variable (shown below in paragraph 3.4).
Besides the above-mentioned costs of the water supply installations, the furnishing of staff facilities, workshop, laboratory, etc. is also part of the installation costs. These installation costs are usually a small part of the investment costs (less than 1 - 3%) for water supply production plants.

Additional costs

The preparation and supervision costs include the costs for the design, preparation of tender documents and building management. It includes both the internal costs of the initiator and the external consultancy costs for all separate project stages (from preliminary research to completion). The preparation and supervision costs typically make up a substantial part of the investment costs (15 - 25%).
These costs are not always equally distinguishable. Some water companies consider the preparation costs as normal activities for the general management. In other cases the construction is put out to tender as a turnkey project, in which case a large part of the engineering costs is included in the contract sum. Also, in a different way of contracting, where the detailed engineering is carried out by the contractor, there is a shifting of this item to the contract sum. When comparing

the different projects, this potential shift has to be taken into account.

The levies contain, among other things, the fees for the building permit. The amount of these fees differs per municipality. Generally, they amount to 0.5 - 1.5% of the overall construction cost (in conformance with the above-mentioned interpretation of NEN 2631), with the lower percentages applied to the higher construction costs.

The financing costs mainly represent interest during construction. Payments are made during the preparation and building stages until the moment of start-up.

The interest during construction depends on the length of time between payments and the moment of start-up, and on the interest rate. When the building period is 2 years, the interest is 10%, and the progress of building is more or less constant (constant monthly costs during the period of building), then the interest on the investment costs amounts to about 10%. The interest costs during construction for drinking water production plants will vary between 5 - 15% of the total investment costs.

Sales taxes include the V.A.T. on the investment costs.
Drinking water companies are exempt from V.A.T., which means that they do not have to pay V.A.T., when making investments. When working with depreciations, the investment costs excluding V.A.T. should, therefore, be taken into account.

Unexpected expenses should not be recorded as a separate entry in the cost presentation, but should be added to as many other expected expenses as possible. The background for this is that, with a seperate cost entry, the post-calculation of projects will be less transparent. The presentation of the cost estimations during the preparation and building stages should reflect estimations in every category of likely costs. Putting one large figure in the "unexpected costs" category gives rise to questions about the total cost estimations.

For drinking water production plants, the remaining additional costs (Section c, d, e, f, and h) are usually small (1 - 3% of the investment costs).

3.3 Index of investment costs

When determining the investment costs for a specific project, often information from comparable projects with comparable process components is used. This applies especially to the beginning of the design process, when detailed design information for the concerned project is still missing.
When the information on the costs of an actual project is used, the following should be considered:
- are all cost components included in the investment costs?
- what was the moment of realization (price level)?
- what was the installed capacity (split treatment, reserve capacity)?

Price level

The cost of goods and services change, in time, which means that investment costs will change too. The basis for this can be either price increases or price decreases. Price increases can be the result of inflation, which means that the cost for loans and materials will rise. Price decreases can be the result of more efficient management, when production is less costly due, for example, to scaling-up, mass production, or automation.

Looking at the potential price difference, it is important to determine when the investment costs were calculated. This is indicated as the price level.

Price-index figures

The development of the price level is described using price-index figures.
Statistics Netherlands, CBS, publishes various price-index figures, like the consumers' price-index (CPI). The CPI shows the development of the price of goods and services that are purchased for consumption by the average household in the Netherlands in a base year (1995 or 2003). The CPI is an important standard for inflation and is often used by companies and government, for

example, within the framework of loan negotiations, creating an index of rents and annuities, and when adjusting tax tables. Inflation is measured as the increase in the CPI over a certain period compared to the same period in the previous year.
In the period from 1996 to 2002 inflation in the Netherlands was an average of 3% per year.

CBS also publishes price-index figures for producers' prices, including those for industry in general and for the construction industry specifically.
For the building industry, the production price-index figures for buildings are published, for house building, for commercial buildings, and for governmental buildings, hospitals, etc.
For the building industry also a couple of price-index figures for land, water and road construction are published, like excavating work, road building and sewage systems.
The price-index for sewerage concerns sewerage within built-up areas for construction and renewal. The index contains, among other things, the demolishing and transporting of brick and asphalt paving, digging of trenches, buying of pipe material (concrete pipes), pipe laying, making house connections, backfilling, and transporting excess earth.

In Figure 5 the progression of the price-index figures for sewage systems within built-up areas is shown. It turns out that the prices have more than doubled in 23 years. Since 1982 the annual price increase has been nearly constant at a level of 2.7% per year (growth rate per year 1.027).

Levelling the price level

When recalculating the investment costs of actualized projects to a desirable price level, price-index figures are used.

The investment costs can be determined to a certain time using:

$$K_a = K_b \cdot \frac{\text{price-index figure time a}}{\text{price-index figure time b}}$$

in which:
K_a, K_b = investment costs at time a and b

For a time in the future there is no price-index figure available. Therefore, an extrapolation of the future price-index figure has to be made.

Based on an expected price development with a fixed increase in the price per year, a future price K_a can be determined from:

$$K_a = K_b \cdot (\text{growth rate per year})^n$$

in which:
n = number of years between time a and time b

Price-index with compound cost components

Drinking water production plants comprise different kinds of construction parts.
The most important of these are:
- civil structures (large-scale construction)
- mechanical installations
- electrical installations
- instrumentation and control installations

The development of the costs will not be the same for these parts. For the civil constructions, the gradual increase in wages will be influential, while for the instrumentation and control installations the relative price decrease of electronics plays an important part.
Therefore, for compound constructions, an index will be determined per kind of construction part to derive a reliable calculation to another price level.
The most important index figures for the realization of drinking water production plants are summarized in Table 9.

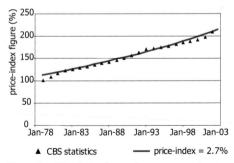

Figure 5   - Price-index figures for sewage systems within built-up areas (CBS 2002)

Table 9   - Price-indices of different parts of compound works

Part	Sub part	Characteristic index figure
Land costs	Acquisition	Consumers Price Index
	Infrastructure	Price Index Civil Engineering
	Site preparation	Price Index Civil Engineering
Construction and equipment costs	Civil engineering	Price Index Utility buildings
	Mechanical engineering	Price Index Machine Industry [1]
	Electrical engineering/instrumentation	Price Index Electrotechnical Industry
	Other	Consumer Price Index
Additional costs	Preparation and supervision	Index government wages
	Interest during construction	Discount rate for promissory notes +1%
	VAT	Ratio of actual value
	Other additional costs	Consumer Price Index

[1] product price index of internal sales of the industry

Suppose that for drinking water plants a compound index figure can be determined. For this example, a certain relationship is supposed for the costs of the different parts, illustrated in Table 9.

In practice the following division of the costs of a conventional water supply plant (with filters and reservoirs constructed in concrete) applies:

- civil structures   40 - 60%
- mechanical installations   20 - 30%
- electrical installations   10 - 20%
- instrumentation and control   5 - 15%

In the period between 1980 and 1995 an analysis was made of the compound index of the WRK surface water treatment plant in Andijk. A compound index showing a 3% rise in the costs per year was acquired. This is reasonably equal to the index figure of commercial buildings.

With an index of 3% per year, the index figure of the investment costs increases up to 1.35 (1.03^{10}) in a period of 10 years and up to 1.81 (1.03^{20}) in a period of 20 years.

3.4   Investment costs and capacity

To transfer the investment costs of a realized project to a future project, the following questions are important to consider:

- is the treatment scheme of the projects equal?
- is the capacity of the projects equal?
- is the complexity and/or "luxury level" of the projects equal?

To compare production plants with different treatment schemes, investment functions per treatment process can be formulated. By adding the costs of the different processes, the total investment costs can be determined.

The complexity may differ per project. Sometimes the building permit only allows a very restricted building area, which means that a complex piled up construction is needed. Therefore, the investment costs are higher.

Also, aspects like representative buildings, with facilities for excursions, influence construction costs.

Because of these variations, the investment costs differ, even when the treatment scheme and capacity are equal. Differences of ±30% are possible, which is a factor of 2 between the most expensive and the least expensive project design.

Scale factor

Of course, the capacity of the plant determines, to an important extent, its investment costs.

For the relation between capacity and investment costs, cost functions can be formulated.

The relation between capacity and investment costs are usually well described by the general formula:

$$K = a \cdot (\text{capacity})^b$$

in which:

K	= investment costs	(E)
a	= costs factor	(-)
b	= scale factor	(-)

In Figure 6 this relationship is given graphically for various scale factors. In this relationship the scale factor is the most important part.

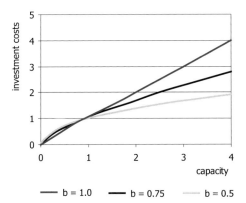

Figure 6 - Relationship between capacity and investment costs for different scale factors

The cost ratio of two different capacities depends only on the scale factor:

$$\frac{K_1}{K_2} = \left(\frac{capacity_1}{capacity_2} \right)^b$$

A scale factor of 1.0 indicates that there is a linear relationship between capacity and investment costs. This usually occurs when more of the same elements are needed for a larger plant, like in membrane filtration in which more of the relatively expensive membrane elements are necessary.

A more or less linear relationship also occurs in very large installations when the process parts already have a maximum capacity and, even more units are required to increase it further. An example is rapid sand filters that, due to restrictions in backwash water facilities, are usually not larger than 30 - 50 m².

A scale factor of 0.6 - 0.7 occurs for process parts for which, at a larger capacity, the size of the elements increases. Reservoirs are a typical example.

When the water height of a reservoir is selected, then with a larger volume the surface of the floor and roof will change on a linear scale with the volume (scale factor 1.0). The surface of the walls will change with the square root of the volume (scale factor 0.5).

In practice the scale factor for units of water production plants will be between 0.6 and 0.9, within the capacity range of factor 2 to 6.

Functions for investment costs

For all sorts of processes or installations, cost functions can be formulated to conform to the general formula for investment costs, based on (uniform) information from field practice.

When deriving these formulas, the range of the cost function is limited and that has to be taken into account. In very small installations, the costs of additional facilities will play a relatively important role; in very large installations, the scale effect will relatively decrease (more of the same elements).

Capacity in the cost function involves different quantities for different processes, like annual capacity, hour capacity, volume, surface area, etc.

The annual capacity is a suitable parameter for global initial cost estimations.

The maximum hour capacity of a process unit is a suitable parameter if the concerned process differs only slightly in design criterion, and, therefore, the size has a fixed relationship with the capacity.

The specific size of a process unit will always give the most reliable cost function. The cost function for rapid sand filters will use the filter surface area as the capacity parameter. A plant with a designed filtration velocity of 4 m/h will be more expensive than a plant with the same hydraulic capacity, but with a designed filtration velocity of 8 m/h. For flocculation, the total volume will be used as the capacity parameter, because large differences in residence time may occur, and different sizes can therefore have the same hydraulic capacity. Also, in reservoirs, volume will be the determining capacity parameter.

The capacity parameters for transport pipes are their length and diameter. For the length, a scale factor of 1.0 (costs are linear with the length) is applied; for the diameter, the same is true. The cost of pipe material and the excavation are more or less proportional to the diameter.

When the scale factor is 1.0 for the diameter, then the scale factor for the capacity of pipes is 0.5. This is because the design velocity is equal to the most economical velocity, which is for all capacities more or less constant.

Investment functions for different design phases

Cost functions used for the initial stage of a project will, in general, have large inaccuracies. One reason for this is that relatively little is known during the initial stage (treatment scheme, specific construction demands, etc.); another reason is that many things can and will change during subsequent designs.

Linear functions are often used for these cost functions (scale factor 1.0), in which the cost factor is chosen within an indicated range, based on the complexity and scale of the considered project.

Table 10 shows some examples of functions for investment costs for initial cost estimations.

The accuracy of these functions will be about ±50%.

In a later stage of the project, like when formulating the draft design, more complex cost functions can be used. Preferably, a scale factor in the cost function will then be included.

The accuracy of certain cost functions per process unit are generally ±30%, assuming that the treatment scheme is known. A greater accuracy will typically not be possible, because, at this stage, it is not yet known what the construction will look like. With this level of accuracy, usually fairly good policy decisions can be made, such as decisions to choose a simpler or more staged plan, or an alternative treatment scheme.

The investment costs account for about 50% - 60% of the production of and/or transportation costs for drinking water. Operation costs (energy, chemicals and staff) are, in general, estimated with a higher degree of accuracy. This will level the inaccuracy in the estimation of the investment costs within the estimation of the production or transportion costs.

Table 11 shows some examples of functions for investment costs for Dutch designs.

During the preliminary and final designs, more and more accuracy in the design is established, and many more details are known. What has been determined is how many and which pumps will be installed, which buffer volume will be chosen, and which additional facilities (e.g., central control room, emergency power, laboratory, etc.) will be used.

The budget of the preliminary design can, therefore, be established with greater detail. Estimations are formulated per discipline (e.g., civil, mechanical or electrical engineering). The estimations will partly be based on more detailed cost functions and partly on figures based on designers' and suppliers' previous experiences.

On the level of tender documents and specifications, the investment costs can be estimated based on estimations in detail (e.g., 300 filter nozzles per filter, 2,500 kg of concrete steel, 50 m² of front/façade element, etc.), in which a large degree of accuracy can be reached. All information used for

Table 10 - Examples of investment cost functions for initial cost estimations

Process / Process part	Cost factor ($€ / m^3$ yearly capacity)
Production from groundwater	1.5 - 3.5
Production from bank filtration	2.0 - 4.0
Production from surface water (direct)	3.0 - 5.0
Production from surface water (soil aquifer recharge)	4.0 - 8.0
Groundwater abstraction	0.10 - 0.15
Aeration	0.10 - 0.15
Degasifying	0.20 - 0.30
Rapid sand filtration	0.30 - 0.55
Filter backwash water treatment	0.05 - 0.15
Raw water pumping	0.10 - 0.15
Microstrainers	0.05 - 0.15
Flocculation	0.10 - 0.25
Floc removal (sedimentation/flotation)	0.5 - 0.25
Rapid sand filtration	0.30 - 0.55
Activated carbon filtration (GAC)	0.50 - 0.90
Softening	0.35 - 0.60
Disinfection	0.05 - 0.20
Membrane filtration	1.00 - 2.00
Slow sand filtration	0.70 - 1.50
Clear water pumping station	0.40 - 0.70
Clear water storage	0.20 - 0.35

Table 11 - Examples of several functions of investment costs (construction plus equipment costs) in sketch design

Process units	Transport pipelines
Rapid sand filters: €0.15 million per m² filter area $^{0.61}$	Normal route: €500 per meter diameter per meter length
Clear water storage: €0.003 million per m³ storage volume $^{0.70}$	Complex route: €1,000 per meter diameter per meter length

Estimating investment costs

A surface water treatment plant of 20 million m^3/y (design capacity 3,200 m^3/h) consists of several processes, like those below.

Process part				
Flocculation	Residence time	20 min	Volume	1,070 m^3
Flotation	Surface load	15 m / h	Surface	215 m^2
Filtration	Surface load	7 m / h	Surface	460 m^2
Activated carbon filtration	Empty bed contact time	15 min	Volume of carbon	800 m^3
Clear water storage	Volume	20,000 m^3		
Clear water pumping station	Capacity	5,760 m^3 / h		

Based on these process units, the investment costs (level of policy plan or sketch design) are estimated using the cost functions for the process units. The table below gives the result of the cost estimation.

Cost element	Costs (million €)
Construction and equipment costs for process units:	
- Flocculation	2.3
- Flotation	2.8
- Filtration	6.8
- Activated carbon filtration	6.7
- Clean water storage	3.7
- Clean water pumping station	7.3
Subtotal process units	29.6
Other (non-process related) investment costs (41% of subtotal process units)	12.1
- Land costs (2% of subtotal process units)	
- Other construction costs (5% of subtotal process units)	
- Additional costs:	
- Preparation and supervision (20% of subtotal process units)	
- Financing costs (10% of subtotal process units)	
- Other additional costs (4% of subtotal process units)	
Total investment costs	41.7

the cost estimation can be taken from the "bill of quantities" and the lists of specifications.
Such a budget usually has the same accuracy as the budget from the contractor (±5 - 10%).

Based on post-calculations of a project, the investment costs can finally be determined.
The post-calculation can also be used to estimate cost functions for various other design phases.

4.   Operational costs

4.1   Definition of operational costs

The operational costs contain all (integral) costs which are made or will be made to use an object, construction or plant.

These costs are made during (parts of) the operation period of the installation or plant and after completion of the construction.

In water supply companies the operational costs can be presented for different configurations, such as:
- the complete company (conform annual report)
- all production plants together (integral production costs)
- a certain production plant (local production costs)
- the complete distribution network (integral distribution costs)
- a certain part of a distribution area (local distribution costs)
- the complete sales department (sales costs)

When estimating the operational costs of a part of the company, it is necessary that the boundaries of this part be clearly defined and that possible overhead costs be assigned in a reliable way.
The sum of the operational costs of all the different parts eventually has to be equal to the operational costs of the total company.

The operational costs are estimated to calculate the total cost price of the different parts of the company. This is important for the calculation of costs to the buyers, because there are different rates charged, such as to large consumers, for bulk delivery to other water supply companies, or for rate differences per part of the distribution area.

The operational costs will also be calculated when determining various alternatives during the preliminary studies. The operational costs will eventually be calculated back into consumers' rates.

4.2 Uniform structure of operational costs

A uniform and unambiguous concept definition is needed to explain and justify the operational costs.

Various systems are developed, sometimes from the formation of company administrations (annual accounts) but also for specific applications. For buildings in the Netherlands, the presentation of operational costs can be used according to NEN

Table 12 - Definition of operational costs (according to NEN 2632)

Part		Sub part	
1	Fixed costs	a1	Interest
		a2	Replacement reserve (depreciation of actual building costs)
		a3	Ground rent
		a4	Owners part real estate tax
		a5	Assurance costs (fire, glass, etc.)
		a6	Governmental contribution (taxes, levies, etc.)
		c1	Rent
		c2	Loss of rent
		c3	Environmental tax
		c4	Users part real estate tax
2	Consumables	b1	Energy costs (electricity and fuels) (maintain)
		c5	Energy costs (electricity and fuels) (use)
			Water
			Chemicals
			Other consumables (regeneration activated carbon, seeding material, etc.)
			Removal waste products
3	Maintenance costs	b2	Technical maintenance (maintain)
		b3	Cleaning maintenance (maintain)
		c6	Technical maintenance (use)
		c7	Cleaning maintenance (use)
4	Administrative management costs	a7	Accounting costs (property)
		b4	Accounting costs (maintain)
		b5	Rental costs
		b6	Administrative staff costs
		c8	Moving costs
		c9	Mediation costs
		c10	Accounting costs (use)
5	Specific operational costs	a8	Surveillance costs (property)
		b7	Surveillance and security (maintain)
		c11	Surveillance and security (use)
			Operation installations
			Quality monitoring

a – costs related to property ownership
b – costs related to ready-to-use maintenance
c – costs related to partial or complete use

2632: "Working costs of buildings - Terminology and classification."
The classification is given in Table 12. In the table a few typical cost items for drinking water supply are included.

Operational costs are represented annually and, because of the fiscal status of water supply companies, those costs are presented excluding VAT. The operational costs minus the fixed costs are also indicated as variable costs.

Interest and replacement reserves (capital costs)

The costs for interest and replacement reserves are indicated as capital costs. The costs for the interest are the actual paid interest costs for loans, but also the costs when using the equity capital.
The cost for replacement reserves is the depreciation based on the current rebuilding value. This way of depreciating is only used for projects within the company, if the company uses the same form of depreciation, to avoid discrepancies in the cost calculations.
The costs for the acquisition of land are often not depreciated, because land is not consumed and has a relatively fixed value. Sometimes, these acquisition costs are revalued based on current acquisition costs.

The depreciation periods are not equal for the various assets. Therefore, the costs for the replacement reserves are determined separately for similar assets (buildings, machines, distribution network, inventories, etc.)

To determine the capital costs, an economic depreciation period is assumed. The economic depreciation period does not necessarily have to be equal to the technical lifetime of an installation. It might be that the condition of an installation is still technically sufficient, but economical operation is no longer possible due to the superfluousness of the process unit or due to high maintenance costs.

To determine the capital costs, a straight-line depreciation, annuity depreciation, or unitary depreciation can be used. Straight-line depreciation is the most common in concerns; annuity and unitary depreciations are most often used in cost comparisons of alternatives.

Straight-line depreciation

In straight-line depreciation, the same depreciation is taken each year.
The annual depreciation, then, is constant over the depreciation period. Therefore, the remaining sum decreases in a line straight over the depreciation period and so does the interest that has to be paid annually.
The annual capital costs consist of depreciation plus interest.

In year t these amount to:

$$A_t = I \cdot \left(\frac{1}{n} + \frac{n + 1 - t}{n} r \right) = I \cdot a_t$$

in which:

I	=	investment costs	(€)
R	=	interest	(-)
N	=	depreciation period	(y)
A_t	=	capital costs in year t	(€ / y)
T	=	year from beginning (t = 1....n)	(y)
a_t	=	annuity in year t	(y^{-1})

Figure 7 shows this development of the capital costs for a depreciation period of 10 years and an interest rate of 7%. The total paid interest amounts to 39% of the loaned sum (a bit more than 10 times half the interest for the first year).

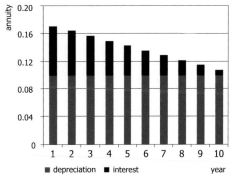

Figure 7 - *Development of depreciation and interest (annuity) with straight-line depreciation (10-year, 7%)*

When the depreciation period is 40 years, then the total paid interest is 144% of the loaned sum (a bit more than 40 times half the interest of the first year).

When the depreciation period is longer, the interest rate has a larger influence on the capital costs. When the depreciation is straight-line, the interest costs are linearly dependent on the interest.

Annuity depreciation

In annuity depreciation the annual capital costs (sum of interest and depreciation) are constant over the depreciation period. This means that in the first few years, the interest share is large and the depreciation share is small.

The depreciation period and the interest rate determine the extent of the annual capital costs, according to the annuity formula:

$$A_t = I \cdot \frac{r \cdot (1 + r)^n}{(1 + r)^n - 1} = I \cdot a_t$$

Figure 8 shows the development of the capital costs for a depreciation period of 10 years and an interest rate of 7%. The total paid interest amounts to 42% of the loaned sum, which is 3% more than with the straight-line depreciation.

When the depreciation period is 40 years, then the total paid interest is 200% of the loaned sum, which is 56% more than with a straight-line depreciation. When the depreciation period is longer, the interest has a bigger influence on the capital costs.

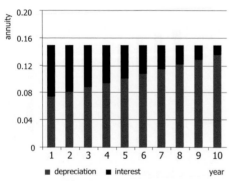

Figure 8 - *Development of depreciation and interest (annuity) with annuity depreciation (10-year, 7%)*

When the depreciation period is 40 years and the interest rate is 3.5%, then the total paid interest would be 87% of the loaned sum.

Unitary depreciation

Unitary depreciation targets a constant cost price of the product over the total depreciation period. Therefore, the expected development in the sales of the product is taken into account.

The development of the capital costs is also dependent on the sales forecast.

When a growth in sales is expected, capital costs over the depreciation period will increase.

Due to delayed repayment, the interest costs will be higher for unitary costs than for annuity depreciation.

Interest

The interest rate is interest paid at the end of each year for the previous year. The discount rate is interest which is paid each year in advance.

To calculate the capital costs, a water company usually works with the average interest of the loan portfolio of the company.

At higher interest rates, investments get more expensive, which makes deliberation of alternatives with relatively lower investment costs more attractive.

Inflation has the opposite effect on this deliberation. Old investments become relatively less expensive because they are repaid when money typically has decreased in value and, therefore, will create a smaller burden.

This combined effect can be taken into account by calculating the investment costs using the net interest rate instead of the raw rate. This is the interest rate (market rate, or average company rate) minus the inflation. When the interest rate is 7% and the inflation rate is 3%, then the net interest rate is 4%.

The net interest rate has been fairly constant the past few years, varying between 2 and 4%, because the interest rate fluctuates with the inflation rate, and the net interest rate actually indicates the real costs of loans or money.

Levies

To the operational costs of a water supply company also belong the various government payments like taxes and levies.

In 2002 the total direct and indirect levies on drinking water in the Netherlands amounted to €0.32 per m^3 (VEWIN- Waterleidingstatistiek). The direct levies (cost price increasing) amounted to €0.14 per m^3 and contained groundwater tax, provincial groundwater levy, and pipeline and concession compensations (precario). The indirect levies amounted to €0.18 per m^3 and contained the tax on tap water and the sales tax (VAT).

An important part of these levies originates from Dutch environmental laws.
Groundwater taxes amount to €0.178 per m^3 of abstracted groundwater and the tax on tap water is €0.136 per m^3 of delivered water, for the first 500 m^3 per connection.

As a result of precario rights, provinces and municipalities are allowed to raise taxes on use by a third party of the space above, on or under the ground (or water) which is reserved for "public service" (a kind of rent). Only a limited number of provinces and municipalities are using this right and, if they do so, large fluctuations in rates (rate for pipes €0.01 - 3.00 per m per year) can exist. For example, the water supply company PWN in Zaanstad has to pay €1.5 million annually to the municipality for the precario tax on their pipes. Of course, these taxes are charged directly to the consumers in this municipality, at €40 per household per year.
In the Netherlands in total, the total precario rights are about €0.01 per m^3 of delivered water.

The provincial groundwater levies are raised for groundwater conservation management. The rates differ per province. In the Netherlands the total provincial groundwater levies are about €0.01 per m^3 of delivered water.

In water companies, received sales taxes (VAT) are deducted from the investments and purchases, and the net amount is remitted to the government.

Private consumers of drinking water pay 6% sales tax as a net expense.

Water companies in the Netherlands are excluded from profit taxes.

Consumables

Consumables are goods which are specifically consumed by the different processes. Also, the replacement of process parts (e.g., UV-lamps, sieves) can be ascribed to this.
The consumables can be divided into the following categories:
- energy (electricity, fuels)
- water
- chemicals (acids, bases, flocculants)
- other consumables (seeding material for pellet reactors, regeneration activated carbon, UV-lamps)
- disposal of waste (sludge, backwash water, pellets)

Consumables do not include general maintenance materials (paint, lubricating oil, tools, etc.). These are included in the maintenance costs.

Energy

The energy costs can be divided into two parts:
- headloss (pressure loss) over the process units (or pressure increase with pumps)
- other energy consumption, specifically for a process unit (UV lamps, saturation in flotation, ozone)

In Table 13 the energy consumption for a few process units is shown conforming to this division.

Table 13 - Specific energy consumption of different treatment processes

Process component	Headloss (Wh / m^3)	Other specific energy consumption (Wh/m^3)
Flocculation	4	20 (mixers)
Flotation	-	50 (saturation)
Degasifying tower	40	40 (RQ = 50)
Filtration	12	-
Softening	20	-
UV disinfection	12	50
Membrane filtration	1,000	-

Chemicals

The cost of chemicals can be globally calculated based on the dosage (mg/l or mmol/l) and the chemical bulk price (cost price equals 100% product per kg or mmol).

The prices for consumables can be very dependent on local circumstances. Of importance, for example, is the size and usage of the goods (bulk transport, quantum discount) and the distance to the production locations (transport costs).

In Table 14 the approximate costs for some frequently used chemicals are shown per unit of dosage.

Other consumables

In a couple of processes it is a question of frequent replacement of process parts to maintain the working of the machine or process. The cost of these consumable goods can be significant. Some typically used consumables for drinking water production are shown below.

Activated carbon has to be regenerated regularly. The annual regeneration volume depends on the load on the carbon, which is expressed in bed volumes (BV). This is the relationship between the treated volume of water (m^3) and the volume of carbon (m^3).

The total cost for this regeneration amounts to approximately €500 per m^3 carbon, which includes emptying, filling, and transport as well as replacement of carbon lost during regeneration.

The cost for new activated carbon is about €800 per m^3 carbon.

Table 14 - Specific chemical costs

Chemical	Dose (unit)	Costs (€ / m^3 per unit dose)
Sulfuric acid	1 mmol / l	0.015
Hydrochloric acid	1 mmol / l	0.015
Caustic soda	1 mmol / l	0.015
Lime	1 mmol / l	0.010
$CaCO_3$	1 mmol / l	0.015
Ferric chloride	1 mg / Fe	0.001
Ferric chloride sulfate	1 mg / Fe	0.0005
PAC	1 mg / l Al	0.001
Cl_2	1 mg / l	0.001
NaOCl	1 mg / l	0.002

In pellet reactors used for softening, seeding material is used, usually about 5% of the total weight of the formed $CaCO_3$.

The cost for this seeding material varies between €150 per ton (sand) and €400 per ton (garnet sand).

The replacement costs for UV-lamps depend on the type of lamp and its lifetime. For high pressure lamps, the replacement cost is about €350 per year per lamp; for low pressure lamps, about €200 per year per lamp.

Maintenance costs

The maintenance costs contain all costs for maintenance, including the repair and replacement of parts of installations within the depreciation period, as far as these are not included in the consumables.

A longer depreciation period often results in the replacement of more parts of the installation within this period and, thus, higher maintenance costs.

The maintenance costs per year are often estimated as a percentage of the construction costs. The civil, mechanical and electrical parts require maintenance to different degrees, therefore, different percentages are used. For the specific parts the percentage has to be estimated as accurately as possible together with the depreciation period.

Generally, the following average percentages for structures and installation costs are used to determine the annual maintenance costs for the total treatment plant:

- civil structures   0.5%
- mechanical installations   2%
- electrical installations   4%
- furnishings   10%

Administrative management costs

The administrative management costs refer exclusively to those costs for the administration (i.e., management) of the installation.

Administrative management costs include:

- costs for the administrative staff
- accounting

Estimating operational costs

A surface water treatment plant of 20 million m³/y (design capacity 3,200 m³/h) exists for several processes, like in the previous example.
The operational parameters are given below.

Process unit				
Flocculation	Energy	24 Wh / m³	Dosing Fe	5 mg / l
Flotation	Energy	50 Wh / m³	Suspended solids (sludge)	20 mg / l
Filtration	Energy	12 Wh / m³	Suspended solids (sludge)	5 mg / l
Activated carbon filtration	Energy	8 Wh / m³	Regeneration	15,000 BV
Clear water storage				
Clear water pumping station	Energy	200 Wh / m³		

Based on this, operational costs (sketch design phase) can be estimated as given below.

Process unit	Total	Fixed costs	Consumables	Maintenance	Specific operational costs	Administrative costs
	(€ / m³)	(€ / m³)	(€ / m³)	(€ / m³)	(€ / m³)	(€ / m³)
Flocculation	0.047	0.017	0.017	0.002	0.006	0.005
Flotation	0.053	0.022	0.017	0.002	0.008	0.005
Filtration	0.088	0.046	0.004	0.006	0.018	0.009
Activated carbon filtration	0.116	0.051	0.030	0.005	0.018	0.010
Clear water storage	0.039	0.025	0.000	0.001	0.010	0.003
Clear water pumping station	0.108	0.058	0.012	0.007	0.020	0.010
Total	0.446	0.220	0.081	0.024	0.081	0.042

- costs for the main office (as far it can be charged to the concerned plant)

Administrative management costs depend on the organization of the company. For estimations, usually 10 - 15% of the remaining operational costs can be used.

Specific operational costs

The specific operational costs in the operation of a treatment plant consist of:
- operating costs:
  - staff costs
  - other costs (including facilities for staff);
- quality monitoring costs:
  - laboratory costs
  - optimization research

Specific operational costs are related to staff size and specific analysis costs.
For an estimate it can be assumed that the percentage of the investment costs (land acquisition costs excluded) is 2% for operation and 2% for quality monitoring.

5.   Cost comparison of alternatives

When a production plant is designed, in most cases, choices have to be made between various alternatives.
The alternatives can differ from each other in the process units, the chemical and energy consumption, maintenance, etc.
Often, alternative choices occur when the investments aren't completely handled at the beginning of the project, but are spread over time (building in stages).
To compare the alternatives unambiguously with each other, it is necessary to have a comparison standard.
In principle two approaches are available:
- comparison of the net present value of investments and operational costs
- comparison of the integral cost price

By using these methods, the alternative investments, together with the accompanying annual operational costs, can be financially and correctly compared with each other.

Net present value

The net present value is the sum that should be paid at the beginning of the project (or operation time) when all costs would have to be paid all at once.

Money that hasn't been spent will bring in interest.

The net present value (at point of time t = 0) of an investment I, at time t can be calculated with:

$$NPV = \frac{I}{(1 + r)^t}$$

in which:

NPV = net present value   (€)
t   = time between moment of investment
         and moment of comparison   (y)

For a plant to be built in the future, it must be remembered that the proposed investment increases in price, because of general money devaluation (inflation).

Taking this into account, the net present value can be calculated with:

$$NPV = I \cdot \frac{(1 + i)^t}{(1 + r)^t}$$

in which:

i = inflation correction   (-)

The formula mentioned above can be approximately rewritten into:

$$NPV = \frac{I}{(1 + (r - i))^t}$$

in which:

r – i = real interest rate   (-)

Integral cost price

In the integral cost price calculation, the costs per product are used for deliberation.

In principle, the same rules apply as discussed under the net present value, such as interest costs, inflation, etc. Only now, the comparison does not aim at an imaginary quantity (NPV), but at the cost to the consumer, which is a more appealing quantity.

In this method (theoretically) the development of the incomes (sales) also has to be taken into

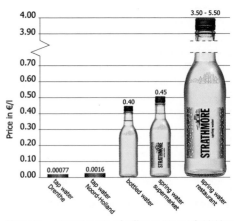

Figure 9   - Integral costs of different types of drinking water

account. Often, calculation of the cost price in the first year is sufficient. The operational costs of the first year are divided by the sales of the first year.

For more or less constant sales, such a simplification is accurate enough to be used for the comparison of alternatives.

Figure 9 gives an example of the eloquence of the concept "integral cost price."

Project horizon and depreciation period

When determining the investments, attention should also be given to the horizon of the project (the time period which is considered in the comparison, typically 30 - 40 years) in relation to the depreciation period (or technical lifetime) of process parts.

When the considered horizon is 30 years and a project is evaluated in which the depreciation period for the buildings is 30 years and the machines are depreciated (replaced) in 10 years, then, for the net present value determination, a reinvestment of the machines after 10 years and after 20 years should be taken into account.

5.1   Comparison of investment costs with phased building

With an increasing demand for water, the capacity of a new production plant could also be realized in stages.

As an example of this, two alternative investment possibilities for the same project are considered. In alternative 1 an investment of I takes place at t=0. In alternative 2 an investment of I1 takes place at t=0 and an investment of I2 after t years.

A postponed investment is of interest if, based on the net present value, an advantage is achieved:

$$I_1 + I_2 \cdot \frac{(1 + i)^t}{(1 + r)^t} < I$$

Assume that a onetime investment of €100 million can be replaced for an initial investment of €60 million, followed by an investment of €50 million after 7 years, in which the operational costs for both alternatives are presumed equal. Both investments together are €110 million, which is 10% more than the onetime investment.

The net present value of the second investment after 7 years is €36 million with an interest rate of 8%, the total net present value of both investments amounts to (60 + 36 =) €96 million.

This is less than the onetime investment of €100 million, so this makes building in stages financially attractive.

With a postponed investment, there is a better connection with the treatment vision at that moment. An extra advantage could be seen if the drinking water consumption does not increase as much as expected, which might extend the period beyond 7 years.

Likewise, there are, of course, all sorts of considerations against investing in stages, like an extra disturbance of the operation, an extra building stage with related attention, etc.

5.2 Comparison of investment and operational costs

Besides estimating the net present value of the investment costs, operational costs should also be taken into account.

How to include this is illustrated below using an example with two alternatives.

Alternative 1 is a project with low investment costs (€60 million) and high operational costs (€7.55 million per year).

Alternative 2 is a project with high investment costs (€100 million) and low operational costs (€4.00 million per year).

Furthermore, it is assumed that the operational costs of both projects are constant during their technical lifetime.

With an annuity of 0.089 (interest rate at 8%, depreciation period 30 years), the yearly capital costs of the projects are €5.34 million and €8.89 million, respectively. This makes the total annual costs for both alternatives (capital and operational) equal (7.55 + 5.34 = 4.00 + 8.89).

Based on this relationship, the conclusion could be drawn that the alternatives are comparable on a financial basis. However, this is not the case, since the above-mentioned comparison is, in fact, one formulated for the first year of operation (t=1). In time, the variable costs will increase, more or less correlated to inflation. This means that, in time, the variable costs will have a more important share in the total annual costs. This can be taken into account now by correcting the variable costs with the inflation percentage and by making all amounts constant to t=0.

Using a formula, the annual variable costs can be made constant as follows:

$$NPV_{Et} = E_{t=0} \cdot \frac{(1 + i)^t}{(1 + r)^t} = E_{t=0} \cdot \frac{1}{(1 + r - i)^t}$$

in which:

NPV_{Et} = net present value of the variable costs in year t

$E_{t=0}$ = variable costs in year t=0

After summing all variable costs over the lifetime of the project, the total net present value is as follows:

$$NPV_E = \sum_{t=0}^{t=n} \left(E_t \cdot \frac{(1 + i)^t}{(1 + r)^t} \right)$$

in which:

NPV_E = net present value of all variable costs over the lifetime of the project

With a 30-year project lifetime, and a real interest rate of 5% (interest 8% and inflation 3%), the total net present value of alternative 1 is €175 million and of alternative 2 is €160 million.

In general, this means that with a conventional comparison of alternatives, the influence of the variable costs is underestimated. From this example, it is clear that the alternative with the higher investment costs is eventually the most economical solution.

When comparing alternatives, inflation should always be taken into account.

This can usually be achieved simply by calculating with real interest figures instead of the interest on the capital market or the average interest of the company loans.

Further reading

Financial concepts and information

- Handbuch der Wasserversorgungstechnik, Grombach/Haberer/Trueb, R. Oldenbourg Verlag (1985)
- Kostenaspecten in planningsmodellen voor de drinkwatervoorziening, Koster, RIVM, H2O 15 (1985)
- Standaardisatie van kosten, DHV Water (1998)
- Investeringskosten van gebouwen, begripsomschrijvingen en indeling, NEN 2631 (1979)
- Exploitatiekosten van gebouwen, NEN 2632 (1980)

- www.worldbank.org/watsan
- www.worldbank.org/watsan/bnwp
- www.adb.org/water
- www.irc.nl

Financial information on water companies

- Waterleidingstatistiek, VEWIN (annual reports)
- Water companies (annual reports)

- www.vewin.nl
- www.ofwat.gov.uk

Questions and applications

Water company as an enterprise

1. What is the content of a financial annual report?

2. Indicate which of the following items belong to the assets and which to the liabilities of a balance sheet.
   a - Contributions for new connections
   b - Realized revaluation reserve
   c - Liquid assets
   d - Loans due banks
   e - Debtors
   f - Provisions
   g - Advance payments for water
   h - Long-term debts
   i - Buildings and land
   j - Provisions
   k - Fixed company assets under construction
   l - Accrued expenses
   m - Issued shares

3. What effects arise for the interest costs and the capital costs if the investment costs are straight-line depreciated?

4. For the items below on a profit and loss account indicate if they belong to the revenues or expenses of a water company:
   a - Standing charge fire hydrants
   b - Materials
   c - Purchase of drinking water
   d - Sales to small users
   e - Third party work
   f - Staff
   g - Capitalized production
   h - Interest
   i - Depreciations

Investment costs

1. To which four groups can the investment costs be divided according to NEN 2631?

2. What can be done to compare production plants with different treatment schemes? How can investment costs be determined?

3. For the capacity in the costs function for different purposes also different quantities can be used. What are these? Explain them.

Operational costs

1. For water companies, the operational costs can be represented for different company parts. Which?

2. Indicate in which 5 groups the operational costs are divided according to NEN 2632.

3. Explain the difference between straight-line depreciation and annuity depreciation.

4. What is meant by consumables? Give some examples.

5. Out of which parts consist the specific operational costs in the operation of a treatment plant.

Cost comparison of alternatives

1. When developing a production plant - in most cases - choices have to be made. The alternatives can differ from each other in the process units, the chemical and energy consumption, the maintenance, etc. Also, alternatives come up in which the investments are not completely made in the beginning of the project, but spread over time (phased building). How can you compare these alternatives in an unambiguous way?

2. Explain the term "net present value."

Applications

1. A water company is a monopoly within the distribution area assigned by the government. Give a couple of arguments for an assigned monopoly.

2. Surface water companies are considerably more expensive than groundwater companies, caused by the more expensive infrastructure required (more complex production and at a greater distance from the consumers). Explain what else can cause the rate differences.

Answers

Water company as an enterprise

1. A financial annual report consists of a balance sheet (list of possessions and debts at the end of the financial year) and a profit and loss account (list of revenues and expenses during the financial year).

2. Assets: c, e, f, l, k
   Liabilities: a, b, d, g, h, j, l, m.

3. The interest costs of a company are high in the beginning and will decrease to zero at the end of the depreciation period. The capital costs (interest and depreciation) for such a company are, therefore, not even over the depreciation period.

4. Revenues: a, d, g
   Expenses: b, c, e, f, h, i

Investment costs

1. - land costs
   - construction costs
   - equipment costs
   - additional costs

2. To compare production plants with different treatment schemes, investment functions per treatment process can be formulated. By adding the costs of the different processes, the investment costs can be determined.

3. The annual capacity is a suitable parameter for initial cost estimations. The maximum hour capacity of a process part is suitable if the concerned process part has hardly any differences in design load, and, therefore, the size has a fixed relation with the capacity.
   The specific size of a process part will give the most reliable cost function.
   The cost function for rapid sand filters will have the filter surface as its capacity parameter.
   For flocculation the total volume will be used as the capacity parameter.

Operational costs

1. For water companies, the operational costs for the different company parts can be indicated, such as:
   - complete company (annual report)
   - all production plants together (integral production costs)
   - a certain production plant (local production costs)
   - the complete distribution network (integral distribution costs)
   - a certain part of a distribution area (local distribution costs)
   - the complete sales department (sales costs)

2. - fixed costs
   - consumables
   - maintenance costs
   - administrative management costs
   - specific operational costs

3. Straight-line depreciation:
   In straight-line depreciation, every year the same depreciation takes place. Because of this, a linear decrease in the remaining amount takes place over the depreciation period and so does the interest that has to be paid annually.

   Annuity depreciation:
   In annuity depreciation the annual capital costs (sum of interest and depreciation) are constant over the depreciation period. This means that in the early years the interest share is large and the depreciation share is small.

4. Consumables are the costs for consumer goods like energy and chemicals. The replacements of process parts (for example, UV-lamps, sieves) can also be included here.

The consumables costs can be divided into:
- energy (electricity, fuels)
- water
- chemicals (acids, bases, flocculants)
- other consumables (seeding material for pellet reactors, regeneration and supplementation activated carbon, UV-lamps)
- disposal of waste (sludge, backwash water, pellets)

Consumables do not include general maintenance materials (paint, lubricating oil, tools, etc.). These are included in the maintenance costs.

5. The specific operational costs in the operation of a treatment plant consist of:
- operating costs:
  - staff costs
  - other costs (among other things, facilities for staff)
- quality monitoring costs:
  - laboratory costs
  - optimization research

Cost comparison of alternatives

1. To compare these alternatives, two methods of approach can be used:
- comparison of the net present value of investments and operational costs
- comparison of the integral cost price

2. The net present value is the sum that should be paid at the beginning of the project (or operation time) when all costs would have to be paid all at once. It takes into account the fact that money that hasn't been spent will bring in interest. For a future construction, it has to be taken into account that the required investment in the future will be higher because of the general money devaluation (inflation).

Applications

1. Arguments for an assigned monopoly are:
- distribution of water determines the price to such an extent that it is never economically attractive to have more suppliers
- the quality and availability of drinking water is of such social importance that it should not be under pressure by companies' economic considerations
- drinking water supply does not qualify for operation by different companies, because this will make quality responsibilities and delivery guarantees very unclear. This is the reason why the government's pursuits of a quality guarantee (always safe and healthy) and a quantity assurance (always in the demanded quantities under sufficient pressure) is, best served by one single company from the source to the tap

2. Rate differences can be explained by differences in:
- age of the infrastructure (capital costs)
- performance on the capital market
- equity capital
- size of the distribution area
- utilization of infrastructure
- staff productivity
- rate policy

Water consumption

TECHNICAL FACETS

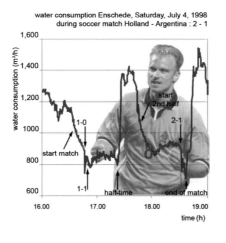

water consumption Enschede, Saturday, July 4, 1998
during soccer match Holland - Argentina : 2 - 1

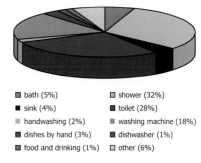

- bath (5%)
- sink (4%)
- handwashing (2%)
- dishes by hand (3%)
- food and drinking (1%)
- shower (32%)
- toilet (28%)
- washing machine (18%)
- dishwasher (1%)
- other (6%)

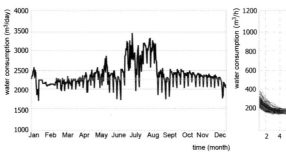

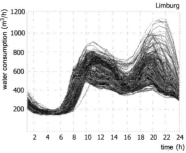

Framework

This module covers the water consumption by households, industries and others. It concerns the supply of water by water companies, as well as the production of water by industries. Water consumption for agricultural purposes (irrigation, etc.) will not be discussed.

Contents

This module has the following contents:

Study goals

After having studied this module you will be able to:
- explain what the terms annual consumption, specific consumption, consumption categories, fluctuation patterns (year, week, day) and peak factors mean
- calculate the consumption of cooling water (from heat discharge and concentration factor)
- calculate overall water consumption (from the specific water consumption)
- explain quality requirements for the different types of consumption
- make consumption forecasts in order to plan new infrastructures
- calculate future water consumption (from extrapolations)

1. Introduction

Water is used for various purposes.
As part of the hydrologic water cycle, water is used for:
- pushing back salt intrusion at river mouths
- replenishing ground- and surface water for water level control (because of "consumption" by evaporation, irrigation, etc.)
- flushing waterways (canals, etc.) for quality control

Water, from the hydrologic water cycle, is also used for household and industrial activities. A few examples of these are water abstraction for:
- public water supplies for domestic use and for the industrial sector (water companies)
- private water supplies (private abstraction by the industrial, agricultural, and horticultural sectors and electricity companies)

In this module the consumption of water will be given a closer look, with the exception of the private abstraction by agriculture and horticulture. This exception is made because of the unusual character of this sector, such as the specific relationship between water consumption and the type of plant or crop, as a result of different climatological circumstances, and specific horticultural needs.

In this module no difference is made between the terms "water usage" and "water consumption." Water is actually never entirely consumed; therefore, under the term "consumption" it is understood to mean the amount of water supplied to a user. The term "consumption" could be applied to situations whereby the quality of the water has been changed to such a degree that the water no longer can be used for the intended purpose. This does not eliminate the fact that the water is suitable for other applications, and therefore, seen from the viewpoint of the hydrologic water cycle, has not been consumed.

Water consumption is defined as a volume per unit of time (m^3/s). This consumption has a significant fluctuation, seen over time. For practical reasons water consumption is considered over an entire year (m^3/y). Sometimes, this is calculated back to consumption per day. In such a case, one speaks of the average consumption per day.
Water consumption is treated in the following subdivisions:
- Annual consumption (with terms such as specific consumption and level of consumption)
- Quality requirements for different uses
- Fluctuations in consumption (with terms such as consumption patterns and peak factors)
- Consumption forecasts in order to plan new infrastructures (with terms such as extrapolation, and unforeseen changes in consumption)

2. Annual consumption

2.1 Water consumption in the Netherlands

In the Netherlands almost 10 billion m^3 of water are consumed yearly (CBS 1996), not including private abstraction by the agricultural and horticultural sectors (Table 1).

Power stations are the largest water consumers (63% of the total consumption). This water is used

Table 1 - Water consumption in the Netherlands (private abstraction by agricultural and horticultural sector not included) (CBS 1996)

	Consumption (mln m³/y)	Percentage (%)	Percentage cooling water (% of consumption)
Power stations	6,199	63	99.5
Industry, refineries and mining	2,529	26	83.2
Households	733	7	-
Small companies and organizations	297	3	-
Water companies	52	1	-
Total water consumption	9,810	100	84.3

Specific water consumption

Specific water consumption = water consumption per characteristic unit
The term "specific water consumption" is used to be able to determine water consumption under other circumstances, or to compare the consumption of different users.

The consumption per capita is a form of specific water consumption. In 1996 the Netherlands had 15.5 million inhabitants.
Thus, the total consumption per capita was
9,810 / 15.5 = 633 m³/p/y
This is equal to 1,730 l/p/d

The household consumption per capita was
733 / 15.5 / 365 • 1.000 = 130 l/p/d

Only 2 - 3 l/p/d was used as drinking water.

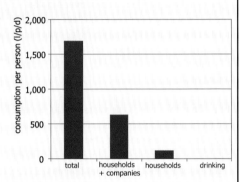

The specific water consumption in the industrial sector is equal to the consumption per produced amount.

In the following table there are a few examples of specific water consumption in the industrial sector.

Industry	Specific unit	Specific water consumption
Paper industry	Per ton paper	15 - 40 m³ / ton paper
Steel mills	Per ton steel	4 - 20 m³/ ton steel
Brewery	Per liter beer	5 - 15 l / l beer
Drinking water companies	Per m³ produced water	1.05 - 1.10 m³ / m³ water

For a good comparison of the data between different industries, the specific water consumption must be subdivided into cooling water, process-related water and non-process-related water.
Moreover, for a clear analysis of the industrial consumption, different specific units will be necessary. For example, the cooling water is determined per consumed amount of energy, the sanitary water and water for climate control as consumption per staff member.

---

almost entirely for cooling (99.5%) by way of their own abstraction of surface water.
Also, industry is a considerable water consumer (26% of the total consumption). A large part of this water, which is mainly abstracted from surface water, is used as cooling water (83.2%) as well.
Households in the Netherlands consume approximately 730 million m³ of water per year. Small companies and organizations consume, in total, approximately 300 million m³ per year. Water consumed by households and small companies is almost entirely produced by water companies.

These water companies also use water themselves during the production process. Losses during distribution are attributed to the consumers.

2.2 Power stations

In 1996 Dutch power plants generated, in total, 211 PJ (58.6 10⁹ kWh) electricity, with an efficiency of 42% (Table 2).
Almost 90% of the residual heat is given off via cooling water. The rest of the heat is dissipated by way of chimneys or given off as radiating heat. The cooling water is withdrawn from rivers, canals or lakes.

Table 2   - Heat balance of the collective Dutch electric
              companies (CBS 1996)

	Energy (PJ = 10^{15} J)
Fuel consumption	504
Electricity production	211
Residual heat	293
Heat discharge by cooling water	263

In 1996, in the Netherlands, a total of 6,200 million m^3 of water was used to discharge 263 PJ of heat.
Per m^3 of water, a total of ($263 \cdot 10^{15}$ / 6,200 $\cdot 10^6$ =) 42 MJ of energy is absorbed.
The specific heat of water is 4.2 MJ/m^3/°C (1 cal/g/°C), as a result of which the average warming of the cooling water amounts to (42 / 4.2 =) 10°C.
The specific water consumption by the power stations in the same year amounted to (6,200·10^6 / 211·10^{15} =) 29 m^3/GJ.

Figure 1 shows that energy production in the Netherlands has definitely increased in the period between 1962 and 1981. The consumption of cooling water made a much smaller increase, as a result of an increase in efficiency in the production of electricity (from 31 to 38%).
As a result of a further increase in the efficiency (42% in 1996) and an increase in water temperature (from 7.0 to 10.2°C), the consumption of cooling water by power stations at the same energy production has decreased considerably over the past 20 years.

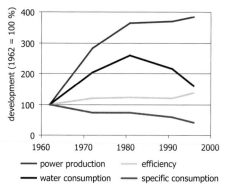

Figure 1   - Development in water consumption of the
              Dutch electric companies

2.3   Cooling water

Calculation for consumption of cooling water (once-through cooling)

For the energy content of the cooling water, the following formula applies:

$$E_c = V \cdot \Delta T \cdot S_h$$

with:

E_c =	energy content cooling water	(J)
V =	volume of water	(m^3)
ΔT =	temperature increase of water	(°C)
S_h =	specific heat	(J/m^3/°C)
	for water: $S_h = 4.2 \cdot 10^6$	(J/m^3/°C)

The amount of energy to be discharged can be calculated by:

$$E_d = E_i - E_p = \left(\frac{1}{\eta}-1\right) \cdot E_p$$

and

$$E_c = \beta \cdot E_d$$

where:

E_d =	energy to be discharged (heat)	(J)
E_i =	imported energy (fuel)	(J)
E_p =	produced energy (electricity)	(J)
η =	production efficiency (= E_i/E_p)	(-)
β =	portion cooling water in energy discharge	(-)

The specific water consumption of power stations (m^3 per produced amount of energy) can be calculated by:

$$\frac{V}{E_p} = \beta \cdot \frac{\left(\frac{1}{\eta} - 1\right)}{\Delta T \cdot S_h}$$

The specific water consumption proves to be highly dependent on the efficiency of the electricity production and on the acceptable temperature increase (Figure 2).

Reduction of cooling water consumption

There are a number of ways to reduce the specific cooling water consumption. Table 3 gives these possibilities. In practice the change from once-

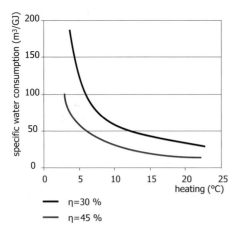

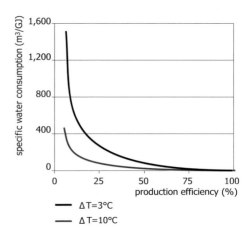

Figure 2   - Specific water consumption of power stations (m³/GJ) as a function of efficiency (η) and temperature increase (ΔT)

through cooling to (open) recirculation cooling is the most effective method for saving water.

Cooling water consumption with open recirculation cooling

The most striking element of open recirculation cooling is the cooling tower. Cooling takes place because water evaporates. The heat produced by the evaporation of water is much higher than heat absorption by a temperature increase. The specific heat of water is 4.2 J/g/°C. If the temperature increases by 10°C, the heat content becomes 42 J/g. The evaporation heat of water is 2,500 J/g, which is a factor of 60 higher. If water consumption with open recirculation cooling is compared with once-through cooling, the following theoretical formula is used:

$$\frac{Q_{circulation}}{Q_{once-through}} = \frac{42}{2,500} = \frac{1}{60} = 1.7\%$$

In this formula the temperature increase is ignored.

In practice this savings is not entirely realized. In open recirculation cooling, evaporation takes place, which results in an increase in the concentration of dissolved substances. This concentration increase results in precipitation of non-soluble salts (scaling) and leads to the dissolving of metals (corrosion). In order to limit this concentration increase, it is necessary to remove dissolved salts by discharging the concentrated water and replenishing it with water of a lower salinity.

For open recirculation cooling there is a recirculation flow approximately equal to the water consumption of the once-through cooling. An equal temperature increase (ΔT) and similar conditions for the heat exchangers in the plant or factory are obtained.

Table 3   - Possibilities for reduction in cooling water consumption

Possibility	Remark
Higher temperature increase	Potential environmental problem
	Temperature increase ΔT_{max} in cooling water is restricted by law to 7°C with reference to 'thermoshock cooling water'
	Temperature increase ΔT_{max} in the receiving water is generally 3°C with reference to protection of the eco-system
Higher energy efficiency	Combined heat and power processes (cogeneration)
Reuse	A higher temperature is no problem for many applications
Open recirculation cooling	The high evaporating value of water can be used
Closed recirculation cooling	Cooling by air (radiator in cars, freon evaporators in refrigerators)

Calculation of cooling water consumption (open recirculation cooling)

Figure 3 shows that for a closed water cycle the amount of added water (make up) must be equal to the amount of evaporated water plus the amount which is discharged (blow down).

For water and salt a mass balance can be made up:

$$in = out$$
$$Q_{in} = Q_{blow\ down} + Q_{evaporation}$$
$$c_{in} \cdot Q_{in} = c_{out} \cdot Q_{blow\ down}$$

where:
Q = the amount of water   (m³)
c = salt concentration   (g/m³)

The cooling water consumption or replenishment, is then:

$$Q_{in} = \frac{J}{J-1}\ Q_{evaporation}$$

where:
J = concentration factor   (-)
J = $c_{out}\ /\ c_{in} = Q_{in}\ /\ Q_{blow\ down}$ (-)
$Q_{evaporation}$ = $\beta \cdot E_a\ /\ (\ 2,500 \cdot 10^6\ )$ (m³)

From the formula it is clear that water consumption has a significant dependence on the concentration factor. The higher the concentration, the greater the water consumption.

During the last few years, better inhibitors and process control systems have been used. Because of these it has become possible to increase the value of the concentration factor from the earlier value of 1.5 - 2.0 to 2.5 - 3.0.

The corresponding decrease in water consumption is desirable because water is becoming more expensive and because a smaller discharge of water results in a reduction of chemicals.
It is now more difficult to reuse the discharged water because of the chemicals (inhibitors) and the higher salt concentrations.

Water consumption within the industry is mainly dependent on the method used for cooling. If water consumption during open recirculation cooling is compared with that of once-through cooling, then, in practice, the following applies (concentration factor 1.5 to 3.0).

$$\frac{Q_{circulation}}{Q_{once-through}} = (\ 1.5/0.5\ to\ 3/2\ ) \cdot 1.7\% = 5.1\ to\ 2.6\%$$

2.4   Industry

In 1996 the total water consumption in Dutch industries, refineries and mining was 2,529 million m³/year (CBS 1996). The water was mainly used for cooling water, and also partly for process water.

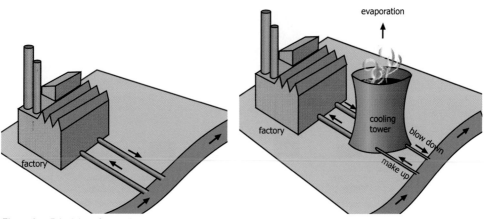

Figure 3   - Principles of once-through cooling and open recirculation cooling

The cooling water consumption is largely covered by private abstraction of surface water, while process water comes from private abstraction or from the water companies.

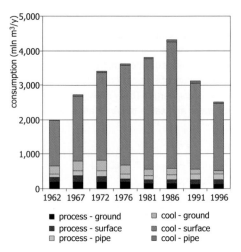

Figure 4 shows the industrial water consumption per sector, as well as what it is used for.
Water consumption within the industry increased considerably between 1962 and 1986 (Figure 5). In 1986 a decrease began and a 42% reduction in consumption was realized within a period of 10 years.This reduction is a result of the more efficient consumption of energy and a more efficient cooling system. This resulted also in the reduction of the number of permits for private abstraction of groundwater to be used as cooling water.

Industrial water has different typical uses. The largest use is for cooling water. Other uses for process water (or process-related water) that can be differentiated are:
- "real" process water
- boiler feed water
- washing and rinsing water

"Real" process water is directly used in the process, boiler feed water is used for steam production, and washing and rinsing water is used for buildings, process installations and bottles.

Figure 5   - Development of industrial water consumption (mln m³/y)

Besides cooling water and process-related water, there is also non-process-related water.
This water is used for:
- sanitary purposes
- climate control (air conditioning, etc.)
- fire protection (including practice/training, etc.)

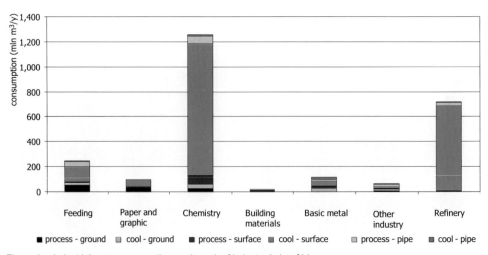

Figure 4   - Industrial water consumption per branch of industry (mln m³/y)

Table 4   - Water supply by drinking water companies (VEWIN 2000)

Kind of water	Own pro- duction	Mutual exchange	Supplied to dis- tribution network	
	(mln m³/y)	(mln m³/y)	(mln m³/y)	(%)
Drinking water	1,183	4	1,187	93
Other water	78	7	85	7
Total	1,261	11	1,272	100

2.5   Water companies

Total supply

In the year 2000 a total of 1,272 million m³ of water was supplied to the distribution network by the Dutch water supply companies (VEWIN 2000).Of this, 93% was drinking water and 7% other water, which was primarily used by the industrial sector.

Seen in Table 4, the amount supplied to the network was not exactly equal to the amount consumed by the users. During the distribution, losses occurred. The amount that is delivered to the network is equal to the company's own production plus the mutual supplies (to/from other water companies).

The amount of water supplied to the network is used as a specific term, because it is easy to measure (water meters). Moreover, it is a useful term that is easily used for planning by water companies. Consumers consider water to have been "supplied" only after it has passed their own meter. The difference between supply to the consumer and supply to the water network can lead to confusion.

Figure 6 shows the historical development of water production (supply to the network) by Dutch water companies.
Up until 1960 the increase in consumption was mainly caused by growth in the population and an increase in the degree of supply (percentage of connected plots).

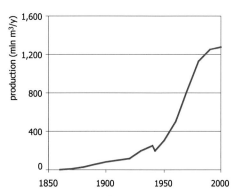

Figure 6   - Production of the drinking water companies (mln m³/y)

In addition to that, the consumption has increased because of a growing water civilization (showering, washing, watering the garden).
Yet, from about 1990 a stagnation in consumption has been visible, which can be explained by the public's awareness of water saving.

Supply by consumer category

For the sake of statistics, consumers of water are annually classified into specific consumer categories on the basis of the amount of water used. Subdivisions are made such that these correspond, more or less, to typical consumer groups. A consumer category can be better defined than a consumer group because of administrative errors (moving, change in connection, distinctions between heavy industry and small companies, etc.).

Table 5 shows the different consumer categories, as well as the typical consumer groups with which they can be associated. The "unbilled consumption" is the difference between that which is supplied to the network and the total amount which is paid for.

Table 5   - Supply of drinking water (VEWIN 2000)

Consumption category (m³/y per connection)	Consumer group	Total consumption (mln m³/y)	(%)	Consumption per person (l/p/d)
< 300	Households	741	63	128
≥ 300 and < 10,000	Small business	214	18	37
≥ 10,000	Industry	172	14	30
Unaccounted for		60	5	9
Supplied to the distribution network		1,187	100	204

Water companies without separate water meters for small consumers (households) cannot determine the unbilled consumption separately and generally include this in the total consumption. For larger consumers, these water companies install water meters.

The unaccounted for is not equal to the "leakage loss," because consumption for firefighting and for cleaning the network (flushing) is not counted as leakage losses.

Households

Households are water companies' largest consumers with approximately 740 million m³/y. The average consumption per person within the household is 128 l/p/d. (with 15.8 million inhabitants in the Netherlands).

Figure 7 shows how the consumption of water is divided.
Almost 50% of the water is used for activities for which a very good quality is required to avoid direct

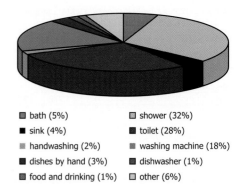

■ bath (5%)	□ shower (32%)
■ sink (4%)	■ toilet (28%)
■ handwashing (2%)	■ washing machine (18%)
■ dishes by hand (3%)	■ dishwasher (1%)
■ food and drinking (1%)	□ other (6%)

Figure 7 - Average household drinking water consumption (VEWIN 2000)

health risks, with taking a shower being the most used (32% of total). For flushing the toilet (28%) and washing machines (18%), a less strict quality is sufficient (household water).

Figure 8 shows that the average consumption per person in households increased between 1970 and 1990. Some of the reasons are the increased

---

Balance terms at water companies

Loss of water occurs during abstraction, production, distribution and supply.

In the following table the losses are shown, as well as typical causes:

Segment	Loss (% of input)	Cause
Abstraction	0 - 1	Flushing, regenerating
Production	4 - 5	Backwash water, concentrate, settling in, cleaning
Distribution	4 - 5	Leakage, measure differences, flushing, firefighting
Delivery	0 - 10	Leaking taps, bursting of frozen pipes

To calculate the total loss, an average loss per segment can be used (for example, during abstraction a loss of 0.5% = 0.005). Then, the remaining amount can be determined (for abstraction 1 - 0.005 = 0.995 · the amount received).

With the losses shown in the table, the following can be calculated:
withdrawal during abstraction = 1 / (0.995·0.955·0.955·0.95) = 1.16 · supplied amount
In order to supply a certain amount of water, 1.16 times that amount must, therefore, be abstracted.

For balance considerations of the distribution network, one must remember that the supplied amount is, in fact, calculated.The payment of water is based on the amount that is read off the consumers' water meters. But, this reading is only done once a year and, based on this, the water consumption per user over the year (Jan. 1 - Dec. 31) is calculated.

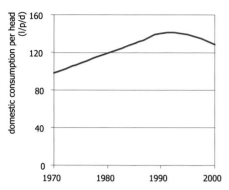

Figure 8   - Trend in water consumption per person for households (l/p/d)

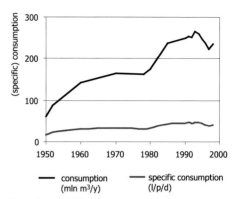

Figure 9   - Trend in water consumption for small business (mln m³/y and l/p/d)

standard of living (larger houses with gardens), but especially because of the increased "water civilization." People started taking showers more often and showered longer; the number of washing machines and dishwashers increased, resulting in more being washed; and, people started watering their gardens more often and for longer periods.

From 1990, consumption per person decreased as a result of large-scale campaigns for water saving. This resulted in the consumer becoming more aware of the environmental influences of water consumption (dessication, consumption of chemicals, electricity, and the production of sludge). Also, the higher price of water, due to the eco-tax, contributed to this savings.

Small business consumers
Small business water consumption can also be indicated as "consumption for commerce, services and government" (CSG) or "consumption for commercial, public, agricultural and recreational reasons" (CPAR).
The small business water consumption is about 210 million m³/y.

In Figure 9 the development of water consumption by small businesses is plotted.
The increase up until 1990 was caused by an increase in consumption for agriculture and horticulture, and by the decrease in large business consumption (classification in another category).

The decrease after 1990 can be explained by water-saving measures, motivated by an increased environmental awareness and the increasing costs.

Per type of company, there are large differences in water consumption. Even similar companies show large differences. In order to be able to compare the different consumers, and to be able to follow the developments, estimates have been prepared for specific consumption by different types of companies.

Industry
The industrial sector consumes approximately 170 million m³ of water per year. This water is used as a supplement to the sector's own abstraction of groundwater and is used where higher quality water is needed, such as for process water and sanitation.
Figure 10 shows the development of drinking water consumption for the industrial sector.
The increase in consumption up until 1990 can be explained by the growth of the industrial sector. It must be pointed out, however, that the increase in consumption was smaller than the increase in production. The decrease after 1990 is again the result of water saving, motivated by environmental issues and increases in the costs.

"Other water"
Water companies supply other types of water besides drinking water. This "other water" is separated from the drinking water by means of a second

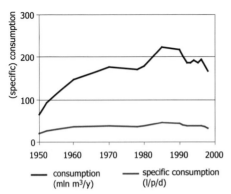

Figure 10 - Trend in reduction of drinking water consumption by the industry (mln m³/y and l/p/d))

network. The costs of construction and operation of a second network are so high that it is only profitable in certain situations to supply other water besides drinking water.

Two examples of other types of water are household water and industrial water.

The idea behind providing household water is that it is wasteful to flush the toilet with expensive drinking water. Is it not possible to use water of a lesser quality, as a result of which costs for treatment can be saved, or an inferior source can be used (surface water instead of groundwater)? With this in mind, in the Netherlands in previous

Figure 11 - Industry water project at Cerestar (Zeeland) with demineralized water from wastewater

years, a number of projects with a dual network for household water and drinking water were undertaken. They proved that the costs of such projects are too high and that contamination of drinking water, because of cross connections, can create large risks.

The total amount of household water in the Netherlands is, consequently, negligible (<0.1 million m³/y).

This certainly does not apply to the amount of industrial other water. The supply of this type of water has steadily increased over the last few years to 85 million m³/y (as of 2000). An industrial water project is frequently profitable because there is a large consumption at one location. The costs of constructing an extra pipeline (network) can, therefore, more easily be earned back by the savings on the costs of the drinking water infrastructure. Also, the risk of cross connections is more easily overcome by the simpler setup.

It is possible that industrial water can have either a higher or lower quality than drinking water, depending on its application in the industry. For higher quality, the water company will naturally negotiate a higher price. For lower quality, the industry will expect a lower price, which could be feasible depending on the savings on treatment costs.

Industrial water provided by the water companies is generally supplementary to the industry's own water abstraction. A number of large industries that have been provided with industrial water include:

- Corus IJmuiden (30 million m³/y process and cooling water, from the WRK system)
- AKZO Delfzijl (10 million m³/y injection water for salt extraction, from Veendam (Figure 12)
- CVG Velsen (4 million m³/y process water, from the WRK system)
- DOW Terneuzen (14 million m³/y process water, demineralized water, from the WBB system and from seawater)
- Shell Moerdijk (5 million m³/y process water, from the WBB system via the Zevenbergen pumping station)

Figure 12 - Industrial water project Veendam (Groningen) with anaerobic injection water from surface water

Figure 13 shows the development in the supply of other water. The increase is mainly the result of the growth of consumption by Corus (steel industry) and of new industrial water projects.

2.6   Water consumption in the world

Table 6 shows that water consumption per capita differs greatly throughout the world. Even in the Netherlands, there are still large differences between urban and rural areas, and between water companies with and without water meters. Also, industrial consumption shows large differences in the world. Differences in specific consumption by a factor of 100 are by no means an exception. Earlier in this chapter we saw that the use of cooling water is the strongest determinant of this.

3.   Quality requirements for consumption

Relationship between use and quality
Different uses require different water quality.

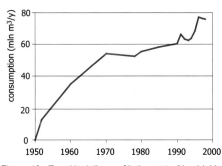

Figure 13 - Trend in delivery of "other water" by drinking water companies (mln m³/y)

Table 6   - Water consumption per person in the world

Location	Consumption per person (l/p/d)	Background
Tanzania (village)	10	Buckets with water from village pump
Maastricht / Tilburg	80	Urban area
Amsterdam / Rotterdam	155	No water meters, big urban area
Zeeland / Drenthe	170	Rural area
Romania	500	No costs, leakage, dissipate
New Mexico (USA)	1,500	Green gardens in desert

197

For each application a (minimum) quality requirement can be formulated. It is, however, impractical to have many different types of water. It is mainly an economic assessment that leads to the clustering of water qualities for multiple uses.

In practice the following elements play an important role in this clustering:
- with different systems, the costs will increase
- with large distances between intake and use, fewer systems will be more feasible
- the production costs are determined by the water with the highest quality requirements
- quality deterioration may occur during transport

Sometimes water with a base quality is supplied, some of which is later upgraded at the place of use.

Uses and types of water
The most common types of water are named in Table 7. The typical quality characteristics have also been shown. For all the uses, "cleanliness" is a general quality characteristic.
Drinking water can be used for drinking as well as for household purposes. The supply of this water is held to legislated quality requirements. Household water must be clean and not transmit microbiological infection. Drinking water must also be safe.
Cooling water must not pollute cooling water systems by settling and/or biological growth, deposit undissolved salts during heating (scaling), or damage the pipeline materials by corrosion.

Rinsing water is most often warm or hot water and must be clean. During the heating process

and evaporation from the cleaned products, no deposits of undissolved salts must occur.

Boiler feed water is used for the production of steam. No deposits may occur in the boilers.

Greenhouse water is mostly used in recirculation systems in horticulture. There nutrients are, as well as pesticides, added to the water for the suppression of plant diseases. Plants evaporate water and are, therefore, sensitive to salts in the water.

4.   Fluctuations in consumption

4.1   Dampening
In the previous paragraphs we spoke about yearly consumption and consumption per capita (average consumption in l/p/d). However, during the year, water consumption exhibits wide variations.
At base level one can look at an individual user, the one who opens the tap. His consumption is extremely erratic.
The average consumption of a larger group of consumers is less erratic. Dampening of the peaks occurs, because not everyone uses water at the same time, and both large and small consumption occur simultaneously.

In order to determine the dampening of the consumption of an amount of water, statistical analysis provides us with a cumulative error law that can be used.

For the total maximum simultaneous capacity, the following applies:

$$Q_t = \sqrt{\left(Q_1^2 + Q_2^2 + .. + Q_n^2\right)} \quad \text{with } n > 20$$

in which:
Q_t = maximum simultaneous capacity   (m³/s)
Q_n = maximum capacity of a certain tap   (m³/s)

This law applies to a sufficiently large number of taps (n>20).

Table 8 shows the calculation for the water use capacity in a house. This shows that the simultaneous maximum capacity is approximately half

Table 7   - Characteristics of different water types

Water type		Characteristics
Drinking water	- household purpose - drinking purpose	Clean + healthy
Cooling water	- once-through - open circulation	Cold, clean + soft/low salt (scaling)
Rinsing water	- cold - warm	Clean + soft (scaling)
Boiler feed water	- low pressure - high pressure	Clean, soft + salt free (scaling)
Greenhouse water	- circulation	Low salt (affect plants)

Table 8 - Capacity of house connections

Connection type	Number of con- nections	Capacity per connection (l/h)
Toilet (free fall), washbasin	2	150
Washbasin	2	300
Shower	1	400
Kitchen tap	2	600
Boiler	-	750
Watering of garden	1	1,200
Toilet (pressure)	-	3,000
Total installed capacity	8	3,700
Total simultaneous capacity (by error law)		1,595
Average consumption with 130 l/p/d and 2.5 p/house		14

Table 9 - Patterns in consumption

Period	Typical cause
Several years	Dry summers
Year	Watering the garden in the summer
Week	Laundry on Monday, Sunday free
Day	Almost no consumption in the night
Hour	Break in soccer match

4.2 Patterns

Water consumption, in larger areas with many users, fluctuates according to typical patterns that are almost totally predictable. From Table 9 we can see that these patterns show large differences in wave length as a result of their cause.

Over several years an autonomous development in consumption occurs, as a result of population growth and developments in the specific consumption. In addition to that, fluctuations occur as a result of dry summers and the resulting consumption caused by the watering of gardens. A year with an extra high consumption means that it has been a dry year.

Figure 14 displays characteristic monthly, weekly and daily patterns. Sundays normally have a lower consumption.

The daily consumption pattern is generally consistent. On Saturdays the consumption starts an hour later and on Sundays (and public holidays) two hours later. Deviations occur in the evenings of the summer months, which is a result of watering the gardens. The difference between the expected

the installed capacity and more than 100 times the average consumed amount.

For house connections with the same maximum capacity, the formula can be simplified as follows:

$$Q_t = Q\sqrt{n}$$

in which:

Q = maximum capacity of the house
        connection   (m³/s)
n = number of house connections   (-)

In practice, deviations occur for a very large number of house connections (n>100). For a larger number of taps, the fluctuations are generally measured to determine the maximum capacity. In general, a lower maximum capacity is found.

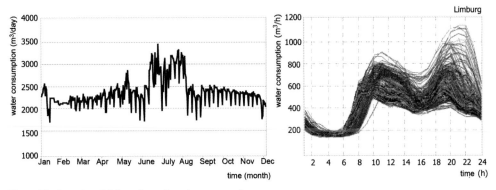

Figure 14 - Annual and daily patterns in water consumption

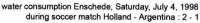

water consumption Enschede, Saturday, July 4, 1998
during soccer match Holland - Argentina : 2 - 1

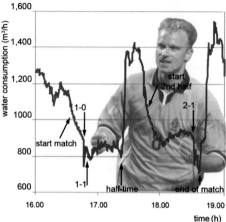

Figure 15 - Water consumption in Enschede during a soccer match: Netherlands - Argentina (quarterfinal WC 1998)

pattern and the actual pattern represents the typical garden watering pattern (trapezium-shaped, between 3 p.m. and 11 p.m. and constant between 4 p.m. and 10 p.m.).

Different areas have different patterns. In Limburg, for example, we find the highest consumption on Saturdays, in Ridderkerk on Mondays. Consumption patterns serve as the "electrocardiograms" of the population. Patterns with a short duration can be seen when there is an important football game on TV. At half-time, a lot of people go to the toilet or make a pot of tea or coffee.
Also, exciting game moments can be deduced from the water consumption. If the game goes well, less water is used because everyone is glued to the TV. And, the same applies to the end of the game (Figure 15). When Johan Cruyff gives commentary during half-time, we see a "dip" in water consumption!

4.3   Peak factors

Because of the specific shape of the consumption patterns, it is obvious that one should use consumption factors, being the ratio of the actual consumption over the average consumption.

Table 10   - Peak factors per period

Period	Peak factors	Difference in relation to
Year (dry / wet)	0.94 - 1.08	Average year consumption (10 years, excl. autonomous growth)
Half a year (summer/winter)	0.94 - 1.07	Year consumption / 2
Month	0.92 - 1.10	Year consumption / 12
Week	0.70 - 1.25	Year consumption / 52
Day	0.65 - 1.40	Year consumption / 365
Hour	0.25 - 1.80	Day consumption / 24
Minute	0.25 - 1.85	Day consumption / 1,440
Days in a week	0.75 - 1.10	Week consumption /7

With changes in the average consumption, the consumption factors will not change, or the change will be minimal. For design and operation, extreme values are especially important. These are indicated with the term "peak factor." Table 10 provides an overview of a number of typical peak factors.

It is customary to relate the consumption for periods of up to a day to the average annual consumption. A commonly used term, in this respect, is the "day factor." Consumption for a period of less than a day is related to the consumption of that day. In this context, the hour factor is frequently used.

As can be seen in Figure 16, the hour pattern on the maximum day is different from that on the average day. Therefore, it can be concluded that the peak factors are not independent. For design purposes, use is made of composite peak factors.

Abstraction, treatment and transport are generally based on the capacity of the maximum day which occurs once every 10 years.

Distribution is usually designed for the maximum hour of the maximum day.
For the average capacity the following applies:
$Q_0 =$ average annual capacity / (365 · 24)

The average capacity of a maximum day in a dry year is then:
$Q_d = (1.08 · 1.40 =) 1.5 · Q_0$

And, the capacity of a maximum hour of a maximum day in a dry year is:
$Q_m = (1.08 · 1.40 · 1.80 =) 2.7 · Q_0$

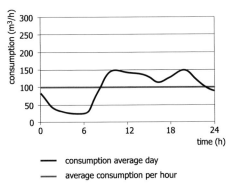 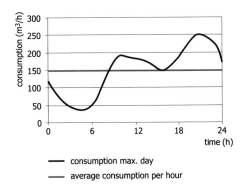

——— consumption average day

——— average consumption per hour

——— consumption max. day

——— average consumption per hour

Figure 16 - Consumption on an average and maximum day (pattern and average)

5. Consumption forecasting

5.1 Goal and timeframe

For the planning of new infrastructures for water supply, future water consumption has to be predicted over a period of 10 to 20 years. For the daily operation of a treatment plant, it is necessary that consumption be reasonably well-predicted for the coming hours. The timeframe of a prediction depends, therefore, on what the prediction is used for. Table 11 gives an overview of this, in which the purpose is also incorporated.

Operational and tactical predictions are based on the consumption patterns described above. Here, management concentrates especially on the deviations to the basic patterns, from which the operational control and management take place. These predictions will not be discussed here.

Strategic predictions are based on the extrapolation of historical data. An analysis of the historical developments in the annual consumption is, therefore, imperative. It is important that one has an understanding of these trends and is able to recognize changes therein.

5.2 Forecasting annual consumption

To predict the annual consumption, two different methods can be examined:

- extrapolation of the total consumption
- extrapolation and summation of the consumption per consumer group

The first method is used for a quick analysis. The second method is more detailed and requires much more data.

Extrapolation is based on the assumption that consumption increases or decreases by a fixed percentage during a number of years. In other words, it has a fixed growth factor.

In formula form this is:

$$consumption_{p+n} = consumption_{p} \cdot GF^n$$

in which:

$consumption_{p}$ = consumption in period p

$consumption_{p+n}$ = consumption in period p+n

n = number of periods (years or decades)

GF = Growth factor per period

For a reliable extrapolation, a good analysis of the history is necessary.

Table 11 - Goal and timeframe of forecast

Goal forecast	Timeframe	Aspect
Planning new production sources	Upcoming years	Strategic
Setting up available capacity	Upcoming year	Tactical
Management infiltration / reservoirs	Upcoming month / week	Operational
Management production / clear water reservoir	Upcoming day / days	Operational
Management transport (pumps, etc.)	Upcoming minutes / hours	Operational

Table 12 - Growth factor per decade and growth per year

	1951 - 1960	1961 - 1970	1971 - 1980	1981 - 1990	1991 - 2000
Growth factor	1.64	1.72	1.16	1.22	0.96
Growth per year	5.1%	5.6%	1.5%	2.0%	-0.4%
Average over:					
Last 50 years	2.7 %	2.7 %	2.7 %	2.7 %	2.7 %
Last 40 years		2.2 %	2.2 %	2.2 %	2.2 %
Last 30 years			1.0 %	1.0 %	1.0 %
Last 20 years				0.8 %	0.8 %
Last 10 years					-0.4 %

Analysis of total drinking water consumption in the Netherlands

In Figure 17 the history of the drinking water consumption in the Netherlands is given ("supplied to the network" in million m³/y).

In Table 12 growth factors for the annual consumption over decades are given (C_{1960} = 1.64 C_{1951}). These growth factors can be converted to a growth factor per year ($GF_d = GF_j{}^{10}$), and expressed as the growth percentage per year (a yearly growth factor of 1.051 equals a yearly growth of 5.1%). The average growth over 50 years amounts to 2.7% per year, with a growth above 5% in the period 1950 to 1970, and even a decrease during the last 10 years.

In the period after 1950 and until the present, two breaks in the trend have been observed.

The first was a result of the implementation of the Surface Water Pollution Act (Wet Verontreiniging Oppervlaktewater - WVO) in 1974, which required that people start paying for the treatment of wastewater.

The second break was the result of public awareness campaigns for water saving, which started

in 1990, and the introduction of a tax on drinking water (eco-tax).

Extrapolation of the total consumption

To formulate an extrapolation of the total consumption, the following steps are distinguished:

- establish growth figures for the future or establish different growth figures over time (trend breaks)
- establish growth figures according to the most probable scenario (average)
- establish growth figures according to the minimum and maximum scenarios (bandwidth)

The maximum scenario is necessary because water companies have a legal supply duty and, therefore, a shortage will never be accepted. The minimum scenario gives the maximum financial risk of a low demand and, therefore, little income.

In Table 13 several growth figures are given for future water consumption in the Netherlands until the year 2030.

It can be assumed that, during the coming 30 years, growth will never be higher than 2.0% per year. This would mean that, beginning with the year 2000, the effect of water saving has been exhausted and water consumption will rise with the average percentage of the last 40 years.

For the minimal scenario it is assumed that water saving will continue until 2010, after which an

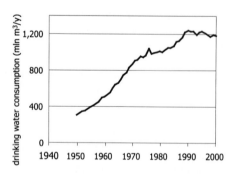

Figure 17 - History of drinking water consumption in the Netherlands (mln m³/y)

Table 13 - Assumption for minimal, average and maximal yearly growth of the total drinking water consumption in the Netherlands

	2001 - 2010	2011 - 2020	2021 - 2030
Minimum	-0.5 %	1.0 %	1.0 %
Average	1.0 %	1.5 %	1.5 %
Maximum	2.0 %	2.0 %	2.0 %

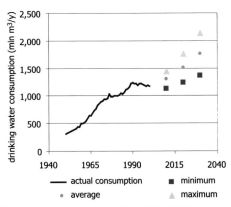

Figure 18 - Actual and predicted total drinking water consumption in the Netherlands (mln m³/y)

actual consumption   ■ minimum
● average   ▲ maximum

Table 14 - Trend prognosis for household consumption (various scenarios)

Year	Specific consumption		Inhabitants		Household consumption	
	(l/p/d)	%	(mln)	%	(mln m³/y)	%
2000	122	100	16.0	100	712	100
2010	120	98	16.8	105	735	103
2020	125	102	17.4	109	794	112
2030	130	107	18.1	113	859	121

In Table 14 a prediction example is given for the development in domestic consumption, according to a random scenario. In the table the indices shown are based on the year 2000. The index values are an accumulation of the growth factors.

increase will occur that is similar to the increase of the past 20 years. In Figure 18 these forecasts for growth are shown.

Extrapolation and summation of consumption per user group

For the prediction of the annual consumption per user group, insight concerning the specific water consumption within the user group can be used. Separate predictions are made for the specific type of consumption and for the specific quantity. These two predictions are more or less independent of each other and are easier to predict separately.

Per user group the following applies:

$$consumption_t = spec. consumption_t \cdot spec. quantity_t$$

In principle a large number of user groups can be differentiated. This will be especially necessary for industrial water consumption, because, per sector, entirely different developments take place.

A few examples of user groups are:
- consumers = l/p/d the number of inhabitants
- power stations = m³/J produced electricity
- industry A = l/kg product A · production of A
- industry B = l/kg product B · production of B

Also, to derive a prognosis from the user groups, minimal and maximal scenarios must be determined.

Trend analysis

Quick insight is necessary when there is talk of a trend break, and these breaks are important for extrapolations.

When analyzing historical data, we see that quite often fluctuations occur that are larger than the trend ("noise"). For a good trend analysis, it is necessary to eliminate the noise.

At water companies, annual consumption fluctuates especially under the influence of the summer weather (maximum fluctuation ± 6%). If we do not correct this, a trend break will only become visible at a later stage.

Consumption in the winter period (November until March) is not dependent on the weather.

For the sake of a trend analysis, consumption during the winter is used, because these figures are easier to predict.

The most probable annual consumption is thus easily derived from the average relationship between annual consumption and winter consumption. For the minimal and maximal annual consumption, the maximal deviations as a result of the summer weather must be ignored.

5.3   Planning for future use

The predictions for water consumption are used to make a plan to cover future water demand. Figure 19 gives an example of this.

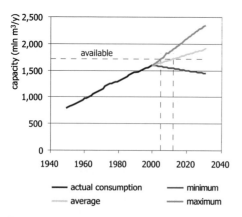

Figure 19 - Capacity expansion planning for various consumption prognoses

For the maximal growth, the capacity increase must be ready within a few years. For the most probable demand (average) this may be some years later, and for minimal demand, the capacity increase will never be necessary.

When planning for future demand, it is important to determine when the capacity increase is necessary.

In this case the legal supply obligation is important, meaning that the available capacity must always be larger than the demand. The water company, therefore, must be able to cover even the maximal demand development.

A large over-capacity, however, is expensive. For this reason, expansions are built in phases, and its realization is postponed as long as possible (the lengthy permit procedure is put into motion, but the actual building activities are not started).

On the other hand, an over-capacity provides a greater reliability of supply and better operational flexibility.

For the planning of future use, one must also look at the impact of potential political and social developments.

Promotion of household water projects and/or industrial water projects from other sources will naturally influence the development of the drinking water demand.

Such developments not only originate from political, but also from technical, issues. Further development of membrane filtration will possibly make it simpler and cheaper to treat water locally, or to reuse wastewater for specific purposes.

Such a development will lead to a reduced demand for drinking water. A reverse development will occur if the "bathing culture" with saunas, steam baths, etc. in private homes increases in popularity.

With all these uncertainties, the water supply engineer will have to choose between certainty and low cost.

Figure 20 - Sufficient drinking water, now and in the future

Further reading

- Waterleidingstatistiek, VEWIN (annual reports)
- Watervoorziening van de industrie, delfstoffen-winning en elektriciteitscentrales, CBS (1996)
- Milieucompendium, RIVM (annual reports)
- Toepassing WAPRO, versie 1999, RIVM (2000)
- Prognose landelijke drinkwatervraag tot 2020, VEWIN (2006)

- www.vewin.nl
- www.rivm.nl
- www.cbs.nl

Questions and applications

Annual consumption

1. Give the definition of specific water consumption, and give two examples.

2. Rank the following water consumers in order of size, from large to small, and give an estimate of the consumption in million m^3/y.
   - Households
   - Power stations
   - Water companies
   - Small companies, institutions and governments
   - Industry

3. Name a few ways to save on cooling water consumption.

4. Explain what is meant by the following terms. What are the similarities and differences between them?
   - Supplied to the net
   - Unbilled consumption
   - The amount which is paid for
   - Flushing
   - Leakage losses

5. Give the average consumption of drinking water per capita for households in the Netherlands in l/p/d and indicate how much it differs from that of Maastricht, Rotterdam, Zeeland, Romania, Tanzania and New Mexico (USA).

Quality requirements for consumption

1. Name a couple of different types of water and, for each type, give a few characteristics.

Fluctuations in consumption

1. Why are peak factors used for determining water consumption? Are these peak factors equal for different periods, or not? If so, in what way(s)? If not, why not?

Consumption prediction

1. In order to predict the total consumption, a number of steps can be distinguished. What are they?

Applications

1. In the Leidsche-Rijn there is a new housing project close to Utrecht. The water company Hydron Midden-Nederland built two water supply networks: one for drinking water and one for household water. As has always been the case, drinking water is connected to most of the taps, the shower/bath connection and the connection for the dishwasher. The toilets, washing machine and the outside taps are, however, connected to the household water.

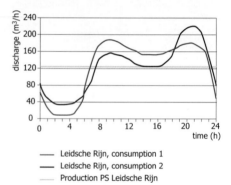

—— Leidsche Rijn, consumption 1
—— Leidsche Rijn, consumption 2
—— Production PS Leidsche Rijn

In the above image, the patterns of drinking water consumption and household water consumption of the Leidsche Rijn are given for the day of maximum consumption. This is the day with the highest water consumption that occurs on an extremely hot day. For the supply of drinking water, Hydron Midden-Nederland will build a new plant, Leidsche-Rijn. The amount of water Leidsche-Rijn must provide on the day of maximum consumption is also given in the figure. The household water will be bought from Water Transport Company Rijn-Kennemerland (WRK). This company produces pre-treated water from the Lek River.

a Which of two consumptions in the figure is the household water consumption and which is the drinking water consumption? Explain your answer.

b Leidsche-Rijn will have 30,000 inhabitants. The total water consumption is 137 liters per inhabitant per day, of which half is drinking water and the other half is household water. For the drinking water consumption, a new plant is designed, Leidsche-Rijn. Determine, from the data of the maximum day from the figure, the peak day factor on which the design of the new plant must be based.

c The outgoing drinking water pipe of Leidsche-Rijn is designed based on the peak hour factor of the consumption. Calculate the peak hour factor.

c Calculate the number of filters that must be built at the new treatment plant, taking into account the following design parameters:
   - flow velocity through the filter: 10 m/h
   - surface area of one filter: 15 m^2

d How many filters can be in use on an average day?

2. A new drinking water treatment plant must provide a city of 100,000 inhabitants with drinking water. From historical consumption data, the following parameters have been calculated:
   - Drinking water consumption: 144   l/p/d
   - Peak day factor: 1.5
   - Peak hour factor: 1.6

a How big is the:
   - average hourly consumption on an average day?
   - average hourly consumption on the day of maximum consumption?
   - maximum hourly consumption on the day of maximum consumption?

b The capacity of the treatment plant is based on which of the three named hourly consumptions from question 2a? Why is this?

Answers

Annual consumption

1. Specific water consumption = water consumption per characteristic unit.

    Paper factory   15 - 40 m³ / ton of paper
    Blast furnaces   4 - 20 m³ / ton of steel
    Breweries   5 - 15 l / l of beer
    Drinking water companies
                           1.05 - 1.10 m³ / m³ of water

2. Power stations   6,199 million m³/y
    Industries   2,529 million m³/y
    Households   733 million m³/y
    Small companies, institutions
    and governments   297 million m³/y
    Water companies   52 million m³/y

3. Larger temperature increase
    Higher electricity efficiency
    Reuse
    Open recirculation cooling
    Closed recirculation cooling

4. The unbilled consumption is the difference between that which is supplied to the network and the amount which is paid for. This is not equal to the leakage losses, because that which is used for firefighting and for cleaning the pipelines (flushing) is not considered leakage losses.

5. The Netherlands   128 l/p/d
    Tanzania   10 l/p/d
    Maastricht   80 l/p/d
    Rotterdam   155 l/p/d
    Zeeland   170 l/p/d
    Romania   500 l/p/d
    New Mexico (USA)   1,500 l/p/d

Quality requirements for consumption

1.

Water type	Characteristic
Drinking water	Clean + healthy
Cooling water	Cold, clean + soft / low salt (scaling)
Rinsing water	Clean + soft (scaling)
Boiler	Clean, soft + salt free (scaling)
Watering gardens	Low salt (affect plants)

Fluctuations in consumption

1. Peak factors are used to relate periods of consumption to the average consumption. The peak factors compare, for example, the hourly pattern on the day of maximum consumption with the average day. For designing, one uses composite peak factors.

Consumption prediction

1. - Establish growth figures for the future or establish different growth figures over time (trend breaks)
   - Establish growth figures according to the most probable scenario (average)
   - Establish growth figures according to the minimal and maximal scenario (bandwidth)

Applications

1. a Consumption 1 is the drinking water consumption, and consumption 2 the household consumption.

    Drinking water consumption decreases at night to almost 0 m³/h; household consumption will not reduce to zero as a result of toilet flushing and washing machines. Drinking water consumption is not higher in the evenings than in the mornings; household consumption is much higher as a result of the gardens being watered in the evenings.

b   Drinking water consumption = 137 · 0.5 = 68.5 l/p/d.
Average hourly consumption = (68.5 l/p/d · 30,000 p.) / 1000 l/m^3 / 24 h/d = 85.6 m^3/h
Maximum average hourly consumption = 120 m^3/h
Day peak factor = 120 / 85.6 = 1.4

c   Average hourly consumption = 85.6 m^3/h
Maximum hourly consumption = 180 m^3/h
Hourly peak factor = 180 /85.6 = 2.1

2. a   Average hourly consumption during an average day is:
(144 l/p/d · 100,000 p) / 1,000 l/m^3 / 24 h/d = 600 m^3/h
Average hourly consumption on the day of maximum consumption is:
1.5 · 600 m^3/h = 900 m^3/h
Maximum hourly consumption during the day of maximum consumption is:
1.5 · 1.6 · 600 m^3/h = 1,440 m^3/h

b   Average hourly consumption on the day of maximum consumption. On this maximum day the treatment plant has to supply the required amount of water. With the help of storage facilities for treated water, the daily modulation (including the hourly peak factor) can be compensated so that the treatment plant can supply the average required amount of water on the day of maximum consumption.

c   The surface area of a filter is 15 m^2
Discharge through one filter is:
10 m/h · 15 m^2 = 150 m^3/h
The number of filters needed is:
900 m^3/h / 150 m^3/h = 6

d   During an average day the average hourly consumption is 600 m^3/h
The number of filters in use can be:
600 m^3/h / 150 m^3/h = 4

Water quality

TECHNICAL FACETS

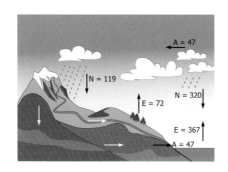

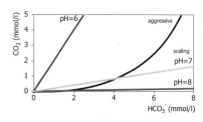

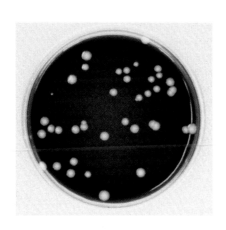

Framework

This module will deal with the quality aspects of the public drinking water supply. Included are the various compounds which may be present in the water and the quality standards for drinking water.

Contents

The module has the following contents:

Study goals

After studying this module you will be able to:

* explain the different compounds in water
* explain the most important chemical processes in water
* describe and quantify the natural processes in water
* explain the background of drinking water quality standards

1. Introduction

Water is the source of life on Earth, but it is not only required for biological processes. Because of its abundant presence and its typical physical and chemical characteristics, water has a very stabilizing effect on interplanetary (sunlight, cosmic radiation) and earthly (climate) processes.

Also, water is the most important means of transport on Earth, not only for the goods that are transported over water in ships, but especially for the dissolved and suspended compounds that are simultaneously transported in it. The types and concentrations of these compounds determine the quality of the water.

This module deals with the quality of water. First, the hydrologic cycle of water on Earth is discussed, as well as all compounds that are transported during this cycle.

Next, the physical and chemical properties of water are dealt with in order to understand drinking water quality standards. For even more information on this subject, one should consult specialist sciences like water chemistry, hydrobiology and microbiology.

Then, the health aspects of drinking water are described, followed by the Dutch legislation regarding drinking water quality.

Finally, the quality requirements for some other applications of water are reviewed.

2. Water on Earth

2.1 The hydrologic cycle

The amount of water on Earth

Water is the most important liquid on Earth; without water, life on Earth is impossible. The total surface area of the Earth amounts to 510 million sq. km, of which 73% consists of water (Figure 1). The total amount of water on Earth is 1,600 million km³, which is equivalent to a layer over the whole Earth having a thickness of 3.1 km (Table 1).

Figure 1 - Water on Earth

Yet, it is said every now and again that water will be the direct cause of future wars. That may be a peculiar saying, but it is understandable when examining the data in more detail. Only 0.5% of all water on Earth is in the form of fresh surface or groundwater. Of this fresh water, the majority is located in the deep underground (over 800 m deep).

In lakes and rivers there are 0.2 million km³ of water, which is equivalent to 40,000 m³ per human being.

If all fresh water was equally distributed over the earth, there would not be such a large water issue. However, the distribution is not equal at all.

In the Netherlands, there is water in abundance (think, for example, of the polders which need to be drained, because they would flood otherwise).

In desert areas where there is hardly any rain and where there are no rivers, there is a large water shortage.

Table 1 - Water on Earth

Type of water	Quantity	
	(mln km³)	(m)
Total quantity of water	1,600	3,100
- chemically bound	230	450
- salt water	1,330	2,610
- ice and snow	30	59
- damp	0.015	0.030
Total quantity of fresh water	8.2	16.1
- in the underground	8.0	15.7
- in lakes and rivers	0.2	0.4

Hydrologic cycle

Water is continuously moving. The properties of water may change (e.g., contamination), or the water may change its phase (vapor, ice), but it remains water.

Due to evaporation, water is present in the atmosphere in the form of vapor. When clouds suddenly ascend, the vapor condenses and the water falls to the surface of the earth in the form of snow, rain or hail. Additionally, water may condense to fog, dew or frost.

Some condensed water will enter into lakes, brooks and rivers, and what doesn't evaporate, will flow over the soil and infiltrate into the ground. Rivers transport water to the sea; groundwater flows through the ground to lower locations and will also reach the sea. From the sea, water will vaporize again (Figure 2).

The water supply from the sea to the land (and the other way around) amounts to 47,000 km^3 per year, which is 1,490,000 m^3/s or 600 times the discharge of the Rhine River. Water in the amount of 119,000 km^3 per year falls on the total land mass on Earth, corresponding to 0.7 m/y or 24,000 m^3/inhabitant/y.

From the hydrologic cycle, the Netherlands receives substantial amounts of water. The majority of the water in the Netherlands comes from across its borders. The Rhine and Meuse rivers supply 80 billion m^3 of water yearly. In some years the discharge is so high that the rivers flood (Rhine and Meuse rivers flooded in 1993 and 1995).

In the Netherlands, the yearly precipitation amounts to 30 billion m^3. A large part of this evaporates, the rest infiltrates into the ground or is transported to the North Sea via surface water.

The average yearly supply of 110 billion m^3 of water to the Netherlands corresponds to over 7,000 m^3 per inhabitant per year. The amount of water that is used by the water companies for drinking water production is 1.2 billion m^3 per year, which is about 1% of the yearly water supply.

Natural compounds in water

In precipitation, gases like oxygen and nitrogen are present. After the rain falls on the land, clay particles, sand and plant matter enter the runoff water. When the water infiltrates into the ground, minerals (e.g., Na, Cl, Ca, Fe) will enter it, because these compounds will dissolve from the soil matrix.

Surface water contains several compounds, such as the biological compounds algae and microorganisms, which are important. The most important compounds in the hydrologic cycle are shown in Figure 3.

Because of very large volume flows within the hydrologic cycle, even with small concentrations of some compounds, there will be a large mass flow. If all rivers contained an average of 100 mg/l of suspended particles and 1,000 mg/l of dissolved salts, then every second a mass of 1,640 tons of this matter would be discharged into the sea.

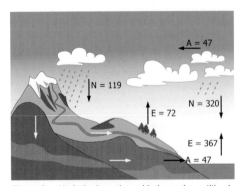

Figure 2 - Hydrologic cycle and balance (quantities in 1,000 billion m^3/y)

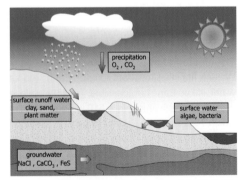

Figure 3 - The most important compounds in the hydrologic cycle

2.2 Water as a means of transport

Contamination of water

Besides the compounds which are present in water naturally, water is also polluted with compounds as a result of human activities (Figure 4). Water is a means of transport for the discharge of diverse matter and also for the discharge of heat.

During the previous century, surface water was highly polluted at several locations in the Netherlands. The Rhine River was even called Europe's sewer. All kinds of industries, and also cities, used the major rivers as sewage systems. Wastewater entered the Rhine and Meuse rivers untreated, thus causing a steep decrease in animal and plant populations. Fortunately, enough people became more and more convinced that they should not continue as they had, and treaties were signed between the different Rhine shore states concerning discharges on the Rhine River.
The Surface Water Contamination Act was adopted in the Netherlands in 1970. The quality of surface water has improved since that time, but there still is a long road ahead before the natural equilibrium is restored.

Not only was surface water contaminated, but similar quality problems actually arose in groundwater areas. For example, at some water companies' pumping stations pesticides were found, or nitrate concentration problems occurred because of overfertilization.

Figure 5 - An example of diffuse pollution

In dealing with pollution, a difference is made between point and diffuse discharges. Point discharges have a high concentration of pollution issuing from one point. Examples of this are the effluent canals of wastewater treatment plants, overflows from sewers, and accidents.
Diffuse discharges are discharges which are located throughout the catchment area of a river. Examples of these are runoff from fertilizers (Figure 5), and the use of pesticides. Therefore, diffuse discharges are more difficult to treat than point discharges.

Water warming

The surface water temperature is determined by meteorological factors primarily. In the Netherlands, this temperature varies between 0°C and 22°C.
The groundwater temperature is rather constant at 10°C, which is the average yearly air temperature (Figure 6). Only the deep groundwater (depth over 500 meters) has a higher temperature than the average surface temperature.

Figure 4 - In the seventies, water contained detergents resulting in foaming in wastewater treatment installations

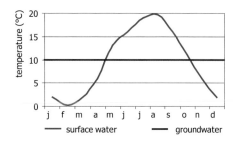

Figure 6 - Natural temperature variation in ground- and surface water

Due to industrial activities, the surface water temperature is artificially increased. This temperature increase is called thermal pollution and has both advantages and disadvantages.

Advantages are that the water freezes less quickly during winter due to the higher temperature. Also, natural self-purification increases because of higher biological activity.

In summer, however, the increased biological activity is disadvantageous because of the more rapid decay of organic matter. This consumes oxygen, while at the same time the oxygen concentration is already lower because of the higher water temperature, which may cause anaerobic conditions, fish mortality, spoilage, and stench.

Another disadvantage is that the water has a lower cooling capacity during summer due to the high water temperature. Limitations have been set for the use of surface water for cooling purposes. The warming of river water can be prevented by using cooling lakes and towers.

2.3   Compounds in water

For discussing the different compounds in water, the following groups are discerned:
- undissolved matter
- dissolved compounds
- vegetable matter
- higher organisms
- pathogenic microorganisms

The distinction between parameters cannot be made very clearly in all cases. Examples of this are the taste and smell of water. Smell and taste are subjective parameters which cannot be detected by any device. The acceptable taste and smell of water are determined using consumer panels, which determine whether they find any unpleasant flavor or odor in a diluted sample of water.

By using different dilution rates, panel members select a taste or smell number. This number indicates the necessary dilution concentration to obtain water without any unacceptable smell or taste.

Undissolved matter

Undissolved matter consists of large or small particles which have not been dissolved in the water.

A distinction based on size is made between suspended and colloidal matter (Figure 7).

The diameter and specific gravity of particles are important for removing them from the water. Particles having a diameter over 10 μm and a specific gravity other than that of water can be removed using either sedimentation or flotation. Suspended particles have a relatively large size, but they may remain in suspension because of turbulent flow. Larger suspended particles will be transported by sliding over the bottom. Suspended particles having a density lower than that of water are transported by floating.

During transport, the suspended matter will be pulverized, transformed first into colloidal particles, and finally into dissolved compounds.

Suspended particles are of mineral or organic origin. Mineral suspended particles originate from sand, clay, loam and other inorganic soil types and enter the water as a result of erosion.

Organic suspended particles originate from the decay of vegetation and from the discharge of untreated domestic and industrial wastewater.

The rivers in Europe have a concentration of suspended matter of about 30 mg/l, while rivers in the tropics may contain up to 10,000 mg/l. The result of those high numbers is that the light entrance is limited and, consequently, oxygen production by means of photosynthesis decreases, the number of fish decreases, and mud will settle when the flow velocity of the water decreases.

In addition to the term suspended matter, the terms suspended solid matter and suspended solids are used.

The amount of suspended and colloidal matter can be expressed in multiple parameters, among

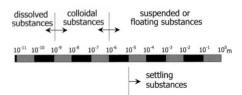

Figure 7   - Dimensions of compounds in water

which are turbidity (sight depth or light passage), suspended solids concentration, and number of particles per size (counting particles).

Suspended particles both absorb and scatter light. Because of this, the intensity of a ray of light passing through a sample will decrease. By comparing the light intensity with that of a standardized dissolution, turbidity is determined. For water analyses, formazine is used as the standard, and the measured values are expressed as Formazine Turbidity Units (FTU). Visually clear water should have an FTU between 1 - 5 (Figure 8).
The suspended solids concentration is determined using a membrane filter and measuring the mass increase of the filter (after dehydration at 103°C).
When counting particles, the size of individual particles in a sample is measured. Then, a distribution of the size of the particles is given.

Colloidal particles are particles having a size between 10^{-9} and 10^{-6} m and a specific gravity around that of water.
Colloidal particles generally have a negative electric charge and their electrostatic repulsion makes it impossible to remove them easily. By adding flocculants, the negative charges are neutralized and the particles may become larger particles which then can be clarified.
Colloidal particles give color and turbidity to the water.

Figure 8 - A low turbidity is desired for the customers' satisfaction with drinking water

Floating undissolved matter
Floating compounds can be subdivided into solids and liquids. Both are often of an organic composition and can be eliminated microbiologically.
Floating matter causes pollution of the shores and an unattractive appearance for recreational activities.

Aquatic plants, decayed organic and animal life, fecal matter and materials from bio-industry belong to this group of solids. Aquatic plants give a pleasant appearance to the water, provided their numbers do not overwhelm.
When there is a high concentration of phosphates in the water (eutrophic water), an explosive growth of aquatic plants may occur, causing an obstacle to navigation. Also, the water may become anaerobic because of the obstruction of light, which will in turn cause fish mortality, spoilage and stench.
Fecal material only enters the water locally, at present. This is because the majority of industrial and residential wastewater is treated.

Oil and waste from chemical plants belong to the liquids group.
Oil enters the water due to accidents and carelessness. Leaking tanks and transportation pipes, ship collisions, illegal discharges of oil into the sewer system by individuals, and the cleaning of oil tanks onboard ships cause the presence of mineral oil in water.

The specific gravity of mineral oil is lower than that of water, causing the oil to form a layer upon the water's surface. This layer prevents oxygen and light from entering the water, thus causing anaerobic conditions, fish mortality and stench. Oil gives an unpleasant taste to water, and removing it from the water is difficult.

Dissolved compounds
Dissolved compounds having a diameter below 10^{-9} m cannot be removed from the water using sedimentation, not even when using flocculants. Only the application of membrane filtration or chemical processes (precipitation, oxidation) can remove those compounds from the water.

In dissolved compounds, a distinction is made on the basis of the chemical composition of the compounds. For example, a distinction is made between inorganic and organic compounds.

A subdivision is also made based on the amounts of chemicals present: macro-pollutants for concentrations over 1 mg/l and micropollutants for concentrations below 1 mg/l (so in the order of micrograms per liter).

Examples of inorganic macro-pollutants are dissolved gases (like O_2 and CO_2), dissolved salts (like $NaCl$, $CaCO_3$, $MgCO_3$) or reaction products from inorganic transformations (Fe, Mn) or organic transformations (NH_3, CH_4, H_2S).

In water several dissolved gases may be present. Rainwater, for example, contains oxygen and nitrogen in concentrations of some mg/l.
Groundwater contains carbondioxide (CO_2), but may contain gases like methane (CH_4) and hydrogen sulfide (H_2S) as well. When groundwater is abstracted from great depths and when there is a high concentration of organic matter in the ground, the water no longer contains any oxygen (anaerobic water).

Because of the long retention times of water underground, the water is able to dissolve several salts or minerals in the soil. Also, chemical or biological reactions may dissolve some compounds into the water. The consequence of this is that the concentration of inorganic salts in groundwater increases (compared to the concentration in rain). The concentration of salts can be as large as some tenths of a milligram up to hundreds of milligrams per liter.

Shellfish in nature produce large amounts of calcium carbonate. Natural phenomena like stalactite caves (Figure 9) and limestone sediments are also examples of calcium carbonate, as well as what gives hard water its hardness.
Hardness is defined as the sum of the concentrations of calcium and magnesium. The hardness of water occurs because the carbon dioxide in water dissolves the calcium carbonate and magnesium carbonate which are present in the ground. Several

units for hardness are used (mmol/l, German hardness degrees, French hardness degrees, American ppm $CaCO_3$).
By discharging wastewater, also considerable amounts of salts can enter the water. Infamous are the waste salt discharges of the French potassium mines into the Rhine River, which doubled the river's chlorine concentration in the past decades.

The total concentration of dissolved salts can be determined by vaporizing the water and weighing the residual (dry residual). This concentration can also be calculated as the arithmetic sum of all dissolved salts. This parameter can also be referred to as Total Dissolved Solids (TDS), which is mostly determined using evaporation.
Water having a TDS below 1,000 mg/l is called fresh water, a TDS over 10,000 mg/l is called salt water. The transition area between 1,000 and 10,000 mg/l is called brackish water.

Instead of determining the dry residual or the TDS, a determination of the electrical conductivity (EC) of the water is often sufficient.

Figure 9   - The stalactites in Remouchamps are an example of precipitation of calcium carbonate

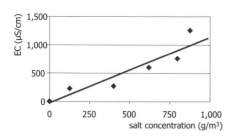

Figure 10 - Relationship between dry residual and electrical conductivity (by approximation)

The EC depends on the concentration and kinds of salts (value and mobility). It may be computed from the concentrations of the different salts. Also, the dry residual can be estimated from the EC, assuming a certain composition of the water. Figure 10 shows a relationship which is often used.

Besides inorganic macro-pollutants, also inorganic micropollutants, such as heavy metals and radio-active compounds, can be discerned. Even in low concentrations, these compounds can be harmful to public health.

Organic compounds are all carbon compounds, except carbon dioxide (CO_2), hydrogen carbonate (HCO_3^-) and carbonate (CO_3^{2-}), which are inorganic carbon compounds. Organic compounds mainly consist of hydrogen and oxygen (in addition to carbon), and to a lesser degree of nitrogen, sulfur and phosphorous. The concentration of organic compounds in ground- or surface water amounts to 1 to 10 mg/l.

The majority of organic compounds are of a natural origin (natural organic matter, NOM, decayed animal or vegetable material), but they also partly originate from the discharge of residential and industrial wastewater.

The number of organic compounds in water is very large. Therefore, it is impossible to measure all those compounds. This causes the concentration of organic compounds to be determined on the basis of some properties of groups of compounds (Table 2).

Many organic compounds can be transformed by microorganisms using oxygen. The amount of oxygen which is used by microorganisms in this transformation is called the Biochemical Oxygen Demand (BOD; unit g O_2/m^3). Instead of being transformed by microorganisms, most organic compounds can be transformed chemically as well (oxidized).

Most pesticides belong to the class of organic micropollutants. There are strict standards for

Table 2 - Classification of organic compounds, or organic parameters

Compound / parameter		Explanation
Organic macropollutants		
Chemical oxygen demand	COD	Oxygen consumption of dissolved organic compounds in water when oxidized with potassium dichromate ($K_2Cr_2O_7$)
Oxidizing capacity with $KMnO_4$	-	Oxygen consumption of dissolved organic compounds in water when oxidized with potassium permanganate ($KMnO_4$)
Biochemical oxygen demand	BOD	Oxygen consumption of biological processes in water
Dissolved organic carbon	DOC	The concentration of dissolved organic carbon
Total organic carbon	TOC	The total concentration of organic carbon
UV-extinction	-	Adsorption of ultra-violet light (254 ηm) is an indication of the concentration of organics
Color	-	Comparison with a solution of Pt/Co is a measure for the concentration of organic humic acids
Organic micropollutants		
Pesticides	-	Occur frequently in water because of usage in agriculture and by discharge of sewage
Polycyclic aromatic hydro-carbons	PAH	Organic compounds with three or more aromatic nuclei per molecule. A number of PAHs are carcinogenic. In nature, they are the result of soot from burning processes
Poly chloride biphenyl	PCB	Compounds of two aromatic rings to which more chlorine atoms are attached
Organic halides	AOX	Halogenated compounds that decay slowly and are likely to have carcinogenic properties
Assimilated organic carbon	AOC	The amount of carbon that can be adsorbed by an organism from the water. This parameter is a measure for the nutrient level of water or the biological stability of water

these pollutants, as they are harmful to public health even in low concentrations.

Vegetation in water

Different kinds of vegetation or vegetative residuals may be present in water. The size of the vegetation varies from very large (e.g., surface water which has been completely covered over by water hyacinths) to microscopically small (phytoplankton). This vegetation forms an essential element in the hydrobiologic cycle, as it decays all kinds of inorganic or organic compounds.

They are not harmful to human health, except for very few poisonous species. However, they may impact the appearance of the water (flavor, odor, color). This larger and smaller vegetation is the food source for other organisms like fish, shellfish and crustaceans.

For the drinking water supply, algae are the most important representatives of vegetable material in water.

Algae are able to build up organic matter from minerals, water, carbon dioxide, nitrate, phosphate, etc. using sunlight energy. This process is known as photosynthesis or assimilation.

When algae die, the reaction is reversed and is called dissimilation. Algae need the nutrients sulfur, nitrogen and phosphorous for their growth, in addtion to carbon and water.

The nitrogen and phosphorous concentrations of water are low by nature, thus limiting algae growth. From the discharge of treated wastewater into surface waters, the concentrations of phosphorous and nitrogen rise, causing increased algae growth. The water becomes turbid and opaque and has an unpleasant green, brown or red color. Then, the water is no longer suitable for recreation and the preparation of drinking water from it is expensive, due to the required advanced treatment techniques.

The concentration of algae in water is determined by counting them under a microscope or by measuring the chlorophyll(a) concentration. Well-known types of algae are blue algae and seaweeds (diatoms). Most algae have a size between 0.01 and 1 mm.

Small animals in water

Besides vegetable compounds, also microscopic animal organisms may be present in water (zooplankton). In nature, these organisms are present in large numbers, and they may also be found in drinking water.

Larger animal species may grow in sand or activated carbon filters at drinking water production plants, and in the distribution network as well. Especially in water having sufficient nutrients (AOC), such higher organisms may flourish.

Table 3 provides an overview of a few of those organisms and the amount in which they may be found in drinking water. The organisms in water are determined by pouring water through a filtration cloth of 0.1 mm. The material (sediment) that remains on the filtration cloth is investigated under a microscope. Based on their external characteristics, the different kinds of organisms are counted. Most of these higher organisms have a size between 0.05 and 10 mm.

Table 3   - Limiting values for higher organisms in drinking water (VEWIN 1993)

Organism	Number (per m^3)
Ciliata	500
Amoeba	100
Testacea	5,000
Foraminifera	100
Turbellaria	100
Nematoda	5,000
Rotatoria	25,000
Gastrotrichia	500
Tardigrada	250
Oligochaeta	100
Gastropoda	50
Hydrachnellae	50
Hydrach larvae	250
Cladocera	2,500
Ostracoda	100
Copepoda	-
Cyclopoida and Calanoida	1,000
Harpacticoida	2,500
Nauplii and Copepodieten	5,000
Asellidea	50
Asellidea (parts)	500
Chironomidae	50
Sediment (ml/m^3)	250

A figure of over 50,000 organisms per m³ gives the impression of a large zoo: unsuitable for consumption and to be avoided by vegetarians.
Characteristic of these higher organisms is that they are harmless to human health. Their presence in drinking water is only aggravating if they are visually discernible by the naked eye.

Pathogenic microorganisms

Not all organisms are harmless. Some are harmful to human health by aggression (shark, crocodile), poison (jellyfish, snake, algae) or by causing disease (pathogenic microorganisms like the Giardia and Cryptosporidium protozoa). Humans can be infected by pathogenic (= disease causing) microorganisms through the intake of drinking water or by contact with infected water (swimming).
Pathogenic microorganisms are not present in water by nature, but they enter the water via feces and urine from humans and animals. Pathogenic microorganisms die in the water because the water temperature is lower than the body temperature of humans or animals.
Mainly because of the continuous supply of untreated or not fully treated wastewater from houses or bio-industry (abattoirs and fatting cattle stables), pathogenic microorganisms are found in water.

Pathogenic microorganisms can cause different diseases (Table 4), which may become epidemic rather quickly via the water.
Cholera epidemics were extensive in the 19th century. Those epidemics took over 65,000 casualties in the Netherlands between 1832 and 1870. In the years 1832, 1833, 1859 and 1866, the number of deaths was over 100 per 100,000 inhabitants per year. After 1900 the epidemics decreased in size and eventually disappeared from the Netherlands.
For several decades, typhus was present in the Netherlands because of the lack of safe drinking

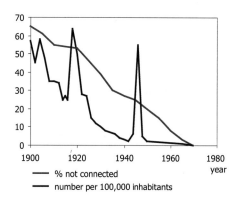

Figure 11 - Deaths due to typhoid fever and percentage of population not connected to drinking water supply

water (Figure 11). To supply good drinking water, water companies were instituted. However, it wasn't until after 1950 before almost all Dutch homes and businesses were connected to central drinking water supply systems.

Since 1976, some cases of Legionnaire's disease have been registered in the Netherlands. It has been proven that Legionella bacteria were common in warm water installations in the Netherlands. It was also shown that some materials may increase the growth of Legionella. In 1986 a committee of the National Health Council advised the Ministry of Health to increase the temperature of warm water installations to 60°C minimum. Also, it was recommended that notification of legionellosis become obligatory, making the tracking of legionellosis hotspots quicker.

Pathogenic microorganisms in water are determined by passing the water through a membrane filter and placing the filter residual on a growth medium for a special organism, then in an incubator at an optimum growth temperature.
To determine the colony number, not even this concentration technique is required, and pouring out a bit of water over a fertile soil is sufficient.
After sufficient growing time in the incubator the number of colonies that have been formed is counted and reported as colony forming units

Table 4 - Pathogenic microorganisms and their resulting diseases

Pathogenic microorganisms	Illness
Bacteria	Typhoid fever, Cholera
Viruses	Hepatitis, Polio
Protozoa (single cell animals)	Diarrhea and stomach complaints

(CFU) per volume. In the case of bacteriophages one speaks of plaque forming units (PFU).

2.4 The purity of water

Water is a very pure product. When the standards for drinking water are observed and the maximum concentration of all the macro-parameters are included, it can be seen that drinking water contains over 99.9% water molecules. When the composition of rainwater is observed, it even consists of 99.995% water molecules (Table 5). Fresh surface water also consists of over 99.5% water molecules.

The most important compounds in rainwater are the dissolved gases, oxygen and nitrogen.

Groundwater that is abstracted from the Veluwe area consists of 99.98% water molecules. Rainwater dissolves inorganic compounds (Ca^{2+}, HCO_3^-, Na^+, Cl^-) during infiltration, thus reducing the purity. However, the composition of the Veluwe water still meets the drinking water standards, so that in some places the water can be distributed directly without any treatment.

As a comparison, the purity of beer is given. In beer the concentrations of the inorganic macro-parameters are slightly higher than in drinking water, but the major difference is the far greater concentration of organic compounds (alcohol).

Besides alcohol, the concentration of carbon dioxide in beer is significantly higher than in drinking water. The carbon dioxide gives the bubbles and fresh taste to beer. Because of these additional compounds, the purity of beer is much less than that of drinking water: it consists of only 88% water molecules.

3. Water: physical and chemical properties

3.1 Properties of water

Pure water is a clear, color-, odor- and flavorless liquid. When exposed to sunlight, thick layers of water appear sky-blue.

Water is a liquid between 0°C and 100°C, but above that temperature it is a gas (water vapor), and below it a solid (ice) (Figure 12).

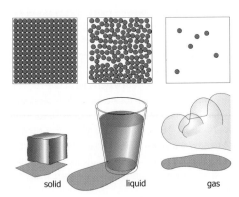

solid   liquid   gas

Figure 12 - The three phases of water

Table 5 - The purity of different products (in mg/l)

	Drinking water guidelines	Rain-water	Ground-water at Veluwe	Beer
Salts:				
- Cl⁻	(150)	3	13	190
- NO_3^-	50	3	7	< 1
- SO_4^{2-}	150	6	9	152
- HCO_3^-	> 60	0	78	630
- Ca^{2+}	(100)	0.2	27	44
- Mg^{2+}	(50)	0.1	2.5	190
- Na^+	150	0.9	9	85
- K^+	(12)	0.2	0.7	300
Gases:				
- CO_2	(< 20)	0.8	7	6,000
- N_2	-	19	19	-
- O_2	> 2	11	4.4	< 20
Heavy metals:				
- Mn^{2+}	0.05	0.03	0.03	0.10
- Fe^{2+}	0.20	0.04	0.04	0.05
Organic compounds	very low	none	none	112,000
Total (mg/l)	900	47	190	120,000
Water (%)	> 99.9	99.995	99.98	88

Figure 13 - Water as a dipole

Table 6 - Density and kinematic viscosity as a function of temperature

Temperature (°C)	Density (kg/m³)	Kinematic viscosity (10^{-6} m²/s)
0	999.87	1.787
5	999.94	1.519
10	999.69	1.307
20	998.19	1.004
30	995.61	0.801
100	958.39	0.294

Table 7 - Solubility product of some relevant salts

Salt	K_s (at 25°C)
$CaCO_3$	$3.8 \cdot 10^{-9}$
$Al(OH)_3$	$2.0 \cdot 10^{-32}$
$Ca(OH)_2$	$4.7 \cdot 10^{-6}$
$Fe(OH)_3$	$2.6 \cdot 10^{-39}$
$CaSO_4$	$7.1 \cdot 10^{-5}$
$FePO_4$	$1.3 \cdot 10^{-22}$
FeS	$1.0 \cdot 10^{-19}$

For the most part, the physical and chemical properties of water are caused by its chemical composition (H_2O) and the atomic configuration of the water molecule. The two hydrogen atoms are located on both sides of the oxygen atom, however, not in a straight line but at an angle of 104°.

Because of the large difference in atomic size between hydrogen and oxygen, water is a strong dipole (Figure 13). This makes water a good solvent and causes increased boiling and freezing temperatures as compared to other compounds having a similar molecular weight, like methane (CH_4).

Many of the physical properties of water strongly depend on temperature (density, viscosity, surface tension, specific heat, vapor pressure, volumetric expansion, compressibility). The large variation in viscosity (gumminess) (Table 6) is important in drinking water treatment as well as for distribution because of the flow resistance in filter media and pipes.

The presence of other compounds will change some properties of water significantly and others not at all. Sea water, for example, has a concentration of dissolved matter of 3.5% (mostly NaCl). This makes the density of water 2.5% higher, the viscosity 10% higher, but the electric conductivity even 5,400 times as large. Freezing only occurs at -2°C.

3.2 Concentrations in water

All inorganic compounds are more or less soluble in water, just like many organic compounds. The solubility, however, is very different between distinct compounds (Table 7). Also because of this, the concentrations (see frame next page) in water vary significantly between different compounds. To illustrate this, Table 8 shows the concentrations for different compounds present in water of a normal composition in an Olympic pool of 2,000 m³. The table shows that the masses of dissolved compounds ranges from 3 truckloads to a fraction of one grain. Investigating a poisonous compound with a concentration of 1μg/l in drinking water is like searching for a single Chinese in China (1 in a billion = 1 ppb). Microbiological research is even on a smaller scale; a bacteria of 1 μm has a volume of 10^{-15} liter. Finding a single bacteria is like finding 1 part in a million billion parts.

3.3 Ions in water

When dissolving compounds in water, most of them dissociate into separate ions. In natural water, significant concentrations of the following ions are present:

- cations: Na^+, K^+, Ca^{2+} and Mg^{2+}, and in smaller amounts of Fe^{2+}, Mn^{2+} and NH_4^+
- anions: Cl^-, HCO_3^-, NO_3^- and SO_4^{2-}

Table 8 - Concentration of compounds in water

Type of compound	Typical concentration	Unit	Mass (kg) in Olympic pool of 2000 m³	
Sea salt	36	g/l	72,000	3 truckloads
Sludge	10 (1%)	g/kg	20,000	1 truckload
Dissolved material	1,500	mg/l	3,000	1 van load
Nitrate	50	mg/l	100	2 barrels
Toxin (light)	10	μg/l	0.02	1 teaspoon
Toxin (heavy)	0.1	μg/l	0.0002	1 grain
Endocrine disrupter	1	ng/l	0.000002	1/100 grain

Concentration – terms and definitions

It is important to know which amount of a certain compound is present in some mixture. Different measurements are used to do so:

- mass (kilogram or equivalents: g, mg, µg, etc.)
- volume (cubic meter or factors of this: dm^3, l, ml, etc.)
- amount of substance (mol or factors of this: mmol, µmol, etc.)

These three different measures have mutual relationships, which are defined by the following properties:

- density of a compound (kg/m^3) = mass / volume
- molar mass of a compound (kg/mol) = mass / amount of substance

The density (formerly specific gravity) is dependent on both temperature and pressure.

The molar mass of a compound has a linear relationship with the molecule as mass, as the number of molecules per mol is equal for all compounds. The molecular mass is the sum of the atomic mass of the different atoms in a molecule.

$$M = N_A \cdot \sum m_a = \sum m_a$$

in which:

m_a = atomic mass of an atom (g)
N_a = Avogadro's constant (number of molecules per mol = $6{,}022 \cdot 10^{23}$)
M_a = molar atomic mass (g)

The molar atomic mass can be found in reference books.

Sometimes, one does not start from the compound itself, but from the solvent before dissolving (and possible subsequent reactions and/or dissociation).
The named measurements and definitions are all used, possibly in the same text.

For a component in a compound, the following terms are used:

- (mass) concentration (kg / m^3) = mass / total volume
- mass fraction (%) = mass / total mass / 100
- (ppm) = mass / total mass - 1,000,000
- molar concentration (mol / m^3) = amount / total volume
- molality (mol / kg) = amount / mass of solvent

In water chemistry, computations of the equilibrium reactions are based on the molar concentrations, expressed in mol/l. This measure is called molarity, having the Molar (1M is 1 mol/l) as its unit.
Pure water itself is 55.6 M (1,000 g/l and 18 g/mol).

Ions are electrically charged. The electric charge of some compound within a fluid depends on the concentration and on the valence of the relevant ion:

- valence concentration (eq / m^3) = molar concentration · valence

The sum of the valence concentrations of all positively charged ions is equal to that of the negatively charged ions (electric neutral).

When more than one compound has dissolved in water, it is typically not possible to trace the origin of the mix. Has the sodium originated from NaCl or from Na_2SO_4, and has the sulphate originated from $MgSO_4$ or from Na_2SO_4? The sum of the valence concentration of the cations is equal to that of the anions, because water is electrically neutral. Using this information one can either check a water analysis or compute an unknown component using an ion balance. Every ion has a specific conductivity, which makes it possible to compute the electric conductivity from the concentrations. One could also compute a single concentration from the known conductivity in reverse.

Ionic strength and activity

At low concentrations there will be no mutual ion influence (ideal solution). When concentrations increase the electrical forces will also increase, causing increased pushing and pulling of ions.

Table 9   - Activity coefficient for ions in water

Water type	Distilled-water	Rhine water	Sea water
Ionic strength	0 mmol/l	10 mmol/l	1000 mmol/l
Valence strength 1-ion	1.00	0.90	0.56
Valence strength 2-ion	1.00	0.66	0.10
Valence strength 3-ion	1.00	0.39	0.06

This prevents some ions from reacting with others. In equilibrium reactions, one does not compute, therefore, using molar concentrations but using adjusted concentrations; these are activities. Table 9 gives some impression of the size of the activity coefficient, depending on the valence of an ion and the kind of water or ionic strength. In subsequent chapters of this module the mutual influence between ions will not be addressed.

Computation ionic balance

A single unknown concentration can be computed using an ionic balance.
In order to do this, the valence concentration for each component is computed:

Compound	Weight concentration (mg/l)	Molar mass (g/mol)	Molar concentration (mmol/l)	Valence	Valence concentration (meq/l)
Cations:					
Na^+	63	23	2.74	1	2.74
K^+	5	39	0.13	1	0.13
Ca^{2+}	45	40	1.13	2	2.25
Mg^{2+}	9	24.5	0.37	2	0.73
Fe^{2+}	4	56	0.07	2	0.14
Mn^{2+}	1	55	0.02	2	0.04
NH_4^+	2	18	0.11	1	0.11
Total	129				6.14
Anions:					
Cl^-	73	35.4	2.06	1	2.06
HCO_3^-	151	61	2.48	1	2.48
NO_3^-	1	78	0.01	1	0.01
SO_4^{2-}	Unknown	96	?	2	?
Total	?				6.14

From the ionic balance it follows that the total valence concentration of the anions should also be 6.14 meq/l.
Therefore, the amount of SO_4^{2-} should be 1.60 meq/l   (= 6.14 - 2.06 - 2.48 - 0.01).
Conclusion: SO_4^{2-} = 1.60 meq/l = 1.60/2 = 0.80 mmol/l   = 0.88 x 96   = 77 mg/l.
The total amount of dissolved matter amounts to 431 mg/l   (= 129 + 73 + 151 + 1 + 77).

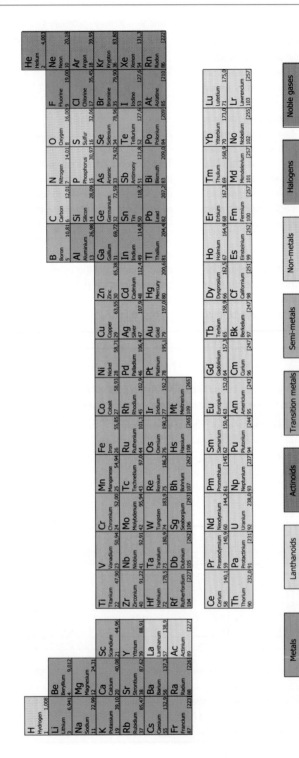

Shown is the average atomic weight, calculated as the average of the natural occurring isotope-mixture.

For quickly declining elements, the [atomic-weight number] for the isotope with the longest half-life is given.

Figure 14 - Periodic table

Computation of gas concentration in water

Compute the oxygen concentration in water, which is in free exchange to open air
(at 10°C, 1 bar = 101,325 Pa).

At sea level, air contains approximately 21 volume percent of oxygen.
The molar fraction of oxygen amounts to 0.21.
The partial pressure is 0.21 bar or (101,325 · 0.21 =)   21,300 Pa.

The oxygen concentration in air is: (21,300 / (8.3143 · (273+10)) =)   9.05 mol/m³.
Having a Henry coefficient of 0.041 for oxygen, the oxygen concentration in water will be:
(0.041 · 9.05 =) 0.37 mol/m³.
At a molar mass of 32 g this amounts to   (0.37 · 32 =)   12 g/m³ (mg/l).

3.4 Gases in water

Gases can dissolve in water. In a condition of free exchange between a liquid and a gas, there will be an equilibrium state for the concentrations of the gas (volatile matter) according to Henry's Law:

$$H = \frac{c_w}{c_g}$$

in which:

c_w = concentration of volatile matter
    in liquid   (mol/m³)
c_g = concentration of volatile matter
    in gas   (mol/m³)
H = distribution coefficient of volatile matter (-)

Henry's Law shows that there is a single defined relationship between the concentrations of volatile compounds in gas and fluid states.

Different compounds have different solubilities, which are temperature dependent.

Table 10 shows the H values for solubility in water at different temperatures. Gases having a low H value are difficult to dissolve in water; gases having high H value dissolve easily. Carbon dioxide is about 30 times as easy to dissolve as oxygen, which in its turn is twice as easy to dissolve as nitrogen. The solubility of methane is comparable to that of oxygen.

The concentration of a volatile matter in the gas state is computed using the general gas law (pV = nRT), which can be formulated as:

$$c_g = \frac{p_a}{RT}$$

in which:

p_A = partial pressure of volatile matter
    in gas state   (Pa)
R = universal gas constant = 8.3143
                          (J/mol/K)
            or (Pa m³/mol/K)
T = temperature   (K)

In a pure gas the partial pressure equals the true pressure. Based on the gas law, a pure gas at 0°C and 101,325 Pa has a concentration of 44.6 mol/m³ (1 mol in 22.4 l).

The partial pressure of a gas can be computed by multiplying the molar fraction (which equals the volume fraction) by the pressure.

At sea level, air contains 78% nitrogen, 21% oxygen,1% argon and 0.032% carbon dioxide. The volume fractions of the other gases (methane, hydrogen sulfide) are even lower. From this information one can compute that water, when it is in

Table 10 - Distribution coefficient H for the solubility in water

Compound		Distribution coefficient H		
		0°C	10°C	20°C
Nitrogen	N_2	0.023	0.019	0.016
Oxygen	O_2	0.049	0.041	0.033
Methane	CH_4	0.055	0.043	0.034
Carbon dioxide	CO_2	1.71	1.23	0.942
Hydrogen sulfide	H_2S	4.69	3.65	2.87
Ozone	O_3	0.64	0.54	0.39

equilibrium with air at 10°C and 1 bar, contains 11.9 mg/l of oxygen (O_2), 17.9 mg/l of nitrogen (N_2) and 0.75 mg/l of carbon dioxide (CO_2).

3.5   Acid-base reactions in water

Ionization of water
One of the most important chemical properties of water is that it can be both an acid and a base, because water ionizes into H^+ and OH^- ions. The H+ ions associate with a water molecule into H_3O^+. In practice, H_3O^+ and H^+ are considered equal and used as equivalents.

These ions are formed at extremely high speeds and, at the same speed, they form water again. Normally, the number of ions at a certain moment is very low.

The ionization is an equilibrium reaction, for which an equilibrium constant can be determined. Because the concentration of H_2O is almost constant (55.6 mol/l), the equilibrium equation for water can be given as:

$$K_w = \left[H^+\right] \cdot \left[OH^-\right]$$

in which

K_w	=	ion product of water
	=	$1.0 \; 10^{-14}$ mol²/l² at 25°C
$[H^+]$	=	concentration H^+ ions (mol/l)
$[OH^-]$	=	concentration OH^- ions (mol/l)

For a neutral solution it holds (at 25°C) that:
$[H^+] = [OH^-] = 1.0 \; 10^{-7}$ mol/l = 0.0001 mmol/l. This proves that there is a very small number of ions.

The concentration $[H^+]$ is usually denoted as the negative logarithm pH:

pH	=	$- \log [H^+]$
pOH	=	$- \log [OH^-]$
pH + pOH	=	14.0 (at 25°C)

A neutral solution has a pH value of 7.0 at a temperature of 25°C. A lower pH, meaning a higher concentration of H^+ ions, indicates an acid solution. A higher pH indicates that a solution is basic.

By adding 0.1 mmol/l H^+ the pH value falls to 4. Adding the same amount of OH^- would increase the pH to 10. Small amounts of acids and bases can have a large impact if there are no other reagents.

Dissociation of carbon dioxide
The most important acid-base reaction in water is related to the dissociation of CO_2.
CO_2 reacts with water:

$$CO_2 + H_2O \rightleftharpoons H_2CO_3$$

Though this reaction requires some time (a few seconds under normal conditions), the transformation is almost complete. In practice, CO_2 and H_2CO_3 are considered identical and are used as equivalents.

The dissociation continues from H_2CO_3 to bicarbonate according to the following equilibrium reactions:

$$H_2CO_3 \rightleftharpoons H^+ + HCO_3^-$$
$$K_1 = [H^+][HCO_3^-] / [H_2CO_3] = 4.5 \; 10^{-7} \text{ (at 25°C)}$$

$$HCO_3^- \rightleftharpoons H^+ + CO_3^{2-}$$
$$K_2 = [H^+][CO_3^{2-}] / [HCO_3^-] = 4.7 \; 10^{-11} \text{ (at 25°C)}$$

From the equilibrium formulas it can be calculated which ionic forms of CO_2 are present at a certain pH value.
For this purpose it is convenient to rewrite the formulas in the pK form (pK = - log K):

$$pK_1 = pH + \log \{ [H_2CO_3] / [HCO_3^-] \} = 6.35 \text{ (at 25°C)}$$
$$pK_2 = pH + \log \{ [HCO_3^-] / [CO_3^{2-}] \} = 10.33 \text{ (at 25°C)}$$

When the concentrations in the logarithmic part are equal, the ratio in that part equals 1 and, because log 1 = 0, it holds then that pH = pK.
Therefore, at a pH value of 6.35, $[H_2CO_3]$ equals $[HCO_3^-]$. For every higher pH unit, the ratio will be a factor 10 lower.
When pH = 10.33, $[HCO_3^-]$ equals $[CO_3^{2-}]$.
For a pH value lower than 8.3, the percentage of CO_3^{2-} is below 1%.

Dissociation of carbon dioxide

A spring water factory puts 4.4 g CO_2 in 1 liter of demineralized water.
What will be the pH value of this water?
What amount of true CO_2 will be in the water?
What will be the pH value when 1 mmol/l HCO_3^- is added?

The inserted amount of CO_2 (or H_2CO_3) is   4.4 / 44 = 0.1 mol.
When x mol of CO_2 dissociates, x mol H^+, x mol HCO_3^- and 1 - x mol CO_2 will be formed (neglecting the amount of HCO_3^- that is transformed into CO_3^{2-}).
From K_1 = x · x / (0.1 - x) = 4.5 10^{-7} it follows that   x = 0.00021 mol/l or 0.21 mmol/l.
Thus, the pH value will be   pH = - log(0.00021) = 3.68.

From K_2 = 4.7 · 10^{-11} = $[H^+] [CO_3^{2-}] / [HCO_3^-]$ and after entering the known values for H^+ and HCO_3^- it follows that CO_3^{2-} = 4.7·10^{-11}.   This can indeed be neglected, so that:
$[CO_2]$ = 100 - 0.21 = 99.79 mmol/l   and $[HCO_3^-]$ = 0.21 mmol/l
(meaning that 0.2% has dissociated)

After adding 1 mmol/l HCO_3^- the pH value will be:
pH = 6.35 - log {99.79 / (0.21+1.00) } = 6.35 - 1.92 = 4.43

A certain pH is linked to a certain ratio between the reaction products, as can be seen in Figure 15.

Because of the HCO_3^- the pH value will change only slightly when adding an acid or a base. Acids and bases will be used by the transformation to CO_2 or CO_3^{2-}. The buffer capacity indicates the amount of acid or base that is required for a pH change (mmol/l/pH).

Determination of CO_2 and HCO_3^- in water
The H_2CO_3 concentration in water is determined by adding a strong base which transforms all CO_2

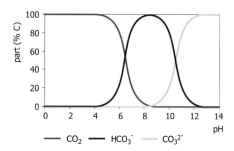

Figure 15 - Relationship between pH, CO_2, HCO_3^- and CO_3^{2-}

into HCO_3^-. At a pH value of 8.3 this transformation is almost complete.
For this titration one can use a pH meter or else the phenolphthalein indicator, which changes from colorless to red at this pH value.
The amount of base equals the amount of CO_2. That amount is sometimes referred to as the base capacity, acidity or the p-number.
For the full pH range it holds that:
p-number = $[CO_2] - [CO_3^{2-}] + [H^+] - [OH^-]$.

The bicarbonate concentration in water is determined by adding a strong acid to water, which will transform all HCO_3^- into CO_2. At a pH value of 4.4 this transformation is almost complete. For this titration one can use either a pH meter or the methyl orange indicator, which changes from yellow to red at this pH value.
The amount of acid corresponds to the amount of HCO_3^-. That amount is sometimes referred to as the acid capacity, the alkalinity or the m-number.
For the full pH range it holds that:
m-number = $[HCO_3^-] + 2 [CO_3^{2-}] - [H^+] + [OH^-]$.

From the definition it follows that:

$m + p = [CO_2] + [HCO_3^-] + [CO_3^{2-}] = TAC$ (Total Anorganic Carbon)

Also for the p and m numbers it holds that they are related to the pH value (3 values, of which 2 are independent). Both can have a negative value; the p-number is always negative at a pH value above 8.3.

The analysis of CO_2 in water is typically very unreliable, because CO_2 escapes during titration, whereby the measurements are influenced.

Therefore, usually the pH value is measured in water under pressure and the m-number is determined by titration. The CO_2 concentration is computed afterwards. The p and m numbers are stochiometric parameters, which are very useful for computations when adding acids and bases or calculating precipitation, etc. From the reaction equations one can determine how both values change. From this information the pH value can be immediately computed, and after that the concentration for the different carbon dissociation products can be calculated.

3.6 Calcium carbonate equilibrium in water

Calcium carbonate is a compound that is difficult to dissolve in water:

$$Ca^{2+} + CO_3^{2-} \rightleftharpoons CaCO_3$$

From a chemical perspective, this is a precipitation reaction, but in natural water also acid-base reactions with carbonic acid are involved. The solubility of calcium carbonate amounts to:

$K_s = [Ca^{2+}][CO_3^{2-}] = 3.8 \; 10^{-9} = 10^{-8.42}$ (at T = 25°C)

From this it can be computed that water will only dissolve 0.062 mmol/l $CaCO_3$ ($x^2 = 3.8 \; 10^{-9}$, $x = 6.2$ 10^{-5}), which corresponds to only 2.5 mg/l of Ca^{2+}. However, when CO_3^{2-} is removed from the water by some acid, the water can dissolve much larger amounts of $CaCO_3$ and the hardness of the water will increase.

In nature, calcium enters the water because the calcium carbonate in the soil reacts with the CO_2 from the water:

$$CaCO_3 + CO_2 + H_2O \rightleftharpoons Ca^{2+} + 2 HCO_3^-$$

For this equilibrium reaction it holds that (at T = 25°C):

$$K = [Ca^{2+}][HCO_3^-]^2 / [CO_2] = 3.6 \times 10^{-5} = 10^{-4.44}$$
$$= K_s K_1 / K_2 = 10^{-(8.42 + 6.35 - 10.33)}$$

When all calcium in the water has originated from calcium carbonate (and not from $CaSO_4$ or $CaCl_2$), it holds that $[Ca^{2+}] = [HCO_3^-] / 2$. Therefore, a third power relationship between CO_2 and HCO_3^- holds for this equilibrium. The graphic presentation of this is known as Tillmans' diagram (Figure 16).

The diagram indicates the calcium carbonate (limestone) equilibrium. Above the equilibrium line, the water is aggressive to limestone, below it limestone will precipitate. At higher temperatures the curve will shift upwards. The water that was in equilibrium will now be limestone precipitating, as is seen in the formation of $CaCO_3$ deposits (scaling) in heating installations.

Aggressive water needs to be alkalized by removal of CO_2. This can be done by gas transfer (shifting along a vertical line), by adding a base (shifting under a 1:1 slope) or by reaction with $CaCO_3$ with marble filtration (shifting under a 2:1 slope).

In limestone-precipitating water there can be a precipitation of $CaCO_3$ (shift under a 2:1 slope).

The equilibrium constants for the calcium carbonate are given in Table 11.

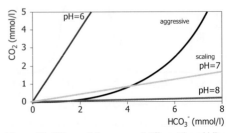

Figure 16 - Tillmans' diagram and different iso pH-lines

Table 11 - Calcium carbonate equilibrium constants
(at pK = - log K, with ion strength = 0)

	10°C	25°C	100°C
		pK	
K_s	8.36	8.42	9.20
K_1	6.46	6.35	6.45
K_2	10.49	10.33	10.16
K_w	14.53	14.00	11.27

Saturation index SI

The degree of over- or under-saturation of calcium carbonate is indicated with the saturation index (SI).

From the equilibrium reaction it can be derived that:

$$SI = \log\left(\frac{[Ca^{2+}]\cdot[CO_3^{2-}]}{K_s}\right) = pH - pH_s$$

Here, the pH_s is the equilibrium pH value of water, with the same Ca^{2+} and HCO_3^- concentrations:

$$pH_s = pK_2 - pK_s - \log([Ca^{2+}][HCO_3^-])$$

Water having a positive SI is limestone precipitating, water with a negative SI is limestone aggressive.

Conditioning

It is preferable that drinking water be slightly limestone precipitating. This will prevent cement-bound materials (concrete, asbestos cement) from corroding. Corrosion of these materials is caused by the dissolution of lime (CaO) from the cement. By a limited precipitation of $CaCO_3$ on metal pipe materials, the dissolution of metals like copper, lead, tin and zinc is prevented or reduced.

Soft water is preferable (total hardness lower than 1.0 - 1.5 mmol/l). Soft water is more pleasant to use (no film on tea, no unpleasant feeling when showering because of higher soap binding, no precipitation or scale in the washing machine, boiler or heater). In natural water the magnesium concentration is almost always limited (<0.5 mmol/l), making the calcium concentration especially important.

Lime

The word lime is used for various chemical substances that have calcium in them.

The exact reference being made is mostly dependent on the person or his occupation.
Some examples of the meaning of lime(stone):
- drinking water consumers and other laypeople often mean calcium (there is much limestone in the water), but also calcium carbonate (limestone scaling in the washing machine)
- geologists use the word for limestone, which mainly consists of calcium carbonate (dripstone caves are present in limestone areas)
- chemists often mean the base compounds CaO and $Ca(OH)_2$ (we use both quick and slaked lime)
- civil engineers use the word for all compounds containing calcium (in concrete, there is both free lime (CaO / $Ca(OH)_2$) and bonded lime (calcium silicates, calcium carbonates, etc.)
- linguists mean 'the carbonic acid of the calcium metal', or 'mortar' or 'plaster' or 'stone', consisting mainly of limestone

Due to these irregularities, the single word lime(stone) should be avoided.
In compound words or in sentences the meaning can be made clear, like in:
- limestone aggressive   able to dissolve $CaCO_3$
- limestone precipitate   able to precipitate $CaCO_3$
- limestone scale $CaCO_3$ deposit due to increasing temperatures
- limestone water   milky mixture of water and $Ca(OH)_2$ (mostly totally dissolved)
- limestone suspense   milky mixture of water and $Ca(OH)_2$ (mostly not dissolved)
- limestone   limestone
- chalk oven   oven for heating (burning) limestone or chalk (for products like CaO).

When softening water in drinking water production plants, mainly the calcium concentration is reduced. At the same time care is taken not to reduce the HCO_3^- concentration too much. The HCO_3^- causes a stable water quality (buffer capacity), making the pH value of the water change only slightly when a small amount of acid forms because of biological activity.

Because of the low hardness, the equilibrium pH value is relatively high (8.0 - 8.3). This increased pH value causes a lower copper and lead solvency of the water.

Besides being advantageous for human health, this is also advantageous for the environment (fewer heavy metals). Because of a lower hardness, fewer environmentally unfriendly phosphates are required in detergents. Phosphates are used in detergents to prevent the precipitation of $CaCO_3$ on clothing and in washing machines.

Because of environmental and health advantages, the Dutch water companies soften drinking water. This central softening is also economically attractive to consumers (less use of soap, lower maintenance costs for hot water installations, no private environmentally unfriendly softening installation required).

3.7   Redox reactions in water

Water can be formed from the reaction of hydrogen and oxygen. In this reaction, oxygen is the oxidant (electron absorber) and hydrogen is the reductant (electron supplier). Such redox reactions (oxidation - reduction) are presented in the form of two half-reactions, from which the total reaction can be added:

$$O_2 + 4 e^- \rightarrow 2 O^{2-}$$
$$H_2 \rightarrow 2 H^+ + 2 e^- \qquad (2 \times)$$
$$\overline{O_2 + 2 H_2 \rightarrow 2 O^{2-} + 4 H^+ \rightarrow 2 H_2O}$$

This reaction can also be reversed under impact of electrical energy, causing the water to be transformed into oxygen and hydrogen again.

Oxidation with oxygen in water

Also in water, oxygen is an important oxidant:

$$O_2 + 2 H_2O + 4 e^- \rightarrow 4 OH^-$$

This oxidation reaction occurs when treating anaerobic groundwater. In this water several compounds are dissolved from the soil, like iron, manganese, ammonium, methane and hydrogen sulfide. Oxidizing these compounds occurs according to the following scheme:

$$Fe^{2+} \rightarrow Fe^{3+} + e^-$$
$$Mn^{2+} + 2 H_2O \rightarrow MnO_2 + 4 H^+ + 2 e^-$$
$$NH_4^+ + 2 H_2O \rightarrow NO_2^- + 8 H^+ + 6 e^-$$
$$NO_2^- + H_2O \rightarrow NO_3^- + 2 H^+ + 2 e^-$$
$$CH_4 + 2 H_2O \rightarrow CO_2 + 8 H^+ + 8 e^-$$
$$H_2S \rightarrow S + 2 H^+ + 2 e^-$$

The extent to which the oxidation reactions above will occur depends on the standard electron potential of the reaction. There are reactions that will start spontaneously (Fe) or be influenced by some catalyst (Mn), or be influenced by bacteria (NH_4, NO_2, CH_4, H_2S).
For the treatment of water it should be considered that sometimes, when adding oxygen during aeration, the CH_4 and H_2S gases are already partly removed.

Oxygen may also oxidize organic matter. This is mainly a biological process.

The redox equation for each compound can be derived from the electron balance.
For the oxidation of iron it needs to be noted that, in order to remove the formed Fe(III), a precipitation reaction to brown iron hydroxide is required:

$$Fe^{3+} + 3 H_2O \rightarrow Fe(OH)_3 + 3 H^+$$

The added reactions, leaving out H_2O itself, are then:

$$Fe^{2+} + 0.25 \; O_2 \rightarrow Fe(OH)_3 + 2.5 H^+$$
$$Mn^{2+} + O_2 \rightarrow MnO_2 + 2 \; H^+$$
$$NH_4^+ + 2 \; O_2 \rightarrow NO_3^- + 6 \; H^+$$
$$CH_4 + 2 \; O_2 \rightarrow CO_2 + 4 \; H^+$$

The reaction equations show a high oxygen demand for ammonium and methane. They also show that all named oxidation reactions are more or less acid-forming. This acid will react with HCO_3^- in water, forming CO_2.

Oxidation in aerobic water
The compounds above entered the groundwater by reduction reactions in the ground. In those, organic compounds, nitrates, and sulfates functioned as oxidants (electron absorbers).
The lower the redox potential of the water, the more compounds that may be used as oxidants.

Oxidation with strong oxidants
During drinking water production, strong oxidants are used. For groundwater treatment, occasionally potassium permanganate is used to support the oxidation by oxygen. This is efficient when the compounds to be oxidized are partly bound to organic compounds.

When treating surface water, strong oxidants like ozone and chlorine are important during disinfection and for the oxidation of organic compounds.

4.   Health and drinking water quality

4.1   The beneficial use of drinking water
Advertisements now and again draw our attention to the beneficial use of bottled water (Spa, Sourcy, Perrier, Reginaris and other brands). Why such a water should be so beneficial for human health mostly remains a mystery. Anyway, it cannot be derived from the composition of the water.

One manufacturer claims that its beneficial use is mainly due to the low concentration of dissolved salts; the other water is, on the contrary, healthy because of the very high concentration of some dissolved mineral.
The mineral concentration of water, however, has a clear influence on the flavor of the water. Some people prefer a very low mineral water (dry residual <50 mg/l), others prefer a high concentration of some or all minerals.

Decidedly, the concentration of dissolved carbon dioxide plays an important role in the taste of drinking water. Sometimes this is wholly absent (Spa Reine), and sometimes one has bubbling water with a concentration of some thousands of milligrams per liter, corresponding with a pH value of 4 to 5.
Drinking water, as is supplied by water companies, does not contain any beneficial elements, nor are those aimed for. This is because citizens feel threatened by the addition of compounds to water. This was the reason why the addition of fluoride to water was forbidden in the Netherlands, though it had been proven that fluoride in drinking water reduced tooth decay.

Drinking water, above all, is not allowed to contain compounds that are harmful to health. If it does, it may not exceed the level at which it has been proven that it has no negative effects on health when used lifelong, even for consumers with reduced resistance levels (babies, diseased or elderly people).

For bottled (packaged) water (natural mineral water and spring water), there is the "Decree for packaged waters" (1998) in the Netherlands. In this decree the standard values for 15 chemical parameters are given, equal to those in the drinking water regulation, which mentions many more parameters (65 in total). For microbiological parameters, the bottled (packaged) water standards are even stricter than those for drinking water. Natural mineral water and spring water do not need to have their original natural quality. Unstable compounds may be removed (iron, sulfur, carbon dioxide) or compounds may be added (carbon dioxide). Table 12 shows an overview of some chemical parameters for different packaged waters.

Drinking water as supplied by water companies shows much smaller quality differences. The supplied water quality, however, would fit well within the above-mentioned brands.

Some brands of mineral water exceed the standards for one or more parameters which have

Table 12 - Chemical concentration (in mg/l) of natural mineral water and bottled water

Mineral		Spa Reine	Reginaris	Extreme values (with brand)		Regulation (*)
Sodium	Na^+	3	low	1,230	Rogaska	> 200
Calcium	Ca^{2+}	5	190	368	Ferarella	> 150
Magnesium	Mg^{2+}	1	110	870	Rogaska	> 50
Chloride	Cl^-	5	low	245	Heppinger	> 200
Sulfate	SO_4^{2-}	4	low	153	Rogaska	> 200
Nitrate	NO_3^-	2	low			
Bicarbonate	HCO_3^-	15	1,950			> 600
Dry rest		33	2,500	4,000	Rogaska	> 1500
Carbon dioxide	CO_2	-	2,500	7,000	Perrier	> 250

* Minimal value for mineral rich water (per mineral)

been set for drinking water in the drinking water regulation.

So, it is not strange that water companies started selling their drinking water in bottles (Prise d'eau, Viteau), and that bottled water producers started putting drinking water in their bottles (Herschi), or using the same groundwater as the adjacent water company (Sourcy).

The beneficial effect of drinking water is not only derived from drinking. For human health its use for washing is important, both washing the human body and washing products for food preparation, or washing the environment. Drinking water is also an important means of removing for human feces (sewage), which also has a major sanitary effect.

4.2 Harmful compounds and organisms in drinking water

Drinking water may not only have beneficial but also detrimental effects.

In water there may be compounds present which could be detrimental to human health. Pathogenic microorganisms can have a direct adverse effect on health, some organic micropollutants are only harmful after years of regular consumption.

Most adverse compounds in drinking water enter the body via the digestive organs, but in some cases via the respiratory organs. Chloroform is an example of a compound in drinking water which typically enters the body by inhaling vapors during showering.

The skin forms a better barrier to alien compounds than the digestive organs. There are no compounds in drinking water which have a direct detrimental effect through the skin.

Generally, there is some maximum boundary value given to a specific harmful compound. However, it could be that the compound cannot or can hardly be analyzed. In that case some indicator parameter is defined. This is the case for many microbiological parameters. Germs like typhus and cholera bacteria are not measured, but E.coli and other coli forms are, because they are indicators for recent fecal contamination and therefore a potential source of harmful viruses and bacteria.

Some harmful compounds will be very harmful even in small concentrations. Some bacteria may be so infectious that very few will cause illness.

Threshold value

For a number of compounds it is assumed that for some concentration in the water there is no harmful effect to health, not even in the case of lifelong exposure. This is the threshold value (also referred to as NOAEL (No Observed Adverse Effect Level) (Figure 17).

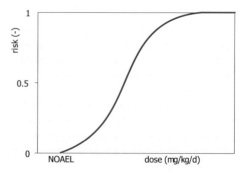

Figure 17 - Toxic compounds with threshold values

The threshold value (NOAEL) is determined from animal tests, and needs to be extrapolated from animals to humans. This is done by dividing the animal NOAEL by a safety factor of 10 to 10,000, depending on the type of study, animal and effect. The tolerable daily intake (TDI) is computed by multiplying safety-corrected NOAEL values by the average weight of some person (60 kg).

Drinking water standards

Drinking water is not the only source of compounds. Man also absorbs compounds from food and inhaled air.

From the TDI for some compound the standard value (maximum allowable concentration) for drinking water is computed, assuming a certain accepted absorption from drinking water and the assumed drinking water consumption.

Mostly a maximum of 10% of the TDI is allowed to be absorbed via drinking water (Table 13).

To arrive at the water standard from NOAEL via TDI can be illustrated by the norm values for nickel. The NOAEL for nickel is 5 mg/kg/d. The extrapolation from animals to man is performed by using a safety margin of 1,000. The NOAEL for man is, therefore, 5 µg/(kg.d).

The TDI at which no harmful effects occur to man is 0.3 mg/d (the NOAEL multiplied by the average weight). The accepted share of drinking water for the TDI is 10% (about 10% of the daily nickel absorption comes from drinking water). The average amount of drinking water consumed per day is 2 liters. The norm value for nickel will be $(0.3 / 2 \cdot 0.1 \cdot 1,000 =) 0.015$ mg/l. Rounded off, the standard is 20 µg/l.

Risk levels

There are carcinogenic compounds having a threshold value, but there are also so-called genotoxic-carcinogenic compounds. Of those compounds it is assumed that any concentration of it may have a harmful effect. Every molecule of a genotoxic-carcinogenic could change a body cell into a cancer cell. The dose-effect relationship for these compounds is shown in Figure 18.

Treatment cannot guarantee that such compounds are fully absent.

In order to come to some standards for carcinogenic compounds, two approaches may be used:
-   setting the standard at the level which is technically and economically feasible
-   determining the acceptable risk and computing the acceptable concentration from it

The acceptable risk is, for example, the chance for an individual to get cancer during his/her lifetime. The risk that is set is 1 in every 1,000,000 people, or a chance of $1 \cdot 10^{-6}$. This corresponds with a yearly risk of 10^{-8} (assuming a lifetime of 100 years).

Every activity carries some risks. Of some risks we are conscious, of others we are not. Risks are subdivided into voluntary and involuntary risks.

Voluntary risks are determined by people themselves. When riding a motorbike or smoking a cigarette, people can choose for themselves whether they take the risk or not.

Involuntary health risks are not chosen by the people themselves. For example, drinking water contains some health risk, however small, which needs to be accepted because one cannot live without water. The health risks from food are, in

Table 13 - Estimated actual share of drinking water in the TDI (norm is 10%) and total daily intake

	The actual share in tolerable daily intake (%)	The acceptable share for drinking water of the total daily intake (%)
Arsenic	< 2	< 4
Cadmium	< 1	< 1
Lead	8	8
Nitrate	< 2	< 4
Copper	< 2	25
Nickel	1	4

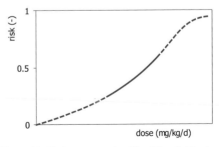

Figure 18 - Toxic compounds without threshold values

Table 14 - Risks per activity

Activity	Risk of dying (per person per year)
Voluntary:	
- smoking	$5 \cdot 10^{-3}$
- riding a motorbike	$2 \cdot 10^{-3}$
- mountaineering	$4 \cdot 10^{-5}$
- plane crash	$2 \cdot 10^{-8}$
Involuntary:	
- drinking water per compound	$1 \cdot 10^{-8}$

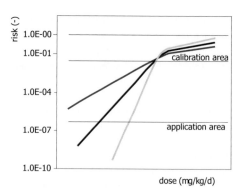

Figure 19 - Risk assessment using animal tests and mathematic models

general, much higher than water because the relative intake of many compounds via food is much higher than the intake via drinking water. The voluntary acceptable risks are higher than the involuntary risks (Table 14).

The determination of involuntary acceptable risks is done by the government. In the Netherlands it was determined that for genotoxic compounds in drinking water the risk should not be above 1.0 10^{-6} per human life.

The determination of the risk of a certain compound without a threshold value is done with animal tests.
Into a certain group of animals, a high concentration of the compound is injected, after which the animals are observed to determine what percentage finally die. To limit the group of animals, a high dose (giving a high risk, about $1 \cdot 10^{0}$ to $1 \cdot 10^{-2}$) is used.
Because the concentrations in drinking water are much lower, an extrapolation using mathematic models needs to be performed. A good calibration of the models is difficult. Generally, they have a logarithmic function, causing calibration in the measurement area to yield a high uncertainty in the application area.

The process is shown in Figure 19. The lines are the output of some model with different parameters. In the calibration region all three lines agree with the data. When, however, the application area is observed, there are large differences.

In order to be sure that the concentration which is absorbed by human beings is not too high, a safety factor of 10 to 10,000 is applied, depending on available data and additional knowledge of the compound.

Ethical levels
Not for all compounds is the standard related to the health risks of the specific compound. This would lead to a very elaborate set of standards. Some compounds, it is believed, do not belong in drinking water. For those compounds, the standard is sometimes based on summation parameters or on arbitrary standards for groups of compounds. For example, for pesticides there is a single ethical standard of 0.1 µg/l in the European drinking water regulations. Within the group there is no differentiation for the different toxicities of the pesticides. Also, standards are set for technical or aesthetic/organoleptic reasons for compounds which are not toxic but which may influence the flavor, color and odor of the water.

Balancing the different health risks
When a standard is exceeded, that does not mean that the water can no longer be drunk. On the one hand, this is because of the applied safety margins. On the other hand, it is because not all standards are toxicological, and exceeding the standard is often only temporary.
A temporary high concentration of trihalomethanes (compounds which are produced during disinfection with chlorine) can be preferred over abandoning disinfection, because the latter may lead to infectious diseases.

Pathogenic microorganisms
Pathogenic microorganisms can be subdivided into bacteria, viruses and protozoa.

Pathogenic microorganisms are present in water due to sewage containing fecal material. In water there are many different kinds of pathogenic microorganisms in low concentrations, making it impossible to measure all of them separately.

Therefore, use is made of indicator organisms, for example E.coli. These are organisms that originate from feces, are present in large numbers, and are typical for a larger group of pathogenic microorganisms.
Besides E.coli, spores of sulfite-reducing clostridia (SSRC) and fecal streptococci are used as indicator organisms.
A few standards for drinking water are formulated on the basis of such organisms. With the absence of indicator organisms, it is assumed that other pathogenic microorganisms will not be present in the drinking water either.

Although drinking water satisfies the standards for indicator organisms, there have been infections with diseases (in the United States and Great Britain) which were caused by drinking water consumption. Therefore, it is desirable to use the same approach for pathogenic microorganisms as is used for micropollutants. The practice is to estimate the risk of infection by a single microorganism (consumption of 2 liters of water per person and one infection in every 10,000 people per year) and determine the acceptable concentration of a microorganism from this information. The standards that originate from this procedure for pathogenic microorganisms are extremely strict. For example, one Giardia protozoa is allowed to be present in every 147 m^3 of water. The measurement of Giardia protozoa in those very low concentrations is, however, a very delicate matter.

The number of Legionnaire's disease cases reported in the Netherlands currently numbers to about 800 per year, which accounts for a yearly disease risk of ca. $50 \cdot 10^{-6}$. Some of these cases are caused by infections during holidays abroad. It is, however, not impossible that the risk of infection from warm water installations is higher than the 1 to 10,000 standard mentioned above.

Harmful chemical compounds
Three compounds are harmful in concentrations above 1 mg/l:
- nitrate   (50 mg/l)
- copper   (2 mg/l)
- fluoride   (1 mg/l)

Too high a nitrate concentration can lead to methaemoglobinemia in small children ("blue babies disease").
Too high a fluoride concentration can lead to bone deformations (fluorosis).
Too high a copper concentration leads to digestive complaints.

Other chemical compounds can even be harmful in concentrations below 1 mg/l.
Arsenic causes the Blackfoot disease, mercury causes brain diseases, and aluminum is related to the early onset of Alzheimer's disease.
The health effects of the different compounds are, as far as they are known, easy to find in literature.
This literature is published by national governments, but also internationally by the World Health Organization (WHO) of the United Nations.

5.   Drinking water legislation in the Netherlands

5.1   Framework for the regulations
Dutch legislation fits within the directives which are set in a European context. New European legislation needs to be absorbed into national law within a certain defined term.
In the formulation and execution of this legislation, many governments and agencies have been involved.

Water Framework Directive
The European Water Framework Directive (December 2000) set a new framework for water management, in which the concepts of "good condition" and "catchment area approach" are central. The directive aims at improving the quality of water systems, and also at the sustainable use of water.

Much of the contents of the directive requires further elaboration.

When examining the framework directive for the drinking water branch, the explanations of the concepts of "protected area," "good condition," "cost recovery" and "priority compounds" are especially important.

The framework directive requires member states to maintain a registry of protected areas. These are also areas that are used for water abstraction for drinking water preparation. The framework directive does not give a system for functional allocation, as we have in the Netherlands for surface water. The Dutch classification "surface water meant for drinking water preparation" will be revoked. This may create a gap in the protection of water which is used for drinking water preparation, especially concerning surface water. In the Dutch Decree on Water Supply standards for surface water are included which are used for the drinking water supply in combination with the treatment process used.

For the water companies "good condition" refers to a quality of ground- and surface water where only simple treatment means are required to produce drinking water. This needs to be clear from the elaboration of the standard for good condition. "Good condition" is one of the central concepts in the Water Framework Directive. The standards which result from an ecological good state are, in a significant number of cases, less stringent than the standards which fit a good condition for drinking water production.

According to the Framework Directive, a reasonable amount of cost recovery for water services needs to be achieved, and the water price policy should stimulate efficient use of the available amounts of water. The principle that the polluter pays is one of the leading principles of the directive. This cost recovery, including external costs, is achieved by the water companies to a sufficient level. However, water companies need to recover very high costs for the removal of pesticides from groundwater. These costs amounted to 227 million euros in the Netherlands over the past ten years.

The Framework Directive requires the formulation of a list of priority compounds, for which emissions into surface water should be reduced or stopped. It is important that those compounds which are problematic in drinking water production be included. The Association of Dutch Water Companies (VEWIN), therefore, supplied measurement data about the occurrence of pollutants in drinking water sources and will, together with the European organization EUREAU, strive for a high priority of specific compounds on the list which are problematic in drinking water production. Atrazine, diuron, isoproturon, and simazine are classified as "harmful priority compounds to be evaluated." Classification as a harmful priority compound implies emission limitations and strict limitations for sewage, emission and losses within 20 years.

National government

The national government creates the framework within which the water companies can produce good drinking water. In the Netherlands the Water Supply Act and the Decree on the Water Supply set the prerequisites that need to be fulfilled. For example, the number of micro- or milligrams of certain compounds that are acceptable in drinking water are exactly described. The sanitary conditions are reviewed by regional inspectors from the Ministry for Housing, Spatial Planning and the Environment (VROM). Within the Health Act, the National Health Council also supervises the drinking water supply. The national government formulates policies; the elaboration of those policies is handed out to the provincial governments.

Also, the national government contributes significantly when it comes to further improvement of the quality of the sources used for drinking water preparation. Especially the ministries of Housing, Spatial Planning and the Environment; Agriculture, Nature and Food Quality; and, Transport, Public Works and Water Management are important in this respect.

The Ministry of Transport, Public Works and Water Management manages the Dutch surface waters. Of vital importance to the drinking water supply are IJsselmeer, Rhine, Meuse. The Ministry makes significant contributions to the improvement of the quality of surface waters. The other waters are managed by the provinces, who mostly delegate this task to regional water boards.

Provincial government

The policy, as it has been formulated by the central government, is elaborated into plans and regulations by provincial governments. For example, the provinces give substance to the measures that are written for the protection of groundwater. In this, they cooperate with the water companies. Also, the provinces hand out permits for the abstraction of groundwater. Not everyone is allowed to dig his own groundwater well; permission needs to be applied for and granted first.

Water boards

The water boards (Dutch: Waterschappen or Hoogheemraadschappen) are, together with the Ministry, responsible for the quality and quantity of regional waters in the Netherlands. The water boards maintain the water level within their regions and, if necessary, discharge water. Additionally, the water boards are responsible for wastewater treatment, checking the quality of surface water, and maintaining canals and city water. Because the Dutch water companies are interested in clean soils, clean rivers and canals, they sometimes cooperate with the water boards. The national organization of water boards is the Association of Dutch Water Boards (Unie van Waterschappen).

VROM-Inspection

Water companies regularly take drinking water samples themselves in order to verify the quality of the product. Supervising them are the regional inspectors of the Ministry of Housing, Spatial Planning and the Environment (VROM) who constantly scrutinize the health effects, the hygiene, and the supply certainty of the Dutch drinking water. If there are problems, the decision of whether or not the supply of drinking water can be continued and what measures are required is made by the VROM inspector.

Water companies

The water companies in the Netherlands provide for a 24-hours-per-day supply of reliable water from the taps.

In case of problems they decide together with the VROM inspector whether the supply of drinking water should be continued. If continuation is impossible, some other supply must be found. The water companies, after all, guarantee continuous supply.

Water companies are united in the Association of Dutch Water Companies (VEWIN). Within the VEWIN, there used to be quality directives for the desired drinking water quality which were stricter than the officially required quality (VEWIN recommendations).

Water companies not only focus on the final product, but, because of their role as guards of the quality of drinking water, they also have a sharp eye on environmental threats and pollution as well. From the perspective of continuity, costs and societal acceptance of water abstraction, they substantially contribute to the repair, maintenance, management and development of nature in water abstraction and protection areas.

5.2   Drinking water quality according to the Decree on Water Supply

The standards to which drinking water in the Netherlands should comply are registered in the Decree on Water Supply, which is an extension of the Water Supply Act. The Decree on Water Supply is regularly adapted to the most scientific insights and to developments in related legislation or European directives, such as EU 98-83-EC.

The Decree on Water Supply also regulates quality standards for surface water suitable for drinking water preparation.

Within the Decree on Water Supply, the following categories of parameters regarding drinking water can be seen:

- health-related, microbiological parameters
- health-related, chemical parameters
- organoleptic / aesthetic parameters
- operational parameters
- signalling parameters

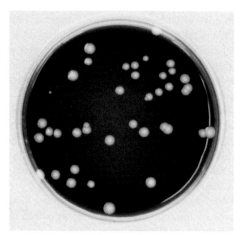

Figure 20 - Bacteria seen in a culture

Health-related, microbiological parameters

The microbiological parameters (Figure 20) having a health-related background are shown in Table 15.

E(scherichia) coli was formerly measured as thermal tolerant bacteria of the coli group (44°C) and Enterococci were measured as fecal streptococci. Microorganisms are not allowed to be present in drinking water in such concentrations that may harm human health. For certain microorganisms like viruses and protozoa, (e.g., Cryptosporidium and Giardia), it is impossible to measure concentrations at the low level that is relevant for human health. Instead, the owner who uses surface water for drinking water production needs to formulate a risk analysis for the water based on measurements of the relevant microorganisms in raw water and data concerning their removal in specific treatment processes, including soil passage in case of infiltration/recovery.

Table 15 - Health-related, microbiological parameters in the Degree on Water Supply

Parameter	Maximum Value	Unit
Cryptosporidium	[1]	
Escherichia coli	0	CFU / 100 ml [2]
Enterococci	0	CFU / 100 ml [2]
(Entero) viruses	[1]	
Giardia	[1]	

[1] Not present in the drinking water in such a concentration that it 's dangerous for the public health

[2] CFU = colony forming units

For the theoretical infection risk computed in this way, there is a provisional boundary value of one infection per 10,000 persons per year. The term 'provisional boundary value' is used to show that the value needs to be verified in practice. Adaptation of the value cannot be excluded.

The verification of this provisional boundary value needs to be performed for Entero viruses, Cryptosporidium and Giardia at least, but, in principle, also for other microorganisms.

If the computed infection risk is higher than the mentioned boundary value, the owner needs to consult the inspector on the measures to be taken. The inspector can decide whether a similar analysis should be performed for groundwater abstraction.

The microbiological parameters in drinking water are quite critical. Even a small contamination may lead to exceeding some standard. In that case, an emergency disinfection is applied and the consumers are advised to boil the water before using it.

Health-related, chemical parameters

The chemical parameters having a health-related background are represented in Table 16. The table shows that for wider standards have been set disinfection by-products (bromate in the case of ozone, trihalomethanes in case of chlorination).

For lead there is a temporary standard because many houses still are equipped with or connected by lead pipes. With lead pipes, it is almost impossible to satisfy the standard if the water is stagnant for some hours.

The temporary increase in the standard value gives the water companies and house owners a chance to change those pipes.

The relatively high values for cadmium and copper originate from a compromise between health effects and technical complexity (many copper pipes with cadmium-containing bronze connections).

For some health-related chemical parameters the VEWIN recommendations are stricter (nitrate 25 mg/l, nitrite 0.05 mg/l, cadmium 1.0 µg/l).

Table 16   - Health-related, chemical parameters in Decree on Water Supply

Parameter	Maximum value	Unit	Remark
Acrylamide	0.10	µg/l	
Antimony	5.0	µg/l	
Arsenic	10	µg/l	
Benzene	1.0	µg/l	
Benzo(a)pyrene	0.010	µg/l	
Boron	0.5	mg/l	
Bromate	1.0	µg/l	With disinfection a maximum value of 5.0 µg/l is allowed (as 90 percentile value, with a maximum of 10 µg/l)
Cadmium	5.0	µg/l	
Chromium	50	µg/l	
Cyanides (total)	50	µg/l	
1.2 – Dichloorethane	3.0	µg/l	
Epichloorhydrine	0.10	µg/l	
Fluoride	1.1	mg/l	
Copper	2.0	mg/l	
Mercury	1.0	µg/l	
Lead	10	µg/l	Until 1-1-2006 the maximum is 25 µg/l
Nickel	20	µg/l	
Nitrate	50	mg/l	
Nitrite	0.1	mg/l	
Polycyclic Aromatic Hydrocarbons (PAHs) (sum)	0.10	µg/l	Sum of specified compounds with a higher concentration than the detection limit
Polychlorinated Biphenyls (PCBs) (individual)	0.10	µg/l	Per substance
PCBs (sum)	0.50	µg/l	Sum of the specified compounds with a concentration > 0.05 µg/l
Pesticides (individual)	0.10	µg/l	Per substance. For aldrin, dieldrin, heptachloor and heptachloorepoxide a maximum of 0.030 µg/l is stated
Pesticides (sum)	0.50	µg/l	Sum of the individual pesticides with a higher concentration than the detection limit
Selenium	10	µg/l	
Tetra- and tri-chloroethene(sum)	10	µg/l	
Trihalomethanes (sum)	25	µg/l	Sum of specified compounds (as 90 percentile with a maximum of 50) Until 1-1-2006 the maximum is 100 µg/l
Vinylchloride	0.50	µg/l	

Organoleptic/aesthetic parameters

The organoleptic or aesthetic parameters concern the appeal of drinking water to the client, for drinking and for cleaning. The organoleptic / aesthetic parameters are shown in Table 17.

For some organoleptic/aesthetic parameters, the VEWIN recommendations are stricter. For turbidity it is 0.8 FTU, for iron 0.05 mg/l, and for manganese 0.02 mg/l.

Table 17   - Organoleptic/aesthetic parameters in Decree on Water Supply

Parameter	Maximum value	Unit	Remark
Aluminum	200	µg/l	
Odor		-	Tolerable level for consumers and no abnormal changes
Color	20	mg/l Pt/Co	
Iron	200	µg/l	
Manganese	50	µg/l	
Sodium	150	mg/l	Yearly average with a max. of 200 mg/l
Taste		-	Tolerable level for consumers and no abnormal changes
Sulfate	150	mg/l	Water may not be aggressive
Turbidity	4 (taps) 1 (from pumping station)	FTU	FTU = formazine turbidity unit
Zinc	3.0	mg/l	After >16 hours of stagnation

Operational parameters

The operational parameters concern the nature of a drinking water company, in which the quality of the drinking water should not be negatively affected during its stay in reservoirs or distribution installations. The operational parameters are given in Table 18.

Some operational parameters concern the danger of growth in the distribution network. This concerns both the organisms themselves, their nutrients (ammonium, DOC/TOC), and the temperature. The minimum concentration of hydrogen carbonate should prevent small CO_2 formation, in case biological growth would lead to a large change in pH value (buffer capacity).The oxygen concentration should be sufficiently high so that, in case of growth, no anaerobic water is formed, with all its negative side effects (stench, etc.). In the VEWIN recommendations, even a minimum value of 4 mg/l for oxygen was included.

An example of growth and scale in drinking water pipes is shown in Figure 21.

Also the aggressiveness of the piping material should be limited (SI, pH, EC, chlorine).

The standards for SI, hardness and hydrogen carbonate are made quite strict (pH range between

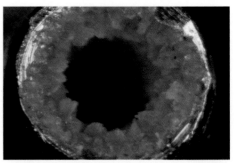

Figure 21 - Example of growth and scale in drinking water pipes

7.6 and 8.5), which is advantageous for the metal dissolving capacity (copper, lead).

The VEWIN recommendations included a pH value within 7.8 and 8.3.

For hardness there is not only a minimum but also a maximum value. Hard water, actually, gives scale in the case of heating in laundry and heating installations. Also, hard water leaves a visible film on tea and causes, by a chemical reaction with soap, a residue on the skin when showering.

To prevent households from softening the water themselves, a maximum hardness is included

Table 18   - Operational parameters in Decree on Water Supply

Parameter	Maximum value (unless stated otherwise)	Unit	Remark
Aeromonas (30°)	1,000	CFU/100 ml	CFU = colony forming unit
Ammonium	0.2	mg/l	
Bacteria of the coli group	0	CFU/100 ml	
Bacteriophages	-	PFU	PFU = plaque forming unit
Chloride	150	mg/l	
Clostridium perfringens (incl. spores)	0	CFU/100 ml	
DOC / TOC	-	mg/l	No abnormal changes
EC (bij 20°C)	125	mS/m	Water must be non-aggressive
Hardness (total)	> 1 and < 2.5 mmol	mmol/l	Total hardness to be calculated as an amount of mmol Ca^{2+} and Mg^{2+}/l. If softening or desalting is used then the 90 percentile value is applied.
Colony number at 22°C	100	CFU/ml	Geometric yearly average. No abnormal changes
Radio activity:			
- Total a	0.1	Bq/l	
- Total ß	1	Bq/l	
- Tritium	100	Bq/l	
- Indicating dose (total)	0.10	mSv/j	
Saturation Index (SI)	> -0.2	SI	Water must be non-aggressive
Temperature	25	°C	Only for cold distributed drinking water
Hydrocarbonate	> 60	mg/l	
pH	> 7.0 and < 9.5	pH	Water must be non-aggressive
Oxygen	> 2	mg/l	

Table 19 - Signalling parameters in Decree on Water
             Supply

Table 19 - Signalling parameters in Decree on Water
             Supply

Parameter	Maximum value	Unit
AOX	-	µmol X/l
Aromatic amines	1 *	µg/l
(Chloor) fenolen	1 *	µg/l
Halogenated monocyclic carbons	1	µg/l
Halogenated aliphatic carbons	1	µg/l
Monocyclic carbons / aromatics	1	µg/l

*   If as metabolite of pesticides then 0.1 µg/l

in the standards. Central softening is better for public health and for the economy than private softening.

Also, for operational parameters, the VEWIN recommendations were stricter. (EC 80 mS/s, ammonium 0.05 mg/l, aeromonas 200 CFU/100 ml, colony number 1 CFU/100 ml.)

Signalling parameters

Signalling parameters are intended to signify possible contaminations.

When the standard value is exceeded, there is no direct risk for public health, but closer investigations need to be performed. This group of parameters is

meant to safeguard the quality of the source. The signal parameters are given in Table 19.

5.3 Safeguarding drinking water quality

The Decree on Water Supply dictates how and when the quality of drinking water should be determined. It also determines the quality which should be safeguarded at the sources and during the treatment process.

Tables 20 and 21 show the safe guard parameters, measurement frequencies, and sample locations for the different parameter groups. Besides using formal standards, the Dutch water companies also use the 'Drinking water hygiene code' (Kiwa 2002), a directive for design and operation for the storage, transport and distribution of drinking water.

6.   Water quality for other applications

There are other applications for water besides drinking. Every application area has specific

Table 20 - Measurement frequencies for controlling and audits as stated in Decree on Water Supply

Daily amount of distributed and processed water within a delivery area in m³	Controlling Number of samples per year	Audit Number of samples per year
<100	2	1
100 - 1,000	4	1
1,000 - 10,000	4 + 3 for each 1,000 m³/d and a fraction of the total amount	1 + 1 for each 3,300 m³/d and a fraction of the total amount
10,000 - 100,000	4 + 3 for each 1,000 m³/d and a fraction of the total amount	3 + 1 for each 10,000 m³/d and a fraction of the total amount
>100,000	4 + 3 for each 1,000 m³/d and a fraction of the total amount	10 + 1 for each 25,000 m³/d and a fraction of the total amount

Table 21 - Controlling parameters in Decree on Water Supply

Parameter group	Sample point t[1]	Sample point p/t[2]
Microbiological parameters	Escherichia coli	-
Chemical parameters	Nitrit	-
Operational parameters	- Ammonium - Bacteria of the coli group - EC - Colony number at 22°C - pH	Clostridium perfringens
Organoleptic / esthetic parameters	- Odor - Color - Taste - Turbidity	Aluminum Iron
Signalling parameters	-	-

[1]   t = at tap point for human consumption
[2]   p/t = after last treatment step at treatment plant and at tap point for human consumption

Table 22 - Quality aspects for different usages

Usage	Specific goal	Aspect
Drinking water	- Household water - Drinking water	Clean, safe + healthy
Cool water	- Circulation - Open circulation	Cold, clean (contamination) + soft / low salt (scaling)
Rinse water	- Cold - Hot	Clean + soft (scaling)
Boiler feed water	- Low pressure - High pressure	Clean, soft + salt free (scaling)
Greenhouse water	- Circulation	Low salt (affecting plants)

requirements for water quality. Those specific requirements may be indicated for every application as rough quality requirements (clean, soft, without salts, etc.). Table 22 shows some examples.

Household water

Household water is used for flushing the toilet, watering the garden, washing the car, and also in washing machines for clothing and dishes. Household water is generally not used for drinking water.

During the test projects that have been performed during the past few years in the Netherlands, however, it has been shown that cross-connections between drinking water and household water frequently occur. Causes are mistakes during construction, but also during use by the inhabitants (fiddling with pipes, using the garden hose for the children's bathtub, etc.). It is, therefore, necessary to make the household water ready for consumption also. Though household water, it is not intended for long-time exposure; the risk of some acute microbiological contamination is not imaginary.

In principle it is possible to prevent such a microbiological contamination by applying chemical disinfection using chlorine. However, this leads to the formation of harmful by-products like trihalomethanes. The question arises as to whether the disadvantages of household water (costs, health risks, environment) are not larger than the intended advantages (savings on drinking water).

These developments have led to very strict regulations for household water projects, which are nowadays discouraged by the government.

Cooling water

In industry, much water is used as cooling water. Of course, the water temperature is important for this application. This makes groundwater attractive, because it has a constant temperature. However, obtaining a permit to use groundwater for this low-end application is almost impossible.

Cooling water is used in heat exchangers and piping systems. In these applications no scaling is allowed to occur and the materials used should not be affected. In order to limit the use of cooling water, often circulation cooling is chosen, meaning that a part of the water evaporates so that concentrations will increase. Nevertheless, pollution, scaling, and corrosion should remain limited.

The quality requirements for cooling water, therefore, are:
- low turbidity (pollution)
- sufficient oxygen concentration, good pH value and low electric conductivity (corrosion)
- low hardness and good pH value (scaling of $CaCO_3$, $CaSO_4$, $Ca_3(PO_4)_2$)
- low silicate concentrations (scaling of SiO_2)

The cooling water directive which is often used is the German directive VGB R455 (1992).

Hot or cold flushing water

In industry, a large quantity of water is used as flushing water. Critical applications of this are found in the food industries (bottle flushing, cleaning of process installations). Less critical applications can be found everywhere (cleaning water for buildings). For good cleaning, warm or hot water is used almost exclusively.

For flushing water in the first instance, the same considerations as for cooling water hold (no scaling and no corrosion). However, in the second instance also a low salt concentration is required,

Figure 22 - Sampling point for quality control at the tap

as all remaining water will evaporate and visible salt residuals can otherwise be formed.

Boiler feed water

Boiler feed water is used for the production of steam. Here, the water will completely evaporate. In industry, considerable amounts of water

are used for this purpose, despite reuse (boiler feed water for the production of boiler water, re-abstracted as condensate).

The quality requirements for boiler feed water depend on the operational pressure of the steam, the kind of steam boiler (large water storage or water pipe), and the possibility of condensate cleaning or reuse.

Typically, fully softened water is used for the production of low-pressure steam, and fully desalinated water is used for high-pressure steam. Frequently applied regulations for boiler feed water are the EEC directive R/54/LEOC/CP 484 (1998) and the German directive for high-pressure steam VGB R450 (2000).

Greenhouse water

Greenhouse water is applied in agriculture and horticulture. The quality of the water is important, because this water is used many times to save water overall, and to limit discharges of nutrients and pesticides.

Plants evaporate water, causing condensation of the circulating water and salt accumulation in the vegetation itself. The sensitivity for salt accumulation differs per type of vegetation.

Generally, a sodium concentration below 60 mg/l is desirable.

Further reading

- Guidelines for drinking water quality, 3th edition, WHO (2004)
- Principles and practices of water supply operations: Water quality, AWWA (2003, student workbook 2005)
- Safe drinking water – Lessons from recent outbreaks in affluent nations, S.E. Hrudey / E.J. Hrudey, IWA (2004)
- Aquatic chemistry, W. Stumm / J. Morgan, Wiley, New York (1996)
- Wasserchemie für Ingenieure, H. Sontheimer / P. Spindler / R. Rohmann, ZfGW-Verlag Frankfurt/ Main (1980)
- De kwaliteit van drinkwater in Nederland, RIVM (annual reports)

- www.overheid.nl/wetten
- www.waterwinkel.com
- www.rivm.nl
- www.mineralwaters.org
- www.who.int
- www.usgs.gov
- www.ukwir.org

Questions and applications

Water on Earth

1. Compounds in water can be subdivided into several categories. Name some of those.

2. Undissolved matter often consists of particles of a relatively large size. These particles can be subdivided according to their sizes. Give this subdivision with names and particle sizes. Also, indicate what size particles need to be in order to settle.

3. There are several parameters in which the amount of suspended or colloidal particles can be expressed. What are they?

4. Indicate whether the organic compounds or parameters listed below are micro- or macro-pollutants. Also explain the terms
   - BOD (Biochemical Oxygen Demand)
   - COD (Chemical Oxygen Demand)
   - Oxidability using $KMnO_4$
   - DOC (Dissolved Organic Carbon)
   - TOC (Total Organic Carbon)
   - UV-extinction (absorption of UV light 254 nm)
   - Color (compared to a certain amount of platinum or cobalt in some solution)
   - AOC (Assimilable Organic Carbon).

5. Explain what is meant by pathogenic organisms, how human beings are exposed to them, whether there is always some amount of them present in water or how they infect the water, how pathogenic microorganisms are subdivided and which diseases are caused by them.

Water: physical and chemical properties

1. What is the saturation index and how can this be determined?

Health and the quality of drinking water

1. Explain the terms below and briefly relate them to one another.
   - NOAEL
   - TDI

Dutch drinking water legislation

1. Which categories of drinking water parameters are discerned within the Dutch Decree on Water Supply?

Applications

1. A soft drink producer uses groundwater as source for cola. A laboratory characterized the composition of the water as follows :
   - chloride   :   14 mg/l
   - sulfate   :   3 mg/l
   - calcium   :   91 mg/l
   - magnesium   :   7 mg/l
   - carbon dioxide   :   13 mg/l
   - hydrogen carbonate   :   279 mg/l

   a   When it is known that the purity of this water is 99.95%, what is the amount of Na^+ in mg/l that is present, assuming that only the Na^+ value is not measured?

   b   What is the hardness of this water? (mmol/l)

   c   Compute the equilibrium concentration of CO_2 in this water using the calcium carbonate equilibrium.

   d   Is this water limestone aggressive or limestone precipitating? Explain your answer using Tillmans' diagram.

   e   To give the water a fresh taste there is, besides flavorings and sugar, also 4,000 mg/l of carbon dioxide added to the water. Compute the pH value of the soft drink using the carbonic acid equilibrium.

2. A sample is taken from groundwater which is located 200 m below the ground's surface. The following composition is measured:

T :	10°C	Na^+ :	? mmol/l
Ca^{2+} :	2.0 mmol/l	Mg^{2+} :	0.5 mmol/l
HCO_3^- :	3.0 mmol/l	SO_4^{2-} :	0.5 mmol/l
Cl^- :	2.0 mmol/l	CO_2 :	4.0 mmol/l

  a Compute the amount of Na^+ (in mg/l) which is present in this water, assuming that only Na^+ has not been measured.

  b Compute the pH value of the groundwater.

  c Compute the amount of CO_2 present in the groundwater.

3. Indicate whether the following statements are true or false (explain your reasoning).

  a The size of colloidal particles is between 10^{-2} and 10^{-6} m.

  b Sulfate is an inorganic parameter.

  c Fresh water has a salinity between 1,000 and 10,000 g/m^3.

  d A sulfate concentration of 159 mg/l corresponds to 3.3 eq/m^3.

  e Chloroform belongs to the trihalomethanes group.

Answers

Water on Earth

1. -   undissolved compounds
   -   dissolved compounds
   -   vegetable matter
   -   higher organisms
   -   pathogenic microorganisms

2. The undissolved compounds are subdivided according to size into:

dissolved particles	$<10^{-9}$ m
10^{-9} m < colloidal compounds	$<10^{-6}$ m
10^{-6} m < suspended compounds	

   Particles settle if their size is above 10^{-4} m

3. Turbidity (visibility depth or light transmittance), suspended solids concentration, and number of particles per unit.

4. Organic macropollutants
   -   BOD (Biochemical Oxygen Demand) is the oxygen demand of biological processes in water.
   -   COD (Chemical Oxygen Demand) is the oxygen demand of dissolved organic compounds when oxidizing using potassium dichromate
   -   Oxidability using $KMnO_4$ is the oxygen demand of dissolved organic compounds when oxidizing using $KMnO_4$
   -   DOC (Dissolved Organic Carbon) gives the concentration of dissolved organic carbon.
   -   TOC (Total Organic Carbon) gives the total concentration of organic carbon
   -   UV-extinction (absorption of UV light 254 nm) is a value indicating the concentration of organic compounds
   -   Color (compared to a certain amount of platinum or cobalt in some solution) gives the concentration of organic humic acids
   -   AOC (Assimilable Organic Carbon) indicates the amount of carbon that can be absorbed from the water by certain organisms and is a measure of the nutrient value of water.

5. Human beings are exposed to pathogenic microorganisms by the intake of drinking water and by exposure to contaminated water (swimming). Pathogenic microorganisms do not belong in water but enter there via feces and urine from humans and animals.

   Pathogenic microorganisms die off in water because the temperature is below that in human or animal bodies.

   Only by continuous supplies from discharges of untreated or partially treated water from households and bio-industries (butcheries) are pathogenic microorganisms found in water. Pathogenic microorganisms are subdivided into bacteria, viruses, and protozoa, which may cause different diseases.

Pathogenic microorganisms	Illnes
Bacteria	Typhoid, Cholera
Viruses	Hepatitis, Polio
Protozoa	Diarrhea

Water: physical and chemical properties

1. SI (saturation index) is the measurement for over- or under saturation with calcium carbonate.

$$SI = \log\left(\frac{\left[Ca^{2+}\right]\cdot\left[CO_3^{2-}\right]}{K_s}\right) = pH - pH_s$$

Health and drinking water quality

1. -   NOAEL

     No-Observed-Adverse-Effect-Level: for some compounds it is assumed that there is no effect harmful to health below a certain concentration.

   -   TDI

     Tolerable daily intake is computed from the safety corrected NOAEL multiplied by the average weight of a person (60 kg).

Dutch drinking water legislation

1. • health-related, microbiological para-
       meters
   • health-related, chemical parameters
   • organoleptic / aesthetic parameters
   • operational parameters
   • signalling parameters

Applications

1. a 99.95% of water and 0.05% of other com-
       pounds means, assuming a density of
       1,000 kg/m³, a total amount of pollution
       of 500 mg/l. The sum of chloride, sulfate,
       calcium, magnesium, carbon dioxide and
       hydrogen carbonate amounts to 407 mg/l.
       So, the sodium concentration amounts to
       93 mg/l.

   b hardness = $[Ca^{2+}] + [Mg^{2+}]$
                = 91/40 + 7/24 = 2.57 mmol/l

   c $CaCO_3 + CO_2 + H_2O \rightarrow Ca^{2+} + 2 \cdot HCO_3^-$

   $$\frac{[Ca^{2+}] \cdot [HCO_3^-]}{[CO_2]_{equilibrium}} = K_a = 4.11 \cdot 10^{-5} \Rightarrow$$

   $$\frac{[2.275 \times 10^{-3}] \cdot [4.57 \cdot 10^{-3}]^2}{[CO_2]_{equilibrium}} = 4.11 \cdot 10^{-5} \Rightarrow$$

   $$[CO_2]_{equilibrium} = 1.16 \text{ mmol/l} = 50.87 \text{ mg/l}$$

   d limestone precipitating, since $[CO_2]$ equi-
      librium is larger than $[CO_2]$ present

   e 4000 + 13 = 4,013 mg/l CO_2 =>
      = 91.2 mmol/l CO_2; $[HCO_3^-]$ = 4.57 mmol/l

   $$pH = pK_1 - \log(3.44 \cdot 10^{-7}) - \log\left(\frac{91.2 \cdot 10^{-3}}{4.57 \cdot 10^{-3}}\right) = 5.16$$

2. a Electron neutrality:
       $2 \cdot 2 + 0.5 \cdot 2 + 1 \cdot x = 3 \cdot 1 + 0.5 \cdot 2 + 2 \cdot 1$
       x = 1 mmol/l

   b pH value = $- \log(3.44 \cdot 10^{-7}) - \log(4/3) = 6.34$

   c $K_2 = [H_3O^+] \cdot [CO_3^{2-}]/[HCO_3^-]$
      $K_2 = 3.25 \cdot 10^{-11}$
      $H_3O^+ = 4.57 \cdot 10^{-7}$; $HCO_3^- = 3 \cdot 10^{-3}$ mol/l
      $CO_3^{2-} = 2.14 \cdot 10^{-4}$ mmol/l

3. a False, the particle size of colloidal particles
      is smaller than 10^{-6} m.

   b True, only compounds containing a C-atom
      (except CO_2, HCO_3^- and CO_3^{2-}) are organic.
      All other compounds are inorganic, so sul-
      fate is an inorganic compound.

   c False, fresh water has a salinity below
      1,000 g/m³.

   d True, the atomic mass of sulfate amounts
      to 96 g/mol. A concentration of 159 mg/l
      thus equals 159/96 = 1.66 mmol/l. The
      valence of sulfate is 2. The equivalence
      concentration is equal to the molarity
      multiplied by the valence = 1.66 · 2 = 3.32
      meq/l or 3.32 eq/m³.

   e True, a trihalomethane is a methane con-
      nected to three atoms of the haloform
      group. Chloroform is part of the group of
      trihalomethanes together with i.e. bro-
      moform, di-bromo-chlorine-methane and
      brome-di-chlorine-methane.

Groundwater

TECHNICAL FACETS

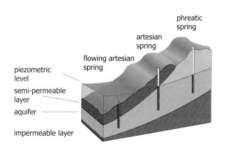

phreatic
spring

artesian
spring

flowing artesian
spring

piezometric
level

semi-permeable
layer

aquifer

impermeable layer

Framework

This module focuses on the production of drinking water from groundwater in the Dutch context. The main points are the different ways of abstracting groundwater, and the different treatment schemes and processes.

Contents

This module has the following contents:

Objective

After studying this module you will be able to:
- explain the different forms of treatment of groundwater
- make calculations for the design of drilled wells
- explain the different types of groundwater (including origin, quality, and treatment schemes)
- make calculations for the water quality in groundwater treatment

1. Introduction

For the large amounts of water which are necessary for the public drinking water supply, the choice for sources is limited to surface water and groundwater.

Groundwater has the advantage that it can be abstracted at many places, which makes transport pipes unnecessary. Furthermore, the water is hygienically reliable and typically has a constant composition. Sometimes, it can even be distributed without treatment, though a simple and cheap treatment is often inevitable.

As a disadvantage, we have to mention that the amounts that can be abstracted are limited, and each abstraction results in a lowering of the groundwater level, which can harm a third party, particularly agriculture and nature.

The abstraction of groundwater is strongly tied to the local situation. An important division can be made between the abstraction of phreatic groundwater (with a free groundwater table) and confined (ground)water (enclosed by a non-permeable layer).

Sometimes, groundwater comes to the surface spontaneously (e.g., a spring), sometimes it has to be abstracted from great depths (in the Netherlands up to 200 m below ground level, in arid areas even up to 1,500 m below ground level).

Groundwater is always connected to surface water. After all, groundwater eventually becomes surface water within the hydrologic cycle (in seas, lakes or rivers). This interaction is accomplished artificially when groundwater is abstracted close to surface water (like riverbank groundwater abstraction along large rivers) and when surface water is added to the groundwater (like artificial recharge in the dune areas). In riverbank groundwater abstraction it is always a matter of the combined abstraction of (older) groundwater and (more recent) surface water. Therefore, a strict division between groundwater and surface water can't really be made. When abstracting water, both water systems are influenced because of this human interference.

Artificial recharge is discussed in the module on surface water, because it is an isolated system in which surface water is infiltrated and re-abstracted completely.

Typical groundwater is generally (especially in sand aquifers) free of suspended solids, microbiologically reliable and practically constant in quality. Treatment mainly aims at the removal of unwanted dissolved substances like iron, manganese, ammonium and methane. In a couple of situations it is also desirable to remove unpleasant dissolved substances like calcium (hardness).

Groundwater is used for drinking water production in the Netherlands at all places where fresh groundwater is present. Because of the influence on the environment by dessication, the national policy aims at limiting groundwater abstraction and at switching, partially, to the use of surface water.

In this module the different aspects of drinking water production from groundwater are discussed. First, an overview is given of the natural environment of groundwater. After that, the possibilities of abstracting groundwater are presented. Subsequently, the treatment of groundwater is explained, followed by the treatment of riverbank groundwater. Finally, the Dutch legislation concerning groundwater is presented.

2. Groundwater in the natural environment

In the hydrologic cycle, groundwater flows to the sea more or less horizontally through the soil. Sooner or later the groundwater reaches the ground level again, invisible by overflow in lakes and rivers, and visible in springs.

The outflow of groundwater can be divided into countless types. However, the most important divisions are, on one hand, between phreatic and artesian outflow and, on the other hand, between outflow by a local depression of the surface or by the presence of an impermeable base. Both divisions together give account for four types of groundwater, which are shown in Figure 1.

Phreatic water

Phreatic groundwater is characterized by a free groundwater table. This groundwater table is strongly influenced by the in- and outflow. Because of rainfall the groundwater table will rise, and out-flow will lower the groundwater table. The ground-water level significantly fluctuates and the dynamic process is fully determined by hydrological and geohydrological conditions. Even without human interference, the natural groundwater table shows large variations.

Artesian water

For artesian water, a confining layer above the aquifer is necessary (Figure 2). Because of this layer, hydraulic pressure can build up which can sometimes cause water to come spontaneously to the surface.

Due to this confining layer, the water has a long residence time in the aquifer. Therefore, natural processes can improve the water quality (micro-

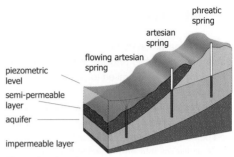

Figure 2   - Artesian water

biological reliability), or they can deteriorate the water quality (dissolving substances in anaerobic circumstances).

Local depression

Springs in phreatic water, as a result of local deep-ening of the surface, are common in nature. Typical examples are draining brooks and streams. The inflow of water is, in these cases, often invisible but can be a significant amount. These brooks and streams are, from a hydrological point of view, functioning the same way as drainage ditches in polder areas.

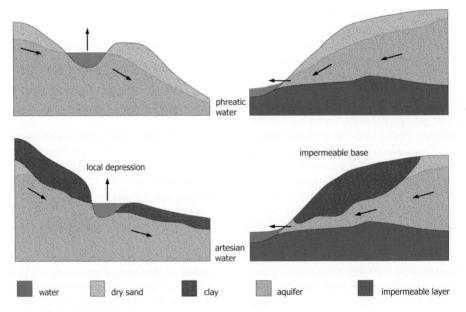

Figure 1   - Subdivision of springs

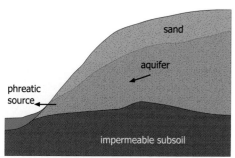

*Figure 3   - Spring in phreatic water over a impermeable
              layer*

In the case of a slight groundwater flow and rivers in their upper reaches, the local depression can run dry. These "dry rivers" or "wadis" are common in desert areas. At first, such rivers mainly transport the surface discharge, which occurs after a rainfall and, afterwards, the water which is infiltrated into the ground.

Rivers, which have cut themselves into the landscape, can also be fed by artesian water, if the river has flushed away the low permeability layer.

Opposite flow situations occur with infiltrating rivers. With this, water flows from the river into the groundwater. In the Netherlands this is a common situation along the large rivers running beside polder areas. In this case, river water feeds the aquifer that exists under the upper clay and peat layers. This infiltrating water is discharged using the ditches and drain facilities of the nearby polder and often drained off into the same river.

Impermeable base
The discharge capacity of springs in a phreatic aquifer above an impermeable layer can be high. After all, the total recharge of the infiltration area with rainfall will discharge from the spring (Figure 3).

3.   Abstraction of groundwater

The abstraction of groundwater is very diverse. With the easiest execution, the freely discharged groundwater can simply be collected (spring capturing).

With the most complicated execution, the groundwater has to be abstracted from depths up to 1,500 meters, and situations can occur where groundwater is under significant pressure and water abstraction becomes more and more like oil drilling, even with spouts.

Facilities for the abstraction of groundwater will be discussed for a number of different types of methods:
- capturing of springs
- types of wells and drain facilities
- horizontal drainage pipes
- dug, driven and spout wells
- drilled wells
- radial wells
- well fields and recharge area

3.1   Capturing of springs
The natural outflow of groundwater (springs) facilitates an easy method for abstracting the groundwater by capturing. With this, groundwater is abstracted just before it becomes surface water. In mountainous areas, natural springs can exist where a significant amount of water flows out at a certain place via cracks in the rock formation. By carefully protecting these springs the microbiological reliability of the groundwater is maintained.

In ancient times spring water was used for a city's central water supply (e.g., Rome, Cologne, Lyon). Spring water is still used on a large scale for the public water supply. It is true that this water often has to be transported over large distances, but abstraction is inexpensive and treatment is usually not necessary.

Capturing water from the numerous springs in rock formations in the Alps, for example, (Figures 4 and 5) accounts for 93% of the water supply in Vienna. This water supply is a modern variant of the old Roman systems, complete with extensive protection areas (approximately 600 km²), two aqueducts with a length of 120 and 170 km (Hochquellenleitungen, Figure 5), and large sealed reservoirs to endure periods with low outflow or high consumption. Next to dosing with chlorine

Figure 4 - Capturing water from one of the springs for the Vienna Hochquellenleitungen

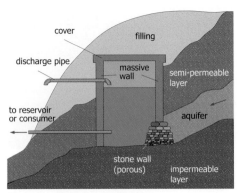

Figure 6 - Capturing spring water

during transport, there is no further treatment. The water is transported to the consumers without the use of pumps.

The capacity of this system is 437,000 m³/d (5 m³/s). Munich and Paris also use spring capturing for substantial amounts.

Smaller outflows near aquifers are also captured. For this, separate facilities have to be constructed to obtain a separate abstraction (Figure 6). To prevent contamination of the water, this capture is provided with a waterproof layer of clay and concrete. The enclosure has to be of such a design and quality that the recharge water stays in the

ground for at least a couple of weeks, before the water reaches the spring.

3.2 Types of wells and drainage facilities

No doubt the oldest method of groundwater abstraction is a hole in the ground with a depth reaching beyond the groundwater level. Obviously, only a small capacity can be obtained in this way.

If a higher capacity is desired, then the contact area with the aquifer has to be enlarged, which is

Figure 5 - The Vienna Hochquellenleitungen accounts for more than 90% of the drinking water supply of Vienna

Table 1   - Types of wells and means of drainage for groundwater abstraction

Thickness layer	Depth of abstraction	Type of abstraction
Small	Shallow	Horizontal, open canals or closed dug drain pipes
	Deep	Horizontal, radial wells
Large	Shallow	Vertical, dug wells
	Deep	Vertical, drilled wells

possible by either enlarging the horizontal dimensions, enlarging the vertical dimensions, or by enlarging both.

Which method has to be executed in a certain case depends on the local circumstances, in particular, the thickness of the aquifer and the depth of the groundwater level beneath the surface. Both dimensions can be small or large, resulting in four different cases, as outlined in Table 1.

Abstraction facilities can be separated into vertical and horizontal wells. When the aquifer has a large thickness and the groundwater level is located at a shallow depth beneath the surface, both horizontal and vertical abstraction facilities can be used. The choice depends on secondary considerations, in which local factors play a large part.

Shallow horizontal abstraction
Considering the required contact area with the aquifer, horizontal abstraction wells have to be designed, if the aquifer has only a small thickness. Open canals and closed, dug drains are used when the groundwater level is located at a shallow depth, at the most 5 - 10 meters below the surface (Figure 7).

Shallow horizontal abstraction is very attractive in areas like the Dutch dunes where the fresh water, which can be abstracted, floats on the underlying salt water. To prevent the salt water from rising, a decrease in the water level has to be as little as

possible, which can be achieved most easily by dividing this abstraction over a great area.

Open canals are inexpensive and easy to construct; they have a large capacity and infinite lifespan. When used for the abstraction of groundwater, these canals have the disadvantage that the abstracted water can be contaminated by contact with animals, birds and the atmosphere. When not constructed with great care, they will deform the landscape. In the Netherlands these open canals were used in several locations for water abstraction in the dune areas.

Today, abstraction facilities for the supply of drinking water are no longer constructed by this method, because of the desired abstraction of hygienically reliable water. Old facilities are more often transformed to closed abstraction facilities with drain pipes.

Closed, dug drain pipes (drains) are more complicated, the construction costs are higher, and the decrease in the groundwater level is greater for the same capacity, because of their smaller diameter. Their lifetime is limited because of clogging. On the other hand, they are located entirely under the ground, making them invisible and protected against contamination, while the surface can be used for other purposes.

Deep horizontal abstraction
In ancient times underground tunnels were dug, for example, in Persia for the collection of groundwater ("qanats"), which are still in use today. Typical for these qanats are the vertical shafts to the surface at regular distances to prevent asphyxiation the diggers. In this way water abstraction was possible at a depth of 15 meters below the surface.

Nowadays, so-called radial wells are used for the abstraction of water from thin aquifers at greater

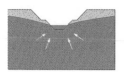
open canal

gravel-packed
drain pipe

Figure 7   - Shallow horizontal abstraction

depths (Figure 8). These wells are also called Ranney-wells, after their inventor Leo Ranney (1933). In principle these radial wells consist of a vertical shaft reaching the aquifer, from where perforated pipes (collectors) are radially arranged and driven almost horizontally into the aquifer.

Every well has 8 to 24 of these collectors with a length of approximately 50 m and a diameter between the 0.2 and 0.5 m. The contact surface with the aquifer is therefore huge, as a result of which large capacities, up to 1 m³/s, are possible. The water is hygienically reliable because of its abstraction at great depths.

However, design and construction is the work of specialists, causing the construction costs to rise. A radial well is only considered economical, when a large amount of water, more than 0.3 to 0.6 m³/s depending on the local circumstances, has to be abstracted.

Shallow vertical abstraction

For the abstraction of shallow groundwater, dug wells are used (Figure 9). These often have a relatively large diameter (1 - 10 m) and a depth of 5 to 25 m. Such wells often have only a small capacity and, therefore, are typically only used for an individual water supply. When well-protected against contamination from above, they are perfectly fit for this use.

A shaft with a large diameter functions as a reservoir, with the result that during short periods a larger amount of water can be abstracted than the amount corresponding to the groundwater supply.

The construction of dug wells is generally easy and inexpensive and does not require special tools or special knowledge.

A number of vertical wells can be beneficial when water has to be abstracted for a central facility from a layer of fine sand with a limited thickness and a deep groundwater level.

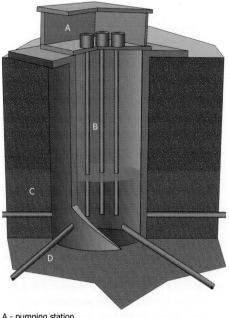

A - pumping station
B - shaft
C - water-bearing stratum
D - radial pipes

Figure 8   - Deep horizontal abstraction

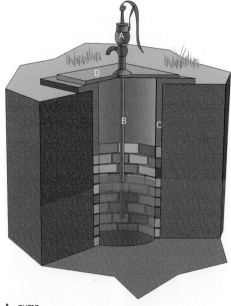

A - pump
B - pump pipe
C - concrete edge
D - wooden cover

Figure 9   - Shallow vertical abstraction (dug well)

Deep vertical abstraction

The most widespread method for the abstraction of deep groundwater is abstraction via drilled tubular wells (Figure 10). Such wells have a diameter of 0.1 to 0.5 m and a depth of several tens to several hundreds of meters. Considering the required contact area with the aquifer, these types of wells can only be used in the case of a larger thickness of the aquifer.

For the construction of tubular wells, many complicated construction methods have been developed. The capacity of each well varies between 0.001 to 0.1 m^3/s. Simple facilities are sufficient to assure hygienically reliable water, because of the great depths.

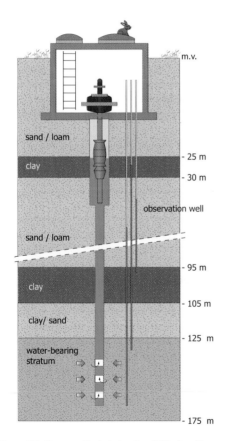

Figure 10 - Deep vertical abstraction (drilled well)

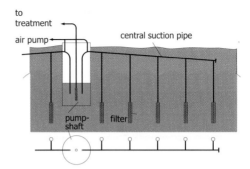

Figure 11 - Series of wells with vacuum system

A single well is sufficient for an individual water supply, to supply water for fire fighting or air-conditioning. A small number of wells is sufficient for small public and industrial water supplies. A series of wells has to be constructed for larger capacities. Every well has to be supplied with its own pump or it has to use central drainage with a vacuum system (Figure 11). On a large scale tubular wells are used for the drainage of building excavations. The construction of tubular wells is usually done by specialized companies. When depths increase, the construction costs can increase significantly.

3.3   Horizontal drainage pipes

Drainage pipes
Drainage pipes are built from tubes, with lengths between 1 to 2 m. These tubes are made with pores, open joints or perforations to allow groundwater to enter (Figure 12).

Porous tubes are normally constructed of fine gravel, sieved between narrow boundaries and attached to each other with cement and water (no-fines concrete). The construction cost for the tubes is low, and they are easy to construct. They may clog quickly, however, due to unfavorable geochemical ratios by deposits of iron, manganese, limestone, etc.

Drainage pipes with open joints are commonly made of concrete or asbestos cement.

vertical openings

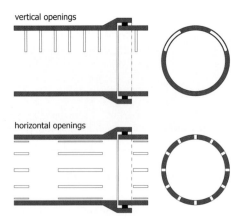

horizontal openings

Figure 12 - Perforated drainage pipes

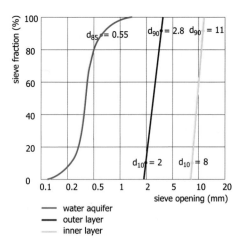

Figure 14 - Sieve analysis for different sand fractions

Cast-iron, copper, wood and synthetic materials are used for the construction of perforated tubes.

Gravel packs
Usually the drain openings are larger than the grain of which the surrounding aquifer is built, and one or more transitional layers of gravel is necessary to prevent the aquifer grains from entering the tubes and to abstract water free of sand (Figure 13).

When this gravel is filtered between narrow boundaries, with the 10% and the 90% diameters differentiating not more than a factor of $\sqrt{2}$, the lower boundary of the outside layer may not be coarser than four times the sieve size through which 85% of the material from the aquifer passes. The transitional layer of gravel connecting the inside may not

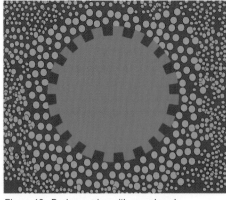

Figure 13 - Drainage pipe with gravel pack

be coarser than a factor of 4, while at last the lower boundary of the inside layer has to be two times larger than the orifices of the drainage pipes.

As an example, a grain distribution in the aquifer is given in conformance with Figure 14. According to the sieve diagram, the aquifer has an 85% diameter of 0.55 mm.
For the gravel deposits and the perforations, this results in:
- outside layer finer than 2.2 - 3.1 mm (chosen as market size 2 - 2.8 mm)
- inside layer 8 - 11 mm
- orifice diameter smaller than 4 mm

This orifice has a large width, so that clogging due to deposits of dissolved contaminants is no longer a threat.

Entry rate
To prevent the clogging of drainage pipes by fine aquifer particles which are carried along, the entry rate v_a of the groundwater at the contact surface of the aquifer and the drainage pipes, including gravel pack, may not be too high.

According to Gross: $\quad v_a < d_{40}$
According to Sichardt: $\quad v_a < \sqrt{k}/60$

in which:
v_a = (superficial) entry rate $\qquad$ (m/s)

k = permeability coefficient (m/s)
d_{40} = sieve size through which 40% of the
material in the aquifer passes (m)

Still, with these entry velocities, the carrying along of the finest aquifer particles cannot be prevented. These particles pass the gravel layer and the perforations, and enter the drainage pipes.

Flow rate in drainage pipes
To prevent deposits in these pipes, the flow rate has to be greater than 0.5 m/s. On the other hand, considering the friction losses which result in a decrease in the water level along the length of the drainage pipes, this rate is not allowed to be too great, preferably not more than 1 m/s. These requirements can generally only be satisfied by enlarging the diameter in a number of steps.

Construction depth
The most difficult decision in the design of a drainage pipe is usually the decision regarding its construction depth. After all, a shallow construction depth lowers the cost of the excavation and maintaining a dry trench. During the operational phase, the danger exists that, due to the shallow depth, contaminations from the surface will contaminate the abstracted water, and that clogging due to iron deposits will occur.

Two types of water flow towards the drainage pipe:
a. water from above, which travels only a short way through the soil and still contains oxygen; and,
b. water from below and sideways, which stayed a longer time in the soil. This water has lost all its soluble oxygen and, therefore, can dissolve iron in the form of ferrous ions.

When both types of water mix near a drainage pipe, the soluble ferrous iron is oxidized to the insoluble ferric hydroxide. Now this will precipitate and block the pores of the gravel pack and the perforations of the drainage pipe. These blockages can hardly be removed afterwards, but they can be prevented by placing the top of the drainage pipe at least 2 to 3 m below the lowest groundwater level during the operation.

Figure 15 - A dug well

3.4 Dug, driven and spout wells

Dug wells
Dug wells are currently constructed with the help of prefabricated concrete rings, which are placed in the ground by excavating the ground on the inside of the ring. Therefore, an inside diameter of at least 1 m is necessary, preferably 1.2 - 1.5 m (Figure 15), so two workman can work there at the same time (Figure 16).

At the end of a dry period, the bottom of the well reaches at least 1 m below the lowest groundwater level and is sometimes finished off with a layer of gravel to prevent the carrying along of fine soil particles.

To prevent the penetration of contaminants from above, many precautions are necessary, like a waterproof filling around the rings and a wide cover above the well. The construction of the filling around the rings is complicated. Therefore, for a system in which rings are used, on-site construction is often chosen instead.

Figure 16 - A dug well under construction

In developing countries, dug wells have the enormous advantage that they can be constructed with local materials and local workers, without the need of specialized tools or knowledge.

In the Western world, dug wells have been almost completely replaced by driven and spout wells.

Driven wells

A driven well consists of a perforated steel tube, also known as a well screen, provided with a massive, tempered steel point on the bottom. This filter is driven into the ground and extended on top with well pipes connected to each other with a screw connection.

After the desired depth is reached, the pump is installed and the driven well can be used (Figure 17).

Considering the possibility of damage occurring during the driving, driven wells can only be constructed in loose, unconsolidated formations and with a small diameter, between 3 and 10 cm, and generally 5 cm.

The capacity per well, therefore, is small, usually not more than 1 l/s (4 m³/h). For an individual water supply, this is nevertheless sufficient, and driven wells have the great advantage that hygienically reliable water can be abstracted.

In the past driven wells were used on a large scale as a temporary water supply, for the water supply of an army in battle, and for the drainage of building excavations. For these purposes, driven wells have been completely replaced by spouted wells.

Spout wells

From the exterior, spout wells look a lot like driven wells, and their areas of use are almost the same.

The steel point on the bottom of the well filter is, in this case, not massive, but hollow and ends in a narrow opening. The water, which is supplied via a lance, is sent through this opening with great force, crushing the underlying ground material.

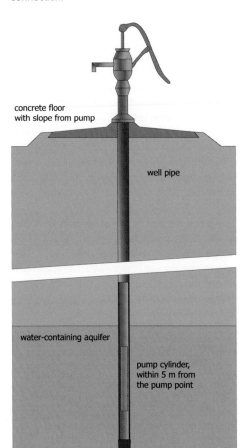

concrete floor
with slope from pump

well pipe

water-containing aquifer

pump cylinder,
within 5 m from
the pump point

Figure 17 - Parts of a driven well

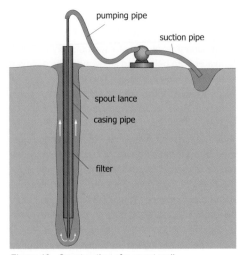

pumping pipe

suction pipe

spout lance

casing pipe

filter

Figure 18 - Construction of a spout well

This crushed material is transported by the water along the well screen and the rising main to the surface (Figure 18). Because of this, the well will sink without any damaging.

Sometimes the required spout water can be abstracted from the water distribution network. Usually, water from a pit or a tanker has to be used, which is put under pressure by a separate pump.

After reaching the desired depth a pump is used or the well is connected to a central suction pipeline.

3.5   Drilled wells

In contrast to the methods described in the previous section, for drilled wells a hole is first made in the ground.

In the case of rock formations, this hole can remain unsupported, but, in the case of loose granular grounds, temporary tubing is necessary to prevent the hole from collapsing. Only when the borehole concerning the diameter and the depth is totally finished, the well screen and the well pipes (casing), are installed together with an optional gravel layer, around the well screen.

For the construction of the borehole, a differentiation has to be made between two activities:
-   the crushing of the material on the bottom of the borehole, with a falling chisel (percussion drilling) or with a turning chisel (rotary drilling)
-   the removal of the crushed material, discontinuing with the help of a bailer or continuing with circulating water or drilling mud (hydraulic drilling)

When combining these activities, four possibilities result. By serendipity, percussion drilling with a bailer, and hydraulic rotary drilling are usually used, so in the next paragraph only these variants will be outlined. In addition, only the simplest methods will be described.

In reality a large number of variants exist for both methods to obtain optimal results under circumstances that vary as to place and time.

Percussion drilling with a bailer

In the case of percussion drilling, the drilling tools have a total length of 5 - 15 m and a total weight of 500 - 2000 kg. They consist of a heavy chisel (drilling bit) which crushes the ground material. The drilling bit is lifted and then the drill cable is loosened. As a result, the bit falls on the bottom of the borehole with great speed. After drilling, according to the method described above, the lower part of the borehole will fill with slurry water and crushed ground material. This slurry slows down the fall of the drilling bit, which slows down the progress of the drill process, and, therefore, has to be removed periodically.

To remove it, the drill tools are replaced by the bailer, in principle consisting of a tube 2 to 8 m long with a somewhat smaller diameter than the borehole and, on the front, equipped with a non-return valve. Just like the drilling tools, this bailer is also moved up and down in the borehole.

Percussion drilling with bailer (also called cable percussion) was employed on a large scale in the Netherlands. It is a safe and reliable method to drill a borehole. It is, however, time and labor intensive, although the workers do not have to be highly educated. Because of these characteristics, cable percussion drilling is still very popular in developing countries.

In the Western world this method has been almost totally replaced by hydraulic rotary drilling.

Hydraulic rotary drilling

Hydraulic rotary drilling, with a continuous removal of crushed ground material, is most often executed with specially fabricated drilling machines, usually assembled on top of a truck (drilling rig, Figure 19).

The drill tools in the borehole are now very simple and consist only of a hollow drilling bit (Figure 20), above which a hollow driver of great weight pushes the bit on the bottom of the borehole. The driver is also of great length to make straight and vertical boreholes.

The hollow drill tube turns the bit around and crushes the material on the bottom of the borehole.

Figure 19 - Hydraulic rotary drilling rig with normal circulation

To transfer the necessary force from the turntable and, at the same time, to lower the bit vertically, the upper section of the drill tube (a kelly), has a square cross-section.

Through the hollow drill tube and the hollow bit, water is pumped down under great pressure. This water spouts with great speed against the bottom of the borehole and aids the crushing work of the turning bit. Next, this water rises in the ring-shaped space between the wall of the borehole and the hollow drill tube and brings the crushed soil material up to a sedimentation tank in which the drill material settles and from which the clarified water is pumped down again.

Figure 20 - Hollow drilling bit for hydraulic rotary drills

Generally, clay and a large variety of other materials are added to this water to increase its specific gravity and viscosity in order to improve the removal of the crushed ground material, to get clean boreholes and a speedy drill process, and to prevent the occurrence of a "blow-out" when drilling for oil and gas. These additions are also necessary for a fourth reason. Unsupported boreholes are used during hydraulic drilling, also in loose granular formations. Because of the previously described additions, the pores in the wall of the borehole will get blocked quickly, causing the hydraulic pressure in the borehole to become so much higher than the pressure in the groundwater that this difference in pressure prevents the borehole from collapsing.

In the case of abstracting groundwater, the use of drilling mud has an important disadvantage: the wall of the borehole becomes impermeable and gives strong resistance to the flow of groundwater to the well screen placed in this hole. There is normally no risk for a "blow-out", and, at a drill depth of a couple hundred meters, a hydraulic pressure difference of a few meters water column is sufficient to prevent the borehole from collapsing. Such a pressure difference can also be obtained when using clean water, even in the case of high groundwater levels, by temporarily constructing the tubes a few meters above ground level. However, to get a quick removal of the crushed ground material with clean water, a higher speed of the upward water flow is necessary, preferably 3 - 4 m/s.

Hydraulic rotary drilling has the advantage of a high drilling speed, allowing holes with a depth between 100 - 200 m to be made in one to a few days. This method is also less labor intensive, however, the operational staff have to be experts to prevent the borehole, with unsupported walls, from collapsing at any time.
When using exploration drilling, this method is hardly suitable, because the layers get crushed and suspended in the drilling mud and are brought to the surface as such, instead of in their original order. Because of the development of geophysical methods for borehole exploration, these objections are now less important.

Completion of the borehole

When the borehole has reached the desired depth with the minimal desired diameter, then the screen and the casing pipes are placed in the center for the borehole. Here, the space between the wall of the borehole and the well is filled with sand or gravel and the temporary casing, when present, is removed.

Casing pipes and screens are built in sections, with a length of 2 to 6 m, and they can be built from a large variety of materials. Presently, steel, with or without protection against corrosion, and synthetic materials are used most often. The internal diameter has to be large enough that the rate at which the abstracted water flows up remains under the 0.5 to 1 m/s to restrict the frictional resistance as much as possible.

The casing pipe is waterproof, but the screen has to be able to abstract the groundwater; it is therefore supplied with a large number of perforations. These perforations are of such a width that during the developing phase of the well, 40 to 80% of the surrounding aquifer material can pass through.

Coarser grains remain and they form a natural gravel layer around the filter with greater porosity and permeability. In fine and moderately coarse sand, the perforation width is small, 0.2 to 0.5 mm and there is the threat of blockage by dissolved contaminants like iron, manganese, calcium carbonate and magnesium. With an artificial gravel pack in 2 or 3 layers, wider perforations can be used and the chance of these blockages occurring can be decreased.

These gravel packs have a thickness from 5 to 8 cm and are constructed in the same way as described for the horizontal drainage pipes. To prevent well clogging by fine ground particles, the entry rate v_a of the groundwater on the contact surface of the aquifer and the well screen or gravel pack may not be too high.

To a certain extent cleaning of vertical wells is possible and, therefore, the previously mentioned values for horizontal drainage pipes can now be doubled:

According to Gross: $v_a < d_{40}$
According to Sichardt: $v_a < \sqrt{k}/60$

Design of drilled wells

For a well with a capacity of 5 l/s = $5 \cdot 10^{-3}$ m³/s = 18 m³/h, the screen and casing pipes must have a diameter of 0.1 m (flow rate in the pipe 0.64 m/s), and with a double gravel pack, the borehole should have a diameter of 0.4 m.

In dune sand with a k-value of $0.15 \cdot 10^{-3}$ m/s = 13 m/d, the permitted groundwater rate at the outer perimeter of the gravel pack is, according to Sichardt, equal to $0.4 \cdot 10^{-3}$ m/s.
The outer perimeter of the gravel pack must have an area of 12.6 m², with a diameter of 0.4 m and a length of 10 m.
According to the sieve diagram of dune sand, the aquifer material has an 85% diameter of 0.25 mm.
For the gravel pack and the perforations, this results in an:
- outside layer of   1 - 1.5 mm
- inside layer of   4 - 6 mm
- slot size of   2 - 3 mm

If the permeability of the aquifer is higher, then the capacity of the well can also be larger.
According to these design criteria, a k-value 10 times higher (coarse sand with grain diameter $\sqrt{10}$ times larger) can result for the same well in a capacity of 50 l/s = $50 \cdot 10^{-3}$ m³/s = 180 m³/h, but only if the screen and casing pipes have a diameter of ($\sqrt{10} \cdot 0.1 =$) 0.3 m.
Because of the necessary space for the gravel pack, a diameter of 0.6 m for the borehole is desired.

Pumps

Naturally flowing (artesian) drilled wells are unusual and, in general, the water has to be abstracted using pumps.

If the groundwater level during the operational phase is just beneath the surface (i.e., not more than 4 - 6 m), then the most desirable solution is central drainage by a vacuum pipe connected to several wells.

In the case of a deeper level of groundwater, every well can be supplied with its own pump, usually set into the shaft.

The pump is usually close-coupled to the electro-motor in submersible pumps (Figure 21). Because

Figure 21 - Submersible pump

of their technological developments, these pumps, have become so attractive that they are even used where it is not strictly necessary, in view of the suction head.

3.6 Radial wells

Radial wells consist of two elements: a vertical shaft and a more or less star-shaped pattern of horizontal filter tubes. The vertical shaft, with an internal diameter of 2.5 to 4 m, is made of reinforced concrete and is brought down by excavating the ground on its inside diameter.

After reaching the desired depth, usually 20 to 30 m below the surface, though sometimes 40 to 60 m, a concrete bottom is poured under water, and, after hardening, the well is pumped dry. At the bottom of the well, near the aquifer, the shaft is supplied with a large number of openings, sometimes in two rows above each other, and then temporarily closed with conical wooden stops on the outside. Through these openings, perforated tubes (or screens) are pushed outside over a distance of 40 to 50 m, and sometimes 100 m. The number of screen tubes is usually 8 to 12, with the extreme values of 4 and 24, while the diameter is normally 0.2 a 0.3 m, but can vary in practice between 0.15 and 0.5.

Even with low numbers and small dimensions of the screens, a large contact surface with the aquifer and a corresponding large potential capacity are obtained.

In the case of a thin aquifer - for which these radial wells are especially developed - this capacity can only be obtained when the permeability is high, like in the case of a gravel layer or an aquifer from which the recharge is secured by nearby surface water.

3.7 Well fields and capture areas

It is outlined in the description of the parts of a drilled well that the maximum well capacity depends on the permeability and thickness of the aquifer and the diameter of the borehole. The designer is only free to choose the last variable.

Because of practical and environmental considerations, the maximum allowable decrease in

Figure 22 - Abstraction well in a recharge area

groundwater levels limits the capacity per well. Calculations of this decrease in groundwater level will not be discussed in detail. One may refer to geohydrological literature for more information. Nevertheless, it can be observed that the underground flow is laminar.

Therefore, the relation between abstraction and drawdown is also linear. For a certain well the specific yield can be determined (in m^3/h per m). In practice this value lies between 5 and 50 m^3/h/m.

For the abstraction of groundwater with vertical wells (Figures 22 and 23), more than one well is usually necessary. These wells influence each other regarding the decrease in groundwater levels. To restrict this, the wells are placed at a practical distance of 50 to 100 m apart. Furthermore, the local drawdown can be limited by spacing the wells over as large an area as possible. In practice, wells are placed in straight rows.

Groundwater abstraction influences the groundwater level in a very large area, not only in the

Figure 23 - Detail of abstraction well

capture area, but also outside it. The capture area is, theoretically, the area in which a closed water balance can be formulated for abstraction and net precipitation. For example, with a net precipitation of 0.3 m/y and abstraction of 3 million m^3/y, the capture area is 10 km^2.

The border of the capture area can be thought of as the watershed of the abstraction. The natural groundwater level on the border of a capture area also decreases due to abstraction. The influence of the abstraction is, therefore, larger than the capture area. In practice this system is more complicated because of the extra recharge of the surface water caused by the decrease in the groundwater level. This surface water can come from both inside the capture area (polders) and outside this area (rivers).

4.   Treatment of groundwater

4.1   Types of groundwater
Groundwater has a near-constant quality. Per location, however, large differences in water composition can be found.

This composition depends on the natural environment from which the groundwater is abstracted, and the route that the water has followed to get there.

Three types of groundwater can roughly be distinguished with respect to the treatment in drinking water production:
- aerobic groundwater (phreatic)
- slightly anaerobic groundwater
- deep anaerobic groundwater

The above list implies that, for the treatment of groundwater, the level of oxygen (aerobic, slightly or deep anaerobic) is very important.

The redox potential is a good indicator for this, but this potential is seldom measured in practice. To what type a certain groundwater belongs can be determined from the concentrations of oxygen, iron, and methane.

The three types of groundwater will be further discussed separately, both their typical characteristics and their typical treatment schemes. After this the different treatment processes will be described.

4.2 Aerobic groundwater (phreatic)

Phreatic groundwater has an open groundwater table and is, therefore, connected to the atmosphere. When the organic matter content of the soil is limited, the water does not lose its oxygen (i.e., become anaerobic). As a result, no anaerobic reactions (e.g., iron dissolution) occur in the soil.

In special cases aerobic groundwater meets the requirements for drinking water.
In the Netherlands a couple of groundwater abstraction facilities are located on the Veluwe from which the abstracted water is directly distributed as drinking water. Normally, some treatment is necessary or desired.
Despite the fact that we are dealing with aerobic (i.e., containing oxygen) groundwater, the first treatment step is an aeration phase. Because of this aeration phase, the concentration of oxygen is increased further and the concentration of carbon dioxide is decreased. If the water complies with the legal standards after this treatment step, then the water can be distributed.

In the case of aerobic phreatic groundwater, only the parameters pH, Ca, SI and HCO_3^- have to be taken into account. The other parameters generally comply with the legal requirements.
Therefore, the treatment scheme of phreatic aerobic groundwater includes, in addition to a possible aeration, conditioning (Figure 24).

Aggressive water

When aerobic groundwater is abstracted from sandy soils (no calcium in the underground), the groundwater is often aggressive to limestone.
Because of a number of breakdown processes, carbon dioxide is present in groundwater, and, because the calcium is missing, the concentration of carbon dioxide is higher than the equilibrium concentration of carbon dioxide. The value of the saturation index, SI, is smaller than 0. To make distribution of this water possible, the saturation index has to be increased.

The SI is increased by aerating the water, which removes carbon dioxide. Then the SI may meet the requirements, but the requirements for pH and HCO_3^- buffering are often not met because the concentration of HCO_3^- is too low. When limestone (marble) filtration is applied, the requirements for SI, pH and HCO_3^- buffering are met. During limestone filtration, the aggressive water is filtered through a filter bed consisting of marble grains (limestone) (Figure 25). Because the water is aggressive, it dissolves the marble grains. After some time, the filter bed has to be refilled with new grains.

Hard water

Aerobic groundwater, which is abstracted from soils rich in calcium (for example, limestone area of Zuid-Limburg), is often very hard (>3 mmol/l). Because of the biological processes in the soil, the concentration of CO_2 can be resulting in substantial dissolution of limestone, forming Ca^{2+} and HCO_3^- in the water. The abstracted water, therefore, is hard.

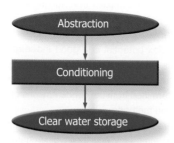

Figure 24 - Treatment of phreatic aerobic groundwater

Figure 25 - Aeration above a limestone filter

Groundwater will sometimes be in equilibrium regarding calcium carbonate (limestone). Water that is supersaturated with respect to calcium carbonate cannot be found in nature; because of the long residence time, a possible supersaturation would already have disappeared due to precipitation. When this water is pumped up and comes in contact with air, the carbon dioxide disappears from the water. The carbon dioxide concentration is, after all, larger than the saturation concentration of carbon dioxide in water being in equilibrium with air. Because of the removal of carbon dioxide from the water, the water becomes supersaturated with respect to calcium carbonate (SI > 0).

To prevent limestone precipitation in the distribution network or in consumers' washing machines and heaters, and to satisfy the recommendation of a maximum hardness of 1.5 mmol/l, the water is softened. This softening occurs by dosing chemicals (NaOH or $Ca(OH)_2$) into the water in cylindrical reactors with upward flow (Figure 26). These reactors contain small sand grains, which are used as crystallization nuclei on which the $CaCO_3$ precipitates.

The softening installation should be followed by granular media filtration, because possible post-precipitation might occur. After all, the time the water stays in the pellet reactor is short (a couple of minutes), and for the complete process of chemical softening more time is needed. When, after the softening, a granular media filtration phase is executed, post-precipitation takes place in the filter bed. If this filtration phase isn't provided, then the precipitation will take place in the distribution network or in the consumers' household machines. Alternatively, acid neutralization can be applied.

Example

As an example of the change in water quality, the Hoenderloo pumping station on the Veluwe is described. Treatment at the Hoenderloo pumping station consists of aeration/gas transfer followed by limestone filtration. The values of the different parameters in Table 2 are the annual averages.

The pH of the treated water is higher than the raw water, because the water is aerated (removal of CO_2) and because the water is filtered through a limestone filter (decrease of the CO_2 concentration, increase of the HCO_3^- and the Ca^{2+} concentration). The SI increases under the influence of the lower concentration of CO_2, and the higher HCO_3^-, and

Figure 26 - Pellet reactor for softening water in Meersen (Limburg)

Table 2 - Quality data of the raw and treated water at the Hoenderloo pumping station (Gelderland)

Parameter	Unit	Raw water	Clear water
Temperature	°C	9.6	10
pH	-	6.1	7.8
EGV	mS/m	9.3	14.3
SI	-	-3.4	-0.3
Turbidity	FTU	-	< 0.1
Na^+	mg/l	8.1	7.9
K^+	mg/l	1	1
Ca^{2+}	mg/l	8.6	22.5
Mg^{2+}	mg/l	1.6	1.6
Cl^-	mg/l	12	12
HCO_3^-	mg/l	21	63
SO_4^{2-}	mg/l	9	10
NO_3^-	mg/l	2.7	2.7
O_2	mg/l	4.2	8
CH_4	mg/l	-	-
CO_2	mg/l	31	2
Fe^{2+}	mg/l	0.06	0.03
Mn^{2+}	mg/l	0.02	< 0.01
NH_4^+	mg/l	< 0.04	< 0.04
DOC	mg/l	< 0.2	< 0.2
E-Coli	n/100 ml	0	0
Bentazon	µg/l	-	-
Chloroform	µg/l	-	-
Bromate	µg/l	-	-

the Ca^{2+} concentrations; the water becomes less aggressive with respect to calcium carbonate.

Because of the use of limestone filtration, the HCO_3^- and the Ca^{2+} concentrations will increase. More ions will get into the water, as a result of which the conductivity (EC) increases.
We can calculate the increase in the HCO_3^- concentration when we assume that all produced HCO_3^- comes from the limestone. For every formed mmol/l Ca^{2+}, 2 mmol/l HCO_3^- are produced. At this pumping station the Ca^{2+}-concentration increases with 0.3475 mmol/l because of the limestone filtration, and the concentration of HCO_3^- has to be increased by $2 \cdot 0.3475 = 0.695$ mmol/l. There was 0.34 mmol/l HCO_3^- present in the raw water and thus, there has to be $0.695 + 0.34 = 1.035$ mmol/l HCO_3^- in the treated water. This corresponds to 63.1 mg/l.

4.3   Slightly anaerobic water

Slightly anaerobic groundwater is found when the groundwater is located under a confining layer, and is characterized by the lack of oxygen and the presence of ammonium, iron and manganese.
The treatment of slightly anaerobic groundwater often consists of aeration followed by submerged granular media filtration (Figures 27 and 28).
Aeration is necessary for the addition of oxygen and the removal of carbon dioxide. The oxygen is used for the oxidation of Fe^{2+} to Fe^{3+} (a chemical process), and it is also needed for the oxidation of NH_4^+ to NO_3^- and of Mn^{2+} to MnO_2.

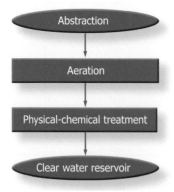

Figure 27 - Treatment of slightly anaerobic groundwater

Figure 28 - Aeration and submerged granular media filtration at the Noord-Bergum pumping station (Friesland)

Aeration is followed by submerged sand filtration. In the filter the oxidized ferric iron reacts with OH^+-ions and is transformed into $Fe(OH)_3$-flocs, which are filtered in the sand bed (a physical process). Manganese undergoes a partly chemical and partly biological transformation, while ammonium is biologically transformed. The transformation of ammonium is accomplished by the bacteria *Nitrosomonas* and *Nitrobacter*. During this transformation a lot of oxygen is used; per mg/l ammonium, the oxygen consumed is 3.55 mg/l. Also, a lot of nitrate is formed; per mg/l ammonium, 3.44 mg/l nitrate is produced.

As a result of the biological transformation of ammonium and manganese and the physical removal of the iron hydroxide flocs, the pore volume between the sand grains decreases, because the pores are filled by either bacteria or by flocs and deposits. The result of this is the increase in the hydraulic resistance of the water when flowing through the filter bed. When this resistance becomes too large, the filter should be backwashed.

Example

As an example of the change in water quality of slightly anaerobic water, the pumping station at the Zutphenseweg will be described. The treatment at the Zutphenseweg pumping station consists of aeration/gas transfer followed by sand filtration and a second aeration. The values of the different parameters in Table 3 are the average values over a year. As a result of aeration the concentration of CO_2 will decrease and the pH of the water will increase. Because of aeration the concentration of

Table 3   - Quality data of the raw and treated water at
Zutphenseweg pumping station (Overijssel)

Parameter	Unit	Raw water	Clear water
Temperature	°C	13.1	13.1
pH	-	7.7	7.9
EGV	mS/m	58	58
SI	-	-0.1	0.1
Turbidity	FTU	-	< 0.1
Na^+	mg/l	75	75
K^+	mg/l	6.7	6.7
Ca^{2+}	mg/l	47	46
Mg^{2+}	mg/l	7.8	8
Cl^-	mg/l	108	110
HCO_3^-	mg/l	185	177
SO_4^{2-}	mg/l	< 1	< 1
NO_3^-	mg/l	< 0.1	2.8
O_2	mg/l	0.4	9.5
CH_4	mg/l	-	-
CO_2	mg/l	7	4
Fe^{2+}	mg/l	0.39	0.03
Mn^{2+}	mg/l	0.03	< 0.01
NH_4^+	mg/l	0.82	< 0.04
DOC	mg/l	2	1,7
E-Coli	n/100 ml	0	0
Bentazon	µg/l	-	-
Chloroform	µg/l	-	-
Bromate	µg/l	-	-

oxygen will increase to a value near the saturation value (ca. 10 mg/l). The concentration of Fe^{2+}, Mn^{2+} and NH_4^+ will decrease due to the influence of oxidation and biological transformations. The nitrate content will increase, because the ammonium is transformed into nitrate. Since the decrease in ammonium is approximately 0.8 mg/l, the nitrate content should increase circa 2.7 mg/l. The oxygen consumption is approximately 2.8 mg/l. To get a high oxygen content, post-aeration is used.

4.4   Deep anaerobic groundwater

Deep anaerobic groundwater is found when the water is abstracted under a confining layer and no oxygen is present in the water. Furthermore, there is also no nitrate present and organic material is broken down with sulfate as an oxidant. Iron, manganese and especially ammonium are present in high concentrations, while hydrogen sulfide and methane are also present in the groundwater.

During the removal of ammonium, a lot of oxygen is used. When the ammonium content is larger

than 3 mg/l, the amount of oxygen necessary for the removal of the ammonium is larger than the total amount of oxygen, which can be dissolved in water (saturation concentration). To prevent anaerobic conditions in the last filter, double submerged filtration or dry filtration followed by submerged filtration is used during groundwater treatment with a high amount of ammonium.

Dry filtration is followed by submerged filtration because, in a dry filter, the breakthrough of particles may occur. When these materials pass through the dry filter, they are filtered in the submerged filter and do not show up in the drinking water.

An aeration phase is present before every filtration step, so the oxygen concentration is high before the water enters the filter and the carbon dioxide is removed (Figures 29 and 30). A dry filter is a filter filled with sand grains with a diameter between 0.8 and 4 mm. A layer of water is not present in the filter, like with submerged filtration. In the dry filter the water flows down past the grains, at the same time air is flowing with the water. The oxygen in the air replenishes the oxygen in the water, which is used by bacteria. In this way more than 3 mg/l of ammonium can be transformed without anaerobic results in the filter.

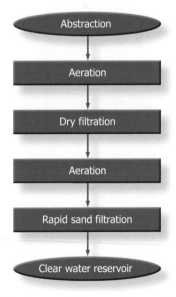

Figure 29 - Treatment of deep anaerobic groundwater

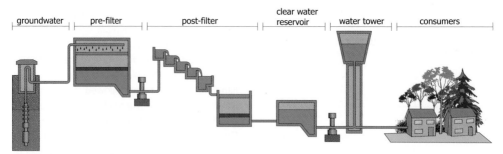

Figure 30 - Treatment of groundwater with double aeration/filtration

Example

As an example of the change in water quality of deep anaerobic groundwater, the St. Jansklooster pumping station is described. The treatment at this pumping station consists of aeration, dry filtration, aeration and submerged filtration. The values of the different parameters in Table 4 are the average values over a year.

As a result of the aeration phases, the amount of carbon dioxide will decrease and the pH will increase. Furthermore, the amount of oxygen will

increase. The concentration of Fe^{2+}, Mn^{2+} and NH_4^+ will decrease because of chemical and biological transformations; the amount of nitrate, on the other hand, will increase. The concentration of nitrate increases less than the theoretical calculation.

4.5 Aeration and gas transfer

Aeration/gas transfer is the process by which water is brought in close contact with air to change the content of the dissolved gases in water. For the treatment of groundwater, this means increasing the oxygen content and decreasing the content of carbon dioxide, methane, hydrogen sulfide and volatile organic compounds. The exchange of gases that occurs in this process always takes place simultaneously: aeration/absorption (gas to water) and gas transfer/desorption (gas from water). The close contact between air and water which is necessary for aeration can be obtained with various systems: by dropping the water through the air in fine droplets (spraying), by dividing the water into thin layers (tower aerators, cascades), or by blowing small bubbles of air through the water (deep well aerators, plate aerators, compressor aerators). Technically, these systems can be realized in a great number of ways.

The choice of a certain system is, to a great extent, determined by the gases that have to be removed. CH_4 and H_2S have to be removed maximally, because the remaining content will affect the post-filters. The removal of CO_2 has to be controlled because its level influences the pH and with that the SI. Table 5 gives a global indication of the effects of the various aeration systems.

Table 4 - Quality data of the raw and treated water at St. Jansklooster pumping station (Overijssel)

Parameter	Unit	Raw water	Clear water
Temperature	°C	10.5	10.5
pH	-	6.9	7.6
EGV	mS/m	51	48
SI	-	-0.4	0.2
Turbidity	FTU	-	< 0.1
Na^+	mg/l	23	21
K^+	mg/l	3	3
Ca^{2+}	mg/l	82	77
Mg^{2+}	mg/l	5.2	6.3
Cl^-	mg/l	41	41
HCO_3^-	mg/l	267	241
SO_4^{2-}	mg/l	18	21
NO_3^-	mg/l	0.07	1.6
O_2	mg/l	0	10.7
CH_4	mg/l	2	< 0.05
CO_2	mg/l	63	11
Fe^{2+}	mg/l	8.8	0.04
Mn^{2+}	mg/l	0.3	< 0.01
NH_4^+	mg/l	2.2	< 0.01
DOC	mg/l	7	6
E-Coli	n/100 ml	0	0
Bentazon	µg/l	-	-
Chloroform	µg/l	-	-
Bromate	µg/l	-	-

Table 5 - Choice for a specific aeration system

Favorable effect	Potential system
Input of O_2	All systems
Low removal of CO_2	Compressor aeration, deep well aeration, cascades
Moderate removal of CO_2	Spraying
High removal of CO_2	Tower aeration
High removal of CH_4	High cascades, plate aeration, tower aeration
High removal of H_2S	All systems, except compressor aeration
Removal of micropollutants	Tower aeration

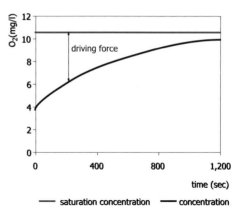

Figure 31 - Change in the oxygen content at aeration in a particular system

Kinetics

Gases are, to some extent, soluble in water. The concentration of a gas in the water phase is in equilibrium linear to the concentration of the gas in the air phase (equilibrium in conformance with Henry's Law). This equilibrium concentration is also called the "saturation concentration." Saturation means "at a fixed concentration of the gas in the air phase." This situation is obtained with a continuous replacement of the air phase. For oxygen in water that is in equilibrium with air, a saturation concentration of 12 mg/l can be calculated (10°C, 21% oxygen, 1 bar).

The equilibrium isn't achieved at once with intensive contact between water and air. Rather, the gas exchange takes place at a rate which is linear to the driving force. This driving force is the difference between the actual concentration and the equilibrium concentration:

$$\frac{dc_t}{dt} = k_2 \cdot (c_s - c_t)$$

in which:

c_t = concentration of a gas in water at time t (g/m³)

c_s = equilibrium concentration of that gas in water (g/m³)

k_2 = gas transfer coefficient (s⁻¹)

The gas transfer coefficient depends on the magnitude of the contact surface between water and air (greater surface area, higher k_2), and on the rate at which this surface is replaced (greater replacement, higher k_2).

For a certain aeration/gas transfer system, the gas transfer coefficient can be assumed to be constant.

Integration of this formula gives:

$$\frac{(c_s - c_t)}{(c_s - c_0)} = e^{-k_2 \cdot t}$$

in which:

c_0 = concentration of a gas in water at time t = 0 (g/m³)

The profile of the oxygen concentration in an aeration device is shown in Figure 31. The oxygen content initially rises quickly and then increases less because of the reduced driving force.

Efficiency

The efficiency of aeration can be defined as the achieved decrease in the driving force divided by the possible decrease in the driving force:

$$K = \frac{(c_s - c_{in}) - (c_s - c_{out})}{c_s - c_{in}} = \frac{c_{out} - c_{in}}{c_s - c_{in}} = 1 - e^{-k_2 \cdot t}$$

in which:

K = efficiency of gas transfer (-)

c_{in} = concentration of the gas before aeration (g/m³)

c_{out} = concentration of the gas after aeration (g/m³)

273

When aerating sequentially the efficiency will be equal per step, because the k_2t-value of the same device is equal. This occurs in aeration with cascades, where the water makes the same falling motion at each step.

The efficiency of the aeration can be increased by increasing the k_2t-value of the device (longer residence time, faster renewal of contact surface, increase of the turbulence in the water phase).

The driving force can also be increased, by increasing the saturation concentration. For aeration this can be done by applying a higher operating pressure (saturation tank, deep well aeration) or by applying pure oxygen instead of air.

Gas transfer can also be executed with a lower pressure (vacuum gas transfer).

An aeration device has different k_2t-values for different gases.

Mass balance

The amount of air needed for the addition of oxygen can be easily calculated. The volume of 1 mol air is 22.4 liters at 1 bar, so 1 liter of air with 21% oxygen is $(0.21 \cdot 32 / 22.4 =) 0.3$ g O_2. To get 10 mg O_2 in 1 liter of water, theoretically, only $(10 / 0.3 / 1,000 =) 0.033$ l air is needed.

The transfer of a gas can be hindered by exhaustion or the accumulation of gas in the air phase. Ventilating the air can limit this.

According to the mass balance, the gas mass that is removed from the water is equal to the gas mass that is transported (carried away) in the air. Therefore, the air-water (volume) ratio (per time unit) is of importance:

$$RQ = \frac{Q_g}{Q_w}$$

in which:

RQ	= air-water ratio	(-)
Q_g	= air (gas) flow	(m³/s)
Q_w	= water flow	(m³/s)

For an increase in the oxygen content, an RQ of 0.5 is sufficient. This is $(0.5 / 0.033 =)$ 15 times more than the amount stated above. To prevent

a limitation in the removal of CO_2, H_2S or CH_4 a minimum RQ of 5 is necessary. When a high level of removal is desired, a higher RQ-value is obviously needed. This is, for example, the case when removing toxic, volatile compounds, like chloroform and trihalomethanes, which can occur in groundwater because of ground pollution.

In the case of bubble aeration the RQ-value is typically smaller than 1. In the case of tower aerators, and plate aerators RQ-values of 10 and higher are applied. The differences in RQ-values cause, to a great extent, the differences in efficiency of these systems for specific gases.

Spraying

By spraying the water against a solid body or against another spray of water, the water is distributed over a large surface.

Over the course of time, a great number of sprayers and spray methods have been developed.

For the treatment of groundwater, the systems can be divided into:

- upwards or downwards spraying
- spraying in a separate room or above a sand filter.

With this, four combinations can be made, which are all being used (Figures 32 and 33).

When an intensive aeration/gas transfer is necessary, double spraying is employed, for example with a spraying room directly above a sand filter. The spraying floor functions as a reservoir for the

Figure 32 - Downward spraying with plate nozzles (Dresden nozzles) over a sand filter at Schiermonnikoog pumping station (Friesland)

Figure 33 - Upward spraying with Amsterdam nozzles in a separate room

Figure 34 - Cascade aeration with distribution from many jets at Heel pumping station (Limburg)

first aeration and also as a dividing system for the second aeration.

Most sprayers have a capacity of 1 - 3 m³/h per sprayer, if 2 - 4 sprayers are placed per m². With this the surface load of spraying (2 - 12 m/h) is approximately equal to the filtration rate of the post-filters. Sprayers have a very limited flow range. In the case of low flows, there isn't a good distribution of the water and a poor aeration results. Therefore, to deal with large fluctuations in capacity one can close off a number of sprayers. The energy used for spraying is limited (0.5 - 2 mwc to provide pressure drop in sprayers and 1 - 2 m as fall height, so 1.5 - 4 m in total).

Spraying is efficient for the addition of oxygen and the removal of CH_4 (for both 80 - 90%), but less efficient for the removal of CO_2 (40 - 50%).

The addition of oxygen results, almost directly, in the oxidation of dissolved iron. Therefore, on the walls and pipes of the spraying systems, iron deposits can be found. This pollution can be limited by using downward spraying directly above the filter. Pollution will always occur in the dividing system and in the sprayers, which will affect a good distribution during spraying. Spray systems will have to be cleaned a few times per year. An open division floor is attractive because of the accessibility of the parts that have to be cleaned.

In the case of dry filtration, spraying is always used to distribute the water evenly over the filter bed. The spraying room has to be ventilated with a flow that results from the desired RQ-value for the aeration/gas transfer. This air is filtered in advance to

avoid contamination of the microbiologically reliable groundwater by contaminants in the atmosphere (aerosols, etc.).

Cascade or waterfall aeration

In cascade or waterfall aeration the water is divided into a thin layer by letting it fall over a sharp edge. In past years many different types of cascades have been developed. In the most efficient types of construction, the water layer is divided into various spouts that fall into a water trough. During this, air bubbles are forced into the water and, because of the turbulence, these separate into many small air bubbles (Figures 34 and 35).

The water trough has a minimum depth of 66% of the fall height to obtain sufficient contact time. The rate of the water depends on the fall height:

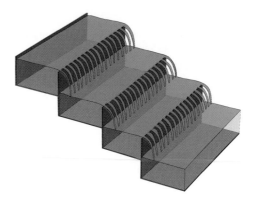

Figure 35 - Principle of the formation of air bubbles in cascade aeration

$$v = \sqrt{2 \cdot g \cdot h}$$

in which:

v	= fall rate	(m/s)
h	= fall height	(m)
g	= gravity acceleration	(9.81 m/s²)

With a height between 0.5 and 1.0, the fall rate is between 3 and 4.5 m/s. With a spout thickness of 1 cm and a fall rate of 3 m/s, the capacity of a cascade is (0.01 · 3 · 3,600 =) 108 m³/h per m overflow length. The efficiency of the addition of O_2 and the removal of CH_4 is more or less linear to the fall height (approximately 50 - 60% per m fall height). Unfortunately, CO_2 is very poorly removed in a cascade (approximately 10 - 20% per step, regardless of the height).

In practice a maximum fall height of 1 meter per step is chosen. The efficiency barely increases above this height. A higher efficiency can be obtained by using more steps. For a very thorough removal of CH_4 cascades with 4 - 5 steps and a total fall height of 4 - 5 m are used.

Many small steps are used if the largest possible CO_2 removal is desired.

The efficiency of a cascade depends little on the hydraulic load (up to 200 m³/h per m). Therefore, cascades are a very robust way of aerating, independent of fluctuation in the production capacity and barely sensitive to deposits of iron on the cascade.

Bubble aeration

Bubble aeration for groundwater treatment occurs in three types of facilities:
- compressor aeration
- deep well aeration
- plate aeration

Bubble aeration has the advantage that, it can be easily incorporated into the treatment scheme. Namely, in the case of bubble aeration, the necessary energy isn't extracted from the water phase (decrease of potential energy), but given to the air phase. This makes the addition of energy and, therefore, the gas transfer much more flexible than the other aeration systems.

Besides, compressor or deep well aerators are used when the removal of CO_2 is undesirable.

Compressor aeration

In the case of compressor aeration, air is directly injected into a water pipe through a compressor.

Calculation for cascade aeration

In the first step of a cascade aerator the oxygen content increases from 0 to 4 mg/l. Calculate the oxygen content after the subsequent steps.

With a saturation concentration c_s of 12 mg/l, the oxygen efficiency of a single step of a cascade can be calculated as follows
    (4 - 0) / (12 - 0) = 0.33

Thus, per step k_2 t = - ln(1 - 0.33) = 0.40
With a residence time of 5 seconds per step is k_2 = 0.40 / 5 = 0.08 s⁻¹

After the second step the oxygen content is	(4 + 0.33 · (12 - 4) = 4 + 2.6 =) 6.6 mg/l
After the third step the oxygen content is	(6.6 + 0.33 · (12 - 66) = 6.6 + 1.8 =) 8.4 mg/l
After the fourth step the oxygen content is	(8.4 + 0.33 · (12 - 8.4) = 8.4 + 1.2 =) 9.6 mg/l

The efficiency per step remains at 33%, but the absolute increase in the oxygen content decreases more and more (from 4 mg/l per step to 1.2 mg/l per step).

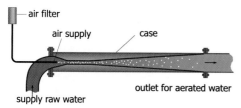

Figure 36 - Venturi aeration, a version of compressor aeration

By a narrowing of the pipe, a higher turbulence is obtained in the water, leading to small air bubbles and good mixing.

For a fast gas transfer it is preferable to inject air at a place where the water has a high pressure, but, when looking at the energy consumption of the gas phase, this is undesirable.
With a pressure of 3 mwc in the water pipe and an RQ of 0.1, the energy consumption of the compressor aeration is (0.1 · 3 =) 0.3 mwc. For the mixing, another 0.5 mwc is needed.
With this system, oxygen can be added, but gas removal almost never occurs.

Compressor aeration is mostly used in combination with pressure filtration.

Venturi aeration is a variant of compressor aeration and was often applied in the past (Figure 36). The air is entrained by a vacuum in the venturi.
Of course this way of aerating is very sensitive to variations in flow, because the vacuum varies with the square root of the water rate in the throat of the venturi.

Deep well aeration
For deep well aeration, air is brought into a vertical tube, where the mixture flows down to a depth of 5 to 20 m (Figure 37). Here, the water flows out of the tube into a larger shaft. Because of the high hydrostatic pressure, a very high transfer of oxygen is achieved, within an exceptionally small space. Furthermore, the energy consumption is very low. The air is injected almost under atmospheric pressure, which consumes little energy. The energy consumption of deep well aeration is mainly the hydraulic resistance of the vertical tube. This is not completely negligible because a rate of 2 - 3 m/s

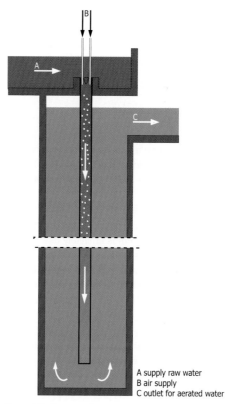

A supply raw water
B air supply
C outlet for aerated water

Figure 37 - Deep well aerator

is necessary to carry along the large air bubbles. Furthermore, the water in the vertical tube has a smaller specific gravity due to the air bubbles and therefore, also a pressure difference will have to be realized to obtain a net gradient.

Oxygen can be added to this system, but gas removal rarely occurs. From a deep well over-saturation of gases can occur and, in the post-sand filters, gas transfer can occur. This may result in faster clogging of the filters.

Plate aeration
With plate aeration, a large amount of air (RQ of 30 - 60) is blown through a thin layer of water (ca. 25 - 30 cm). The air is injected through many small holes (ca. 1 mm) in the bottom (Figures 38 and 39). The large amount of air causes strong turbulence and a good gas transfer, despite the short residence time (10 - 20 s).

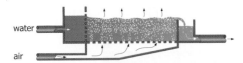

Figure 38 - Principle of plate aeration

The energy consumption in the water phase is very low (slow flow in an open trough), but in the air phase the energy consumption is very high. With an RQ of 50 and a water height of 0.30 m, the energy consumption is (50·0.30 =) 15 mwc.

With this system a very good methane removal is possible (90 - 95%) and considerable CO_2 removal (60 - 70%). This system is definitely used if extra methane removal is necessary afterwards, and if there is no hydraulic gradient available. The system is very sensitive to fouling, meaning that the small holes can clog due to iron and calcium deposits. Therefore, cleaning of the bottom plates is necessary several times a year. To limit the amount of outside air that has to be filtered, recirculation of used air is warranted.

Tower aeration

In the case of tower aeration, water is distributed over a column with packing, through which air is blown (Figures 40 and 41).

Tower aeration is easily configured for the removal of gases by:
- choice of bed height (1 - 5 m)
- choice of packing material (course, fine, open, filled)

Figure 39 - Plate aeration at Oldeholdpade pumping station (Friesland)

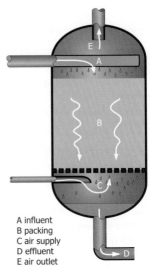

A influent
B packing
C air supply
D effluent
E air outlet

Figure 40 - Principle of tower aeration

- choice of air direction (co-current, counter-current)
- choice of RQ (1 - 100)

Due to such design choices, a very good removal of gases is possible. Tower aeration is not very sensitive to variations in hydraulic load (50 - 150 m/h). It is, however, sensitive to fouling, which makes regular replacement or cleaning of the packing material necessary if the water contains iron. In some cases this cleaning is performed by backwashing the aeration tower.

Tower aeration is also sometimes realized in a pressure vessel.
With a vacuum, gases can be removed without gases being added to the water (vacuum gas transfer).

With high pressure, over-saturation can occur. This is used in saturation for flotation.

4.6 Filtration

Filtration of groundwater is a process similar to the filtration of surface water. Both consist of a filter (sand) bed of 1 - 2 m through which water flows. The filter is backwashed (almost) daily, cleaned

Figure 41 - Tower aeration at Valtherbosch pumping station (Drenthe) for removal of volatile micropollutants

by an upward water flow, almost always with extra backwash air.

When treating groundwater, the filter is more like a "reactor" than a "filter." Groundwater is mainly abstracted from sand layers, as a result of which the water is completely free of suspended material. The sand of groundwater filters is, above all, contact material on to which bacteria and reaction products can adhere.

In groundwater filters, various chemical and biological processes take place, which all relate to the oxidation of dissolved groundwater components. These processes don't take place simultaneously. Because of differences in reaction kinetics, various zones, where a certain process dominates, can be determined in the filter.

Table 6 shows an overview of these processes.

Table 6   - Processes used for groundwater filtration (in order of performance)

Process	Dominant mechanism
Oxidation and hydrolysis of Fe^{3+}	Chemical
Oxidation of CH_4	Biologic
Oxidation of H_2S	Biologic
Oxidation of NH_4^+	Biologic
Oxidation of Mn^{2+}	Chemical (catalytic)

Iron (Fe^{2+})

Abstracted anaerobic groundwater in the Netherlands contains iron in concentrations of several milligrams per liter and, in exceptional cases, up to 25 mg/l.

In the oxidation and hydrolysis of iron, first the ferrous iron is oxidized, after which hydrolysis takes place and iron hydroxide flocs are formed. These flocs are filtered in the sand bed:

$$4\,Fe^{2+} \qquad\qquad \rightarrow 4\,Fe^{3+} \qquad\qquad +\,4\,e$$
$$4\,e \quad +\,O_2 \;+\; 2\,H_2O \rightarrow \qquad\qquad 4\,OH^-$$
$$8\,H_2O \rightarrow \qquad 8\,OH^- + 8\,H^+$$

$$4\,Fe^{2+} + O_2 \;+ 10\,H_2O \rightarrow 4\,Fe(OH)_3\,(s) \;\; + 8\,H^+$$

The rate at which oxidation and the hydrolysis of iron takes place depends on the pH. With a low pH the process develops slower than with a high pH. For that reason, when treating groundwater with a low pH, an aeration method is applied in which much of the CO_2 is removed and, therefore, a higher pH is achieved.

During the oxydation and hydrolysis of iron, acid is formed, so the process slows down itself. In practice it appears that the pH of the water is generally such that a fast reaction still can be achieved. While the formed acid reacts with the present HCO_3^- which forms CO_2, there is only a relatively small decrease in the pH.

The reactions of iron occur during aeration. On the one hand, this is positive because the used oxygen can be replaced and the formed CO_2 can (partially) be removed.
On the other hand, the iron flocs which are formed prove to be harder to filter than the flocs that form and grow in the filter itself.

The formed iron flocs usually get caught in the top 0.3 - 0.5 m of the filter bed. The deposits are always noticeable because of their rusty brown color.

Methane (CH_4)
Abstracted anaerobic groundwater in the Netherlands contains methane in concentrations up to several milligrams per liter.
Methane that is not removed during aeration will be "burned" by methane-oxidizing bacteria (methanotrophic) in the filter:

$$CH_4 \quad + 2\,H_2O \rightarrow CO_2 \quad + 8\,H^+ + 8\,e$$
$$8\,e + 2\,O_2 \quad + 4\,H_2O \rightarrow \quad 8\,OH^-$$
$$\overline{CH_4 \quad + 2\,O_2 \quad\quad\quad \rightarrow CO_2 \quad + 2\,H_2O}$$

The speed of the transformation will be relatively high, if there are sufficient methanotrophic bacteria present in the filter. In practice it has been seen that after a few days/weeks this is the case, even without the seeding of bacteria. These bacteria exist, typically, in nature (air, materials, etc.) and grow relatively fast.
Based on the redox potential, CH_4 (and also H_2S) would oxidize before Fe^{2+}. However, without bacteria, the oxidation of CH_4 and H_2S doesn't happen fast enough. So, in fact, the actual removal doesn't occur before the filtration, because only in the filter a sufficient mass of bacteria can grow.

Many methanotrophic bacteria produce mucus/slime. They can stick securely to the sand grains and are poorly removed when backwashing the filter.

The accumulation of a bacteria mass can occur with the result being the growth of other bacteria, like Aeromonas, and even the formation of anaerobic zones in the biomass itself. Also in the aeration systems and softening reactors, mucus-producing methanotrophic bacteria can cause problems. These problems don't occur when the concentration of methane is low (less than 0.5 mg/l). Such a low concentration is, therefore, considered a goal of the aeration. This can only be achieved by high efficient aeration systems.
The methane which isn't removed by the aeration is usually removed in the upper 0.3 - 0.5 m of the filter bed.

When applying dry filtration with a forced airflow through the filter bed, the methane is mainly removed by gas transfer, instead of by biological transformation.

Hydrogen sulfide (H_2S)
Abstracted anaerobic groundwater in the Netherlands contains H_2S in concentrations up to several milligrams per liter. The gas has the typical smell of rotten eggs. In general, it is satisfactorily removed with aeration because of the low concentrations of H_2S in the air. The remaining H_2S is transferred to the elementary sulfide (S) by a few sulfide-oxidizing bacteria, and then to sulfate:

$$H_2S \quad\quad\quad\quad \rightarrow S \quad + 2\,H^+ + 2\,e$$
$$S \quad + 4\,H_2O \rightarrow SO_4^{2-} + 8\,H^+ + 6\,e$$
$$8\,e \quad + 2\,O_2 + 4\,H_2O \rightarrow \quad 8\,OH^-$$
$$\overline{H_2S \quad + 2\,O_2 \quad\quad \rightarrow SO_4^{2-} + 2\,H^+}$$

H_2S is also already partially removed as a result of the increase in pH because of the removal of CO_2. H_2S is transferred to HS^- (with pH = 6.9 is $[H_2S] = [HS^-]$ and with pH=7.9 is $[H_2S] = 0.1\,[HS^-]$).

The processes mentioned above develop quickly, completely and without problems in groundwater treatment.

Ammonium (NH_4^+)
Abstracted anaerobic groundwater in the Netherlands contains ammonium in concentrations up

to several milligrams per liter and, in exceptional cases, up to 10 mg/l.

NH_4^+ is at first oxidized to nitrite by the *Nitrosomas* bacteria and subsequently oxidized to nitrate by the *Nitrobacter* bacteria:

$$2 NH_4^+ \quad + 4 H_2O \rightarrow 2 NO_2^- + 16 H^+ + 12 e$$
$$12 e \; + 3 O_2 + 6 H_2O \rightarrow \qquad 12 OH^-$$
$$\overline{}$$
$$2 NH_4^+ \quad + 3 O_2 \qquad \rightarrow 2 NO_2^- + 2 H_2O + 4 H^+$$

followed by:

$$2 NO_2^- \quad + 4 OH^- \rightarrow 2 NO_3^- + 2 H_2O + 4 e$$
$$4 e \; + O_2 \; + 2 H_2O \rightarrow \qquad 4 OH^-$$
$$\overline{}$$
$$2 NO_2^- \quad + O_2 \qquad \rightarrow 2 NO_3^-$$

in total:

$$NH_4^+ \quad + 2 O_2 \qquad \rightarrow NO_3^- \; + 2 H^+$$

The biological transformations take place simultaneously. Nitrite is found in the filtrate only in the case of an oxygen shortage. Ammonium is transformed to nitrate in the middle of the filter bed, below the iron zone. This requires sufficient biomass being deposited in the filter which sometimes takes several weeks after start-up of a new filter. Filters with new filter material first experience a conditioning or ripening period to obtain filtrate of good quality. For the removal of ammonium good management of the biomass is of great importance. With a backwash program that is too intensive, the amount of biomass can become too small; and, with a backwash program that is too conservative, accumulation of biomass can occur. This accumulation will result in the growth of other bacteria, like Aeromonas, and even in the formation of anaerobic zones in the biomass itself. Big fluctuations in the supply of ammonium (flow and concentration) to the filter should also be avoided.

Despite good biomass management, it might still be necessary to replace the filter material annually, or to clean it externally. In case this external cleaning takes place with only a fraction of the filter material, a substantial biomass will remain and conditioning might not be necessary.

Manganese (Mn^{2+})

Abstracted anaerobic groundwater in the Netherlands contains manganese in concentrations of less than 1 mg/l and, in exceptional cases, up to 2 mg/l.

Mn^{2+} is oxidized in a sand filter to Mn^{4+}:

$$2 Mn^{2+} \qquad + 4 H_2O \rightarrow 2 MnO_2(s) + 8 H^+ + 4 e$$
$$4 e \; + O_2 \; + 2 H_2O \rightarrow \qquad 4 OH^-$$
$$\overline{}$$
$$2 Mn^{2+} + O_2 \; + 2 H_2O \rightarrow 2 MnO_2(s) + 4 H^+$$

The speed of this transformation is very slow, unless a certain amount of MnO_2 has already been deposited, working as a catalyzing agent for the further transformation.

The formed MnO_2 adsorbs free Mn^{2+}:

$$Mn^{2+} \; + MnO_2 (s) \qquad \rightarrow Mn^{2+}.MnO_2 (s)$$

The adsorption reaction is much faster than following oxidation with oxygen to MnO_2. With this adsorption, also the oxygen consumption for the removal of manganese is lower than would be expected based on a complete oxidation. In practice 30 - 90% of the manganese will be oxidized.

The black color shows that manganese is deposited in the lower part of the filter. Furthermore, when the filter is being conditioned, the removal of manganese will only start if the removal of ammonium is substantial.

The deposits of manganese are hard to wash out, because they stick steadfastly to the sand grains, much more so than the flaky iron deposits and the biological deposits belonging to methane and ammonium removal. If the filter bed is too low (or the filter load too high), then manganese can also deposit on the filter nozzles and, as a result, the hydraulic resistance over the filter bottom can get very large. This can lead to damage of the filter floor when backwashing. Because of the manganese deposits, the filter material will have to be replaced regularly (sometimes annually), or externally cleaned.

Calculation of oxygen consumption and carbon dioxide production

Calculate the oxygen consumption and carbon dioxide consumption of groundwater after aeration:

Component	Raw water (mg/l)	Oxygen consumption (mg O_2/l)	Carbon dioxide production (mg CO_2/l)
Fe^{2+}	10	1.4	15.7
CH_4	1	4.0	-
H_2S	0.1	0.2	0.6
NH_4^+	3	10.7	14.7
Mn^{2+}	0.5	0.2	0.8
Total		16.5	31.8

The oxygen consumption is more than the saturation concentration so dry filtration has to be used. The carbon dioxide consumption is almost 32 mg/l, or (32/44=) 0.73 mmol/l.

This shows that an aeration type has to be chosen in which a substantial CO_2-removal is achieved, or an additional filtration over limestone ($CaCO_3$) must be chosen.

Oxygen consumption and acid production

All processes mentioned above have in common the consumption of oxygen and the production of acid.

In submerged filters the available amount of oxygen is limited to approximately 10 - 12 mg/l. If the process needs more oxygen, then dry filtration should be used. In this case, oxygen is added continuously during filtration resulting in the water from the dry filter almost always becoming saturated. Methane and ammonium are the large-scale consumers of oxygen.

Also, acid production has to be considered. If the acid production is too high, the pH will decrease and, with this, the speed of oxidation.

In natural groundwater there will always be sufficient HCO_3^- present, as a result of which the produced acid will transform into CO_2:

$$HCO_3^- + H^+ \rightarrow CO_2 + H_2O$$

Table 7 shows a total overview of the oxygen consumption and acid production for various groundwater constituents.

Filtration process

In the filtration process water flows from top to bottom through a filter bed, usually sand with a more or less uniform diameter.

For the filtration of groundwater the diameter of the filter material has to be chosen carefully.

A smaller diameter results in a larger contact area for chemical and biological processes and leads to better removal and particles retention by the filter. A larger diameter results in a more equal load over the filter bed height (deep-bed filtration) and a lower hydraulic resistance. And thus, the filter will have longer running times before it gets clogged and has to be backwashed.

With a high load (of iron and ammonium), the choice should be made for a larger grain diameter in dry filtration, as a result of which possibly post-submerged filtration will be necessary to remove washed out particles.

Table 7 - Oxygen consumption and acid production during groundwater filtration

Components	Molar mass (g/mol)	Oxygen consumption		Acid production	
		(mol O_2/mol)	(mg/l O_2 per mg/l)	(mol H^+ /mol)	(mg/l H^+ per mg/l)
Fe^{2+}	56	0.25	0.14	2	1.57
CH_4	16	2	4.00	-	-
H_2S	34	2	1.88	2	5.50
NH_4^+	18	2	3.56	2	4.89
Mn^{2+}	55	0.5	0.29	2	1.60

Moreover, the diameter of the filter material has to be between narrow boundaries. When backwashing the filter, small filter grains will be washed up because these particles have a lower sedimentation rate. The finest grain fraction is the determining factor for clogging at the top of the filter, because the load is also largest there, due to sizable iron deposits.

For a uniform grain diameter the ratio between the upper and lower boundaries of the grain particles (90%) has to be between 1.5 (fine sand) and 1.2 (coarse sand).

Filter material is produced by sieving sand or broken gravel between two sieves with a mesh width that conforms to the upper boundary as well as to the lower one.

The filtration rate (in m/h) is defined as the water flow (in m^3/h) per m^2 filter area. The actual water rate in the filter bed is of course higher.

Clean filter material has a total porosity of 35% to 45%. With a filtration rate of 5 m/h the hydraulic resistance (clean bed resistance) is 0.1 - 0.3 m, depending on the grain diameter.

Biomass is situated in the pores and the oxidation products are deposited there as well.

Due to ongoing deposition, the hydraulic resistance increases. With a filter resistance of 1.0 - 1.5 m, the filter is backwashed.

A backwash with air (60 - 80 Nm/h, 2 - 4 min) precedes the backwash with water. Then, at a high rate (superficial rate, 25 - 40 m/h), clean water is led through the filter in an upward direction.

For backwashing a total volume of about 3 - 5 times the total water volume of the filter is needed.

The deposits in the filter require abrasive backwashing. This requires high density filter material (sand, gravel), so dual media filters are not used in groundwater treatment plants.

The diameter of the filter material and the filtration rate are naturally also related to the height of the filter bed. The filter bed height has to be high enough to allow the chemical and bacteriological processes to develop (almost) completely. It is true that these processes occur sequentially, but the zones in which the processes occur run more or less simultaneously. An incomplete process could result

in fouling of the filter bottom, requiring the complete filter being taken out for a thorough cleaning.

Above the filter bed is a layer of water. The height of this supernatant layer cannot be too great, because a longer residence time between the aeration and the filter bed results in more oxidation and the hydrolysis of iron and, therefore, a faster clogging of the upper layer of the filter. A small supernatant water level can result in a vacuum in the filter bed, which can lead to gas release and faster clogging because of gas bubbles.

The following design parameters are employed for open submerged filters:

- grain diameter   2.0 - 2.5 mm (coarse)
                        or 0.8 - 1.2 mm (fine)
- bed height   1.5 - 2.5 m
- filtration rate   5 - 7 m/h
- supernatant   0.3 - 0.5 m

Construction

A rapid sand filter consists, most often, of an open tank of reinforced concrete.

The height of this tank is 4 to 5 m, a height that is determined by the supernatant water level, the filter bed height, and the height of the bottom construction.

In Figure 42 a cross-section is shown of an open rapid sand filter.

The construction of the bottom consists of a false floor with filter nozzles (Figures 43 and 44). These filter nozzles have small perforations with a width between 0.5 to 1.0 mm, which prevent the loss of filter sand.

The function of the filter nozzles is mainly to distribute the backwash water and air equally. The height below the filter floor has to have a minimum of 0.5 m for an equal distribution of backwash water and air. In practice, a much greater height is used (1.0 - 1.5 m) because of the desired accessibility of the space for maintenance and cleaning.

Backwash troughs are employed above the filter bed in a number of installations for an even collection of backwash water. In a good filter design, equal drainage is possible over a spillway next to

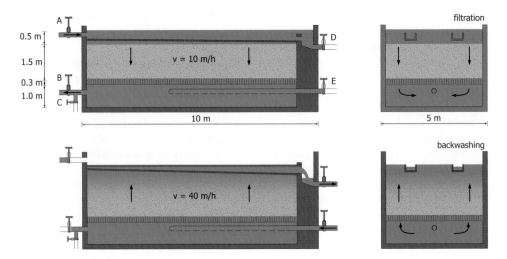

Figure 42 - Construction of an open rapid sand filter

the filter bed, even with a horizontal flow length of 5 - 7 m.

The shape of the filter is rectangular with a surface area often between 15 and 40 m². The surface area per filter is mainly determined by the desired number of filters. A minimum of four filters is used because, in maintenance and filter backwashing, a certain production capacity is desired.

When the yearly capacity is 1 million m³/y, the average production, then, is 115 m³/h and the production on the maximum day is approximately 170 m³/h (peak factor 1.5). With a filtration rate of 5 m/h a filtration area of 34 m² is needed, which is 8.5 m² per filter with four filters. With a larger yearly capacity, first a larger surface area per filter will be chosen and then the number of filters will be increased.

It is preferable that every filter be located in its own enclosed space. This will make maintenance possible without microbiological contamination of any nearby filters. In the space above the filter, most often, the aeration is situated, as a combined treatment unit. The air should be filtered to prevent contamination.

Figure 43 - Filter bottom with perforations in which nozzles can be placed

Figure 44 - Filtrate cellar with nozzles, seen from below, and foundation poles

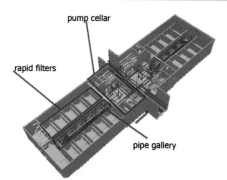

Figure 45 - 3D image of a rapid sand filter building with several filters

Figure 46 - A pressure filter is placed at Hendrik Ido Ambacht pumping station (Zuid-Holland)

Operation

During operation the raw water is supplied via valve A (Figure 42), and flows through the filter bed and the filter floor to leave the filter as treated water via valve B. As the filtration continues, the valve in the discharge pipe have to open further to compensate for the filter resistance caused by deposition of suspended solids. When this regulator is completely open, if continuing the filtration process, the filtration rate and the hydraulic capacity will decrease.

To avoid this, the filter is taken out of service for backwashing, valves A and B are closed, and valves D and E opened. Via valve E water is supplied which rises through the filter bed, expands the bed, loosens the depositions, and transports the water via backwash troughs and valve D out of the filter. The filter is put back into service by closing valves E and D and opening valves A and B.

In case the quality of the filtered water is unacceptable in the beginning of the run, then valve B remains closed and the filtrate is returned to the raw water supply pipe through valve C. Sometimes the effluent pipe is provided with a regulator, which only opens slowly during the first half hour to limit the filtration rate to a lower level.

Pressure filtration

Next to the open rapid sand filters described above, closed filters of the same construction, but placed in a waterproof steel vessel (Figures 46 and 47), are also used.

Now the driving force during filtration is the difference in water pressure above and below the filter bed. This pressure difference can be dramatically increased to a 5 to 15 m water column. With this, despite a fast clogging of the filter bed, long run times can be achieved. The attractiveness for industrial use lies in the low investment costs and the ability to place these filters at a random place or level.

The accessibility for maintenance of pressure filters is much worse than for open filters in an enclosed space.

Pressure filters can easily be combined with compressor aeration, which makes them unsuitable for a good removal of CO_2, H_2S and CH_4.

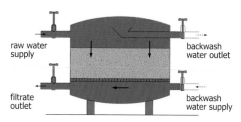

Figure 47 - Standing pressure filter

Because of the excessive injection of air in compressor aeration, pressure filters have to be provided with a ventilation valve on top of the filter vessel.

Dry filtration

Open and closed filters can also be used as dry filters. Dry filters lack a regulation valve, or an overflow at the height of the filter which makes sure there is always water on top of the filter. In the case of dry filtration, the filter is continuously emptied via a free outflow under the floor; the top of the filter will remain "dry." Because of the absence of water, there is always air in the filter bed and the used oxygen can be replenished. Due to the natural movement of the water, air will be carried along if the space below the filter is ventilated. This air circulation can be improved by sucking the air out of the space below the filter bed.

Theoretically, counter-current aeration would be more effective. This aeration, however, demands a lot of energy because of the small pore size in the sand bed and results in an uneven airflow and waterflow (flooding).

Also with dry filtration, usually a coarser sand fraction is used (1.5 - 2.5 mm).
The deposits in dry filtration are more evenly spread over the bed height, because the free water flow carries the particles deeper into the filter bed, due to the high water rates in the filter.

For this reason a dry filter will always have a higher breakthrough of turbidity than a comparable submerged filter. Subsequently, dry filtration almost always demands a post-submerged filtration.

The (gross) filtration rates for dry filtration are comparable to submerged filtration. Yet the residence time is much shorter, because most of the pores of the filter are filled with air instead of water.
In a submerged filter the total residence time is in the range of 15 - 25 minutes, and in a dry filter in the range of 1 - 2 minutes.

4.7 Neutralization

Groundwater often has a high carbon dioxide content as a result of all sorts of breakdown processes of organic material in the soil. If this carbon

---

Neutralization by aeration/gas transfer

The raw water (10°C) of a pumping station has the following composition:
Ca^{2+} = 2.0 mmol/l, HCO_3^- = 4.0 mmol/l,   pH = 6.46.
What is the pH in equilibrium after aeration, and how much CO_2 has to be removed?

From $pK_1 = pH + log \{ [CO_2] / [HCO_3^-] \}$ results that
$log \{ [CO_2] / [HCO_3^-] \}$ = 6.46 - 6.46 = 0 , that is $[CO_2] / [HCO_3^-] = 10^0 = 1$
so $[CO_2]$ = 4.0 mmol/l = 4.0 · 44 = 176 mg/l.

From $pH_s = pK_2 - pK_s - log \{ [Ca^{2+}] \cdot [HCO_3^-] \}$ results that
    pH_s = 10.49 - 8.36 - log (2.0 10^{-3} · 4.0 10^{-3}) = 2.13 + 4.80 = 7.23 and
    SI = $pH - pH_s$ = 6.46 - 7.23 = -0.77 , so the raw water is limestone aggressive.

When removing CO_2, $[Ca^{2+}]$ and $[HCO_3^-]$ remain equal and thus pH_s remains equal.
Therefore, in equilibrium $pH = pH_s$ = 7.23.

With pK_1: log { $[CO_2]$ / [4.0 10^{-3}] } = $pK_1 - pH$ = 6.46 - 7.23 = -0.77   so
$[CO_2]$ = $10^{-0.77}$ · 4.0 10^{-3} = 0.34 · 4.0 10^{-3} = 0.68 10^{-3} mol/l = 0.68 mmol/l
During aeration 4.0 - 0.68= 3.32 mmol/l CO_2 is removed, that is 3.32 · 44 = 146 mg/l.
Therefore, the required efficiency is (146 - 1 / 176 - 1 =) 83%.

dioxide isn't completely neutralized in the soil, the water will contain "aggressive CO_2" that can react with limestone and materials like concrete. Neutralization aims at conditioning the water so it no longer contains aggressive CO_2. Through neutralization, the pH of water will always increase (thus becoming less acid).

To remove aggressive CO_2 the following methods are employed:
- aeration/gas transfer
- limestone filtration
- dosing of a base

The method chosen is, to an important extent, determined by the desired water quality. Aggressive CO_2 is not permitted in drinking water, and the water needs to contain 1 mmol/l HCO_3^- at a minimum, while a content of 2 mmol/l is desirable for a sufficient buffer capacity. Furthermore, the pH should be as high as possible to limit the dissolving of lead and copper into the water from the pipe materials.

Neutralization by aeration/gas transfer
The choice for an aeration system depends on the desired removal of CO_2. By neutralizing with aeration the water is brought in contact with air. Water that is in equilibrium with air will contain approximately 1 mg/l CO_2. Because the carbon dioxide content in groundwater is much higher than equilibrium, it will transfer from the water to the air.

Due to the removal of carbon dioxide, only the CO_2 concentration of the water changes, the other concentrations remain equal. Neutralizing with aeration can then be done if the HCO_3^- concentration is already high enough. In this case, aeration/gas transfer is also the right method for neutralizing because this results in a high pH.

If the hardness of the water is high, then there is the possibility that, because of aeration, the carbon dioxide concentration will get lower than it in equilibrium. This may lead to limestone deposits in the aeration system and in the post-filtration.

Neutralizing by limestone filtration
With limestone filtration, aggressive water flows through a filter bed filled with calcium carbonate (marble) grains. The filter bed functions the same way as a sand filter.
However, in this case, the marble grains dissolve slowly. When the grains have become very small, they will be removed during backwashing.

Neutralization by limestone filtration

Raw water (10°C) of a pumping station has the following composition:
Ca^{2+} = 2.0 mmol/l, HCO_3^- = 4.0 mmol/l,   pH = 6.46, CO_2 = 4.0 mmol/l
What is the pH in equilibrium after limestone filtration and how much $CaCO_3$ is required?

When x mol $CaCO_3$ reacts, then x mol CO_2 is removed and x mol Ca^{2+} and 2x mol HCO_3^- are formed.
From K = $[Ca^{2+}] \cdot [HCO_3^-]^2 / [CO_2]$ = $10^{-(8.36+6.46-10.49)}$ = $10^{-4.33}$ results:
$\quad$ $(2.0 + x) \cdot (4.0 + 2x)^2 / (4.0 - x) \; 10^{-6} = 10^{-4.33}$ so that x = 1.20 mmol/l

Thus in equilibrium is:
Ca^{2+} = 3.20 mmol/l, HCO_3^- = 6.40 mmol/l, CO_2 = 2.80 mmol/l.
From pH_s = $pK_2 - pK_s - \log\{ [Ca^{2+}] [HCO_3^-] \}$ results:
$\quad$ pH_s = 10.49 - 8.36 - $\log\{ [3.20 \; 10^{-3}] [6.40 \; 10^{-3}] \}$ = 2.13 + 4.69   = 6.82
After limestone filtration the pH (or pH_s) is lower than after aeration/gas transfer.

During filtration 1.20 mmol/l CO_2 is transformed and 1.20 mmol/l $CaCO_3$ is consumed, that is $(1.20 \cdot 100 =) 120$ g/m³.
A production of 1 million m³ per year corresponds to 120 tons per year.

The filter bed is regularly replenished with new grain material.

In the case of limestone filtration, aggressive CO_2 is removed with the following reaction:

$$CaCO_3 + CO_2 + H_2O \rightarrow Ca^{2+} + 2\ HCO_3^-$$

The hardness and mainly the bicarbonate content increase in limestone filtration. Limestone filtration is used for water with a low bicarbonate content and, therefore, a low buffer capacity. The amount at which the hardness and bicarbonate increase can be influenced by the choice of the preliminary aeration method, with a lot or a little CO_2 removal.

The reaction mentioned above is an equilibrium reaction. This means that, on one hand, the dosage of $CaCO_3$ added is never too much. On the other hand, the driving force decreases because of the reaction, and the reaction rate also decreases. The equilibrium is obtained after an infinitely long contact time, in theory.

In practice, only a limited contact time is used. A bed height of 1.5 - 2 m with a filtration rate of 5 m/h is common. With a porosity of 0.35, a contact time of $(0.35 \cdot 1.75/5 =)$ 0.15 hour is realized and usually an SI of -0.3 is achieved.

Larger bed heights are needed if aiming at the removal of iron, manganese and ammonium simultaneously. The increase in pH has a positive influence on oxidation rates.

Neutralizing by a base

By dosing a base, carbon dioxide can be neutralized.

In practice (sodium hydroxide, NaOH), lime $(Ca(OH)_2$ or soda (Na_2CO_3) is used for this.

The following reaction then occurs:

$$NaOH + CO_2 \rightarrow HCO_3^- + Na^+$$
$$Ca(OH)_2 + 2\ CO_2 \rightarrow 2\ HCO_3^- + Ca^{2+}$$
$$Na_2CO_3 + CO_2 + H_2O \rightarrow 2\ HCO_3^- + 2\ Na^+$$

When dosing a base, carbon dioxide is transformed into bicarbonate. The dosed amount has to match exactly the amount of CO_2 that has to be transformed. In the case of an underdose, the water remains acid, and in case of an overdose, oversaturation occurs and the precipitation of $CaCO_3$.

Neutralization by dosing caustic soda

Raw water (10°C) of a pumping station has the following composition:
Ca^{2+} = 2.0 mmol/l, HCO_3^- = 4.0 mmol/l, pH = 6.46, CO_2 = 4.0 mmol/l.
What is the pH in equilibrium after dosing caustic soda and how much NaOH is required?

When x mol NaOH is dosed, then x mol CO_2 is removed and x mol HCO_3^- is formed.
From $K = [Ca^{2+}] [HCO_3^-]^2 / [CO_2] = 10^{-(8.36+6.46-10.49)} = 10^{-4.33}$ results:
$(2.0) \cdot (4.0 + x)^2 / (4.0 - x) \cdot 10^{-6} = 10^{-4.33}$ so that x = 2.30 mmol/l

Thus, in equilibrium is:
Ca^{2+} = 2.00 mmol/l, HCO_3^- = 6.30 mmol/l, CO_2 = 1.70 mmol/l
From $pH_s = pK_2 - pK_s - log\{ [Ca^{2+}] [HCO_3^-] \}$ results:
$pH_s = 10.49 - 8.36 - log\{ [2.00\ 10^{-3}] [6.30\ 10^{-3}] \} = 2.13 + 4.90 = 7.03$
After dosing caustic soda, the pH is lower than after aeration/gas transfer, but higher than after limestone filtration.

Because of dosing caustic soda, 2.30 mmol/l CO_2 is transformed and 2.30 mmol/l NaOH is consumed, that is $(2,30 \cdot 40 =)$ 92 g/m³.
A production of 1 million m³ per year corresponds to about 92 tons NaOH (100%) per year.

The dosage of a base for neutralization is only used when a small pH increase is desired. The two previously mentioned methods (aeration/gas transfer or limestone filtration) are simpler in operation and cheaper. Thus, dosing a base is only applied as a final correction of the pH.

4.8   Softening

Groundwater can have a high hardness if a lot of carbon dioxide, formed by organic breakdown, has reacted with limestone rock in the soil.

The hardness (Ca^{2+} + Mg^{2+}) of drinking water, according to Dutch regulations, may not be more than 2.5 mmol/l. Furthermore, a pH as high as possible is desired to limit the lead and copper solvency. For a higher pH, a lower hardness is required. However, softening is not allowed lower than 1 mmol/l. After all, the drinking water has to contain a minimum of 1 mmol/l HCO_3^-, though 2 mmol/l is considered desirable.

Softening for the production of drinking water is almost always executed using pellet reactors. In these reactors calcium is removed by dosing a base (caustic soda or lime) in the course of which $CaCO_3$ pellets are formed, which are reusable as chicken feed (for producing eggshells), or for neutralization purposes.

Alternative methods (sludge process, ion exchange or nanofiltration) are not applied for softening because these processes are more expensive and produce large waste flows which can't be reused.

The quantity of magnesium in natural water is usually less than 0.5 mmol/l.
With such a level the removal of magnesium is not desirable because of health concerns (magnesium deficit). Under process conditions in pellet reactors, magnesium isn't removed.

Softening with sodium hydroxide

By dosing sodium hydroxide (NaOH) the following reactions occur:

$$NaOH + CO_2 \rightarrow HCO_3^- + Na^+$$
$$NaOH + HCO_3^- + Ca^{2+} \rightarrow CaCO_3 + Na^+ + H_2O$$

NaOH is consumed for the neutralizing reaction (removal of CO_2) and for the softening reaction (removal of Ca^{2+}). A partial removal of CO_2 is necessary because a higher pH means a lower CO_2 content.

For the softening reaction, as much NaOH is needed as the desired reduction of hardness (ΔCa^{2+}).
For neutralizing, almost all the CO_2 has to be removed if the final equilibrium pH is to be approximately 8. When a much higher pH is desired, then even extra NaOH is needed to transfer HCO_3^- to CO_3^{2-}. The latter is negligible in drinking water practice.
Per mmol/l reduction of hardness, the content of HCO_3^- will drop with less than 1 mmol/l; 1 mmol/l $CaCO_3$ will form and the content of Na^+ will increase with more than 1 mmol/l.

Sodium hydroxide is available as a bulk chemical in a 50% solution. For drinking water treatment, this is usually diluted directly at delivery, because it can then be stored at a lower temperature.
Diluted sodium hydroxide is a clear fluid that is easy to pump. Of course, the water for dilution has to be free of carbonate or calcium, otherwise small particles of $CaCO_3$ can form during dilution; these particles are hard to remove afterwards or can result in deposits in the sodium hydroxide installation.

Softening with lime

By dosing lime the following reactions occur:

$$Ca(OH)_2 + 2 HCO_3^- + Ca^{2+} \rightarrow 2 CaCO_3 + 2 H_2O$$
$$Ca(OH)_2 + CO_2 \rightarrow CaCO_3 + H_2O$$

For the softening reaction, as much as $Ca(OH)_2$ is needed as the desired reduction of hardness (ΔCa^{2+}).
For neutralizing, almost all the CO_2 has to be removed.
In drinking water practice, the final pH is such that formation of CO_3^{2-} and OH^- can be neglected.
When dosing lime, CO_2 is transformed into $CaCO_3$ and not into bicarbonate, as with sodium hydroxide. This is because the calcium in the lime also has to be removed to obtain a net softening.
Per mmol/l reduction of hardness, the content of

Softening by dosing sodium hydroxide

Raw water (10°C) of a pumping station has the following composition:

Ca^{2+} = 2.0 mmol/l, HCO_3^- = 4.0 mmol/l, CO_2 = 1.0 mmol/l

What is the required dosing with sodium hydroxide for softening down to Ca^{2+} = 1.0 mmol/l and what is the final water composition?

The content of Ca^{2+} has to be lowered with 2.0 - 1.0 = 1.0 mmol/l, for which 1.0 mmol/l NaOH is needed, then 1.0 mmol/l HCO_3^- is removed and 1.0 mmol/l $CaCO_3$ is formed.

The amount of CO_2 that has to be removed can be calculated assuming that x mol NaOH is dosed, then x mol CO_2 is removed and x mol HCO_3^- is formed.

From $K = [Ca^{2+}] [HCO_3^-]^2 / [CO_2] = 10^{-(8.36+6.46-10.49)} = 10^{-4.33}$ results:

$(1.0) (4.0 - 1.0 + x)^2 / (1.0 - x) \cdot 10^{-6} = 10^{-4.33}$, so x = 0.71 mmol/l

Therefore 1.0 + 0.71 = 1.71 mmol/l NaOH is needed, that is $(1.71 \cdot 40 =) 68$ g/m³.

The production of 1 million m³ per year corresponds to 68 tons NaOH (100%) per year.

1.0 mmol/l $CaCO_3$ is formed, that is $(1.0 \cdot 100 =) 100$ g/m³.

A production of 1 million m³ per year corresponds to 100 tons $CaCO_3$ per year.

After softening:

Ca^{2+} = 1.00 mmol/l, HCO_3^- = 3.71 mmol/l, CO_2 = 0.29 mmol/l, $Na^+ = Na^+_0$ + 1.71 mmol/l, pH = pH_s (equilibrium)

From $pH_s = pK_2 - pKs - \log\{ [Ca^{2+}] [HCO_3^-] \}$ results :

$pH_s = 10.49 - 8.36 - \log\{ [1.00\ 10^{-3}] [3.71\ 10^{-3}] \} = 2.13 + 5.43 = 7.56$

The pH mentioned above equals pH_s. This shows that it is permissible to neglect the formation of CO_3^{2-}.

Softening by dosing lime

Raw water (10°C) of a pumping station has the following composition:

Ca^{2+} = 2.0 mmol/l, HCO_3^- = 4.0 mmol/l, CO_2 = 1.0 mmol/l

What is the required dosage of lime to soften up to Ca^{2+} = 1,0 mmol/l and what is the water composition?

The content of Ca^{2+} has to be lowered with 2.0 - 1.0 = 1.0 mmol/l, for which 1.0 mmol/l $Ca(OH)_2$ is needed, then 2.0 mmol/l HCO_3^- is removed and 2.0 mmol/l $CaCO_3$ is formed.

The amount of CO_2 that has to be removed can be calculated assuming that x mol $Ca(OH)_2$ is dosed, then x mol CO_2 is removed and x mol $CaCO_3$ is formed.

From $K = [Ca^{2+}] [HCO_3^-]^2 / [CO_2] = 10^{-(8.36+6.46-10.49)} = 10^{-4.33}$ results:

$(1.0) (4.0 - 2.0)^2 / (1.0 - x) \cdot 10^{-6} = 10^{-4.33}$ so that x = 0.91 mmol/l

And thus 1.0 + 0.91 = 1.91 mmol/l $Ca(OH)_2$ is needed, that is $(1.91 \cdot 77 =) 147$ g/m³.

The production of 1 million m³ per year corresponds to 147 tons $Ca(OH)_2$ per year.

2.0 + 0.91 mmol/l $CaCO_3$ is formed, that is $(2.91 \cdot 100 =) 291$ g/m³.

The production of 1 million m³ per year corresponds to 291 tons $CaCO_3$ per year.

After softening:

Ca^{2+} = 1.00 mmol/l, HCO_3^- = 2.00 mmol/l, CO_2 = 0.09 mmol/l, pH = pH_s (equilibrium)

From $pH_s = pK_2 - pK_s - \log\{ [Ca^{2+}] [HCO_3^-] \}$ results:

$pH_s = 10.49 - 8.36 - \log\{ [1.00\ 10^{-3}] [2.00\ 10^{-3}] \} = 2.13 + 5.70 = 7.83$

With this pH it is permissible to neglect the formation of OH^-.

HCO_3^- will decrease by 2 mmol/l, and more than 2 mmol/l $CaCO_3$ will form.

Compared to sodium hydroxide, the bicarbonate content is significantly lowered with lime. This demands that the raw water contain sufficient bicarbonate when applying lime to satisfy the quality requirements with the desired reduction of hardness. If this is not the case, then lime is preferred over sodium hydroxide, because a higher pH is achieved.

Also the sodium content of the drinking water might require the use of lime instead of sodium hydroxide.

Lime is made by decomposing $CaCO_3$ in a chalkoven into CaO and CO_2. The CaO is a hydrophilic (moisture-attracting) powder. The natural reaction with water (vapor) in the air transforms a part of the powder into lumps that are difficult to process. The hot lime is therefore often directly flushed with a stoichiometric amount of water, in the course of which $Ca(OH)_2$ forms. This is called slaked lime as opposed to the more reactive quicklime. Both forms react with CO_2 in the air forming $CaCO_3$ lumps, which hamper a correct dosing.

The dosing of a powder at the bottom of the pellet reactor is not practical, so lime is first dissolved in the water from which carbonate is removed.

The solubility of $Ca(OH)_2$ is low (ca. 1 g/l). Usually, a suspension (mixture of water and particles) is produced with 1 - 2% $Ca(OH)_2$ and is pumped into the pellet reactor.

The lime particles first have to dissolve in the reactor, which doesn't happen immediately. This is why lime requires a longer residence time than sodium hydroxide in the pellet reactor. As a result of this, the size of the reactor is larger.

The lime particles in suspension have to be very small, to avoid their being wrapped by a layer of $CaCO_3$ limiting the lime's effectiveness, and being washed out as small particles. In a careful design of the production installation and an accurate operation, in practice, almost complete use of the lime is possible.

It is true that, as a chemical, lime is cheaper than sodium hydroxide, but the dosing installation is much more complicated, and therefore more expensive for materials and operation. Therefore, for small installations, sodium hydroxide is used, also in cases in which lime would give a better water quality.

Lime is also available as a stable lime suspension, which makes a make-up installation unnecessary. However, this lime is considerably more expensive than lime in powder.

Pellet reactors

In drinking water production softening is almost always executed using pellet reactors. Water flows with high rates (superficial rate 70 - 100

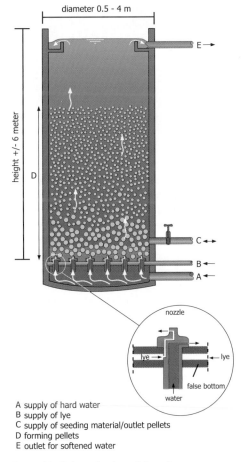

A supply of hard water
B supply of lye
C supply of seeding material/outlet pellets
D forming pellets
E outlet for softened water

Figure 48 - Schematic of a pellet reactor

Figure 49 - Pellet reactors in Assen (Drenthe)

m/h) upward through a reactor filled with pellets. The pellets flow freely through the water (fluidized bed) (Figures 48 and 49). The bed height at rest in a pellet reactor is about circa 2 m when sodium hydroxide is added, and about 4 m with lime. Depending on the upward water rate and the pellet diameter, the expansion of the bed when operating is between 50 - 120% of the bed height at rest. At the bottom of the reactor sodium hydroxide or lime is dosed so $CaCO_3$ precipitates on the pellets and the pellets grow. Because of the consistent quality of groundwater, the dosing pumps can almost pump a proportional amount (fixed relationship between water and base discharges). The pH and the conductivity (with lime) of the effluent are variables for controlling the process.

The pellets should not grow uncontrollably. Large pellets result in a smaller crystallization surface and, therefore, a poorer reactivity. Pellets should also not be too small, because then they would contain too much seeding sand.

At the bottom of the reactor, grown pellets (1.0 - 1.5 mm) are regularly drawn off and new sand grains (0.4 - 0.6 mm) are added.

With a pellet growth from 0.5 to 1.2 mm, the increase in volume is a factor of $(1.2/0.5)^3 = 13.8$, so the use of seeding sand is $1/(13.8 - 1) = 8\%$ of the $CaCO_3$ production. Before new seeding sand is added, it is first washed to remove small particles and disinfected with a caustic solution.

The pellets are drawn off under gravity. This suspension can be directly transported in a drainage container.

In the reactor no complete chemical equilibrium is obtained because of the limited residence time. Usually, an effluent is achievable in which 0.05 - 0.15 mmol/l $CaCO_3$ could still precipitate. This

Softening in split-treatment

Raw water (10°C) of a pumping station has the following composition:
Ca^{2+} = 2.0 mmol/l, Mg^{2+} = 0.2 mmol/l, HCO_3^- = 4.0 mmol/l, CO_2 = 1.0 mmol/l
How much has to be removed by the softening reactors for softening down to a total hardness of 1.0 mmol/l?

With a total hardness of 1.0 mmol/l Ca^{2+} is
(1.0 - 0.2 =) 0.8 mmol/l (content of Mg remains equal).
In the pellet reactor softening down to
Ca^{2+} = 0.5 mmol/l (on condition that $[HCO_3^-]$ softened >1.0 mmol/l)
Assume that a fraction x is softened, then a fraction (1-x) will not be softened.
When mixing both flows, the following Ca-balance applies:

$x \cdot [Ca]_{softened} + (1-x) \cdot [Ca]_{not\ softened} = 1 \cdot [Ca]_{mixture}$
$x \cdot 0.5 + (1-x) \cdot 2.0 = 0.8$, so
$x = (2.0-0.8) / (2.0-0.5) = 1.2 / 1.5 = 0.8$

Thus, a minimum of 80% of the discharge has to be treated in the pellet reactors.

happens in the post-filters when not enough acid is dosed, or when unsoftened water is not added (softening with split-treatment).

In a pellet reactor, calcium cannot be removed completely. For sufficient reaction rates, the effluent should contain $[Ca^{2+}]$ > 0.5 mmol/l, $[HCO_3^-]$ > 0.5 mmol/l and $[Ca^{2+}] \cdot [HCO_3^-]$ > 0.5 $mmol^2/l^2$.

In the case of softening non-aerated groundwater, next to $CaCO_3$ Fe^{2+} and Mn^{2+} will also precipitate as $FeCO_3$ and $MnCO_3$. However, softening non-aerated groundwater could lead to problems if there is more than 0.5 mg/l PO_4^{3-} in the groundwater. This disturbs the crystallization process in such a way that the pellets contain some water, and excessive growth of the bed occurs. In the aeration phase before softening, however, this phosphate binds to iron and this phenomenon doesn't occur.
With a methane content of more than 0.1 mg/l CH_4, biological growth of methane bacteria could also occur in the reactor.

4.9 Nanofiltration

At a few locations in the Netherlands, groundwater is abstracted that contains a noticeable quantity of organic material and, therefore, has a yellow color (humic acids). The legal limit for color is 20 mg/l Pt/Co, but only with less than 10 mg/l Pt/Co color will the customers experience their bath water as "colorless."

Nanofiltration is an effective removal process for humic acids. Water is forced through a membrane under high pressure, and large molecules are retained. Next to the humic acids, the divalent ions are effectively removed, including dissolved iron, manganese and hardness.
This requires anaerobic conditions in the membranes units to avoid oxydation of irons and manganese which would cause fouling of the membranes.

The largest installation in the Netherlands with nanofiltration of anaerobic groundwater is in Zwolle (Figure 50). For this, hydraulically optimal pressure vessels (Optiflux®) are used.

Figure 50 - Anaerobic nanofiltration for the drinking water supply in Zwolle (Overijssel)

4.10 Treatment of backwash water

In the case of groundwater treatment, waste flows are produced mainly as backwash water of filtration.

Figure 51 - Backwash water treatment with tubular membranes (Air-flush®) at Spannenburg pumping station (Friesland)

In total the backwash water production is usually 2 - 4% of the total drinking water production. Due to the scarcity of groundwater, such a production loss is undesirable. Furthermore, the backwash water can't be discharged, untreated, on surface water.

Backwash water treatment consists of a buffer reservoir and a treatment installation. The buffer reservoir usually consists of two reservoirs which can both store two backwashes. This makes it possible to take one reservoir out of operation for maintenance and still have a buffer volume, though a limited one. The treatment installation has two to four parallel process units.

For disposal on to surface water, tilted plate sedimentation is the most suitable process. When using backwash water for drinking water production, ultrafiltration (Figure 51) is the most suitable process. In ultrafiltration water is put under pressure and forced through a tubular, or capillary, membrane; with this, all suspended contaminants are removed. Each 10 - 20 minutes the membrane has to be backwashed and concentrated backwash water is released.

The settled sludge or concentrated backwash water can be thickened further in a storage and thickening buffer. The thickened sludge can be reused as an additive for the production of bricks or as phosphate binder (after acidification) in wastewater treatment.

If the thickened sludge can't be reused, then it will be dumped at a dump site. In a few cases the backwash water sludge has a high content of arsenic. In anaerobic groundwater this arsenic is sometimes present in very low concentrations. In groundwater treatment, arsenic removal is very effective due to its strong binding to oxidized iron. With an unfavorable ratio of arsenic to iron, sludge can be formed with a high arsenic content, making it a chemical waste. However, the arsenic won't leach from the sludge in a sludge dump, so there will be no real threat to the environment.

5. Treatment of riverbank groundwater

5.1 Types of riverbank groundwater

Riverbank filtration is groundwater that is abstracted directly adjacent to surface water, usually from a river. The abstraction takes place in such a way that the abstracted water consists mostly of surface water. This surface water is infiltrated into the soil via the riverbank on the river bottom. In this way, a mixture of surface water and natural groundwater is abstracted.

Figure 52 - Riverbank groundwater well in Germany

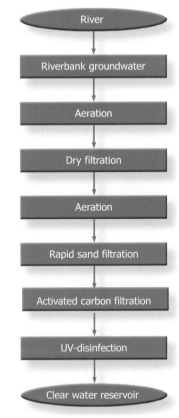

Figure 53 - Treatment of riverbank groundwater

The residence time of the infiltrated surface water in the soil can be several years. In this case we call it riverbank groundwater. This groundwater has the characteristics of groundwater, but the chemical composition also reveals surface water. In the Netherlands such abstractions are found along the Lek and the IJssel. The distance between abstraction wells and the river vary between 200 and 1,000 m.

In Germany most abstraction wells are placed much closer to the river (Figure 52). Residence times of several weeks are common. It is then called riverbank filtrate. It is clear that the existence of surface water in such cases is easier to recognize. A well-defined boundary between riverbank groundwater and riverbank filtrate doesn't exist.

5.2   Riverbank groundwater

The treatment of riverbank groundwater has many similarities to the treatment of slightly anaerobic groundwater. Riverbank groundwater is actually for a large part "natural" groundwater. The other part is surface water that has some of the characteristics of groundwater due to a long residence time in the soil.

The treatment scheme for riverbank groundwater is shown in Figure 53. Depending on the soil composition, higher concentrations of iron, ammonium, manganese and methane can be found. Furthermore, the hardness can be fairly high because of infiltration of river water. Due to

high concentrations of ammonium, which are biologically transformed to nitrate, a lack of oxygen can occur in the treatment; therefore, an extra dry filtration stage is often included (Figure 54).

Figure 54 - Aeration over a dry filter in Zwijndrecht (Zuid-Holland)

Activated carbon filtration is also used for the treatment of riverbank groundwater because of taste problems and problems with pesticides. A part of the water is surface water and, thus, it also contains substances associated with surface water.

For riverbank groundwater, UV-disinfection is often applied as the last disinfection stage, especially if activated carbon filtration is used in the treatment. In the activated carbon filters grow microorganisms due to the breakdown of organic material; these can subsequently end up in the water.

With UV-disinfection the microorganisms are killed, without the formation of disinfection by-products which are typical for chemical disinfection.

Example

As an example of riverbank groundwater, the Nieuw-Lekkerland pumping station of Hydron Zuid-Holland is described. Table 8 shows that the water contains a high concentration of ammonium and that there are pesticides present in the water.

Table 8 - Quality data of raw and treated water at Nieuw-Lekkerland pumping station (Zuid-Holland)

Parameter	Unit	Raw water	Clear water
Temperature	°C	12	12
pH	-	7.3	7.4
EC	mS/m	78.4	77
SI	-	-0.2	-0.1
Turbidity	FTU	-	< 0.1
Na^+	mg/l	69	70
K^+	mg/l	4	4
Ca^{2+}	mg/l	84	84
Mg^{2+}	mg/l	12	12
Cl^-	mg/l	128	135
HCO_3^-	mg/l	223	187
SO_4^{2-}	mg/l	55	59
NO_3^-	mg/l	< 0.1	2.3
O_2	mg/l	0.8	5.7
CH_4	mg/l	1	< 0.05
CO_2	mg/l	20	14
Fe^{2+}	mg/l	3.8	0.02
Mn^{2+}	mg/l	0.9	< 0.01
NH_4^+	mg/l	3	< 0.03
DOC	mg/l	3	2.5
E-Coli	n/100 ml	0	0
Bentazon	µg/l	0.32	< 0.05
Chloroform	µg/l	-	-
Bromate	µg/l	-	-

Hence, the treatment scheme is as follows: aeration, dry filtration, aeration, submerged filtration, activated carbon filtration, and UV-disinfection.

Chloride can be a problem for riverbank groundwater treatment plants along the Rhine. In the treatment, chloride isn't removed. When the concentration in the Rhine is too high, then the standard for chloride may be exceeded.

Oxygen increases because of the aeration steps. Manganese and iron decrease because of the combination of aeration and filtration. Ammonium decreases because of transformation in the dry and submerged filters. Because of that the nitrate content increases. Because of activated carbon filtration, the Bentazon content decreases.

There are no E-coli in the raw water because the raw water passes through the soil. During UV-disinfection, possible organisms are killed that grow in the activated carbon filter.

5.3 Riverbank filtrate

The treatment of riverbank filtrate doesn't show many differences from the treatment of riverbank groundwater. Only in this case, the share of surface water is larger, which makes activated carbon filtration and post-UV-disinfection more important.

Dosing with ozone is applied in a number of cases for riverbank filtrate, oxidizing the micropollutants.

Dosing with ozone is, in this case, not necessary for disinfection. When the water is passing through the soil, all (harmful) bacteria are removed, even with a relatively short residence time.

For soil passage the filtration of microorganisms is the most important removal mechanism. For this, reference is made to the good microbiological water quality, obtained with slow sand filtration in surface water treatment. In a slow sand filter a good disinfection is obtained with a residence time of only 0.5 - 1.0 days.

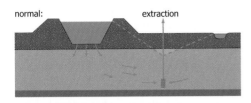

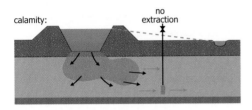

Figure 55 - Water (plus contamination) will drain into the well even after abstraction is stopped

5.4 Risks of riverbank groundwater

In the past riverbank groundwater has been considered a historical mistake. The reason for this is that the spreading of pollutants in the soil near the river cannot be prevented.

In the Netherlands the water level of the rivers is higher than the water level in the surrounding polders. Thus, there will always be a flow from the river in the direction of the polders. If pollution in the river occurs, then these pollutants will drain in the direction of the polders (Figure 55). Riverbank ground-

water has the name "historical mistake" thanks to the limited controllability of the pollutants.

However, the disaster at the Sandoz factory in Basel showed that the limited controllability of pollutants does not have to be a problem for the water supply. On November 1, 1986, the Sandoz chemical factory in Basel caught fire. When putting out the fire, large amounts of pesticides (10 to 30 tons, including Disulfoton and Thiometon) ended up in the Rhine. In Germany great panic arose because all life in the Rhine was feared to be destroyed for 10 years. Directly downstream of the Sandoz factory all fish and insect larva were killed. Water companies with riverbank filtration along the Rhine stopped the abstraction of water. The disaster was even compared to the Chernobyl disaster.

In the Netherlands the effects of the disaster were limited (Figure 56). For a couple insect species (water fleas, mosquito larva) the mortality was large. High concentrations of the disposed pesticides weren't measured in the Netherlands because of dilution, dispersion and breakdown. The WRK in Nieuwegein closed the intake of water for one week. Their reason for this wasn't the high concentrations of pesticides, but public opinion.

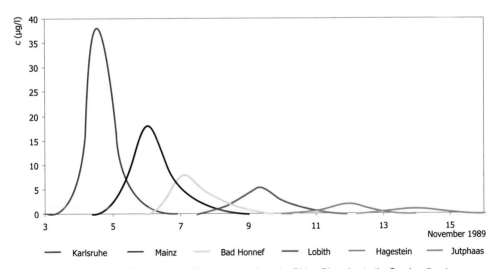

Figure 56 - Concentration of Disulfoton at different points along the Rhine River due to the Sandoz disaster

In Germany the Sandoz disaster was used to start a large-scale investigation into the safety and reliability of riverbank filtration with possible new pollutions of the river.

The levelling of concentration peaks occurs due to a difference in the residence time of the flow in the soil. This occurs especially during disasters where, in a short period, high concentrations are found in the river. Because of levelling, there is hardly a rise in concentration in the abstraction wells.

Within the framework of the research mentioned earlier, the influence of levelling was examined in Cologne. On the 7th, 8th and 9th of November concentrations higher than 1 g/l were present.

Only after a month, a rise in the Disulfoton concentration was found in one of the riverbank filtrate wells some distance from the Rhine.

The maximum concentration (0.05 µg/l, lower than the standard for drinking water) was found after two months in a well and was a factor of 66 lower than the concentration in the Rhine. Thus, the pollutants did not end up in the wells in high concentrations, however they continued to appear in low concentrations over a longer period.

The research also demonstrated that some pesticides were broken down during soil passage and that some substances were well-absorbed by activated carbon.

Based on that research, the Germans drew an important conclusion:

Und die Moral von der Geschicht
Die Stoßbelasting stört uns nicht

(The conclusion of this story is
  The pulse load is not harmfull)

It does not matter how big a spill is, because of levelling and breaking down, the concentration in the abstraction wells of riverbank groundwater will stay sufficiently low.

Besides this, another important conclusion can be drawn:

Was uns dargegen gar nicht paßt
ist auch am Rhein die Dauerlast

(On the other hand, the real problem
  is the prolonged overloading)

Naturally, it is better to apply treatment at the source, rather than letting the contamination flow into the water, as a result of which the contamination accumulates in nature.

5.5   Future riverbank groundwater

It can be concluded that riverbank groundwater has incorrectly been named a historical mistake in the past. From research after the disaster near Sandoz, it has become clear that riverbank groundwater is a reliable source of drinking water supply, which in some respects can be seen as a golden compromise between groundwater and surface water.

Compared to groundwater, riverbank groundwater has the advantage that the groundwater level decreases less. This means that fewer effects on nature and agriculture occur and abstraction is more sustainable.

Compared to surface water, riverbank groundwater has the advantage of microbiological reliability and a much more stable and predictable quality. This means that no large reservoirs and infiltration facilities are needed and less sludge is produced.

This does not suggest that riverbank groundwater is an irreproachable source for drinking water supply. In artificial infiltration schemes the surface water is treated before infiltration in the soil, as a result of which the spreading of contaminants from the surface water is limited. In the case of riverbank groundwater, this is not possible and also not useful, because the surface water naturally infiltrates into the soil in the Netherlands, as a result of which the surface water will spread to the surrounding polder lands.

Another point of discussion is the groundwater tax. The treasury considers riverbank groundwater as groundwater, for which a groundwater tax has to be paid. In reality, a part of the abstracted water always comes from surface water. A number of drinking water companies have challenged the legitimacy and the efficacy of the groundwater tax for this kind of abstraction. After all, the effects of riverbank groundwater abstraction on the groundwater level are on a totally different order of magnitude than from "normal" groundwater abstraction.

Other, more technological, discussion points include the minimal required residence time in the soil to guarantee hygienic reliability. In the past, 60 days were used, but research has shown that with shorter residence times good results can also be retrieved. Another item is the optimal design of the well field to achieve as much levelling as possible of the differences in quality (for this it is useful to locate the wells perpendicular to the river).

These considerations are notably interesting when designing future abstractions and when the goal is to retrieve good water quality with minimal effects on nature and the environment. In this way it seems to be possible to create a combination of drinking water abstraction and environmental development along the big rivers in the future.

5.6   *Activated carbon filtration*

Activated carbon filtration is a treatment process based on adsorption. With this, substances adhere to the surface under the influence of surface and Van de Waals forces. In drinking water production this is the adsorption of apolar (not charged) micropollutants, such as most pesticides like Bentazon and Atrazine. The water flows now downwards through a filter bed of activated carbon grains.

Process

Adsorption can be approached in the relatively narrow concentration range by an equilibrium reaction, like the dissolving of gases:

$$K = \frac{c_s}{c_w}$$

in which:

K = (isotherm) equilibrium constant $\quad$ (-)
c_s = concentration in the carbon $\quad$ (g/l carbon)
c_w = concentration in the water $\quad$ (g/l water)

This linear isotherm indicates that the equilibrium concentration in the water becomes higher when the carbon is more loaded.

With new carbon the desired effluent concentration is reached in the top of the filter bed, because of the carbon's low loading. When the carbon becomes more loaded, this front shifts down.

Because of the kinetics process, this is not a sharp front, but a transitional area. At the top, the concentration in the carbon is in equilibrium with the influent; at the bottom, the carbon is in equilibrium with the desired effluent concentration. During further loading, the effluent concentration will exceed the target value and the filter will have to be taken out of service.

An important process parameter during carbon filtration is the time in which the equilibrium has to be reached. For practical purposes, empty bed contact time (EBCT being the residence time in an empty carbon bed) is used. Often an EBCT between 12 and 40 minutes is used. The true contact time is, of course, shorter depending on the (macro) porosity of the grain bed.

The amount of water that can be treated in the filter before breakthrough occurs is expressed as the number of bed volumes (again formulated as empty bed volume). In practice, lifetimes of 10,000 to 30,000 bed volumes are possible, depending on the contaminants that have to be removed. At a bed height, for example, of 3 m and 10,000 bed volumes, the total amount of water treated is $(3 \cdot 10,000 =) 30,000$ m. At a (superficial) filtration rate of 5 m/h, this corresponds to a lifetime of $(30,000/5 =) 6,000$ hour, or almost 0.7 year.

Next to the microcontaminants, which have to be removed, natural organic matter (NOM) also sticks to the surface, which results in biological growth of a large variety of bacteria and higher organisms. The biological activity has positive and negative effects. Because of the biological breakdown, the adsorbed material is transformed so more surface area is available, but the biological material covers a large surface area itself. The net effect is usually that the biological activity increases the lifetime of the activated carbon.

In situations where the previously mentioned breakthrough covers a substantial part of the bed height, much of the carbon at the bottom of the filter is not heavily loaded. In this situation often a two-staged system is employed, by locating two filters in a series. At breakthrough both filters are taken out of service. Only the carbon in the first filter is replaced by new carbon. The original second filter is now used as the first filter with the new carbon as the second filter. This system is also referred to as a pseudo moving bed, because the carbon bed is not replaced but only the hydraulic sequence of the filters is reversed. From the equilibrium kinetic it follows that the carbon bed has to be disturbed as little as possible, for example, by backwashing. A loaded carbon particle, originating from the upper part, may desorb the adsorbed contaminants (equilibrium at a low concentration in water) at the bottom.

Construction

Activated carbon filtration shows great similarity to the previously described rapid sand filtration process. Structurally, all the external characteristics are the same (dimensions, bed height, floor construction, measurement tools, etc.). For activated carbon filtration, the filter bed consists not of sand grains, but of activated carbon grains, with a diameter between 0.5 and 1.5 mm and a gravity between 300 - 500 kg/m³.

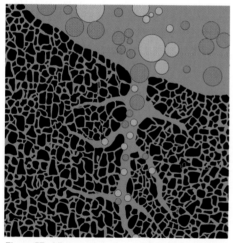

Figure 57 - Micropores and pore channels in an activated carbon grain

Activated carbon is made by heating organic carbon (wood, peat, coal, coconut), resulting in a very porous material with a very high specific surface (500 - 1,500 m²/g). The pores have very diverse dimensions (0.1 - 1,000 nm). The smallest pores are the most important ones for the surface effects, while the larger pores serve as a transport channel to the smaller pores (Figure 57).

Contaminated carbon can be regenerated. In this process the carbon is heated again. The adsorbed contaminants are burned or volatilized during this process. At such regeneration 5 - 10 % of the carbon is lost by burning or pulverizing.

5.7   UV - disinfection

Radiation with ultraviolet light (UV) in which microorganisms are present will result in the destruction of the DNA of the microorganisms. This destruction blocks further metabolism and cell growth. To get this effect, the organisms have to be hit by sufficient radiation and of the right wavelength. The highest sensitivity occurs at 254 nm (250 - 260 nm). The UV radiation is made with the help of UV lamps (Figure 58) located in a contact room where the water, which has to be treated, flows through.

The required UV dosage is defined as the amount of radiation energy with a wavelength of 254 nm per m² that is located as far as possible from the radiation source at a certain exposure time. The

Figure 58 - UV-disinfection after activated carbon filtration at Heel riverbank groundwater treatment plant (Limburg)

Figure 59 - Dutch sign of a groundwater protection area

unit is W/m^2 · s or J/m^2. The required radiation differs per microorganism.

Water blocks UV light to some extent. This is why the lamps have to be placed together tightly. The extent to which UV light is blocked differs for every type of water. It can be measured as UV transmission. The radiation from a lamp decreases over time. This loss in radiation has to be compensated for by other lamps or by an overdose in the previous period. Most lamps have a lifespan of 6,000 to 10,000 working hours. UV disinfection is a relatively easy and inexpensive way to disinfect.

6. Groundwater legislation in the Netherlands

Groundwater lies within the influence area of the European Water Framework Directive, which was published in 2000.
This framework directive has consequences for the Dutch water legislation:
- Groundwater Act
- Environmental Management Act
- Water Management Act
- Surface Water Pollution Act
- Soil Protection Act

The Dutch framework for the public drinking water supply is established in the Policy Plan for Drinking and Industry Water Supply.

Groundwater Act
Abstraction of groundwater is an activity in the Netherlands controlled by the Groundwater Act. The Groundwater Act names the provincial government as executors of the groundwater policy, including the distribution of permits for abstraction. Provincial governments formulate these policy and management plans, as well as decrees. Large groundwater abstractions have to carry out an Environmental Impact Assessment (EIA) for their permit granting.

Groundwater protection areas
Within the legal framework provincial governments formulate policy and management plans for the protection of groundwater for the supply of

drinking water. In these documents, groundwater protection areas are identified, usually indicated as water abstraction areas (Figure 59).

Environmental Management Act
Within the Environmental Management Act the resolution about the EIA is formulated. In this resolution it is stated that an EIA procedure has to be executed before the construction of a new groundwater abstraction facility with a capacity of more than 3 million m^3 per year.

Further reading

- Principles and practices of water supply operations: Water sources, AWWA (2003)
- Principles and practices of water supply operations: Water treatment, AWWA (2003, student workbook 2005)
- Groundwater monitoring in Europe, EEA (1996)
- Groundwater quality and quantity, EEA (1999)
- Groundwater recovery, L. Huisman, Winchester Press (1972)

- www.eea.eu.int
- europe.eu.int
- www.vewin.nl
- www.kiwa.nl
- www.overheid.nl/wetten
- www.epa.gov
- www.awwa.org
- www.groundwater.org

Questions and applications

Groundwater in the natural environment

1. Describe the 4 types of outflow of groundwater.

Abstraction of groundwater

1. Describe the well-known types of wells and drainage utilities for groundwater abstraction. Also, indicate the depth of abstraction and the thickness of the aquifer.

Treatment of groundwater

1. The hardness of raw water is 2.4 mmol/l (0,2 mmol/l Mg^{2+} and 2.2 mmol/l Ca^{2+}). In the softening reactor the water can be softened down to 0.8 mmol/l. Determine the minimum amount of water that has to flow through the pellet reactor.

Treatment of riverbank groundwater

1. For the abstraction of water along the banks of rivers and lakes, there are two situations:
   - riverbank groundwater
   - riverbank filtration

   Describe the different types of treatment with their similarities and differences.

Groundwater legislation in the Netherlands

1. Indicate which laws are important for groundwater abstraction.

Applications

1. A drinking water company uses two types of groundwater for the production of drinking water: anaerobic and aerobic groundwater. Water analyses are regularly conducted in the laboratory of the drinking water company. In the table the results of the analyses of the water types are shown.

Analysis results in two different types of groundwater

Parameter	Unit	Anaerobic groundwater	Aerobic groundwater
K^+	mg/l	3	2.2
Na^+	mg/l	23	13
NH_4^+	mg/l	2.2	0
Fe^{2+}	mg/l	8	0
Mg^{2+}	mg/l	5.2	1.6
Ca^{2+}	mg/l	82	8.6
Cl^-	mg/l	41	12
HCO_3^-	mg/l	267	21
NO_3^-	mg/l	0.06	2.7
SO_4^{2-}	mg/l	18	9
CO_2	mg/l	80	32
O_2	mg/l	0	9.7
CH_4	mg/l	2.2	0
Temperature	°C	10	10

a Calculate the molar concentrations of the deep anaerobic groundwater.

b Calculate the pH of both types of water.

c Calculate the pH of the water when both water types are mixed.

d Demonstrate that deep anaerobic groundwater is limestone aggressive.

e Deep anaerobic groundwater is located at a depth of 230 meters. Calculate the saturation value of carbon dioxide at this depth.

2. Indicate if the statements are true or false (explain your answers).

a In the aerobic groundwater on the sand grounds of the Veluwe, the nitrate and calcium contents increase due to environmental pollution.

b In slightly anaerobic groundwater, methane is formed because of a reduction in organic material.

c In deep anaerobic groundwater, there is no nitrate present due to denitrification.

3. In the east of the Netherlands a new drinking water treatment plant is built. The source for the treatment station is groundwater. The treatment scheme consists of: aeration - dry filtration - softening - submerged filtration.

a The new drinking water treatment plant is built close to a large river. Give possible reasons why groundwater is chosen and not surface water as a source for the treatment?

b Why is groundwater aerated?

c Describe three systems which are used in practice to aerate groundwater.

d Which substances are removed during dry filtration? Name a minimum of three substances.

e Which substance in groundwater plays a crucial role when considering dry filtration instead of submerged filtration and why?

4. The groundwater that is abstracted by the Helden pumping station (for the water composition see table below) follows this treatment process: aeration (spraying) - dry filtration - limestone filtration

a Describe which type of water this is.

b Because of spraying, the concentration of CO_2 decreases by 50% and the oxygen concentration increases up to 8 mg/l. Calculate the composition of the water (fill in the missing values in the second column).

c In the dry filter iron removal occurs. Calculate the effect of iron removal on the concentrations of Fe^{2+}, Ca^{2+}, Mg^{2+}, O_2, CO_2, HCO_3^- and the pH. Fill in the missing values in the third column of the table.

d Why is the dry filter backwashed after some time?

e To satisfy the demands on drinking water, the last treatment step is limestone filtration. Calculate the effect of the limestone filtration on the concentrations of Fe^{2+}, Ca^{2+}, Mg^{2+}, O_2, CO_2, HCO_3^- and the pH. Fill in the missing values in the last column of the table.

Water quality data

Parameter	Raw water	After spraying	After dry filtration	After limestone filtration
Temperature	10			
Na^+ (mg/l)	15			
Ca^{2+} (mg/l)	28			48
Mg^{2+} (mg/l)	9.7			
HCO_3^- (mg/l)	12.2			
pH	5.75			
Fe^{2+} (mg/l)	8			
O_2 (mg/l)	0			
CO_2 (mg/l)	44			

Answers

Groundwater in the natural environment
1. - Phreatic water
     - local deepening
     - impermeable base
   - Artesian water
     - local deepening
     - impermeable base

Abstraction of groundwater
1.

Thickness layer	Depth of abstraction	Type of abstraction
Small	Shallow	Horizontal, open canals or closed dug drain pipes
	Deep	Horizontal, radial wells
Large	Shallow	Vertical, dug wells
	Deep	Vertical, drilled wells

Treatment of groundwater
1. Calcium balance
   $x \cdot 0.8 + (1-x) \cdot 2.2 = 1.3$
   $x = (2.2 - 1.3) / (2.2 - 0.8) = 0.65$
   Therefore 65% of the flow has to pass the reactor.

Treatment of riverbank groundwater
1. Riverbank groundwater:
   Riverbank groundwater is water that is mostly groundwater. It has the characteristics of groundwater and the treatment is based on groundwater treatment (aeration and rapid filtration). Riverbank groundwater is abstracted at a distance of approximately 1 kilometer from the bank of a river.
   Riberbank filtration:
   In riverbank filtration about 90% of the water is river water. The abstraction wells are close to the river (from several meters up to 100 meters), which makes the residence time in the soil short, circa 1 month. The levelling that is achieved is also lower, a factor of 50 - 100 can be achieved.

Groundwater legislation in the Netherlands
1. - Groundwater Act
     - Environmental Management Act
     - Soil Protection Act

Applications
1. a From the analysis record, the concentration of substances can be calculated in mmol/l
   $HCO_3^- = 4.38$ mmol/l
   $SO_4^{2-} = 0.19$ mmol/l
   $Cl^- = 1.16$ mmol/l
   $Na^+ = 1.0$ mmol/l
   $Ca^{2+} = 2.05$ mmol/l
   $Mg^{2+} = 0.21$ mmol/l

   b Deep anaerobic groundwater:
     $HCO_3^- = 267$ mg/l = 4.38 mmol/l
     $CO_2 = 48.4$ mg/l = 1.1 mol/l
     $pH = 6.46 + \log (1.1 / 4.38) = 7.07$
     Aerobic groundwater:
     $HCO_3^- = 21$ mg/l = 0.344 mmol/l
     $CO_2 = 32$ mg/l = 0.727 mmol/l
     $pH = 6.46 + \log (0.344 / 0.727) = 6.14$

   c Add the concentration of HCO_3^- and CO_2 and divide them by 2
     $HCO_3^- = (4.38 + 0.344) / 2$
     $= 2.36$ mmol/l
     $CO_2 = (1.1+0.73)/2 = 0.914$ mmol/l
     $pH = 6.46+\log(2.36/0.914) = 6.87$

   d The pH in equilibrium is:
     $pH_s = 10.49 - 8.36 - \log (2.05 \cdot 4.38 \cdot 10^{-6}) = 7.17$
     $SI = pH - pH_s = 6.14 - 7.17 = -1.03$
     SI is negative, thus limestone aggressive
     This can also be determined with Tillmans' diagram, the point is above the equilibrium line.

   e The absolute pressure on a depth of 230 meters is 24 bar; the molecular weight of carbon dioxide is 44 g/mol; and, the temperature is 283 K; the volume fraction carbon dioxide = 0.032% = 0.00032;

c_g = 0.00032 · 2,400,000·44 / (8.31·283)
= 17.7 mg/l;
H of carbon dioxide at 10°C is 1.23; so
c_w = 1.23 x 17.7 = 21.8 mg/l

2. a False, the content of nitrate increases due to manure dumping (ammonium is transformed into nitrate with oxygen).
However, in sand grains there is no calcium carbonate present, so the calcium concentration can't increase.

b False, only in deep anaerobic water is methane used as an oxidator for organic material.

c True, in deep anaerobic water there is no oxygen present because the oxygen is used as an oxidator. Consequently, nitrate is used as an oxidator for the transformation of organic material.

3 a Groundwater
- microbiologically reliable
- constant temperature
- not polluted
- insensitive to calamities
Surface water
- not microbiological reliable
- no constant temperature
- polluted (organic micropollutants)
- sensitive to calamities

b To remove carbon dioxide and methane from the water and to add oxygen.

c 1. Spraying, with sprayers the water is distributed over the filter bed; during the fall the water is in contact with air above the filter bed.
2. Cascade, water flows from one water trough into the other, the contact with air is mainly due to the dragging of air bubbles.
3. Aerating and gas transfer tower, water flows from the top downwards through a tower which is filled with plastic material. Air is blown through the tower from top to bottom or from bottom to top so gas transfer occurs in the cylinder.

d Iron, manganese and ammonium.

e Ammonium, because during the biological transformation of ammonium a lot of oxygen is consumed.

4. a From the water composition the result is that no oxygen is present in the water, so the groundwater is anaerobic.

b During spraying only the values of the gases CO_2 and O_2 change. Since the pH depends on the CO_2-concentration, this will also change. The values of the remaining parameters remain the same. The CO_2-concentration decreases down to 22 mg/l, the oxygen concentration increases to 8 mg/l. The pH changes from 5.75 to 6.06.

c In the dry filter iron removal occurs according to the equation:
$$Fe^{2+} + \tfrac{1}{4} O_2 + \tfrac{1}{2} H_2O + 2\ OH^- \rightarrow Fe(OH)_3$$
Transformation of 8 mg/l Fe^{2+} results in an oxygen consumption of 1.14 mg/l. However, next to the consumption of oxygen in the dry filter, oxygen is also added. The oxygen concentration will rise up to 10 mg/l. OH^- is consumed, an amount of 0.29 mmol/l. Because only a few OH^--ions are present in water, HCO_3^- is transformed into OH^- and CO_2. Yet there is less than 0.29 mmol/l HCO_3^- present, so the pH will decrease significantly (the buffer of HCO_3^- disappears completely).
The concentration of HCO_3^- will be 0 mg/l after iron removal.

d In the dry filter, transformation of iron to iron hydroxide occurs. Iron hydroxide deposits in the pores of the dry filter; this will clog the dry filter in the course of time. To remove this clogging the dry filter should be backwashed.

e As a result of limestone filtration the quantity of Ca^{2+}, HCO_3^-, CO_2 and the pH will change. The relationship in which this happens results from the equation:
$$CaCO_3 + CO_2 + H_2O \rightarrow Ca^{2+} + 2\ HCO_3^-$$

The table shows that the calcium content rises with 20 mg/l or 0.5 mmol/l. The concentration of HCO_3^- will increase with 1.0 mmol/l or 61 mg/l. The concentration of CO_2 will decrease with 0.5 mmol/l or 22 mg/l.

Water quality data

Parameter	Raw water	After spraying	After dry filtration	After limestone filtration
Temperature	10	10	10	10
Na^+ (mg/l)	15	15	15	15
Ca^{2+} (mg/l)	28	28	28	48
Mg^{2+} (mg/l)	9.7	9.7	9.7	9.7
HCO_3^- (mg/l)	12.2	12.2	0	61
pH	5.75	6.06	4	7.2
Fe^{2+} (mg/l)	8	8	0	0
O_2 (mg/l)	0	8	10	10
CO_2 (mg/l)	44	22	30	8

Surface water

TECHNICAL FACETS

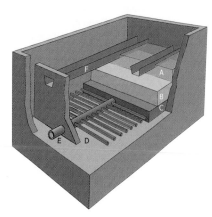

Framework

This module focuses on the production of drinking water from surface water. The focal points are the different possibilities for abstracting surface water, and the different treating schemes and processes.

Contents

This module has the following content:

1. Introduction
2. Surface water in the natural environment
3. Intake of surface water
    3.1   Rivers and canals
    3.2   Shallow lakes
    3.3   Deep lakes
    3.4   Reservoirs
    3.5   Polders
4. Direct treatment of surface water
    4.1   Historic development
    4.2   Contemporary treatment
    4.3   Future treatment
    4.4   Reservoirs
    4.5   Screens and strainers
    4.6   Coagulation
    4.7   Sedimentation and flotation
    4.8   Rapid filtration
    4.9   Slow sand filtration
    4.10 Disinfection
    4.11 Other treatment methods
    4.12 Treatment of backwash water and sludge
5. Indirect treatment of surface water through infiltration
    5.1   Surface water through open infiltration
    5.2   Surface water through deep infiltration
    5.3   Pre-treatment
    5.4   Transport to infiltration area
    5.5   Infiltration
    5.6   Post-treatment
    5.7   Deep infiltration
6. Legislation on surface water in the Netherlands

    Further reading
    Questions and applications
    Answers

Study goals

After studying this module you will be able to:
- explain the different forms of intake of surface water
- explain the different forms of treatment schemes for surface water
- solve computations for self-purification in reservoirs
- solve computations for sedimentation rate and surface load

1.   Introduction

Populated areas are often located in river deltas, where surface water is abundantly available and where it can be abstracted rather easily in large amounts.

However, compared to groundwater, surface water shows very large variations in available quantity as well as in quality. The variations in quantity and quality can be such that the water is temporary not available or not suitable for the production of drinking water. For these periods, large storage facilities are required. Storage reservoirs or facilities are always required, because contamination of river water by ships or industrial wastewater cannot be prevented.

In the production of drinking water from surface water, two different approaches can be distinguished:
- direct treatment of surface water
- indirect treatment of surface water via infiltration

Especially in the western parts of the Netherlands, surface water is used as a source for drinking water. However, in the future it will be necessary for water companies, traditionally using groundwater, to use surface water as well, because of the reduction in groundwater allowances and the increase in water consumption.

This module will describe the different aspects of drinking water treatment from surface water. First, an overview will be given of the natural environment of surface water (Figure 1). After that, different possibilities to produce drinking water from surface water will be described.
Then, the direct treatment of surface water will be explained, followed by indirect treatment via infiltration.
Finally, the Dutch legislation concerning surface water will be presented.

Figure 1   - Surface water in a "natural" environment

2.   Surface water in the natural environment

In its natural environment, surface water can be found in several forms:
- rivers
- lakes
- seas
Besides, these natural water forms, man-made forms can also be included:
- canals
- reservoirs
- artificial lakes and buffer reservoirs
- gravel pits and sand extraction pits

Only very rarely do surface waters form a closed system. Typically, there is direct interaction with the groundwater via seepage or infiltration.
Surface water systems will always be flushed through with fresh water, which will almost always end up in the ocean. In very rare cases, such as salt lakes, surface water is discharged by means of evaporation.

Rivers
High up in the mountains river water is only minimally contaminated and contains few dissolved minerals. Therefore, it is highly attractive as the source for water supply for people and industries.
In the middle course of the river, the flow is greater and less variable, and the amount of dissolved solids will also be greater. In some cases this river water can be used for the production of drinking water without any reservoirs.
In the lower course of the river, the water is highly mineralized and contaminated with residential and

industrial wastewater. Accidental contaminations are always to be feared.

In the Netherlands, the Rhine, Meuse and Drentse Aa rivers are used for drinking water supply.
The Rhine is a glacier/rain river with peak flows in winter and spring (ca. 2,500 m³/s) and a relatively high minimum flow (ca. 1,500 m³/s). The catchment area includes large parts of Switzerland, Germany, France, Luxembourg and the Netherlands (Figure 2). High population density, strong industrialization and extensive navigation leave definite marks on the water quality (e.g., a high salt content).
For drinking water production in the Netherlands, Rhine water is mainly abstracted indirectly from canals and lakes fed by the river, or by riverbank filtration along the Lek and IJssel rivers (which are fed by the Rhine).

The Meuse is a rain river with a high flow rate in winter (ca. 400 m³/s) and a minimum flow rate in summer (ca. 100 m³/s). Its catchment area includes large areas of France, Belgium and the Netherlands. The discharge of industrial and residential wastewater is less than in the Rhine River, but because of the highly fluctuating discharge, the quality is variable as well.

Figure 2 - Catchment area of the Rhine

Meuse water is abstracted at the Biesbosch reservoirs (ca. 200 million m³/y, max. 7 m³/s) and indirectly from the Lateraalkanaal in Limburg (total 20 million m³/y, max. 1 m³/s). Additionally, water is abstracted from the Andelse Maas (ca. 70 million m³/y, max. 2 m³/s), but because of the long residence time and the large quantity of seepage from the nearby polder, this dammed branch is characterized more as a (flushed) lake than a river.

The Drentse Aa is a small rain river. The catchment area encompasses a large part of the Drenthe province where there are mainly untouched and agricultural areas. Yearly, about 6 million m³ (ca. 0.2 m³/s) of surface water are abstracted to supply drinking water to the city of Groningen, which uses drinking water both from surface water and groundwater.

Canals
Often, canals have characteristics similar to a river. For example, canals are not only used for navigation but also as a means to transport surface water. This is done for both irrigation purposes and for the drainage of surplus rainwater, or for the prevention or limitation of salt intrusion.

In the Netherlands the Amsterdam-Rhine Canal, the Lekkanaal, the Lateraalkanaal and the Twentekanaal are used as sources for drinking water supply.
The Amsterdam-Rhine Canal is a navigation canal that is used for the transportation of (fresh) Rhine water to the Noordzeekanaal (ca. 25 m³/s). Near Loenen, Amsterdam-Rhine Canal water is used for mixing with polder water from the Bethunepolder for the direct treatment of drinking water (intake max. 20 million m³/y, ca. 1 m³/s).

The Lekkanaal is a side branch of the Amsterdam-Rhine Canal. By controlling the discharge in this canal, the quality of the water can be influenced somewhat. Near Nieuwegein, where the Lekkanaal is located, water is abstracted for the production of industrial and residential water. As a result of turbulence caused by ship movement, the level of dissolved solids can be temporarily increased. This water is also used for the production of drinking water via infiltration into the dunes (total 150 million m³/y, max. 6 m³/s).

The Lateraalkanaal is a lock-controlled navigation canal parallel to the Meuse River. By controlling the discharge, the quality of the water can be somewhat influenced. Water from this canal is used for the production of drinking water via bank filtration alongside a closed gravel pit (total 20 million m³/y, max. 1 m³/s).

The Twentekanaal, near Enschede, is a "dead end" canal with locks. It is flushed with water from small creeks and wastewater treatment plants. Water is abstracted from this canal and used for the production of drinking water via infiltration into the soil (total 10 million m³/y, ca. 0.4 m³/s).

Lakes

Because of their large surface area, lakes have a less variable supply capacity, and their large volume causes the water quality to be stable as well. When incidental discharges of pollutants are expected, there should be a reservoir separated from the lake. However, because of self-purification, the water quality will typically improve on its own. For example, sedimentation clarifies the water, the permanganate index and biochemical oxygen demand will decrease because of the oxidation of ammonium and organic matter, and the hygienic quality will improve because fecal bacteria will die of natural causes. The rate of self-purification not only depends on the mean residence time, but also on the minimum residence time, which can be rather brief in lakes because of short-circuiting. By constructing lead dams in lakes, the shortcut currents can be minimized. However, these dams are rather costly to construct.

For water abstraction, stratification in deep eutrophic lakes is rather disadvantageous. The water below the metalimnion (Figure 3) is useless because of its anaerobic condition, while the water above the metalimnion is unattractive because of its high algae content. A significant quality improvement can be achieved by mixing, as this will bring the deep water temporarily to the surface, while the algae growth is slowed by the lack of light in deep waters.

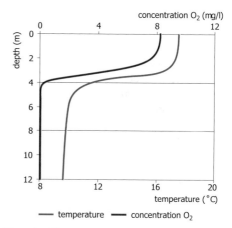

Figure 3 - Thermocline in eutrophic lakes

In the Netherlands, the IJsselmeer and Haringvliet lakes are used to supply drinking water.
The IJsselmeer is a large, shallow lake (depth 3 - 5 m, 1,100 km²) that is flushed with Rhine water (via the IJssel River) and drainage water from surrounding polders. Residence time in the lake is about four months. The water is abstracted at Andijk and is used for the direct production of drinking water (ca. 25 million m³/y, ca. 1 m³/s), and for the production of drinking water by means of infiltration into the dunes as well as for industrial water (total 110 million m³/y, ca. 4 m³/s).

The Haringvliet is a large, shallow lake (80 km², depth ca. 2 - 15 m) that is flushed by water from the Rhine and Meuse rivers and by drainage water from surrounding polders. Residence time in the lake is about one to two weeks. The water is abstracted at Stellendam and is used for the production of drinking water by means of infiltration into the soil (total 5 million m³/y, ca. 0.2 m³/s).

Reservoirs

Reservoirs are artificial lakes, created by the construction of a dam (Figure 4) or by the construction of a surrounding dike. Reservoirs dampen the variation in a river's flow, making a steady abstraction of water possible for irrigation, water supply or energy production via a power plant.
Reservoirs are typically constructed at a great distance from the supply area. Often, that is not a

Figure 4 - Hoover Dam in the Colorado River (USA)

problem because simple treatment is usually sufficient, due to self-purification in the reservoir.

Seas

Globally, most water is found in seas and oceans. Because of the high salt level, the water cannot be used for most applications. In rare cases sea water is used for the water supply, especially in arid areas, like the Middle East, and on small tourist islands, like in the Caribbean and the Mediterranean. However, those applications require a costly desalination process.

3. Intake of surface water

The intake of surface water is rather easy. However, special arrangements need to be made in order to abstract the water at the right place and to prevent shore erosion.

Equally valid considerations when determining the right abstraction site are whether there is a sufficient supply, even at the minimum water level, and

an absence of danger or damage to the installation by ships, floating ice or high water discharge.

Intake facilities for the abstraction of surface water will be described below for:
-   rivers and canals
-   shallow lakes
-   deep lakes
-   reservoirs
-   polders

3.1   Rivers and canals

Because of strong turbulence in flowing river water, a significant mixing will occur, causing the water composition to vary only slightly over the cross-section of the river. Because of upper stream sewerages, some difference may occur between the left and right banks. The level of suspended solids can vary a bit more and will be less in the inner curve of a river or between two dams, but this affects mostly the coarser particles that have a high settling speed, making it inexpensive and easy to remove them when producing drinking water.

To prevent the transport of coarser particles and the obstruction of the inlet installation, the intake velocity should be low, below 0.1 - 0.2 m/s. The intake of material that rolls over the riverbed can be prevented from doing so by constructing the inlet openings slightly higher. The intake of floating material can be prevented by abstracting the water below the surface.

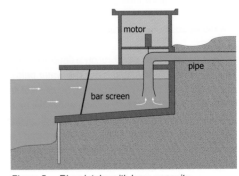

Figure 5   - River intake with large capacity

Figure 6   - Intake station at Heel production plant (Limburg)

A strainer (bar screen or trash rack) is necessary to avert larger floating material like woodblocks, which might damage the pumps (Figures 5 and 6).

3.2   Shallow lakes

In shallow lakes the water composition will vary little over the depth. Only the level of suspended solids will be slightly higher near the water's surface (e.g., algae) and near the bottom (e.g., scoured soil particles). Due to contact with humans or animals, water contamination may be greater near the shore, as mixing in a horizontal direction is minimal.

This potential contamination requires water to be abstracted some distance from the shore, and some meters above the bottom to prevent too much sludge from being abstracted as well. For the discharge of the water a conduit needs to be constructed, either as a tunnel in solid rock or as a pipe in a dredged trench (Figure 7).

Figure 8   - Intake structure with hinged pipe in Loenen (Utrecht)

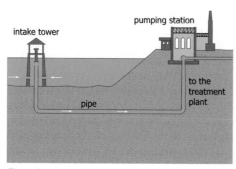

Figure 7   - Inlet structure in a lake, with an intake tower

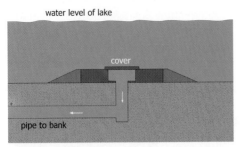

Figure 9   - Intake structure in a lake without an intake tower

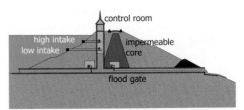

Figure 11 - Dam with intake structures for abstraction at different levels

A hinged pipe can also be used between a solid construction in the lake and the shore (Figure 8).

When no obstacles are allowed in the lake (in view of boats, floating ice, etc.), the design shown in Figure 9 should be used.

3.3   Deep lakes

In oligotrophic deep lakes a high water quality can be found at any depth, making it advantageous to abstract water at a depth below 30 meters because of the constantly low temperatures.

Like with shallow lakes, the vicinity of the shore should be avoided and the intake should be some 3 - 5 meters above the bottom to prevent the intake of sludge. Because of these two cautions, it is difficult to construct the connection pipe along the shore.

Figure 10 shows the use of a hinged pipe to solve this intake problem. These pipes may be designed with ball hinges or with cheaper, flexible connections of elastic plastics.

In eutrophic deep lakes the best quality during the summer stability can be found just above the metalimnion. However, the metalimnion does not have a constant depth; it increases during summer and autumn. At the end of autumn or at the beginning of winter, the stratification is destroyed, turning the contents of the lake upside-down and necessitating withdrawal of the best water quality at greater depths.

This means that the abstraction needs to be possible at different levels. Hinged intakes or intake towers with openings at different heights may be used for this end.

3.4   Reservoirs

Reservoirs are of the same nature as deep lakes. The inlet is usually constructed near the dam. The inlet can be constructed either inside the dam (Figure 11) or in separate towers (e.g., variable height) near the dam (Figure 12).

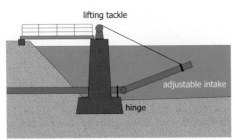

Figure 10 - Hinged intake structure

Figure 12 - Intake tower with variable inlet height

316

3.5 Polders

In polders a constant groundwater level is maintained. In low countries like the Netherlands, such a constant groundwater level can only be achieved by draining surplus water.

This drainage water does not form only by rain falling inside the polder area. In polders situated lower than their immediate surroundings, drainage water can develop from seepage. The amount of seepage water is relatively constant over the year, making drainage water available permanently. Therefore, it can be used for the supply of drinking water.

An important part of the water supply of Amsterdam is based on drainage water from the Bethune polder. Per year about 25 million m³ of drainage water are abstracted from a polder of about 5 km², having a level 1 - 2 m below the water level in surrounding lakes.

This amount is equivalent to 5 m/y, which is considerably more than the rain surplus of 0.3 m/y. The drainage water is transported through a 7 km long open canal (Waterleidingkanaal) to the pretreatment plant at Loenderveen.

This method of abstracting surface water is more like groundwater abstraction. Because of the open abstraction, the water is of a worse microbiological quality than groundwater, but the chemical composition leaves no doubt of its groundwater origin.

Abstraction from the Andelse Maas for the water supply of the The Hague area is mainly determined by drainage water from polders upstream. The Andelse Maas is a dammed side-branch of the Meuse River, from which Meuse water is taken in artificially by means of sluices and pumps. The amount abstracted for drinking water production is less than the amount of drainage water available.

4. Direct treatment of surface water

From a global point of view, the direct treatment of surface water is the most applied method for drinking water production. This is mainly because large cities have developed along river banks, making surface water directly available.

In order to be suitable for drinking water, suspended solids must be removed together with pathogenic bacteria. Over the years the removal of micropollutants has become necessary as well, together with the construction of storage basins, to use when the concentration of micropollutants is too high. Micropollutants often originate from human activities upstream.

The next section will describe the historical development of the direct treatment of surface water. Then, the contemporary treatment schemes will be described, followed by a description of future developments. Finally, the individual treatment processes in those schemes will be explained.

4.1 Historic development

Throughout the ages, because of both the increasing quantitative demand (population growth, consumption growth) and the increasing qualitative demand (worse sources, more stringent quality legislation), direct treatment methods for drinking water production have changed drastically.

Traditionally, direct treatment was performed by clarification in large sedimentation basins and subsequent slow sand filtration. Characteristic of this procedure was the enormous spatial demand and the labor intensive operation (manual removing of the "Schmutzdecke" from the slow sand filter).

By adding rapid filtration, the load on the slow sand filtration was decreased, making an increased production capacity with traditional means possible. To guarantee the bacteriological quality of the drinking water, a safety chlorination was applied as a final step in the treatment process. This caused a small amount of chlorine to be present in the water at the customers' taps.

In time production needed to be increased further. This caused the rapid filtration system to be heavily loaded, resulting in run times that were too short between backwashing. The problem was solved by adding a flocculant before sedimentation, thus increasing the effectiveness of the sedimentation.

When production demands increased further, the surface area of the slow sand filtration installation became the bottleneck. The slow sand filtration not only removed suspended solids, but removed (pathogenic) bacteria as well. Slow sand filtration was increasingly replaced by chemical disinfection (e.g., break-point chlorination). Break-point chlorination oxidizes ammonium (NH_4^+) to nitrogen (N_2) as well.

Increased river contamination necessitated the construction of reservoirs to be able to stop the direct intake of river water. Additionally, micropollutants needed to be removed by activated carbon (i.e., dosing of powdered activated carbon, PAC). This traditional treatment process (Figure 13) is still widely applied around the world.

The reservoirs were shallow basins at first. However, in these shallow reservoirs, a considerable algal population can develop during spring and summer.

Because of algal bloom, the first step in the treatment process is the application of microstrainers. Algae are quite difficult to remove by way of sedi-

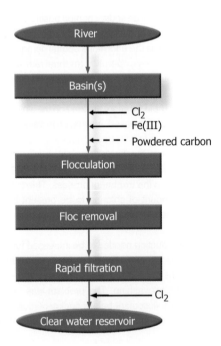

Figure 13 - Traditional treatment scheme for direct treatment of surface water

mentation, which is, in fact, only possible when using very high doses of flocculants. Additionally, algae can cause taste and odor problems.

Since the 1970s mainly deep reservoirs have been used. In these deep reservoirs, algae growth can be quite well controlled, making the microstrainers obsolete. Using deep reservoirs with a very long residence time will yield a considerable amount of self-purification in the basins as well.

Water from such reservoirs is typified by a low concentration of suspended solids (<5 mg/l), few algae, and a low ammonium concentration. With this water quality, sedimentation is sometimes unnecessary, and a very low dose of flocculant followed by rapid sand filtration can be used.

4.2   Contemporary treatment

Problems with the traditional treatment process

Contemporary treatment originated from the chlorination issue and the increased river water pollution. In 1974 J. Rook, of the Rotterdam Water Company, discovered harmful by-products from the chlorination process (disinfectant by-products). These are mainly trihalomethanes (THMs), from which chloroform ($CHCl_3$) is produced at the highest level. THMs are created by the reaction of chlorine with humic acids present in the water, and are harmful to human health. The Dutch Decree on Water Supply sets a standard of 25 µg/l (sum) for THMs. Chlorination may lead to exceedence of this standard; but without sufficient chlorination, the disinfection would be inadequate, a worse condition from the point of view of public health. This caused the Dutch Decree to temporarily allow a THM value to 100 µg/l (until January 1, 2006).

In 1987 the insecticide Bentazon was found in Amsterdam's drinking water. Like many micropollutants, this insecticide proved to be insufficiently removed in the treatment process, even in the case of artificial infiltration into sand dunes. Other insecticides, like Atrazin and Diuron, have also been shown to pass through a traditional treatment process. Because activated carbon filtration does remove these pollutants sufficiently, it has become a typical element in any contemporary treatment process.

In 1993, a severe Cryptosporidium outbreak occurred in Milwaukee, Wisconsin (USA), resulting in 400,000 ill people and 100 deaths. Chlorination did not prove to be a sufficient barrier to cysts like Cryptosporidium and Giardia. Using higher doses and longer contact times will produce trihalomethanes (THMs). Alternatives to this are stronger disinfectants like chlorine dioxide (ClO_2) or ozone (O_3).

Chlorine dioxide also produces by-products, but less than when using chlorine or hypochlorite. Disinfection using ozone can produce bromate, which is also harmful to public health. However, because sufficient disinfection is essential for the drinking water supply, the Dutch Decree on Water Supply allows an increase in the maximum bromate concentration from 1.0 µg/l to 5.0 µg/l when using ozone disinfection.

Characteristics of temporary direct treatment

Characteristics of the current treatment of surface water for production of drinking water are:

- storage reservoirs with a retention time of 1 - 3 months, making an intake stop possible in case of severe river contamination, and with a depth of over 20 meters to control algae growth
- process reservoirs with a retention time of about 1 month and a depth of over 20 meters, leading to a significant self-purification (sedimentation of suspended solids, ammonium oxidation) while still keeping algae growth under control
- removal of suspended solids by coagulation (adding flocculants), flocculation and floc removal by filtration, possibly preceded by sedimentation or flotation
- primary disinfection using a minimum amount of chlorine or ozone
- removal of micropollutants by activated carbon filtration
- secondary disinfection using a minimum amount of chlorine or chlorine dioxide

Example of contemporary direct treatment (chlorine and activated carbon filtration)

An example of current direct treatment can be found at the Berenplaat production plant (Figures 14 and 15).

At this site drinking water is produced from Meuse water, which has first been stored in the Biesbosch storage reservoirs. At the Berenplaat plant, microstrainers form the first step in the treatment scheme. This process was selected because, previously, the water, stored in a shallow basin, led to algae growth. In the current scheme the microstrainers could have been left out, but, actually, they have been left in service.

To disinfect the water, hypochlorite is added (about 1 mg/l as Cl_2). This needs to contact the water for half an hour, which is done in a tank with a canal labyrinth. After this phase a flocculant is added (ca. 5 mg/l Fe^{3+} in the form of $FeCl_3$) for the coagula-

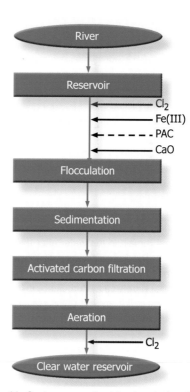

Figure 14 - Contemporary direct treatment of surface water (Berenplaat)

Figure 15 - Drinking water production at the Berenplaat production plant (Zuid-Holland)

tion of suspended solids, and then lime is added to correct the pH value of the water (ca. 6 mg/l in the form of CaO). When necessary, a flocculant aid (ca. 1 mg/l in the form of Wispro in winter) and powdered activated carbon (ca. 7.5 mg/l in case of severe pollution) are added. The added chemicals are mixed with the water using mechanical stirrers for rapid mixing.

The adding of $FeCl_3$ is for removing suspended solids that remain in the water after the storage reservoirs. The Fe^{3+} together with the lime OH^- form small $Fe(OH)_3$ flocs around the particles. Mechanical stirrers cause turbulence in the water, and the flocs collide and grow (flocculation). A flocculant aid can accelerate this process.

Because the flocs are heavier than water, they can be removed by sedimentation. This is done in the floc-blanket clarifier (floc removal). The total retention time in the floc-blanket clarifier is about one hour at a sedimentation rate of not more than

4.8 m/h. The settled flocs (sludge) are drained into a very large sedimentation basin, where they accumulate at the bottom.

To remove the remaining turbidity, taste, odor, and micropollutants, the water is treated using activated carbon filters. The filters consist of a layer of granular activated carbon at a height of 1.1 meters, applied over a supportive gravel layer. The filtration rate is no more than 9.4 m/h, equivalent to an approximate retention time (empty bed contact time) of 7 minutes minimum.

Because the filters will slowly clog, they need to be backwashed with clean water in an upward direction every few days. Because carbon activity decreases over time, the carbon must be reactivated every 1 - 1.5 years.

Cascades (five steps with a total height of about 2 meters) bring oxygen into the water; before that water is pumped into the clear water reservoirs. Aeration is included in the treatment process in order to add oxygen which could be low in the raw water because of biological processes. Chlorine dosing causes the biological activity during the treatment process to be minimal.

To prevent regrowth during transportation, hypochlorite is added before the clear water reservoirs (ca. 0.5 mg/l as Cl_2).

The data shown in Table 1 indicate the water quality of the untreated and treated water. The raw water has a high pH value, caused by sodium hydroxide softening in the Biesbosch reservoirs.

By forming $Fe(OH)_3$ the pH value is reduced, and by adding lime it is raised again to the desired level. The suspended solids are mainly removed in the floc-blanket clarifiers and during (activated carbon) filtration. Chlorination causes an increased chloroform concentration and a reduced E.coli number.

Example of contemporary direct treatment (ozone with activated carbon filtration)

Another example of contemporary treatment is found at the Kralingen production plant (Figures 16 and 17). Here, drinking water is also produced from Meuse water from the Biesbosch reservoirs. At the Kralingen plant a flocculant is added first (ca. 4 mg/l Fe^{3+} in the form of $FeCl_3$), before the water goes through a static mixer. This causes small $Fe(OH)_3$ flocs to form and to include pollutants from the water. If necessary, another flocculant aid (ca. 1 mg/l in the form of Wispro, during winter) is added. In four serial flocculation compartments having a total retention time of at least 20 minutes, slowly rotating mixers cause the flocs to grow. The mixing decreases in intensity in each consecutive compartment in order to prevent flocs from being destroyed. The flocs are

Table 1   - Quality data of the raw and clear water at the Berenplaat drinking water production plant (Zuid-Holland)

Parameter	Unit	Raw water	Clear water
Temperature	°C	11.9	11.9
pH	-	9	8.1
EC	mS/m	51	54
SI	-	0.9	0.1
Turbidity	FTU	2	0.1
Na^+	mg/l	46	49
K^+	mg/l	6	6
Ca^{2+}	mg/l	51	54
Mg^{2+}	mg/l	8	8
Cl^-	mg/l	72	74
HCO_3^-	mg/l	87	95
SO_4^{2-}	mg/l	64	83
NO_3^-	mg/l	3	3
O_2	mg/l	11.1	10.8
CH_4	mg/l	-	-
CO_2	mg/l	0.3	1.3
Fe^{2+}	mg/l	-	-
Mn^{2+}	mg/l	-	-
NH_4^+	mg/l	-	-
DOC	mg/l	3.6	2.6
E-Coli	n/100 ml	100	0
Bentazon	µg/l	0.2	< 0.1
Chloroform	µg/l	0	38
Bromate	µg/l	< 2	2.0

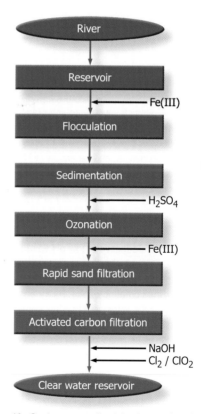

Figure 16 - Contemporary direct treatment of surface water with ozonization (Kralingen)

Figure 17 - Kralingen drinking water production plant (Zuid-Holland)

removed in a lamella separator where they settle between ascending plates. This arrangement creates an enormous settling surface in a relatively small area. Particles with a sedimentation rate of over 1.2 m/h are all separated in this installation. The settled flocs slide down over the plates into a sludge thickener, which is equipped with stirrers. The thickened sludge is pumped to sludge-drying beds for dewatering.

After the flocculation and floc removal, sulfuric acid is added first to lower the pH, because ozone is more effective at low pH values. Ozone is produced locally from liquid oxygen. In ozone generators the oxygen is exposed to high electric voltages, thus creating ozone. By means of a diffuser, the ozone is injected into the water (ca. 1.2 - 2.0 mg/l in the form of O_3). The ozone spreads through the water in the form of fine dissolving bubbles, being active there during a contact period of 8 - 10 minutes. The ozone gas that is released at the water's surface is destroyed thermally. Ozone kills bacteria and viruses, destroys micropollutants, and improves the taste of the water.

To remove the remaining turbidity, the water is treated in a dual-layer sand filter. For an effective performance of this filter, first an extra flocculant is added (ca. 0.5 mg/l Fe^{3+} in the form of $FeCl_3$).

The sand filters have a surface area of 9 by 4 m and consist of a sand layer of 0.7 m and an anthracite layer of 0.8 m. Below these layers there is a gravel support layer. The filtration rate is 20 m/h maximum. Because the filters clog, they are backwashed daily with air (max. 80 Nm/h) and water (max. 45 m/h) in an upward direction.

Subsequently, the filtered water is treated with activated carbon for an approximate contact period (empty bed contact time) of 10 minutes. The remaining micropollutants and the taste and odor are removed. Because the activated carbon activity decreases in time, it needs to be reactivated every 1 - 2 years. Also, every two to three weeks the filters need to be backwashed in order to remove suspended solids. After the activated carbon treatment, sodium hydroxide is added to correct the pH value.

322

To make sure that microbiological regrowth does not occur during distribution, hypochlorite is added (ca. 0.3 mg/l in the form of Cl_2).

Table 2 shows the water quality of both the raw and treated water. The raw water has a high pH value, caused by the softening with sodium hydroxide in the Biesbosch reservoirs. Due to formation of $Fe(OH)_3$ and sulfuric acid, the pH value is reduced, and by adding sodium hydroxide it is increased again to the normal value. The suspended solids are mainly removed in the lamella separators and the dual-layer filters. Adding ozone results in an increased bromate content and a reduced E.coli number.

Mainly, the concentrations of DOC and Bentazon are reduced during the activated carbon filtration. With ozone, the increased retention time, and the greater biological activity, DOC removal is better at Kralingen than at the Berenplaat production plant. The low chlorine dosing results in a small increase in chloroform in the water.

Table 2   - Quality data of the raw and clear water of the Kralingen production plant (Zuid-Holland)

Parameter	Unit	Raw water	Clear water
Temperature	°C	11.9	12.1
pH	-	9	8.2
EC	mS/m	51	55
SI	-	0.9	0.1
Turbidity	FTU	2	0.05
Na^+	mg/l	46	52
K^+	mg/l	6	6
Ca^{2+}	mg/l	51	51
Mg^{2+}	mg/l	8	8
Cl^-	mg/l	72	73
HCO_3^-	mg/l	87	94
SO_4^{2-}	mg/l	64	85
NO_3^-	mg/l	3	3
O_2	mg/l	11.1	10.2
CH_4	mg/l	-	-
CO_2	mg/l	0.3	0.9
Fe^{2+}	mg/l	-	-
Mn^{2+}	mg/l	-	-
NH_4^+	mg/l	-	-
DOC	mg/l	3.6	1.9
E-Coli	n/100 ml	100	0
Bentazon	µg/l	0.2	< 0.1
Chloroform	µg/l	0	1.8
Bromate	µg/l	< 2.0	3.9

4.3   Future treatment

Problems of contemporary treatment

Contemporary treatment techniques still face some problems, such as the by-products (THMs and bromates) that are formed during disinfection and oxidation, due to the discovery of new emerging micropollutants, and the required prevention of Legionella.

Effective removal of Cryptosporidium and Giardia requires high dose ozone. The tightened regulations regarding bromate make this more difficult. Besides, new and difficult to remove polar micropollutants have been discovered. These compounds may require an oxidation process with high doses, which will again give rise to the formation of undesirable by-products.

Also, the increase of hormones in surface water (i.e., estrogen) and materials which act as endocrine disruptors and lead to hormonal deviations will be important in future drinking water production from surface water. Finally, the Legionella issue will require an improved water quality in order to reduce Legionella growth in the distribution network. This will require a further reduction in the amount of assimilable organic matter (AOC) in the water.

The above developments will necessitate a renewed orientation of the integral setup of treatment schemes for the direct production of drinking water from surface water. It may be that biological and physical processes will increasingly take over the role of the chemical processes for disinfection and oxidation (Figure 18).

Figure 18 - Future treatment of surface water: physical or chemical

Figure 19 - *Biologically activated carbon filtration at Berenplaat production plant (Zuid-Holland)*

Biological processes

In biological processes, many pollutants are assimilated by biomass and removed in this way. Also, biological processes will result in reduced amounts of organic matter (DOC, AOC, etc.). The treated water should be biologically stable, so that the biological activity in the distribution network will be low and residual disinfection is unnecessary.

The biological treatment processes that are currently considered for large-scale application are:
- biologically activated carbon filtration (Figure 19)
- slow sand filtration

For Amsterdam's water supply some steps in this direction have been taken in recent years, and some aspects of it are currently operational. A further optimization of the contemporary treatment processes is being researched.

Physical processes

Physical processes currently being considered for large-scale applications are:
- UV disinfection
- membrane filtration

By exposing the water to UV radiation, the DNA structure of organisms is destroyed, thereby stopping growth. It has proved to be very effective to combine UV disinfection with hydrogen peroxide as a strong oxidant. Both processes have not shown any harmful side-effects to date. An example of such a system is the Noord-Holland (Andijk) water supply (Figures 20 and 21).

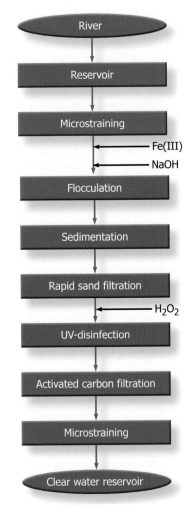

Figure 20 - *Direct treatment of surface water at Andijk production plant (2005)*

Figure 21 - *UV / H_2O_2 (Andijk)*

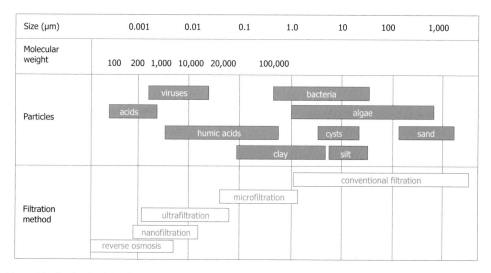

Size (μm)	0.001	0.01	0.1	1.0	10	100	1,000
Molecular weight	100 200 1,000 10,000 20,000		100,000				
Particles	acids / viruses / humic acids / clay			bacteria / algae / cysts / silt / sand			
Filtration method	reverse osmosis / nanofiltration / ultrafiltration		microfiltration	conventional filtration			

Figure 22 - Application fields for membrane filtration

With membrane filtration, the water is pressurized through a membrane. These membranes are available in several different pore sizes (Figure 22).

Ultra- and microfiltration mainly retain the coarser pollutants like suspended solids, cysts and bacteria. Nanofiltration also retains divalent ions, like Ca^{2+}, SO_4^{2-} etc., most larger organic compounds (humic acids), and most micropollutants. Here, cysts, bacteria and viruses are entirely filtered out. Reverse osmosis increases the filtration to monovalent ions and almost any micropollutant.

There are some objections to the application of membrane filtration:
- risk of membrane defects and thus incomplete disinfection
- disposal of concentrate
- high costs of construction and operation

Recently, a treatment plant based on membrane filtration (ultrafiltration followed by reverse osmosis, Figures 23 and 24) was started up in Noord-Holland (Wijk aan Zee). The produced water is mixed with drinking water from a system of artificially infiltrated surface water.

Figure 23 - Membrane filtration plant in Heemskerk (Noord-Holland)

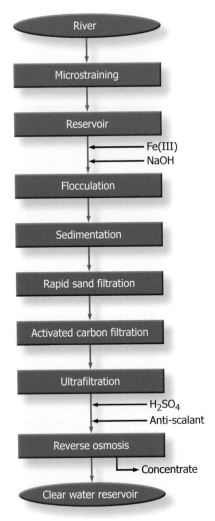

Figure 24 - Direct treatment of surface water at Heemskerk production plant

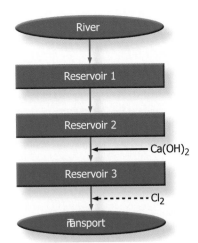

Figure 25 - Process scheme at the Brabantse Biesbosch water production plant

4.4 Reservoirs

The direct production of drinking water from surface water requires the use of deep reservoirs in order to cope with inlet stops (e.g., due to contamination) and to increase the natural process of self-purification.

Table 3 shows the three different types of reservoirs. Analysis reservoirs and process reservoirs are best when constructed in such a way that a plug flow is obtained. Sometimes, lead dams are constructed. Plug flow is advantageous for any time-dependent process, such as many biological processes.

In the case of the Biesbosch reservoirs (Figure 25), open storage consists of a series of three deep reservoirs. These basins are equipped with aerators to achieve a homogeneous water quality to prevent stratification and limit algae growth by

Table 3   - Different types of reservoirs with their specific functions

Type of reservoir	Retention time	Function
Analysis reservoir	ca. 1 week	Analysis of the intake water. Based on this analysis it is decided whether the water can be used for intake or if the intake has to be stopped
Process or mixing reservoir	ca. 3 - 5 weeks	Quality improvement due to mixing or dosing of chemicals Self-purification of the water due to decay and sedimentation
Storage reservoir	ca. 1 - 3 months	Storage during times of bad water quality (due to a disaster or low river discharge) Water quality dampening due to mixing Self-purification of the water due to decay and sedimentation

Figure 26 - The Biesbosch reservoirs system (Noord-Brabant)

reducing light. The three reservoirs have different functions and are controlled in different ways. The first reservoir (Figure 26) has a storage function and will, therefore, have level fluctuations. The second reservoir has a self-purifying function. The second and third reservoirs are both controlled without level fluctuations.

Softening is achieved in the third basin by adding milk of lime. This causes the pH value to rise. Transport chlorination is applied only when too high a growth in the transport pipelines is expected or found. This would increase the hydraulic resistance and, thus, the energy costs, and will reduce the quality of the water during transport. Because of the formation of undesirable by-products, chlorination is used as little as possible.

As can be derived from Table 4, the Biesbosch reservoirs have a self-purifying capacity. The amount of suspended solids and the turbidity are reduced by means of sedimentation. Heavy metals, like cadmium and nickel, are removed together with the suspended solids (to which they are attached). By softening, the pH value increases and the calcium and bicarbonate levels decrease.

Table 4 - Quality data for the Meuse water and for the water after the reservoirs of the Brabantse Biesbosch (Noord-Brabant)

Parameter	Unit	Raw water	Clear water
Temperature	°C	13.5	11.9
pH	-	7.9	9
EC	mS/m	51	51
SI	-	0.2	0.9
Turbidity	FTU	10	2
Na^+	mg/l	37	46
K^+	mg/l	6	6
Ca^{2+}	mg/l	63	51
Mg^{2+}	mg/l	8	8
Cl^-	mg/l	61	72
HCO_3^-	mg/l	154	87
SO_4^{2-}	mg/l	52	64
NO_3^-	mg/l	4	3
O_2	mg/l	9.7	11.1
CH_4	mg/l	-	-
CO_2	mg/l	3.5	0.3
Fe^{2+}	mg/l	-	-
Mn^{2+}	mg/l	-	-
NH_4^+	mg/l	-	-
DOC	mg/l	4.1	3.6
E-Coli	n/100 ml	4,800	100
Bentazon	µg/l	0.2	0.2
Chloroform	µg/l	0	0
Bromate	µg/l	< 2.0	< 2.0

During the retention time in the reservoirs, persistent organic micropollutants, like Bentazon, will not be removed. Neither will conservative elements like chloride be affected on a yearly average, but peaks will be dampened nevertheless.

It is obvious that pathogenic micro-organisms will die in the basins. This can be seen from the reduction of the E.coli level, which is an indicator for those microorganisms.

Biochemical oxidation

When organic matter enters surface water, it will be transformed by microorganisms, thus using oxygen. The amount of oxygen used by the microorganisms is indicated by the BOD parameter, the Biochemical Oxygen Demand, with units of $g\ O_2/m^3$.

To determine the BOD value, a water sample is stored for five days at a temperature of 20°C in the dark, to prevent green algae from producing oxygen by means of photosynthesis. Then, the oxygen concentration at the end is compared to that at the beginning of the test. The difference between the two is the BOD. During the standard BOD test procedure, not all organic matter is transformed.

When it is assumed that organic matter is removed according to a first-order process, it holds that:

$$b_t = b_0 \cdot \exp(-k_1 \cdot t)$$

in which:

b_0 = concentration of organic matter at
    the start   (mg O_2/l)
b_t = concentration of organic matter
    after t days   (mg O_2/l)
k_1 = rate constant   (d^{-1})
t = time   (d)

The rate constant k_1 is a function of the temperature and can be computed using the following equation:

$$k_1 = 0.23 \cdot \exp(0.046 \cdot (T - 20))$$

in which:
T = temperature   (°C)

Table 5   - Correction factor alpha as a function of the temperature

T (°C)	5	10	15	20	25	30
α	0.7	0.8	0.9	1.0	1.1	1.2

The measured value of the BOD in the initial test is the difference between the starting concentration of organic matter and the concentration after $t = 5$ days at $T = 20°C$, or:

$$BOD_5^{20} = b_0 - b_t = b_0 - b_0 \cdot \exp(-k_1 \cdot t)$$
$$= b_0 \cdot (1 - \exp(-0.23 \cdot 5)) = 0.684 \cdot b_0$$

After five days at a temperature of 20°C, slightly more than 2/3 of all organic matter has been transformed. For the transformation of all organic matter, the oxygen demand amounts to:

$$b_0 = \frac{1}{0.684} \cdot BOD_5^{20} = 1.46 \cdot BOD_5^{20}$$

The biochemical oxygen demand during t days at a temperature of T °C is computed as follows:

$$BOD_t^T = 1.46 \cdot BOD_5^{20} \cdot$$
$$(1 - \exp(-0.23 \cdot t \cdot \exp(0.046 \cdot (T - 20))))$$

In reality, at higher temperatures, a larger portion of the organic matter is biochemically transformed than at lower temperatures. Therefore, the BOD found in the former formula is multiplied by a factor α which is temperature dependent (see Table 5).

Algae

Algae are able to produce organic matter from water, carbon dioxide, and the energy from sunlight. This process is known as photosynthesis.

$$n \cdot CO_2 + n \cdot H_2O + energy \rightarrow (CH_2O)_n + n \cdot O_2$$

When algae die, the reaction is reversed, and referred to as dissimilation:

$$(CH_2O)_n + n \cdot O_2 \rightarrow n \cdot CO_2 + n \cdot H_2O + energy$$

Besides light, carbon and water, algae need the nutrients sulfur, nitrogen and phosphorous for their growth. Naturally, the nitrogen and phosphorous levels in water are low, limiting algae growth in this way. By discharging treated wastewater on surface water, the amount of phosphorous and nitrogen strongly increases, causing an increased algae growth. The water will appear turbid and will have an unpleasant green, brown or red color. The water is unsuitable for recreational activities, and the preparation of drinking water will be quite expensive due to the advanced treatment techniques required.

In spring, when the temperature of the water rises, algae growth occurs. This causes the carbon dioxide level of the water to fall and the oxygen level to increase. The water may contain three times as much oxygen as the saturation level.

In summer, algae growth is more or less equal to algae mortality. Both assimilation and dissimilation reactions occur. The assimilation reaction works mainly during daylight (light yielding the necessary energy); the respiration reaction works mainly during the night. These reactions cause the oxygen level to be high during the day, while the water may become anaerobic during the night (Figure 27).

When algae die during autumn, organic matter will be produced, which will be broken down in a respiration reaction with oxygen. This results in the oxygen level falling possibly causing major fish mortality. Eutrophication of the water can be prevented by removing one of the nutrients from the water that limits excessive algae growth.

Stratification

In deep lakes and reservoirs (depth over 15 m), temperature stratification may occur. During summer the temperature of the upper layer of a lake is higher than that of the lower layers. The density of water decreases at temperatures above 4°C. Therefore, the upper layer of the lake (to a depth of about 7 m) is warm and has a lower density than the lower layer of the lake. The lighter water floats on the heavier water.

No mixing of these layers will occur. The upper layer, which is rich with oxygen, is called the epilimnion, the lower layer is the hypolimnion (Figure 28). The layer between the two is called the metalimnion or thermocline.

Algae growth is only possible in the epilimnion, because the light cannot enter the deeper layers. These algae cause the high oxygen levels in the upper layer.

When the algae die, they will settle to the bottom of the lake, where they will be broken down by bacterial respiration in the lower regions. This will cause the oxygen level in the lower layer to fall and, because no oxygen is added, cause anaerobic conditions. Because of the production of carbon dioxide, the pH value of the lower layer decreases. Also, anaerobic conditions cause iron and manganese to dissolve from the bottom sediment.

In autumn the upper layer cools, becoming even heavier than the lower layer. When a storm disturbs the already unstable equilibrium, the contents of the lake may reverse within a few hours. The anaerobic water will come to the surface and the aerobic water will go towards the bottom. The lake's water will no longer be suitable for the production of drinking water. Preventing this side effect of the

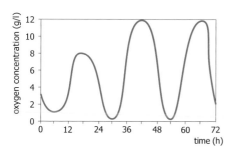

Figure 27 - Variation in the level of oxygen due to algae growth in a mesatrophic lake

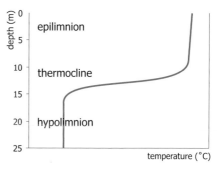

Figure 28 - Stratification in a deep lake

Table 6   - Trophic states of water

Trophic state	P (g/m²/y)	N (g/m²/y)
Oligotrophic	< 0.25	< 5
Mesatrophic	0.25 - 1	5 - 20
Eutrophic	> 1	> 20

reversing of layers can be accomplished by limiting algae growth, for example, by removing the nutrients from the water (Table 6), or by injecting air into the lower layers, causing a continuous circulation of water and thus preventing stratification.

Self-purification
Natural water bodies will always receive pollutants. Fortunately when left to itself, the quality of water will improve after some time.

Self-purification is a natural process on which many treatment processes are based. Because this process is time-dependent, the flow pattern in the surface water is important, as the flow pattern influences the retention time and its variance.

During the retention of water in reservoirs, the quality will improve. Particles with a density higher than the water's will settle, organic matter will be converted, and the temperature of the water will change because of a heat exchange with the atmosphere. Pathogenic microorganisms will die and be unable to propagate in the cold water. The concentrations of non-destructible compounds will be dampened because of mixing. All processes described above are summarized in the concept of self-purification.

Plug flow or mixing?
When water particles in a river or in a pipe are followed, they may have about the same retention time at turbulent flow conditions. In this case one speaks of plug flow. The water particles move like a cluster through a narrow and long system, in which no mixing with other water particles occurs. This means that the concentration in the water particles may differ.

Water particles in a lake are seen to have different retention times. One particle will have a longer retention time, another a shorter. The concentration of the particles, on the other hand, will be constant.

plug flow

$$T = \frac{L}{v}$$

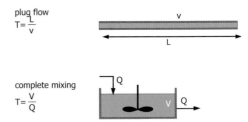

complete mixing

$$T = \frac{V}{Q}$$

complete mixing (n reservoirs in series)

$$T_1 = \frac{V_1}{Q} \qquad T_{tot} = \frac{V_{tot}}{Q}$$

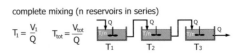

Figure 29 - Different flow conditions

When it is assumed that the water entering the lake will immediately mix with the lake water, one speaks of complete or ideal mixing (Figure 29). Plug flow and complete mixing are two extremes regarding retention time and concentration differences.

One can determine the differences in the retention time using tracer tests. These tests will add some compound to the water from an initial period t = 0 continuously. When there is a plug flow in the system, the concentration will suddenly jump to the concentration added, after the retention time. When there is complete mixing, the concentration will gradually rise to the final concentration (Figure 30). When multiple mixed systems are used consecutively, the system will approach plug flow.

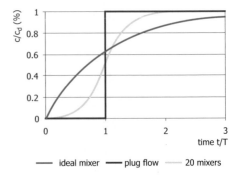

Figure 30 - Residence time distribution for different flow patterns

Mass balance

As a simple example of a mass balance, the discharge of chloride into a river is considered. A river has a flow of 30 m³/s and contains a chloride amount of 134 g/m³ (inlet). Into this river 400 m³/h of drainage water containing 13,000 g/m³ of chloride is added (addition). Compute the chloride concentration after the discharge of the wastewater (outlet).

Chloride inlet in river: $(Q_1 \cdot c_1) = 30 \cdot 134 = 4{,}020$ g/s

Chloride addition in wastewater: $(Q_2 \cdot c_2) = 400/3{,}600 \cdot 13{,}000 = 1{,}444$ g/s

Total chloride in: $(Q_1 \cdot c_1 + Q_2 \cdot c_2) = 5{,}464$ g/s

Total river flow after discharge point: $Q_3 = Q_1 + Q_2 = 30 + 400 / 3{,}600 = 30.11$ m³/s

Chloride concentration after discharge point: $c_3 = 5{,}465 / 30.11 = 181.5$ g/m³

Plug flow and complete mixing are important in the self-purification of water. For example, for the decay of bacteria, it is important to know the retention time in the system (e.g., river, lake). A plug flow will cause the retention time to be the same for all water particles and bacteria. A mixed system makes it possible for bacteria either to leave the system immediately or to stay in the system a long time.

The large differences in retention times in a mixed system causes the effectiveness for decay to always be lower than that of a plug flow. For dampening concentration peaks, on the other hand, a mixed system will be more efficient than a plug flow system.

Mass balance
Mass balance applies to any system (Figure 31). The law of conservation of matter holds for this balance: no matter can be lost.
Mass balance has the following appearance:

inlet + addition = outlet + removal + storage

In some cases parts of this balance are negligible. Generally, it is supposed that the volume of a lake or river is constant (no variance in water level, water inlet equals water outlet). This removes the storage factor from the balance. For conservative compounds which will not be removed, like chloride, the removal term may be neglected.

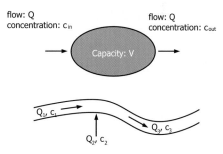

Figure 31 - Schematic figure of mass balance

Decay and mortality in plug flows
In a plug flow it is assumed that over any length, dx, the mixing is ideal throughout the cross-section (Figures 32 and 33). Additionally, the flow is assumed to be constant throughout the section.

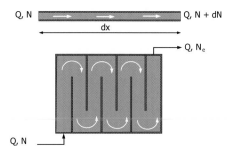

Figure 32 - Schematic figure of plug flow

Figure 33 - Plug flow reservoir at Berenplaat production plant (Zuid-Holland)

Assuming that no storage exists in a plug flow system, the following mass balance can be formulated:

inlet = outlet + decay

$$Q \cdot N = Q \cdot (N + dN) + k_0 \cdot N \cdot A dx$$

in which:

k_0 =	decay or mortality coefficient	(s^{-1})
N =	number of bacteria	(m^{-3})
A =	cross-sectional area	
	(= river width x depth)	(m^2)
Q =	flow	(m^3/s)
dx =	length	(m)

When removing equal terms it follows that:

$$Q dN = -k_0 \cdot N \cdot A dx$$

or:

$$\frac{1}{N} dN = -k_0 \cdot \frac{A}{Q} dx$$

The value of the decay coefficient amounts to 0.2 - 4 d^{-1}.

Two boundary conditions can be formulated for this system:

- at x = 0 it holds that $N = N_0$
- at x = L it holds that $N = N_e$

Applying these boundary conditions results in:

$$\ln N]_{N=N_e}^{N=N_0} = -k_0 \cdot \frac{A}{Q} x]_{x=L}^{x=0}$$

$$\Rightarrow \ln(N_0) - \ln(N_e) = k_0 \cdot \frac{A}{Q} \cdot L$$

$$\Rightarrow N_e = N_0 \cdot \exp(-k_0 \cdot T)$$

Thus, it is clear that decay in a plug flow will conform to an exponential function.

Decay and mortality in a complete mixing system

A complete mixer is represented as a tank having a volume V (m^3) which is fed by a flow Q and a concentration N_0 (Figures 34 and 35).

complete mixing (reservoir)

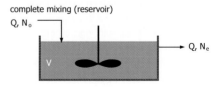

Figure 34 - Schematic figure of an ideally mixed tank

Figure 35 - Mixing system reservoir in the Biesbosch

From the reactor the flow Q leaves (equal to the inlet flow) having a concentration N_e. Because the flow entering the tank is equal to the flow leaving the tank, no storage will occur.

The following mass balance may be formulated for the tank:

inlet   = outlet + decay

$$Q \cdot N_0 = Q \cdot N_e + k_0 \cdot V \cdot N_e$$

This results in the following solution:

$$N_e = \frac{N_0}{1 + k_0 \cdot T}$$

Figure 36 shows the results of the decay in a plug flow and in a complete mixing system at the same decay coefficient k_0 and as a function of residence

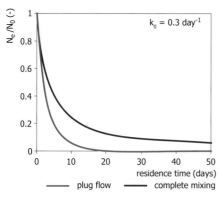

Figure 36 - Decay and mortality for a plug flow and for an ideally mixed tank, with equal decay coefficients

time. At first sight it seems that the results are not very different. However, when t = 20 days is considered, then N_e/N_0 in a plug flow system equals 0.0025 and in a full mixing system equals 0.14. This makes a difference factor of 58!

Decay and mortality in consecutive mixed systems

For the removal of microorganisms (mortality), it is always better to use a plug flow system. However, the disadvantage of such a system is that it is rather expensive to construct. First, a reservoir needs to be built, and, second, lead dams need to be constructed inside the reservoir. Because of this, multiple consecutive reservoirs are used instead. Multiple reservoirs, used consecutively, will approach a plug flow.

We have seen that the residence time variance will decrease when more multiple reservoirs are used consecutively. By constructing multiple reservoirs consecutively, we obtain a situation which is between an ideal mixer and a plug flow.

When we formulate a mass balance for multiple consecutive reservoirs, we obtain the following formulas:

Reservoir 1:

$$N_1 \cdot Q = N_2 \cdot Q + k_0 \cdot V_1 \cdot N_2$$

$$\frac{N_2}{N_1} = \frac{1}{1 + k_0 \cdot \frac{V_1}{Q}}$$

The outlet concentration of Reservoir 1 is the inlet concentration of Reservoir 2.

Reservoir 2:

$$N_2 \cdot Q = N_3 \cdot Q + k_0 \cdot V_2 \cdot N_3$$

$$\frac{N_3}{N_2} = \frac{1}{1 + k_0 \cdot \frac{V_2}{Q}}$$

When the volume of both reservoirs is the same $(V_1 = V_2)$ and when the residence time in the two

Table 7 - Mortality as a function of time, $k_0 = 0.30\ d^{-1}$

N_e/N_0 (-)	T (days):	15	30	60
Plug flow		$1.11 \cdot 10^{-2}$	$1.23 \cdot 10^{-4}$	$1.52 \cdot 10^{-8}$
Complete mixing (one reservoir)		$1.82 \cdot 10^{-1}$	$1.0 \cdot 10^{-1}$	$5.2 \cdot 10^{-2}$
Complete mixing (four reservoirs in series)		$4.90 \cdot 10^{-2}$	$8.96 \cdot 10^{-3}$	$1.09 \cdot 10^{-3}$

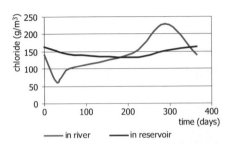

Figure 37 - Levelling concentration due to mixing

reservoirs together equals the residence time of one ideal reservoir, the two equations may be rewritten as:

$$\frac{N_3}{N_1} = \frac{1}{\left(1 + \dfrac{k_0 \cdot T}{2}\right)^2}$$

For a series of n reservoirs the general equation holds:

$$\frac{N_e}{N_0} = \frac{1}{\left(1 + \dfrac{k_0 \cdot T}{n}\right)^n}$$

In Table 7, the mortality in the different systems is given as a function of time. The mortality in the plug flow system is larger, by far. The mortality in a series of reservoirs is higher than when one single large reservoir is used.

Levelling in a mixing system

Levelling is important for any water company using river water as a source for drinking water production. A river has large flow fluctuations, causing concentrations to vary dramatically. When the water is directly abstracted from the river, it may happen that concentrations temporarily exceed the standards. However, when water from a reservoir is abstracted, levelling of the concentration occurs and the standard might be achieved.

In order to determine the required size of a reservoir, the following equation is employed:

$$\text{inlet} = \text{outlet} + \text{decay}$$
$$Q \cdot c_0 \cdot dt = Q \cdot c_e \cdot dt + V \cdot dc_e$$

This corresponds to a first-order linear differential equation:

$$\frac{dc_e}{dt} = \frac{Q \cdot (c_e - c_0)}{V}$$

It is beyond the scope of this text to elaborate on the solution of the equation above, but the example in Figure 37 may illustrate levelling in a mixed reservoir.

A river having a varying chloride concentration flows through a reservoir. Concentration peaks in the river are levelled in the reservoir. When the river water is the source for drinking water production and the standard for chloride is 175 mg/l, abstraction of the river water should be delayed for about 100 days (day 225 to 325 from Figure 37). When a reservoir is used and fed by the same river, levelling will take place causing water abstraction to be possible throughout the year.

4.5   Screens and strainers

Coarse strainers with openings between 2 and 8 centimeters are used at surface water inlets to prevent the inlet of large objects which would otherwise lead to congestion in pipes or the damage of pumps or other machines.

Bar screens or trash rakes are coarse strainers consisting of round or rugged steel grids, which are connected by strips and which are placed at a slight angle from the vertical (Figures 38 and 39).

The coarse openings retain only the very large material. These allow for minimal cleaning either by hand or by mechanical means, on a daily basis or less. The cleaning frequency is further reduced

Figure 38 - Coarse strainers

Figure 40 - Microstrainers at Berenplaat production plant (Zuid-Holland) for removal of floating material (mainly algae)

by a low entrance rate, using either a large strainer width and/or smaller angle of the bars.

Most often, leaves and duckweed also have to be retained by finer strainers. The smaller openings (0.5 - 2 cm), however, require more frequent or continuous cleaning.

Openings of 0.5 mm seem very small, but even then they are about 5 to 15 times larger than the granular filter bed pores. Because of their opening size, strainers can only slightly relieve the load on the subsequent sand filters. A better result can be obtained by a microstrainer (Figure 40) being spun with a very fine mesh. The microstrainer is continuously rotated while being backwashed from the top.

Not only does the mesh have very small openings, 10 to 40 μm, but it is situated in such a way as to require the water to pass through it at an angle perpendicular to the flow direction. This significantly increases its effectiveness. Originally, microstrainer were designed to retain algae from storage reservoirs to prevent a rapid blocking of the sand filters.

4.6   Coagulation

Large suspended particles can be removed by sedimentation, as part of the self-purification in reservoirs.

As suspended particles become smaller, the sedimentation rate decreases; sedimentation stops altogether below 1 μm by Brownian movement.

If the particles are electrically neutral, they could be brought together by stirring, after which the London-van der Waals forces would make them cluster to larger aggregates that may be clarified. However, particles occurring in natural waters are electrically charged. Those charges are always of an equal sign, mostly negative, and, therefore, the Coulomb's forces cause them to repel and make aggregation impossible.

This force can be reduced by increasing the electrolyte level of the water, which provides positively charged ions to neutralize the particles. The total charge of the particle decreases, thus reducing the Coulomb forces to a value below the strength of the London-van der Waals forces and thus enabling aggregation.

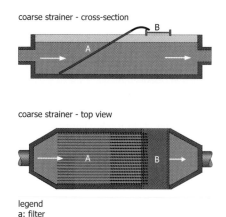

coarse strainer - cross-section

coarse strainer - top view

legend
a: filter
b: inspection platform

Figure 39 - Coarse strainers

Table 8   - Flocculants for coagulation with the applied doses and chemical side-effects

Product		Ferric chloride	Ferric chloride sulfate	Aluminum sulfate	Polyalumumchloride
		$FeCl_3$	$FeClSO_4$	$Al_2(SO_4)_3 \cdot 18H_2O$	$Al(OH)_xCl_y(SO_4)_z$
Trade form		solution	solution	powder	solution
Producer (Kiwa-ATA)		Kemira	Melspring	Kemira	Kemira
		AKZO		Rhodia	Rhodia
		Sidra			Sachtleben
		Tessenderlo			Nalco
Flocculation component		Fe^{3+}	Fe^{3+}	Al^{3+}	Al^{3+}
Floc (precipitation)		$Fe(OH)_3$	$Fe(OH)_3$	$Al(OH)_3$	$Al(OH)_3$
Dosing (as Al or Fe)	(mmol/l)	0.1 - 0.4	0.1 - 0.4	0.1 - 0.4	0.1 - 0.4
mg/l		4 - 20	4 - 20	2 - 10	2 - 10
OH^- usage (ratio)		3	3	3	0.9 - 2.2*
Increase of Cl^- (ratio)		3	1	0	0.9 - 1.9*
Increase of SO_4^{2-} (ratio)		0	1	1.5	0.1 - 0.3*

* different per product

In a natural environment this occurs when river water flows into the sea with high levels of sodium ions (10,000 mg/l).

However, trivalent ions are 600 times as effective as monovalent ions. Of course, flocculants need to be harmless to public health, so iron and aluminum ions are used in drinking water treatment. They are added to the water in the form of soluble salts, like $FeCl_3$, $FeClSO_4$ or $Al_2(SO_4)_3$ (Table 8). By rapid mixing they are equally distributed through the water in about 15 seconds, forming microflocs immediately.

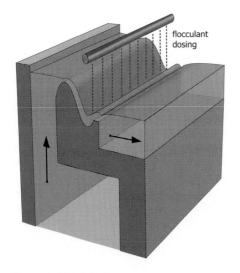

flocculant dosing

Figure 41 - Waterfall mixer

The rapid mixing can best be achieved in a waterfall mixer (Figure 41). This converts gravity energy of about 0.5 m to a high mixing energy (turbulence). By using a threshold downstream, the mixing energy is used within a short time (< 3 seconds). The iron and aluminum salts form flocs of iron- or aluminum hydroxide : $Me^{3+} + 3\ OH^- \rightarrow Me(OH)_3$. The rate of this reaction is optimal at a certain pH value. For iron this pH value needs to be around 8.0 and for aluminum about 6.5. To obtain these pH values for iron salts, usually a base, like lime or caustic soda, is added.

The addition of flocculants causes the salt content in the water to rise slightly.

Flocculation

To unify flocs into larger aggregates having higher sedimentation rates, they need to contact one another. This is done by slow mixing for about 20 - 30 minutes in a flocculation tank.

Flocculation needs to be done within a plug flow, because shortcut currents result in small flocs being difficult to remove. Therefore, the mixing units have their axes aligned parallel to the flow direction (Figure 42). During retention in the flocculation tank, the diameter of the flocs increases. Mixing is slowed to prevent floc breaking.

The total mixing energy in flocculation is significantly less than the energy input during the mixing process.

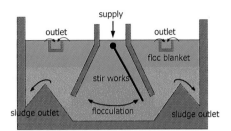

Figure 44 - Vertical sedimentation tank with floc-blanket

Figure 42 - Flocculation installation for preliminary treatment at Katwijk (Zuid-Holland)

Floc-blanket clarifiers

Flocs can be formed and removed quite well in a vertical flow tank.

In the upward flowing wedge-formed tank seen in Figures 43 and 44, the flow rate decreases with height. At a certain height the flow rate is equal to the sedimentation rate of the particles. The particles remain there. The floating particles form a floc-blanket, enclosing small particles. This makes the application of a higher surface load than for sedimentation possible (4 - 6 m/h instead of 0.8 - 1.2 m/h).

Floc-blanket clarifiers are generally used with preliminary flocculation.

These clarifiers are used less frequently these days because of the uncontrollability of the process. Usually, a system is chosen that has a separate flocculation, followed by lamella sedimentation or by flotation.

Figure 43 - Floc-blanket clarifiers at Berenplaat (Zuid-Holland)

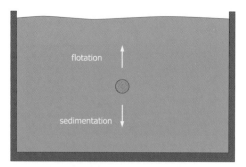

Figure 45 - Sedimentation versus flotation

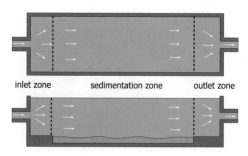

inlet zone   sedimentation zone   outlet zone

Figure 47 - Rectangular sedimentation tank with horizontal flow

4.7   Sedimentation and flotation

Sedimentation and flotation velocity
If the suspended particle has a density higher
than that of the surrounding fluid, it descends in a
process known as sedimentation. If the opposite
is true, the particle rises and the process is called
flotation (Figure 45).
For smaller particles, which are frequently present
in drinking water treatment, Stokes' law holds:

$$s = \frac{1}{18} \cdot \frac{g}{v} \cdot \frac{\rho_s - \rho_w}{\rho_w} \cdot d^2$$

in which:

s	=	sedimentation or flotation rate	(m/s)
g	=	gravity acceleration	(m²/s)
v	=	kinematic viscosity	(m²/s)
ρ_s, ρ_w	=	density of the particle and	
		the fluid	(kg/m³)
d	=	diameter of the (spherical)	
		particle	(m)

This formula shows that the rate s is greater and
the sedimentation process takes less time when
the difference between the density of the particle
and the fluid are great and when the size of the
particle is larger.
The density of the particle can be increased by
adding heavy materials like crushed limestone, or
decreased by introducing air. The latter process is
so inexpensive and easy to do that it is currently
used for the removal of algae, which are heavier
than water. Enlarging the particle size is achieved
by the processes of coagulation and flocculation,
which were described earlier.

In natural waters, particles have different sedimentation rates. These rates can be measured
in laboratories, yielding the cumulative frequency
distribution shown in Figure 46. Figures 47 and
48 show a rectangular sedimentation basin. The
basin inlet equally distributes the water with the

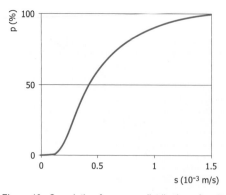

Figure 46 - Cumulative frequency distribution of sedimentation rates

Figure 48 - Rectangular sedimentation tank in Nieuwegein
(Utrecht)

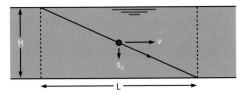

Figure 49 - Sedimentation rate of particles is equal to the surface load; all particles settle

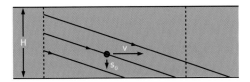

Figure 50 - Sedimentation rate of the particles is less than the surface load; particles settle partly

suspended particles over the basin's cross-section, and the outlet steadily withdraws the water and the remaining particles from the entire cross-section of the basin.

Surface load

The flow rate v is constant over all contents in the sedimentation zone. Figure 49 shows a section of the sedimentation zone with a particle having the special sedimentation rate s_0, being the rate at which it just reaches the bottom (lower right side after beginning on the upper left side). This suggests that all particles having a sedimentation rate $s = s_0$ or greater will be removed entirely, while according to Figure 50 the effectiveness for particles with a lower rate falls to:

$$r = \frac{h}{H} = \frac{s \cdot T}{s_0 \cdot T} = \frac{s}{s_0}$$

in which T is the residence time.

Considering the frequency distribution of sedimentation rates, as shown in Figure 51, the effectiveness is:

$$s \geq s_0 \quad r_1 = 1 - p_0$$

$$s < s_0 \quad r_2 = \int_0^{p_0} \frac{s}{s_0} \, dp$$

$$r = (1 - p_0) + \frac{1}{s_0} \int_0^{p_0} s \, dp$$

in which the integral corresponds to the shaded area.

On the left side of Figure 51 there is a horizontal line drawn in such a way that both shaded areas are equal, and the total effectiveness can be read out immediately. This effectiveness depends on the frequency distribution of the sedimentation rate on the one hand, and on the value of s_0 on the other. Figure 51 shows this on the right side.

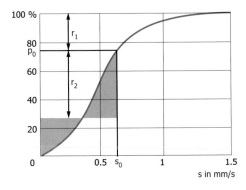

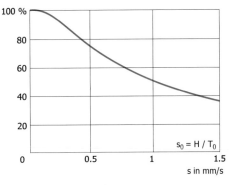

Figure 51 - Effectiveness calculation for a sedimentation tank with horizontal flow

According to Figure 50 it holds that

$$\frac{s_0}{v} = \frac{H}{L} \quad \text{or with} \quad v = \frac{Q}{B \cdot H}$$

$$s_0 = \frac{Q}{B \cdot L} = \frac{Q}{A}$$

in which

Q = the flow to be treated   (m³/s)

A = the basin surface area   (m²)

The relationship of s_0 is called the surface load. It varies in practice between 0.05 and 0.5 mm/s (0.18 and 1.8 m/h). Even in basins with a totally arbitrary surface form, this equation describes the sedimentation rate. After all, during the residence time T, all particles will be removed for which the sedimentation rate is above:

$$s = \frac{H}{T} = \frac{H}{\left(\dfrac{A \cdot H}{Q}\right)} = \frac{Q}{A} = s_0$$

Flow pattern

The effectiveness or removal ratio at the surface load rate s_0 on the right side of Figure 51 will be achieved only if neither disturbing turbulence nor unstable currents occur. This requires low Reynolds' number values (v · D / v) and high Froude number values (v² / g · R). In rectangular basins (Figure 52) this can be approximated by establishing a horizontal rate of about 5 mm/s (18 m/h).

Inlet and outlet constructions

Whatever form is chosen, much attention needs to be paid to inlet and outlet constructions. In particular, the inlet of the water needs to be designed in such a way that water and suspended particles are equally distributed across the basin.

Figure 52 - Rectangular sedimentation tank with horizontal flow

Figure 53 - Rectangular sedimentation tank with extra floors

Leaving the basin, the water rate is accelerated and the current become more stable. The outlet construction can be simpler, like a weir construction.

Lamella sedimentation

According to sedimentation theory, the depth of the basin does not influence its effectiveness. This means, when stated another way, that by adding extra floors (Figure 53), the surface load can be reduced and the effectiveness can be increased. The distance between the floors should be large enough, about 0.8 m, to install and maintain chain scrapers.

When the plates, shown in Figure 54, are positioned at a 60° angle, gravity suffices for removing the settled flocs, thus making a reduction in the mutual distance to 5 cm possible. This creates the possibility of housing an enormous sedimentation capacity in a relatively small volume. For example, an effective surface load of 1.0 m/h can be achieved in a much smaller sedimentation basin, with an approximate (gross) surface load of over 10 m/h.

Flotation

In the case of flotation, air bubbles stick to suspended particles. For good results, every suspended particle should stick to multiple bubbles.

Figure 54 - Rectangular sedimentation tank with sloping plates

Figure 55 - Lamella separator

These bubbles can be very small, but should be present in tremendous numbers (about $10^9/m^3$). This cannot be achieved by injecting air, but is possible with the method shown in Figure 56. Here, part of the effluent is circulated and saturated with air in a high pressure tank. At a pressure of 6 bar, the solubility of air in water increases sevenfold to 7 $\cdot$ 30 = 210 gram per m^3. When pressure is reduced to normal values by means of a reducing valve, 6/7 parts of the air is freed in the form of microbubbles, roughly equal to 0.13 m^3 of air per m^3 of water. This is sufficient for the desired results, especially when the particles have aggregated because of flocculation. With flotation, a surface load of 8 - 12 m/h can be achieved.

Flotation is less robust than lamella sedimentation, because of the additional required installations. On the other hand, with flotation, one can

Figure 57 - Flotation with saturated air

vary the amount of air introduced according to the circumstances. Flotation also works well with smaller flocs.

4.8 Rapid filtration

Practical forms
In America, rapid filtration was first employed in 1885, and in 1895 in Europe. As indicated by its name, the water to be treated flows at high rates, 2 - 5 mm/s (7 - 18 m/h) down through the granular filter bed. This decreases the necessary surface as compared to slow sand filters, thus also decreasing the construction costs per capacity unit.
Because of resistance to the water by a granular bed, the rates mentioned above can only be achieved when using coarser and more regular filter material, which will store the contaminants from the untreated water at greater depths and which will make high sludge storage possible. However, clogging will occur rather quickly, requiring the filter to be cleaned every few days. Because of the

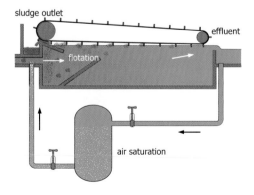

Figure 56 - Flotation with saturated air

deep bed filtration, this cleaning process needs to include the whole filter bed.

Formerly, cleaning was done by hand by inserting injection needles from the upper side. Today, hydraulic filter cleaning is used without exception, by reversing the water flow and flushing the filter from the bottom at high rates (5 - 15 mm/s, 18 - 54 m/h). These rates are so high that an expansion of the filter bed occurs (Figure 58), causing the sludge between the grains to loosen and be taken out by the backwash water.

As is shown in Figure 59 schematically, an open rapid filter basically consists of a rectangular concrete basin with a surface area of 10 to 100 m². From top to bottom the influent water is in this basin, then in the filter bed, and finally in the drainage system. The raw water has a layer thickness between 0.4 and 1.5. The filter bed, having a thickness between 1.0 and 2.0 m, typically consists of a layer of anthracite (light), above a layer of finer sand (heavy). This comprises a so-called dual-media filter (coarse and fine filters).

A filter layer is composed of uniform grains, the size of which can vary between 0.6 and 2.0 mm. The drainage system supports the filter, drains the filtered water, and supplies the backwash water. A system of perforated pipes covered with transition layers of gravel or a false floor equipped with nozzles is commonly used.

The filter is connected to several pipes. These pipes are equipped with valves and control instruments in order to keep the upper water level, the filtration rate, and the backwash rate at the desired level.

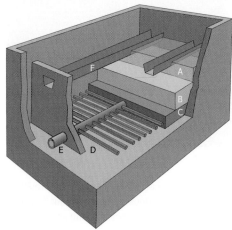

A - raw water
B - sand layer
C - gravel layer
D - perforated drainage pipes
E - effluent
F - discharge gutter for backwashing

Figure 59 - Filter bottom constructed of perforated pipes and gravel layers

A rapid filtration plant consists of a number of filters, usually between 4 and 40. The common setup is to have filters on both sides of a corridor (Figures 60 and 61). At about the halfway point, this corridor is interrupted by a building containing all central facilities, like backwash pumps and reservoirs, heating and air-conditioning units, workshop, laboratory, office, etc. In warmer climates the filters themselves are built in the open air, but, in the Netherlands, indoor construction is necessary to prevent freezing in winter.

Figure 58 - Backwashing of an open rapid filter for preliminary treatment in Katwijk (Zuid-Holland)

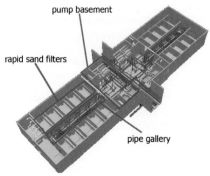

pump basement

rapid sand filters

pipe gallery

Figure 60 - Design for a rapid filtration plant

Figure 61 - Rapid filtration plant in Nieuwegein (Utrecht)

Rapid filtration mainly removes particles from the raw water by sedimentation, and by other mechanisms to be described later. However, as compared to slow sand filtration, the stored particles in the filter bed need not be eliminated by biochemical oxidation, but can be removed periodically by means of backwash. In combination with the deep penetration of suspended particles, backwashing permits rapid filtration to be useful even for highly polluted water. The resulting effectiveness, however, is much less than with traditional slow sand filtration, making it only applicable when the raw water is of good quality, for example from groundwater or clear surface water from reservoirs. Rapid filtration is most often used in combination with other treatment techniques.

Surface water is mainly treated by means of coagulation or sedimentation. However, the product of both still contains some particles, necessitating rapid filtration to remove the remaining contaminants. This requires finer filter material (0.5 to 0.8 mm), which is applied in smaller layer thicknesses (0.6 to 1 m), and requires slower filtration rates, usually between 1 and 2 mm/s (4 to 7 m/h).

Processes

Filtration is the process by which the water is treated by flowing through a bed of granular material, as a result of which pollutants are removed. This bed usually is a layer of sand through which the water flows from top to bottom at a rate v between 0.05 and 0.5 mm/s (0.18 and 1.8 m/h). At these rates suspended matter is retained, the number of bacteria and other organisms is signifi-

cantly reduced, and (important) changes occur in the chemical composition of the water. This effect is caused by several processes, such as mechanical filtration, sedimentation, adsorption, chemical and biological oxidation, bacteriological activity, and the like, which will be described separately, but which cooperate and can influence each other in reality.

Mechanical filtration removes suspended particles which are larger than the pores between the sand grains. As such, this treatment process is limited to the upper layer of the filter bed, is independent of the flow rate and is unable to remove suspended solids or bacteria (Figure 62).

Removal of suspended solids or bacteria is possible with sedimentation, which works in the same way as the process described for sedimentation basins. The main differences are that, in the filtration case, the surface area on which the suspended material may settle is significantly larger, and the surface load is proportionately smaller. After all, this surface is the total surface area of the upper sides of the grains, in an amount that is not covered by other grains nor exposed to erosion. Depending on the layer thickness or the grain size, this surface area varies between 100 and 1,000 m^2 per square meter of filter bed.

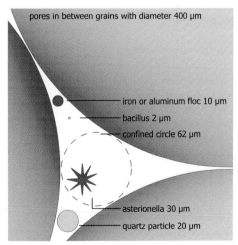

Figure 62 - Size of the pores and suspended particles in a filter bed

Suspended particles do not move to the grain surface only because of gravity, but also because of hydrodynamic force and inertia or of laminar and turbulent diffusion as well. When the suspended particle approaches the granular surface, it will stick to it because of the London-van der Waals and Coulomb's forces.

Mass attraction acts at any time and on any particle, but electrical attraction is only possible when the granules and the suspended particles are oppositely charged. Sand is negatively charged naturally, thus it is able to adsorb all positively charged ions like iron, manganese and the like.

At some places in the filter bed, enough positively charged particles might be adsorbed so that the charge changes, making the granules now able to attract all negatively charged ions like colloidal particles, organic matter, bacteria, and the like. This situation may repeat a few times; the total charge, however, always is decreasing, reducing the purifying capacity of the filter to such a level that no longer sufficiently cleans the water. Then, the filter needs to be backwashed in order to regain its purifying capacity.

Because of the adsorption of colloidal, molecular and ionized dissolved pollutants described above, the concentration at the granular surface increases, accelerating diverse chemical and biological processes. Oxidation can (partly) remove ammonium and organic matter. These reactions are performed by microorganisms.

The latter (i.e., oxidation) is especially important for organic matter, which is used by the surface bacteria as food. In part, this food is used for maintaining life processes and is oxidized into water, carbon dioxide, and several metal and metalloid oxides in this way; and, in part it is used for growth (assimilation), transforming dissolved organic matter into suspended organic matter, which is later filtered out.

4.9   Slow sand filtration

Slow sand filtration was first used for drinking water production in 1829, by James Simpson of Chelsea Waterworks, London.

When it became clear after the middle of the 19th century that this method might also yield water which was microbiologically reliable, the use of it increased dramatically throughout the world. Except for the use of newer building materials, the same slow or biological sand filters are still used today.

In principle the design consists of a basin of reinforced or normal concrete having a depth of 3 to 4 meters and a surface area of some hundreds or thousands of square meters. From top to bottom the following are present in the basin:

- the raw water which needs to be treated, at a depth of 1 to 1.5 m, in some cases extended to 2 m
- the filter bed, consisting of fine sand, with 10% of the grains being smaller than 0.15 to 0.3 mm, in a layer of 0.8 to 1.3 m
- the drainage system, for example consisting of perforated pipes with some number of gravel transition layers

Figure 63 shows the raw water being supplied at a constant upper water level. The water descends through the filter bed at a slow rate, usually between 0.1 and 0.15 mm/s (0.3 - 0.5 m/h), and at a maximum production rate 20 - 50% higher. The water is captured by a system of perforated drainage pipes, which end in a clean water canal running next to the full width of the basin. The filtered water is drained via a vertically adjustable telescopic pipe, which can be used to set the desired filtration rate.

As the filter is operational for a longer time and as the filter resistance H increases, this pipe should be lowered in order to obtain the same filtration velocity. When the lowest position is reached, a further increase in the filter resistance would imply

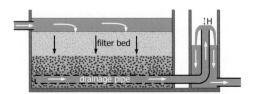

Figure 63 - Slow sand filter construction

Figure 64 - Slow sand filters at Weesperkarspel (Noord-Holland)

a decrease in the filtration rate, necessitating the filter to temporarily stop operation for cleaning.

The low filtration rate causes the filter to clog slowly and to be functional for many weeks or even months, before cleaning is necessary. By using fine filter material having extremely small pores, the suspended material is mainly removed by sieving. This process is, however, limited to the surface of the filter, causing clogging to occur only in the upper centimeters of the filter bed (the so-called "schmutzdecke").

This resistance can be eliminated by removing the upper 1 or 2 centimeters of the filter, thus restoring its capacity. Previously this was done, without exception, by hand. Today, mechanical systems have been designed for this purpose. An example of these is shown in Figure 66.

When the raw water contains nutrient salts (nitrates and phosphates), a rich growth of algae may occur in the upper layer of the water above the sand bed. This will increase the clogging of the filter and decrease its operational period. When algae growth is unacceptable, the filter should be covered, thus removing the light necessary for algae growth.

Doubtless, slow sand filtration is a good treatment process. By using fine sand having narrow pores and an enormous grain surface all suspended contaminants are removed. This yields clear water, either by sieving or adsorption, where the same adsorption followed by chemical and biological oxidation will remove a considerable amount of iron, manganese, ammonium and organic matter. These processes will stabilize the water, reducing potential problems in the distribution network because of iron scale, bacteria growth and the like. The long retention time in the filter bed also creates a significant bacteriological-biological treatment, which will yield hygienically safe water, free of pathogenic organisms, when the water quality conditions are not too bad. Because of the shallow depth to which contaminants penetrate, however, the pollution load is small, and acceptable run lengths can only be obtained when the raw water is relatively clean.

Figure 65 - Slow sand filters at Weesperkarspel (Noord-Holland)

Figure 66 - Mechanical cleaning of a slow sand filter

Figure 67 - Slow sand filters at Leiduin (Noord-Holland) take the largest part of the treatment plant

Despite the excellent water quality which may be obtained by using slow sand filtration, these filters are decreasingly used in the Western world. They are actually expensive to construct, expensive to operate and require enormous amounts of land. Technology now makes it possible to obtain reliable water by other treatment means (e.g., disinfection with chlorine, ozone and the like).
In developing countries the situation is exactly opposite. Land and unskilled labor are abundantly available, and building a slow sand filter can be done with local materials and by local labor without spending scarce capital. The hygienic reliability of the water causes disinfection to be unnecessary, thus chlorine disinfection is unnecessary as well. However, slow sand filtration, in developing countries, suffers from the idea that this technique is obsolete and, therefore, no longer used in the Western world.

When slow sand filters are used to obtain hygienically reliable water, a slow filtration rate needs to be used (0.05 mm/s), and the filtrate should not be used during the first days after cleaning, but should be discharged or circulated until the flora and fauna of the filter have been fully restored (start-up period).

4.10 Disinfection
In order to be hygienically reliable, drinking water should contain none to minimum amounts of E.coli bacteria only, less than 1 per 100 ml according to EU regulations. In most countries the guideline is even stricter (1 per 300 ml). Groundwater fulfills this requirement naturally, but surface water is

always contaminated and, even in good cases, contains 10 to 1000 E.coli per liter. This number may even increase to 10,000 to 1,000,000 per liter because of discharges of domestic sewage. Therefore, a thorough reduction of this population by means of treatment is required. Usually this removal of bacteria is described as a log-removal. This means that a log-6-removal amounts to a reduction of 1,000,000 to 1 (10^6 to 10^0 or log 6 – log 0 = log 6). Any treatment process does reduce the bacteria population somewhat. When there is a series of treatment processes, the total result can be found by adding the log values of the individual processes (Table 9).

Slightly contaminated surface water, having only 10 - 100 E.coli per liter, can be sufficiently treated by slow sand filtration. When the water is more heavily contaminated with 1,000 E.coli per liter, sedimentation and rapid filtration need to be added. For Rhine water (with about 100,000 E.coli per liter), the treatment process consists of coagulation, sedimentation, rapid filtration, and slow sand filtration (total reduction log 5). When the contamination is even more severe, either a reservoir (reduction log 2 to 3), double coagulation and sedimentation, or double sand filtration should be applied. However, any of these treatment schemes is much more thorough - and, so, more expensive - than would be required to remove the suspended and dissolved turbidity. A cheaper solution can be obtained by reducing the above treatment methods to the level necessary to remove dissolved turbidity and adding disinfectants for removing bacteria only.

Disinfection destroys bacteria by boiling, by irradiating them with UV-light or ultrasound oscillations, or poisoning them with chlorine or chlorine compounds, bromine, iodine, ozone and a wide range

Table 9   - The removal of E-coli for different treatment processes

Treatment process	Removal of E-coli (log)
Sedimentation (reservoir)	0.3 - 1.0
Microstrainer	0.2 - 0.3
Coagulation and sedimentation	1.0 - 2.0
Rapid sand filtration	0.8 - 1.2
Slow sand filtration	2.0 - 3.0

of other chemicals. These chemicals need to be added only in small amounts, are easy to dose, inexpensive, and 100% effective, causing them to be used on a large scale for drinking water preparation, even when their use is not strictly necessary as part of a multiple barrier system.

Ozone

When attention is paid only to the quality of the water, ozone is the most attractive disinfectant. After all, it decomposes, after having completed its task, to molecular and atomic oxygen, which are quite desirable drinking water components.

$$O_3 \rightarrow O_2 + O$$

This decomposition process is accelerated when the water contains oxidizable organic matter, which binds atomic oxygen and accelerates the reaction above towards the right side. So much ozone can be abstracted from the water, in this case, that the remaining amount is insufficient for disinfection.

Sufficient disinfection requires higher doses of ozone to be added, which becomes very expensive. For disinfection only, this high price has little meaning, as a dose of 0.1 mg/l is sufficient. However, when large amounts of organic matter are present, a considerably larger amount of ozone (a few mg/l) needs to be added, which would increase the price of the water by a few eurocents per cubic meter.

Figure 68 - Ozone generator at Weesperkarspel (Noord-Holland)

A severe disadvantage of using ozone is the formation of bromate when it reacts with bromide, which is often present in surface water.

Chlorine

Chlorine is the disinfectant most commonly used in the world. This disinfectant reacts in water:

$$Cl_2 + H_2O \rightarrow HOCl + H^+ + Cl^-$$
$$HOCl \rightleftharpoons H^+ + OCl^-$$

in which the uncharged HOCl easily reaches the protoplasm of the negatively charged bacteria. Finally, it holds that:

$$Cl_2 + H_2O \rightarrow 2H^+ + 2Cl^- + O$$

in which the reaction is accelerated because of the presence of organic matter, requiring a higher dose of chlorine to be added for disinfection.

Chlorine is so inexpensive that this would not cause any economic problem, but the fall of the pH value and the increase in the chlorine taste of the water may be unpleasant.

Compared to ozone, which decomposes spontaneously, the solution of chlorine in water is rather stable after the removal of organic matter, causing it to remain present at a few tenths of mg/l until the final home taps. The water has a definite chlorine flavor now, which most Europeans find rather unpleasant. Americans, however, tend to see that as proof that the water is hygienically reliable. When the chlorine flavor is unacceptable, it can be removed by activated carbon filtration after oxidation and disinfection.

Chlorine does not destroy all organic matter. Some compounds (e.g., phenol) form rather unpleasantly flavored substances after reacting with the chlorine. These are removed during activated carbon filtraton.

A severe restriction on the use of chlorine is due to the formation of THMs and other undesirable by-products during its reaction with humic acids which are ever-present in surface water.

In addition to the use of chlorine gas, disinfection can also be accomplished with solid or fluid chlorine compounds like calcium ($Ca(OCl)_2$) and sodium hypochlorite ($NaOCl$):

$$Ca(OCl)_2 \rightarrow Ca^{2+} + 2OCl^-$$
$$NaOCl \rightarrow Na^+ + OCl^- \quad \text{and}$$
$$OCl^- + H^+ \rightleftharpoons HOCl$$

These compounds are easy to handle and less dangerous to the environment. However, they are considerably more expensive and they decompose during storage, reducing their disinfecting capacity.

4.11 Other treatment techniques

Adsorption

Adsorption may remove non-charged micropollutants from the water. Adsorption is based on the principle that different particles will attract each other because of the surface forces (van der Waals force, surface tension). By creating a very large surface area, a relatively good removal can be achieved.

In drinking water production, two different types of adsorption are used:
- granular activated carbon treatment (GAC)
- powdered activated carbon treatment (PAC)

Granular Activated Carbon filtration (GAC)

Activated carbon filtration uses activated carbon as the granular filter material in a system similar to the one described above.

In these filters, the activated carbon is present as granules having a diameter of 0.8 - 1.5 mm. These granules have a highly porous structure, thus creating a very large surface area (400 m^2/g).
The water flows through the bed of granules, making the micropollutants adsorb to the surface. Because of the surface forces of the grains, these pollutants are transported inwards, decreasing the load at the grain surface.
After the filter has been used for treating several thousands of bed volumes of water, it will no longer adsorb any pollutants, referred to as breakthrough. This breakthrough differs across the compounds to be adsorbed; some do adsorb better than others.

Figure 69 - Activated carbon filtration at Weesperkarspel (Noord-Holland)

When the filter bed is saturated with pollutants, the filter material is removed. Activated carbon can be regenerated. At high temperatures the contaminants are partly burned and partly vaporized, without burning the activated carbon itself.

Powdered Activated Carbon treatment (PAC)

Activated carbon can also be used for adsorption by adding it in a powdered form to the water (some milligrams per liter). The powder is removed after a certain retention time by filtration or sedimentation.
Powdered carbon cannot be regenerated.

Oxidation

Some pollutants in the water can be removed by oxidation. This process destroys or transforms pollutants into components which are either harmless or can be removed in a successive treatment process (mostly biological).

The concept of oxidation is used in drinking water production when strong oxidants, which are also used for disinfection (e.g., ozone, hydrogen peroxide), are applied. Oxidation with oxygen, like when aerating anaerobic groundwater, is not usually called oxidation but rather iron removal, ammonium removal, or manganese removal.

Membrane filtration

Membrane filtration is a relatively young technique that is still in development. With membrane filtration, water is pressed through an extremely thin film. The pore size of the film is chosen so that it will stop all undesirable particles.

These particles may be suspended particles (micro-filtration is used), colloidal matter (ultrafiltration or nanofiltration is used) or dissolved particles (nanofiltration, reverse osmosis is used).

Because of the small size of the pores, a very large filter surface is necessary (filtration rate ca. 0.001 - 0.1 m/h) besides requiring relatively high pressures (2 - 200 mwc).

4.12 Treatment of backwash water and sludge

During the treatment of surface water, considerable amounts of wastewater are produced:

- backwash water from microstrainers (<0.5% of the flow)
- sludge from sedimentation and flotation (<1% of the flow)
- backwash water from rapid filtration (2 - 3% of the flow)
- backwash water from activated carbon filtraton (<0.5% of the flow)

Computation of sludge amounts

A surface water treatment plant having a capacity of 20 million m^3/y treats water having a suspended solids concentration of 25 mg/l.

For coagulation 8 mg/l Fe^{3+} is dosed before sedimentation and 0.5 mg/l Fe^{3+} before filtration.

Both sedimentation and filtration have a removal efficiency of 95% (meaning that 5% remains in the effluent).

The sludge stream leaving the sedimentation tank has a dry solids level of 0.5% and 4% after thickening.

The sludge stream leaving the filters has a dry solid concentration of 100 mg/l (0.01% dry solids) and of 3% after clarification and thickening.

The thickened sludge will be dewatered to a dry solids level of 30% and discharged.

Compute this plant's sludge production and sludge flows.

The effluent of the sedimentation contains (0.05 · 25=) 1.25 mg/l of suspended particles and (0.05 · 8=) 0.4 mg/l Fe^{3+}.

The effluent of the filters contains (0.05 · 1.25=) 0.06 mg/l of suspended solids and (0.05 · (0.4 + 0.5)=) 0.045 mg/l Fe^{3+}.

The iron is removed in the form of $Fe(OH)_3$, of which the mass is ((56 + 3 · (16+1)) / 56 =) 1.92 as large as the mass of Fe^{3+}.

During sedimentation (25 - 1.25 + (8 - 0.4) · 1.92 =) 38.3 mg/l will come free, as to (1.25 + 0.4 · 1.92 =) 2.0 mg/l during filtration.

The sludge flow leaving the sedimentation unit contains (0.5 / 100 · 10^3 =) 5 g/l, causing the sedimentation unit to have a concentration factor of (5 · 10^3 / 38.3 =) 130 or (1 / 130 =) 0.77% of the flow.
The sludge flow leaving the filtration unit contains 0.1 g/l, causing the filtration to have a concentration factor of (0.1 · 10^3 / 2.0 =) 50 or (1 / 50 =) 2.0% of the flow.

The discharged sludge contains 300 g/l, yielding a concentration factor of (300 · 10^3 / (38.3 + 2.0) =) 7.400 for the whole plant, or (1 / 7.400 =) 0.013% of the flow.
On a yearly basis (0.013% · 20 · 10^6 =) 2,600 m^3 of sludge is discharged, containing (30% · 2,600 =) 780 tons of dry solids.

- flushing water from slow sand filtration (<0.1% of the flow)

All waste streams contain some suspended matter. The treatment of these waste streams includes:
- flow equalization (to reduce backwash water peaks)
- sedimentation (for dilute flows like backwash and flushing water)
- thickening
- dewatering
- discharge to landfill

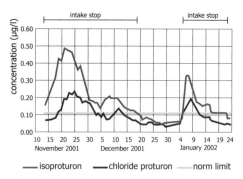

Figure 70 - Pollution at the intake point of the WRK Nieuwegein

5.   Indirect treatment of surface water through infiltration

5.1   Surface water through open infiltration

The source of infiltration water is surface water. However, disadvantages of surface water are that the temperature and the salinity vary throughout the year, that it is contaminated with pathogenic microorganisms, and that, even after treatment, growth and settling of particles in the distribution network may occur.

By infiltrating the surface water into the ground its quality is improved. This means that the pathogenic microorganisms are degraded and that the water is in a better biological and chemical state, causing no settling and no regrowth to occur.

Also, the temperature changes are levelled. Both the temperature and the salinity will be more or less constant.

Water can be infiltrated into freatic groundwater. When the supply of treated surface water is obstructed somehow (e.g., accident, network repair), it is possible to continue the abstraction for some time. During this time the groundwater level decreases, but this is, to some extent, acceptable without damaging the natural biology.

Infiltration projects cover large areas that also need to be protected, because they mainly deal with large amounts of water. However, as the infiltration area is always developed as a natural area, it will have a high recreational value.

Figure 70 shows an example of an intake stop because of contamination of the surface water by insecticides. Because the contamination occurred in winter, an intake stop of some weeks could be taken without damaging the environment in the infiltration area.

5.2   Surface water through deep infiltration

Expansion of natural infiltration into the dunes is not always possible because of environmental aspects. A water company using water from the dunes has, nevertheless, two possibilities to increase capacity.

First, the pre-treated surface water can be purified directly (see direct treatment), after which the water is mixed with the infiltrated water.

Second, the company may apply deep infiltration. Deep infiltration infiltrates the water into a confined aquifer. Because of the enclosing clay layers, there is almost no exchange with the freatic water above, so the infiltrated water does not influence the ecosystem. When using deep infiltration, care has to be taken during the preliminary treatment. The fewer particles that are present in the water, the smaller the chance that the infiltration wells will clog. Storage in deep infiltration is limited. When extracting water without supplying the necessary water for a long period, the chance of salt water intrusion exists.

Deep infiltration is not pursued only in the dunes. Also in other parts of the Netherlands, deep infil-

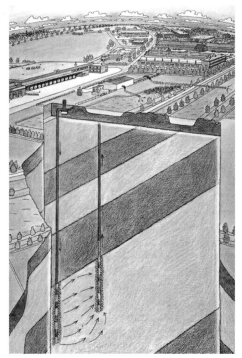

Figure 71 - Deep infiltration at Someren (Noord Brabant)

tration is used for the production of drinking water (Figure 71). The requirements are that the soil is sufficiently permeable and that there are confining layers in the underground.

5.3 Pre-treatment

To make the surface water suitable for transport and infiltration, suspended particles need to be removed first.
The standard pre-treatment of surface water consists of flocculation followed by floc removal and rapid filtration (Figure 72).

Flocculation is achieved by adding a flocculant, which removes the negative charge of the colloid particles, thereby making flocculation possible. These flocs can be removed by means of sedimentation in large ponds or in compact lamella separators, or by means of flotation.
Not all flocs are removed in sedimentation. Small flocs remain suspended and need to be removed by means of rapid filtration.

In the flocs, many other materials are removed like heavy metals (being positively charged and adsorbed to the flocs), and microorganisms. As a flocculant, mostly a trivalent metal salt, like iron chloride ($FeCl_3$), iron chloride sulfate, or aluminum sulfate, is used.

At the WRK Nieuwegein production plant (NV Watertransportmaatschappij Rijn-Kennemerland), flocculation is accomplished with iron chloride, followed by settling in a large sedimentation tank, and rapid filtration (Figure 72 and Table 10).

The quality of surface water varies throughout the year. For example, the turbidity at the Nieuwegein site varies between 5.5 and 25.5 FTU and the temperature between 2 and 23°C. This influences the settling behavior, the filtration, and the biological processes.

During the treatment process the composition of the water changes. The quantity of suspended solids, the turbidity, the amount of heavy metals, like cadmium and nickel, and the colony count decrease.
By adding iron chloride, the chloride concentration of the water rises. On average 3 mg/l Fe^{3+} is added, implying an increase in the chloride concentration of 5.7 mg/l. The ferric ions form a compound

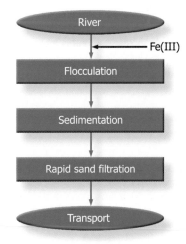

Figure 72 - Preliminary treatment of surface water for infiltration

351

Table 10 - Quality data of the raw and treated water at Nieuwegein (Utrecht)

Parameter	Unit	Raw water	Clear water
Temperature	°C	12.5	12.5
pH	-	8	7.8
EC	mS/m	80	80
SI	-	0.4	0.2
Turbidity	FTU	10.4	0.2
Na^+	mg/l	80	81
K^+	mg/l	6	6
Ca^{2+}	mg/l	81	81
Mg^{2+}	mg/l	11	11
Cl^-	mg/l	149	155
HCO_3^-	mg/l	157	156
SO_4^{2-}	mg/l	66	67
NO_3^-	mg/l	4	4
O_2	mg/l	9.2	7.3
CH_4	mg/l	-	-
CO_2	mg/l	2.6	4.4
Fe^{2+}	mg/l	-	-
Mn^{2+}	mg/l	-	-
NH_4^+	mg/l	-	-
DOC	mg/l	3.9	3
E.Coli	n/100 ml	5,000	50
Bentazon	µg/l	0.2	0.2
Chloroform	µg/l	0	0
Bromate	µg/l	< 2.0	< 2.0

pre-treatment process for infiltration water does not remove organic micropollutants like insecticides. This requires the preliminary treatment process to be expanded with activated carbon filtration (Figure 74).

At the WRK Andijk site, the preliminary treatment process consists of a reservoir, flocculation, floc removal (lamella settling), rapid filtration and activated carbon filtraton. Iron chloride sulfate ($FeClSO_4$) is used as a flocculant.

In the IJsselmeer there is algae growth. Therefore, the amount of organic matter (DOC) and the turbidity are high (Table 11). To reduce the algae the flocculant needs to be added in relatively large amounts, 20 mg/l Fe^{3+} on average. This causes the pH value of the water to decrease. To increase the pH value, lime ($Ca(OH)_2$ is added.

Because WRK Andijk water is now used for both deep infiltration and membrane filtration, the requirements regarding the turbidity and the clog-

together with the hydroxide ions, thus removing hydroxide ions and reducing the pH value.

The quality standards for infiltration water have been made stricter.
Originally, preliminary treatment was performed in order to prevent contamination of the transport pipelines and the clogging of the infiltration ponds. Nowadays, another demand is that no elements foreign to the infiltration environment will accumulate (like organic micropollutants). The standard

Figure 73 - Open sedimentation pond at Nieuwegein (Utrecht)

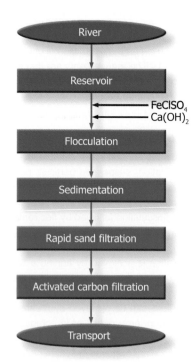

Figure 74 - Treatment scheme of infiltration water where organic micropollutants are removed

Table 11 - Quality data of the raw and treated water at Andijk (Noord-Holland)

Parameter	Unit	Raw water	Clear water
Temperature	°C	11	11.1
pH	-	7.8	7.8
EC	mS/m	95	80
SI	-	0.1	0.2
Turbidity	FTU	8	0.2
Na^+	mg/l	113	81
K^+	mg/l	9	6
Ca^{2+}	mg/l	70	81
Mg^{2+}	mg/l	14.5	11
Cl^-	mg/l	150	160
HCO_3^-	mg/l	138	115
SO_4^{2-}	mg/l	37	67
NO_3^-	mg/l	4	4
O_2	mg/l	10.1	9.5
CH_4	mg/l	-	-
CO_2	mg/l	2.6	1.3
Fe^{2+}	mg/l	-	-
Mn^{2+}	mg/l	-	-
NH_4^+	mg/l	-	-
DOC	mg/l	8	3.3
E.Coli	n/100 ml	5,000	50
Bentazon	µg/l	0.2	< 0.1
Chloroform	µg/l	0	0
Bromate	µg/l	< 2.0	< 2.0

ging capacity, expressed as MFI (membrane fouling index), have been increased. Those demands may be met by the current treatment process given that the process is well-controlled.

At WRK Andijk no inexpensive iron chloride nor caustic soda is added, because the IJsselmeer contains large concentrations of chloride and sodium, which should not be further increased.

5.4 Transport from pre-treatment to the infiltration area

Pre-treatment is sited at the intake point of the surface water. This site is rather remote from the infiltration area.

Infiltration, therefore, requires long transport pipes. Because of the large size of surface water production plants, these pipes will also have a considerable diameter. Sometimes, a double transport pipeline is constructed in order to improve the reliability of the system in case of breakdown.

However, it should be considered that the buffer capacity of the infiltration system is sizable and able to cover water supply during intake stops.

During the transport of pre-treated surface water to the dunes, energy is lost because of the resistance in the pipes. The smaller the diameter and the longer the pipe, the larger the energy loss. This energy loss needs to be compensated for by the pumps.

5.5 Infiltration

Figures 75, 76 and 77 show pictures of open infiltration in dune areas.

The pre-treated surface water infiltrates into the soil, which results in a quality improvement, including the levelling of concentrations.

A retention time of two months is deemed enough to make the water reliable, from a microbiological point of view.

The spatial need for infiltration is easily computed from the desired retention time in the ground:

$$T = \frac{V}{Q} \quad \Rightarrow \quad A = \frac{T \cdot Q}{D \cdot p}$$

in which:

T = the average retention time in the ground (s)
V = the volume flowing through (m³)
Q = the flow through the ground (m³/s)
D = the thickness of the aquifer (m)
p = the porosity of the ground (-)

With the above formula, the spatial demand for an infiltration of 50 million m³ per year will amount to 5.6 million square meters, at a retention time of two months, an aquifer of 5 m thickness, and a porosity of 0.3. This can be achieved in an area of 1 x 5.6 km.

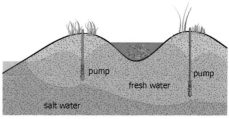

Figure 75 - Infiltration systems in the dunes

Figure 76 - Infiltration pond in the dunes

This spatial demand is equal to a surface load of 8.9 m/y, which is about (8.9 / 0.3 =) 30 times as much as the net precipitation (rainfall minus evaporation) of 0.3 m/y.

Within this infiltration area there is an abstraction of about (1/30 =) 3.3% rain water, assuming the water balance in the area is closed.

When infiltration is interrupted, it will be possible to abstract water for a long time. A delay of a month results in a maximum reduction of the groundwater level with (8.9 / 12 / 0.3) = 2.5 m.

Pre-treated surface water is mainly infiltrated into the dunes by means of open infiltration. In the dunes there is a system of ponds and artificial canals.

Based on a filtration rate of 0.1 to 0.4 m/h in the case of slow sand filtration, an infiltration rate from the infiltration facilities of 2 m/d (730 m/y) appears possible. Therefore, the example above would require an infiltration area of (8.9 / 730 =) 1.2% of the total area necessary for infiltration.

The distance between the infiltration facility and abstraction is determined by the porosity of the ground. A limiting factor is the acceptable reduc-

tion of the groundwater level (drop is linear with porosity and flow).

The system of infiltration facilities is constructed in such a way that all ponds can be dried separately in order to clean accumulated matter on the bottom. Because the water evaporates, cracks will develop in the sludge above the soil (Figure 78).

The composition of the infiltrated water is different from the composition of the original dune water. Foreign water is infiltrated into the dunes. This will cause nutrients to enter the normally poor sand soil, thus changing the vegetation. In this way infiltration can affect natural areas.

There are many animal species in the dunes. The dunes in which water is infiltrated are protected areas. Visitors may only enter these areas on foot. Expansion of the dune infiltration is complicated. Work should only be conducted during winter or it may otherwise disturb the breeding season. Additionally, any installation requiring oil is not allowed, in order to prevent contamination of the area. Also, the level of noise should be limited as much as possible.

The system of infiltration (open infiltration, open abstraction) has developed over time. However, the removal of microorganisms from the water is compromised when recontamination occurs after infiltration. Birds and other animals will contaminate the water with their feces. Therefore, most water companies turn towards a system of closed abstraction.

After being abstracted out, the dune water is transported through pipes to the final treatment plant.

Figure 77 - Infiltration pond (drying up)

Figure 78 - Sludge in infiltration pond

5.6   Final treatment of infiltrated water

After being abstracted, the water requires a final treatment.

The soil passage in the dunes removes micro-organisms and, at the same time, iron, manganese, and ammonium ions from the soil are dissolved. These ions need to be removed from the water. In case the water was not treated with activated carbon before infiltration, organic micro-pollutants may be present in the water. Those need to be removed as well.

The simplest procedure for the final treatment of infiltration water is similar to a groundwater treatment plant: aeration followed by rapid filtration (Figure 79).

As an example of the final treatment of infiltration water, the Bergen plant in Noord-Holland is considered.

Pre-treated water from the IJsselmeer (with activated carbon filtration) is infiltrated into the dunes. Abstracting is done by means of a closed system. The final treatment consists of aeration and rapid filtration.

Despite the fact that the hardness of the water is rather high (2.25 mmol/l), no softening process is applied.

Table 12 - Quality data of the raw and treated water at Bergen treatment plant

Parameter	Unit	Raw water	Clear water
Temperature	°C	11.7	12
pH	-	7.6	7.7
EC	mS/m	86	86
SI	-	0.1	0.0
Turbidity	FTU	-	0.1
Na^+	mg/l	78	78
K^+	mg/l	7	7
Ca^{2+}	mg/l	89	90
Mg^{2+}	mg/l	13	12
Cl^-	mg/l	147	149
HCO_3^-	mg/l	192	198
SO_4^{2-}	mg/l	92	93
NO_3^-	mg/l	1	1
O_2	mg/l	0.2	8
CH_4	mg/l	0	0
CO_2	mg/l	9	7
Fe^{2+}	mg/l	0.6	0.03
Mn^{2+}	mg/l	0.1	< 0.01
NH_4^+	mg/l	0.31	< 0.03
DOC	mg/l	3	3
E.Coli	n/100 ml	0	0
Bentazon	µg/l	< 0.1	< 0.1
Chloroform	µg/l	0	0
Bromate	µg/l	< 2.0	< 2.0

The abstracted water has a low turbidity, because it has been filtered by the dunes (Table 12). During the retention time in the ground, the oxygen concentration is reduced. During the aeration phase the oxygen rate will rise again.

During aeration the iron and manganese ions are oxidized. To remove the iron hydroxide and manganese oxide, rapid filtration is used. The ammonium is transformed into nitrate in the rapid filter.

The concentrations of Bentazon and Diuron (pesticides) are low when abstracting water from the dunes. This is because of the activated carbon filtraton before infiltration. The concentrations will not be reduced further during the final treatment phase.

Generally, the applied treatment process is more extensive in practice. This is partly due to the treatment processes chosen in the past. Then, final treatment of infiltrated water consisted of slow sand filtration only. Later, other treatment techniques were added. The slow sand filters are still

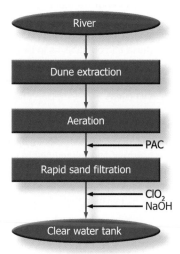

Figure 79 - A simple post-treatment scheme of infiltration water

Figure 80 - Infiltration area and post-treatment plant near Scheveningen

functional when the abstraction of water is done in an open system. In that case, the slow sand filters remove pathogenic microorganisms.

Infiltration water from the large rivers and from the IJsselmeer has a high hardness. Softening with pellet reactors is undertaken to reduce the hardness to about 1.5 mmol/l. These pellet reactors are used after aeration and before rapid filtration, in order to remove the carry-over.

When they have not been removed during preliminary treatment, organic micropollutants are removed by means of powdered carbon or activated carbon filtration. The addition of powdered carbon is done before weir aeration, because that process will sufficiently mix the powder with the water. When activated carbon filtration is used, it is done after rapid filtration.

To improve the removal of organic micropollutants, ozonation can be used. Ozonation oxidizes organic macro-molecules into smaller organic molecules, which can be removed more easily during activated carbon filtraton. A disadvantage of the combination of ozonation and activated carbon filtration is that there will be a high rate of biological activity in the activated carbon filters. This may cause microorganisms to be present in the water, which will require disinfection after activated carbon filtration. This disinfection is done in the slow sand filters.

All in all this makes for quite an extensive treatment process, especially considering the fact that the water has been pre-treated before infiltration and transported over large distances. Therefore, the price of drinking water prepared from infiltration water is higher than that of water produced from groundwater.

6.   Dutch surface water legislation

Surface water is included in the European Water Framework Directive, which was issued in 2000. This directive has an impact on Dutch water legislation:
- Groundwater Act
- Environmental Management Act
- Water Management Act
- Surface Water Pollution Act
- Soil Protection Act

The Dutch framework for public water supply is laid down in the Policy Plan for Drinking and Industry Water.

Environmental Management Act
The Environmental Management Act includes the Environmental Impact Assessment (EIA) Regulation. This requires an EIA-procedure for the construction of any large transport pipes (longer than 10 km, diameter above 1,000 mm), which are frequently used in surface water projects. This act applies also to the construction of any reservoir having a capacity above 10 million m^3 and any surface water infiltration project having a capacity over 3 million m^3/y.

Water Management Act
Abstraction of surface water is dealt with in the Water Management Act. This act requires that permission be requested (and given) for any abstraction.

Water Supply Act
The Water Supply Act contains the Decree on the Water Supply. This decree spells out the quality standards for surface water in order to allow it to be used for drinking water supply.

Soil Protection Act
The Soil Protection Act includes the Infiltration Decree for soil protection. This decree details the standards for the artificial infiltration of surface water.

Further reading

- Principles and practices of water supply operations: Water sources, AWWA (2003)
- Principles and practices of water supply operations: Water treatment, AWWA (2003, student workbook 2005)
- Surface water quality monitoring, EEA (1996)
- Artificial groundwater recharge, L. Huisman / T.N. Olsthoorn, Pitman (1983)
- Slow Sand Filtration, L. Huisman / W.E. Wood, WHO (1974)
- Slow Sand Filtration for Community Water Supply in Developing Countries: A design and construction manual, J.H.C.M. Oomen / J.C. van Dijk, IRC (1978) (also in French and Spanish)

- www.eea.eu.int
- europe.eu.int
- www.vewin.nl
- www.kiwa.nl
- www.overheid.nl/wetten
- www.wrk.nl
- www.gwa.nl
- www.wbe.nl
- www.epa.gov
- www.awwa.org

Questions and applications

Surface water in its natural environment
1. Give a few examples of surface water in a natural or man-made environment.

Intake of surface water
1. Name a few types of surface water which are used for drinking water production.

Direct treatment of surface water
1. Mostly, in the case of direct treatment, reservoirs are used prior to treatment. There are three types of these reservoirs. Name the types, the retention times and their functions.

Indirect treatment of surface water through infiltration
1. What are the opportunities in case expansion of natural infiltration into the dunes is impossible?

Legislation on surface water in the Netherlands
1. Indicate which laws apply to the use of surface water in the Netherlands.

Applications
1. Meuse water is extracted from the Andelse Maas reservoir near Brakel and transported to Bergambacht, a distance of 30 km. The water is pre-treated in Bergambacht and then transported to the dunes near Katwijk, a distance of 60 km.

   a Provide reasons for the preliminary treatment being performed in Bergambacht instead of in Brakel.

b Why is aluminum sulfate added in the Andelse Maas reservoir?

c What are the requirements for pre-treated water which is to be infiltrated into the soil, and are those requirements fully met in practice?

d Describe the functions of all steps in the treatment scheme and describe which compounds are removed and to what extent.

e Indicate some reasons for the existence of slow sand filters.

2. A town having 600,000 inhabitants discharges its wastewater on a river. The river's cross-sectional area amounts to 66.7 m^2 and the flow is 26 m^3/s.
   Decay coefficients for different types of water:
   - reservoir: 0.3 d^{-1}
   - slow flowing river (v < 1 m/s):   0.5 d^{-1}
   - fast flowing river (v > 1 m/s):   0.8 d^{-1}

   a Compute the average E.coli content in the river if any person produces $1 \cdot 10^{11}$ E.coli daily.

   b At what distance from the discharge point will the content of E.coli be below 10^7 per m^3?

   c A drinking water production plant has its inlet downstream from the discharge point. In order to obtain a sufficient decay of E.coli, several reservoirs are used serially. The retention time in a single reservoir is 45 days. How many reservoirs are required to keep the E.coli content below 10^6 per m^3?

   d In a swimming pool, per swimmer $2 \cdot 10^9$ germs enter the water daily. The germ number in any swimming pool should not be above $5 \cdot 10^8$. Compute the minimum size of the pool if the daily number of swimmers is 200.

3. At the Berenplaat production plant there is a reservoir (volume - 7,300,000 m³), which is currently only used for the intake of Meuse water in case of emergency. The capacity of the inlet pumps is 22,000 m³/h. The reservoir is shallow and a few lead dams have achieved a plug flow in it.

a Which compounds do you expect to be present in the water and indicate the expected amount in which they will occur.

b Compute the protozoa removal percentage during the retention in the reservoir. Assume a decay for protozoa of 0.5 per day.

c What would have been the removal percentage for protozoa in case there was full mixing in the reservoir?

d A common problem in reservoirs is algae growth. Argue whether this problem will be present in the reservoir mentioned.

4. Next to a small river in a natural area there is a factory. To reduce the waste load of the river, the factory has two emergency reservoirs with a net volume of 1,000 m³. In case of emergency the wastewater can flow through those reservoirs first before being discharged into the river. The question pertains to the way these reservoirs should be operated in order to reduce the waste load as much as possible. There are three possibilities:

- The reservoirs are operated parallel, which means that the wastewater is equally divided among the reservoirs.

- The reservoirs are operated serially, meaning that the total waste flow will first pass through one reservoir and then through the other.

- The reservoirs are used intermittently, which means that they will be emptied after an emergency and filled during the next one.

a Compute the equilibrium concentration in the effluent when using parallel reservoirs and a continuous flow of 1,000 m³/d having a concentration of 100 mg/l and a decay coefficient of 1 d⁻¹.

b What will the equilibrium concentration be in case the reservoirs are operated serially and the same amount of wastewater flows through them?

c When the reservoirs are filled with 1,000 m³ of wastewater once (intermittent operation), what will be the concentration in the basins after 1 day and after 10 days?

In practice, it will often be unknown how often, how long, and how much wastewater will flow in an emergency.

d Which practical advice can nevertheless be given for the best operation of the reservoirs? Deal with parallel, serial, or intermittent operation, depending on the situation of the company.

Answers

Surface water in its natural environment

1. - Rivers
   - Lakes
   - Seas
   - Canals
   - Reservoirs
   - Gravel and sands pits
   - Artificial lakes and storage reservoirs

Intake on surface water

2. - Rivers
   - Shallow lakes
   - Deep, oligotrophic lakes
   - Deep, eutrophic lakes
   - Reservoirs
   - Polders

Direct treatment of surface water

1.

Type of reservoir	Retention time	Functions
Analysis	ca. 1 week	Analysis of the intake water, based on this analysis the intake can be stopped temporarily
Process or mixing reservoir	ca. 3 - 5 weeks	Quality improvement by dosing of chemicals Self-purification of water by decay and sedimentation
Storage reservoir	ca. 1 - 3 months	Storage during periods of bad water quality (due to disaster or low river discharge Self-purification of water by decay and sedimentation

Indirect treatment of surface water through infiltration

1. First, the pre-treated water may be purified directly, after which mixing is applied with infiltrated water. Second, deep infiltration may be applied.

Legislation on surface water in the Netherlands

- Groundwater Act
- Environmental Management Act
- Water Management Act
- Surface Water Pollution Act
- Soil Protection Act

Applications

1. a In former days, Bergambacht was the inlet site, but this was moved to Brakel because of salinity problems.

   b Aluminum sulfate is mainly meant for P-removal and reduction of algae growth.

   c Pre-treated water should comply with the requirements, meaning that the concentrations of the following compounds should not exceed the standards:
   - suspended solids
   - phosphate, nutrients
   - organic micropollutants /insecticides (these standards are not met)
   - heavy metals

   Pre-treatment is also for limiting clogging in the dunes, so suspended solids removal.

   d Andelse Maas Reservoir:
   - Processes: levelling, settling, nutrient removal, buffer
   - Compounds removed: suspended solids (70%), nutrients (70%), heavy metals (90%)

   Rapid filtration:
   - Processes: removal of suspended solids, disinfection
   - Compounds removed: suspended solids (70%), algae (70%), microorganisms (80%)

   Dunes:
   - Processes: buffer, smoothing, disinfection, nitrification
   - Compounds removed: microorganisms (>99%), organic matter (20%)

Cascade aeration:
- Processes: gas exchange
- Compounds removed: carbon dioxide (80%)
- Compounds injected: oxygen (80%)

Pellet softening:
- Processes: softening
- Compounds removed: calcium (60%)

Rapid filtration:
- Processes: post-softening
- Compounds removed: carry-over $CaCO_3$, Fe^{2+} (90%), NH_4^+ (90%), Mn^{2+} (90%)

Slow sand filtration:
- Processes: disinfection
- Compounds removed: microorganisms (>99%), AOC (80%)

e   Removal of bacteria, suspended solids, AOC

Slow sand filtration is, strictly speaking, obsolete in the case of closed abstraction, but as the abstraction was open in former days, the slow sand filters are still present.

2. a   Daily $(1 \cdot 10^{11}) \cdot 600,000$ E.coli are discharged into the river. The amount of E.coli then equals:

average E-coli =
$$\frac{1 \cdot 10^{11} \cdot 600 \cdot 10^3}{26 \cdot 3,600 \cdot 24} = 2.67 \cdot 10^{10} \ m^{-3}$$

b   It is assumed that the river flow is a plug flow, making the exponential solution applicable:

$$\frac{N_e}{N_0} = \exp(-k_0 \cdot t)$$

in which $N_e = 1 \cdot 10^7$ E.coli per m^3 and N_0 equals the number of E.coli at the discharge site ($N_0 = 2.67 \cdot 10^{10} \ m^{-3}$).

The flow rate of the river equals the flow divided by the cross-sectional area or 26 / 66.7 = 0.38 m/s. As it is a slow-flowing river (v < 1 m/s), the decay coefficient equals 0.5 d^{-1}. The point at which less than 10^7 E.coli per m^3 are present in the water can be computed by using the exponential solution.

$$t = \frac{-\ln\left(\dfrac{N_e}{N_0}\right)}{k_0} = \frac{8.22}{0.5} = 16.5 \ days$$

After 16.5 days the number of E.coli falls below $1 \cdot 10^7$ per m^3. The distance to the discharge site is computed by multiplying time by the velocity of the river:

x = v·t = 0.38·(60·60·24)·16.5 = 541,000 m = 541 km

c   The decay is achieved in reservoirs with full mixing. As multiple basins are used serially, the solution for decay in multiple reservoirs.

$$\frac{N_e}{N_0} = \left(\frac{1}{1 + k_0 \cdot t}\right)^{-n}$$

in which $N_e = 1 \cdot 10^6$ E.coli per m^3 and N_0 equals the number of E.coli at the discharge site ($N_0 = 2.67 \cdot 10^{10} \ m^{-3}$). The decay coefficient k_2 in a reservoir amounts to 0.3 d^{-1} and the retention time amounts to 45 days per reservoir. The number of reservoirs n needs to be computed. When all known values are filled in, the following equation is obtained:

$$\left(\frac{1}{1 + k_0 \cdot t}\right)^{-n} = \frac{N_e}{N_0} \Rightarrow$$

$$\left(\frac{1}{14.5}\right)^{-n} = \frac{10^6}{2.67 \cdot 10^{10}} \Rightarrow$$

$$14.5^n = 26,700 \Rightarrow n = 3.8$$

d A germ balance can be formulated for the pool. It holds that:

inlet   = outlet + decay

$(2 \cdot 10^9) \cdot 200 = 0 + 0.3 \cdot 5 \cdot 10^8 \cdot V$

It follows from this that the volume of the swimming pool should be 2,660 m³ in order to keep the germ number below $5 \cdot 10^9$.

3. a.

Compounds	Order of magnitude
Bacteria / viruses	100,000 / l
Organic micropollutants	in micrograms / l
Pesticides	in micrograms / l
Colloids, suspended solids	in milligrams / l
Oxygen	0 - 10 mg / l
Carbon dioxide	0 - 1 mg / l
Salts	100 - 500 mg /l

b. The retention time (T = V/Q) in the reservoir needs to be computed first, this amounts to 13.8 days. The current in the reservoir approaches the plug flow model and, therefore, the following equation is used:

$$\frac{N_e}{N_0} = \exp(-k_0 \cdot t)$$

The relationship between the number of protozoa leaving the reservoir and the number of protozoa entering the reservoir is computed using the equation above. After filling in this equation it follows that this relationship amounts to 0.001. The removal amounts to:

$$\text{removal} = \left(1 - \frac{N_e}{N_0}\right) = (1 - 0.001) = 0.999$$

The removal percentage (removal•100%) amounts to 99.9%.

c If the reservoir would be a full-mixed system, another equation needs to be used to compute the relation between the leaving and entering numbers of protozoa. It is the following:

$$\frac{N_e}{N_0} = \frac{1}{1 + k_0 \cdot T} = \frac{1}{1 + 0.5 \cdot 13.8} = 0.1266$$

The removal amounts to 1 - 0.1266 = 0.8734 and the removal percentage amounts to 87.34%.

d Yes, it is a shallow reservoir. Because sunlight enters the reservoir, algae growth will certainly be a problem. However, as the retention time is short, algae growth will be somewhat limited.

4. a Full mixing, retention time per reservoir amounts to 1,000/500 = 2 days, $c_e = c_0/(1+k \cdot t) = 100/3 = 33$ mg/l

b Full mixing, retention time per reservoir = 1 day
concentration after first reservoir amounts to $c_e = c_0/(1+k \cdot t) = 100/2 = 50$ mg/l
concentration after second basin amounts to $c_e = c_0/(1+k \cdot t) = 50/2 = 25$ mg/l

c Plug flow, so $c_e = c_0 \cdot \exp(-k \cdot t)$
After one day the concentration amounts to 36.8 mg/l
After 10 days the concentration amounts to 0.0045 mg/l.

d Preferably emptying the reservoirs when the quality is high; in case of emergency, fill intermittently; first the one, then the other (serially); if the emergency lasts for too long, continue serial operation; when the emergency is over, wait until quality has improved and then empty.

Distribution

TECHNICAL FACETS

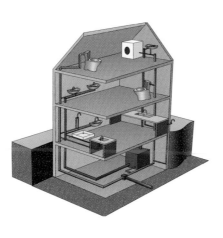

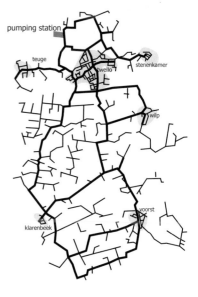

Framework

This module deals with the technical aspects of a drinking water distribution system. This not only covers a distribution network, home connections and house installations, but also pumping systems, transport pipes and storage reservoirs.

Contents

This module has the following contents:

Study goals

After studying this module you will be able to:
- name the parts of a distribution system and explain their functions
- make calculations for transport systems (hydraulic resistance, economic velocity)
- calculate the required volume of storage reservoirs
- explain the basis for the calculations of a distribution network
- explain the scheme for drinking water installations

1.   Introduction

In the past people got their water from a village pump or tap in the neighborhood, or from the water salesman on the market square. This situation is, in many developing countries, still true (Figure 1). Wealthy people would have their drinking water brought to their home. This is also the case in many countries. Water is delivered in a container truck to a reservoir in the garden and then the water is pumped to a reservoir on the roof; this reservoir supplies the taps in the house.

In Western society, drinking water is delivered to consumers by a distribution network, with sufficient pressure to supply the various taps in the house.

Distribution is a very important factor in modern drinking water supply systems.

Distribution is important because of:
-   comfort of supply
-   quality of the supplied product

From the point of view of comfort, the user does not want the drinking water only supplied at home,

Figure 1   - Drinking water distribution by truck

but he or she also wants it available at various consumption points, and in sufficient amounts with sufficient pressure. This requires a very large network of pipes from the production locations to the taps. From the point of view of quality, it should not decline (too much) during distribution. Therefore, there should be no harmful interaction between drinking water and pipe material, and also no pollution of the drinking water from outside the distribution network (through infiltration of ground- or surface water, or diffusion of pollutants from the soil). Also, biological growth in the water and accumulation of pollutants in the distribution network should be avoided.

With these initial requirements, the sanitary engineer has to make sure that, with a good design, these two requirements can be realized at the lowest costs possible. Naturally, there should be sufficient drinking water available at all times, even in times of extreme demand.

It is also important that there is sufficient supply reliability, so in case of failure at one part of the distribution network, the supply will continue undisturbed; this is also considered standard practice by the consumers.

It is not unnatural that consumers have become used to this. Because of the importance of good drinking water, supply requirements have been established with legal standards for the public's drinking water supply.

For good drinking water supply, distribution is as important as production. Distribution may be, due to numerous pipes underground, less visible than production. It is of such a size that, in the end, the annual costs for distribution are often higher than those for production.

This module deals with the main aspects of drinking water distribution, from the production reservoirs to the taps. First, the various parts of distribution are presented. Subsequently, a closer look is given to the transport of drinking water. Special attention is paid to the hydraulic aspects of transport and the design aspects of the transport pipe systems.

After this, the storage of drinking water is dealt with. For this, the calculation of the volume of a reservoir is important, and so are the design aspects of drinking water reservoirs. Next, there will be an examination of the different aspects of the distribution network.

Finally, drinking water or residence installations are briefly discussed.

2. Parts of a distribution system

In general, the public drinking water supply has a technical scheme as shown in Figure 2.

Production consists of the abstraction of "raw water" (groundwater from the soil, or surface water from rivers, canals and lakes), followed by a treatment process, after which the water is stored in a production reservoir.

If the supply area is a great distance from the production location, the water is first transported by transport pumps and transport pipes.

To level the daily variation in water consumption, distribution reservoirs are used. From the reservoirs the drinking water is brought, under pressure, to supply the distribution network.

In the distribution network a dense system of pipelines is present (Figure 3). From this network the drinking water is delivered to the consumers at home by a "service connection."

After registering on the water meter, the drinking water enters the residence installation or a collective pipe network. Here, the water is divided among

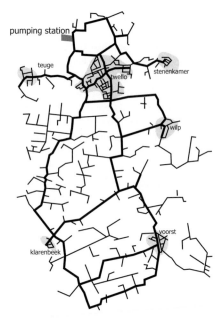

Figure 3 - A distribution network in a rural area

all the taps in the house(s), like kitchen, toilet, bathroom, bedroom, garden, central heating, etc. A share of the water flows via the hot water installation, which consists of a heater or boiler and pipes to the taps in the bathroom, kitchen, bedroom, etc.

In practice several variants of the general scheme shown in Figure 2 exist. Often, the transport stage

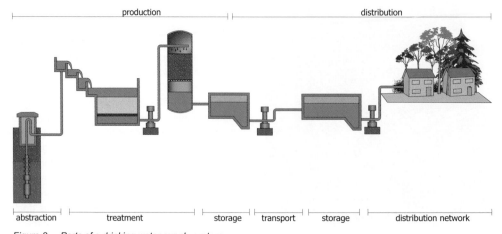

production		distribution	
abstraction	treatment	storage	transport	storage	distribution network

Figure 2 - Parts of a drinking water supply system

is missing and the production reservoir corresponds to the distribution reservoir.

In several cases the distribution reservoir is located in the distribution network itself. This can be a high reservoir on a hill above the city (working as a very large water tower), or a low supplemental reservoir. Such a reservoir is filled at night from the distribution network and delivers water back into the distribution network (supplement) during the day via its own distribution pumps.

3.   Transport

3.1 Hydraulic aspects

In long transport pipes a uniform flow predominates (independent of place), because of a constant flow profile. Non-uniform flow occurs at the changes in pipe diameter and at the outflow in reservoirs.

In principle, the flow in pipes is non-stationary (dependent on time), because of the fluctuating demand. However, the changes develop gradually, as a result of which, for the calculations of hydraulic resistance, a stationary flow is assumed.

Furthermore, for the calculations of transport pipes for water, it is assumed that water is non-compressible.

The hydraulic resistance in pipes consists of 2 components:
- friction losses, by a uniform flow along a circular wall
- local losses, by an irregular change in the flow profile

In transport pipes rapid changes in the flow can also occur, like when turning off and on the pumps and the sudden closure of valves. This results in pressure changes which travel through the pipes as a pressure wave and is reflected in profile changes. This phenomenon is called a "water hammer."

In this module, water hammer is not described in more detail.

Transport and distribution

The terms transport and distribution are often used interchangeably in practice.
Naturally, in a distribution network also transport of drinking water takes place. As a matter of fact, that is precisely the function of a distribution network.

In this module, for a clear understanding, the following definition of a distribution network is used:
all pipes which directly supply consumers with water, as well as the pipes which are directly, hydraulically connected with these.
Directly, hydraulically connected means without a pressure increase by pumps, or pressure regulation by valves.

In a distribution network the minimum pressure for the consumers is a normative quantity (200 kPa above street level). Furthermore, the discharge fluctuates directly with the variation in water demand.
In a transport system the pressure is not determined by the minimum supply pressure, but only by the hydraulic conditions of the transport itself.

Between the transport system and the distribution network is, most often, a considerable storage, therefore the flow variation in the transport system is much smaller than in the distribution network.
The transport system is measured on the maximum daily consumption, the distribution system on the maximum consumption per second. This demand per second often equals the maximum demand per hour due to levelling. Naturally, this doesn't count for dead-ends of the network, where the consumers' consumption fluctuations are significant.

Calculation of friction losses

discharge	=	10,000	m³/h	=	2.78	m³/s
transport distance	=	54	km	=	54,000	m
pipe diameter	=	1,500	mm	=	1.5	m
wall roughness	=	1.0 mm		=	1.0 10⁻³	m

$$\text{velocity in the pipe} = \frac{2.78}{0.25 \cdot \pi \cdot 1.5^2} = 1.57 \text{ m/s}$$

$$Re = \frac{v \cdot D}{v} = \frac{1.57 \cdot 1.5}{1.0 \cdot 10^{-6}} = 2.36 \cdot 10^6$$

The value of λ can be determined fairly precisely by calculating λ without the term with Re and then filling the calculated λ in the complete formula.
Iterative: λ = 0.0180 (without Re term: λ = 0.0178)

$$\Delta H_F = \lambda \cdot \frac{L}{D} \cdot \frac{v^2}{2 \cdot g} = 0.0180 \cdot \frac{54,000}{1.5} \cdot \frac{1.57^2}{2 \cdot 9.81} = 81.4 \text{ m}$$

Gradient = ΔH/L = 81.4/54 = 1.5 m/km

Friction losses

Friction losses can be determined with the formula of Darcy-Weisbach and Colebrook-White:

$$\Delta H_F = \lambda \cdot \frac{L}{D} \cdot \frac{v^2}{2 \cdot g}$$

$$\frac{1}{\sqrt{\lambda}} = -2 \cdot \log\left(\frac{k}{3.7 \cdot D} + \frac{2.51}{Re\sqrt{\lambda}} \right)$$

$$Re = \frac{v \cdot D}{v}$$

in which:

ΔH_F	=	friction losses	(m)
λ	=	friction factor	(-)
L	=	length of the pipe	(m)
D	=	diameter of the pipe	(m)
v	=	velocity in the pipe	(m/s)
g	=	gravity constant	(m²/s)
k	=	wall roughness	(mm)
Re	=	Reynolds number	(-)
v	=	kinematic viscosity	(m²/s)

In the formula for friction losses the velocity can be rewritten to discharge and diameter. With v² = Q²/A² and A = 0.25·π·D² is:

$$\Delta H_F = \lambda \cdot \frac{8 \cdot L \cdot Q^2}{g \cdot \pi^2 \cdot D^5}$$

In the past also simplified formulas were used (like Chézy, Manning), but because of the use of computers, these simple formulas have lost their usefulness.

In practice the friction factor λ lies between 0.01 and 0.04. For the first estimation of λ often 0.02 is used (Chézy coefficient C=50).

The friction factor especially depends on the relative wall roughness (k/D).
Table 1 shows that wall roughness differs widely per material. In time wall roughness can noticeably increase due to corrosion, deposits and the formation of slime. Because of this a doubling of the friction factor can be found in practice.
The friction factor also depends on the type of flow (laminar if Re<2,300, turbulent if Re>10,000). In practice, turbulence is often of such a size that the term with Re in the formula for the friction factor is negligible.

Table 1 - Wall roughness of pipe materials

Type of material	Wall roughness (mm)
Masonry	1.0 - 5.0
Concrete	0.5 - 2.0
Metal	0.1 - 0.3
PVC	0.01 - 0.05

Local losses

When the flow velocity is reduced, the kinetic energy (velocity height = $v^2/2g$) is not completely transformed into potential energy (pressure height). Local losses occur when the pipe diameter gets larger or at the outflow in a reservoir.

Local losses also occur after a narrowing and after contraction of flow at inflow in pipes, at joining pipes, and at bends.

In a pipe system, local losses occur at various locations. The total local losses can be calculated with:

$$\Delta H_L = \sum \xi \cdot \left(\frac{v^2}{2 \cdot g} \right) = \sum \xi \cdot \frac{8 \cdot Q^2}{g \cdot \pi^2 \cdot D^4}$$

in which:

ΔH_L	=	local losses	(m)
ξ	=	loss factor	(-)

In this formula the loss factors are related to the velocity in the pipe.

For different flow situations, local losses can be determined in an empirical way. The determined loss factors can be found in hydraulic engineering books (as formulas, values or nomograms). In there, local losses are often referred to as "minor losses."

Table 2 shows the loss factors for a number of typical flow transitions. This shows that a designer can influence the local losses not only by chang-

Table 2   - Loss factors (ξ) for some flow transitions

Transition	ξ
Inflow from reservoir (incoming pipe)	1.0
Inflow from reservoir (sharp inflow)	0.5
Inflow from reservoir (rounded inflow)	0.1
Bends 90° (abrupt bend)	1.2
Bends 90° (r = D)	0.2
Bends 90° (r = 4D)	0.1
Movable valve (open)	0.1
Butterfly valve(open)	0.2
Check valve (non-return valve or one-way valve)	2.5
Outflow in reservoir (sharp outflow)	1.1
Outflow in reservoir (widening outflow)	0.2

ing the pipe diameter, but also by the shape of the transitions. Narrowings are more critical transitions than widenings because of contraction.

In pipes the largest local losses occur near check valves (non-return or one-way valves) ($\xi = 2.0 - 2.5$) because of the significant change in the flow profile.

In the case of outflow in still water (like the inflow in a reservoir), the complete velocity height is lost ($\xi = 1.0$). In the outflow in larger pipes, the loss is dependent upon the size of the difference in velocity ($\xi = 0.01 - 1.0$).

Butterfly valves in opened state also disturb the flow ($\xi = 0.2 - 0.5$).

In the case of inflow in pipes, the local losses are dependent upon the shape of the pipe entrance spout ($\xi = 0.01 - 0.5$).

In practice a ξ_{total} between 1 and 4 can be used for short pipe pieces. For longer pipes with many

---

Calculation of local losses

discharge	=	10,000 m³/h = 2.78 m³/s
transport distance	=	54 km
pipe diameter	=	1,500 mm
number of bends	=	30 ($\xi = 0.5$ average per bend)
number of valves	=	10 ($\xi = 0.3$ average per valve)
number of check valves	=	1 ($\xi = 2.5$)
inflow	=	1 ($\xi = 0.5$)
outflow	=	1 ($\xi = 1.0$)

$$\text{velocity in the pipe} = \frac{2.78}{0.25 \cdot \pi \cdot 1.5^2} = 1.57 \text{ m/s}$$

$$\Delta H_L = ((30 \cdot 0.5) + (10 \cdot 0.3) + 2.5 + 0.5 + 1.0) \cdot \frac{1.57^2}{2 \cdot 9.81} = 22 \cdot \frac{1.57^2}{2 \cdot 9.81} = 2.8 \text{ m}$$

bends, appendages, joints, etc., a much higher value can be employed.

Total losses

The total losses for flow in a pipe can be described with:

$$\Delta H_{dynamic} = \Delta H_F + \Delta H_L = c_F \cdot Q^2 + c_L \cdot Q^2$$

in which:

$\Delta H_{dynamic}$	=	total dynamic losses	(m)
Q	=	discharge through pipe	(m³/s)
c_F	=	coefficient for friction losses	(s²/m⁵)
c_L	=	coefficient for local losses	(s²/m⁵)

The friction losses are linearly related to L and (approximately) D^{-5}.
The coefficient for local losses is linear to ξ_{total} and D^{-4}.
The quadratic relationship between discharge and resistance can be found in the pipe characteristics.

For long pipes (L/D>500), the local losses are "minor," but for very short pipes (L/D<20), the local losses are major.

Pressure line and gradient

The dynamic losses and altitude of the water levels in reservoirs determine the pressure line along the transport pipe.
Figure 4 shows an example of the pumping head and pressure line for two different discharges.
The pressure line shows the change in the energy height in the pipe. For transport pipes, a linear relationship can be considered.
The pressure height is equal to the energy height minus the velocity height. For transport pipes the velocity height is usually negligible.
The slope of the pressure line is called the gradient:

$$i = \frac{H}{L}$$

in which:

i	=	gradient	(-)

The internal pressure in the pipe equals the pressure height minus the location height of the pipe.

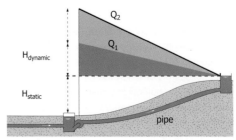

Figure 4 - Pumping head and pressure lines for a transport main for two different flow rates

In the example of Figure 4, the internal pressure is highest near the pumping station.

The maximum admissible pressure in the pipe is determined by the strength of the pipe, which is for a certain pipe material determined by the thickness of the pipe wall. This establishes the maximum internal pressure and, therefore, also the maximum supply capacity of a transport pipe.
In principle the pipe wall could be made thinner along the length (lower internal pressure). In practice such a weakening is not applied because of the water hammer and its large temporary pressure surges.
Changes in pipe strength are made in mountainous areas, where the static pressure shows large differences (thicker pipes in valleys).

Pumping head and pumping energy

The pumping head of the pumps in the pumping station should, at a minimum, equal the level difference between the reservoir at the pumping station and the receiving reservoir (static head). The water flows only if the pumping head is higher than the static head.

The required pumping head in the pumping station can be calculated with:

$$H_{pumping} = H_{static} + H_{dynamic}$$

in which:

$H_{pumping}$	= total pumping head	(m)
H_{static}	= static pumping head	(m)
$H_{dynamic}$	= dynamic pumping head	(m)

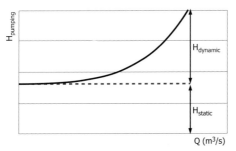

Figure 5 - The pipe characteristics represent the relationship between flow rate and pumping head
for a transport main

The relationship between pumping head and the
discharge through the pipe is shown in the pipe
characteristics (Figure 5).

The required power and the energy consumption
of the pumps are calculated with:

$$P = \frac{Q \cdot H_{pumping} \cdot \rho \cdot g}{\eta}$$

$$E = P \cdot t$$

in which:

P = required power   (W)
ρ = density of the liquid   (kg/m³)
η = efficiency of the pumping installation   (-)
E = energy consumption   (Ws)
t = operation time of pumps   (s)

With a higher pumping head, the discharge through
the pipe increases.

If the available $H_{dynamic}$ is doubled, then the discharge through the pipe increases by a factor
$\sqrt{2} = 1.41$ (a quadratic relationship between flow
resistance and discharge).

3.2 Economic velocity

When designing a transport pipe, the length L, the
static pumping head H_{static}, and the discharge Q(t)
are already known, only the internal diameter D
still has to be chosen.

With a small diameter the construction costs are
low, yet the energy costs are high, and the opposite
is true for large diameters. Somewhere between
these extremes lies the most economic diameter
for which the sum of the construction costs and
the capitalized energy costs are minimal.

Construction costs

The construction costs of a transport pipe depend on
the pipe material, the subsurface, and the surface.
For a rough estimate, the construction costs can
be calculated using:

$$K_c = 500 \cdot D \cdot L$$

in which:

K_c = construction costs   (€)

Calculation of pumping energy

discharge   = 10,000   m³/h = 2.78   m³/s
pumping head =   81.4 + 2.8 = 84.2 m
efficiency   =   0.75 · 0.9   = 0.68 (efficiency pumps · efficiency electric installation)
water density =   1,000   kg/m³
operation time =   365   days per year
energy costs   = € 0.08   /kWh

required power = 2.78 · 84.2 · 1000 · 9.81 / 0.68 = 3,380 kW

energy consumption =   3,380 · 365 · 24 = 29.6 million kWh per year
pumped amount   = 10,000 · 365 · 24 = 87.6 million m³ per year
specific demand   =   29.6 / 87.6   =   0.34 kWh per m³

energy costs   = 29.6 · € 0.08   = € 2.37 million per year
specific costs =   0.34 · € 0.08   = € 0.024 per m³ (2.4 cents per m³)

Energy costs

The energy costs for the static pumping head are independent of the diameter and can, therefore, be excluded from the optimization.

The annual energy costs for the dynamic pumping head can be calculated with (λ= 0.02, no local losses, efficiency 0.68, continuous supply, energy costs € 0.08 per kWh):

$$K_e = 16.7 \cdot Q^3 \cdot D^{-5} \cdot L$$

in which:

K_e = annual energy costs   (€/year)

Assuming a real interest of 5% (interest 7%, inflation 2%), the present value of the energy costs $K_e(n)$ in year n are related to the energy costs in the first year $K_e(1)$ as follows:

$$K_e(n) = \frac{K_e(1)}{(1.05)^n}$$

With a lifetime of 50 years, the net present value of the total energy costs is:

$$NPV_e = 19.2 \cdot K_e(1)$$

in which:

NPV_e = net present value energy   (€)

The annual maintenance costs of the pipe are not considered, because these barely depend on the diameter (within the considered diameter range).

Total costs

The total costs K_{total} can be calculated with:

$$K_{total} = 19.2 \cdot 16.7 \cdot Q^3 \cdot D^{-5} \cdot L + 500 \cdot D \cdot L$$

Figure 6 shows the construction costs and the net present value of the energy costs of a transport pipe as a function of the pipe diameter (Q = 0.6 m³/s, L = 54 km).

Optimal velocity

In Figure 6, it can be seen that the optimal diameter is between 0.9 and 1.0 m. Within the range of 0.8 and 1.2, the total costs differ less than 10% from the lowest possible costs. The graph of the total costs shows that the risks are smaller for a diameter that is too large than too small, from the point of view of costs.

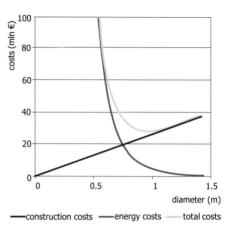

——construction costs ——energy costs ——total costs

Figure 6 - Construction costs and net present value of the energy costs as a function of the pipe diameter

The optimal diameter $D_{optimum}$ can be calculated analytically with $K'_e(D) = 0$. This results in:

$$D_{opt} = \frac{1.2}{\sqrt{Q}}$$

The formula shows that the optimal diameter is independent of the pipe length. The formula can be rewritten for the flow rate in the pipe:

$$v = \frac{Q}{A} = \frac{\left(\frac{D}{1.2}\right)^2}{\frac{\pi \cdot D^2}{4}} = 0.88 \text{ m/s}$$

The optimal velocity proves to be independent of the discharge Q.

Table 3 shows the optimal pipe diameter and accompanying gradient for several discharges. This illustrates that the optimal gradient is larger

Table 3 - Optimal velocity, diameter and gradient for transport mains (constant flow)

Flow (mln m³/y)	Flow (m³/s)	Velocity (m/s)	Diameter (mm)	Gradient (m/km)
1	0.032	0.88	210	3.7
2	0.063	0.88	300	2.6
5	0.158	0.88	480	1.6
10	0.32	0.88	680	1.2
20	0.63	0.88	960	0.8
50	1.58	0.88	1,510	0.5
100	3.2	0.88	2,140	0.4

Table 4 - Optimal velocity at design flow rate (100%) at different operational situations

Operational situation	Velocity (m/s)
Constant maximum flow rate (50 years, 100%)	0.88
Increasing load (from 50% to 100% in 25 years), afterwards 25 years maximum flow rate (100%)	1.18
Yearly maximum flow with (stepwise) seasonal fluctuations (constant + or - 10%)	0.85
Yearly maximum flow with (stepwise) seasonal fluctuations (constant + or - 50%)	0.68

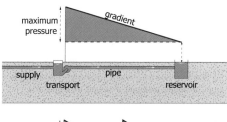

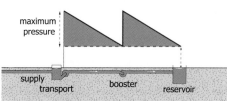

Figure 7 - Capacity increase by boosters

for small diameters (circa 2 m/km) than for large pipes (circa 0.5 m/km).

For a transport main, the available $H_{dynamic}$ is in the order of magnitude of 60 mwc (maximum internal pressure 65 mwc and a static pumping head of 5 mwc).
The optimal gradient implies that a transport distance between 30 - 120 km requires a less optimal diameter, or booster installations along the main.

Optimal velocity with fluctuations
In the above calculations a constant and full loading of the transport main is assumed.

Table 4 shows several typical operational situations and consequences at the optimal velocity. For a transport main with an increasing load, the energy costs are initially low, while the energy costs in the last stage mildly influence the present value. Because of this, the optimal velocity is much higher than with constant full loading.
With fluctuations during the year, the raised energy costs are much greater during peak periods than the lowered energy costs during low periods ($K_e = f(Q^3)$). Because of this, the optimal velocity during full load decreases. The greater the fluctuations, the lower the optimal average velocity.

3.3 Capacity

Capacity increase by boosters
The transport capacity of a pipe system is especially limited by the maximum permissible pressure. The transport capacity can be increased by

applying boosters along the pipe. A booster is a pumping installation placed directly into the pipe. Figure 7 illustrates that with a single booster pump the transport capacity is increased up to 141% (=√2), due to a doubling of the available gradient. With two boosters, an increase of 173% (=√3) should be possible. Because of the quadratic relationship between gradient and flow velocity, the relative capacity increase decreases with every extra booster.

Boosters are also used in transport mains with very short-term peak loads and in transport mains with a high static level difference (e.g., in mountainous areas).

Supply reliability with double pipes
During a disturbance (pipe fracture, collapse, mechanical damage, route modification, etc.), transport pipes can be out of service for a long time. This means a complete stoppage of supply for a single transport pipe.

With a double transport pipe, at least half of the transport capacity is available.

When a connection is made between two pipes, then two segments are obtained. During a disturbance in a segment, the complete discharge is led through one single pipe (Figure 8). Because of the double discharge, the pressure drop in this segment is four times as large as in the other seg-

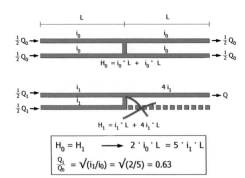

$$H_0 = i_0 \cdot L + i_0 \cdot L$$

$$H_1 = i_1 \cdot L + 4 i_1 \cdot L$$

$$H_0 = H_1 \longrightarrow 2 \cdot i_0 \cdot L = 5 \cdot i_1 \cdot L$$

$$\frac{Q_1}{Q_0} = \sqrt{(i_1/i_0)} = \sqrt{(2/5)} = 0.63$$

Figure 8   - Security of supply with two segments

ment. The resulting transport capacity is now 63% $(\sqrt{(1+1)/(1+4)})$.

Table 5 shows the resulting pipe capacity of a double pipe system with segmentation.

3.4   Design aspects

Choice of material

In the past, various materials were used for the construction of transport pipes; in chronological order they were terracotta, bronze, lead, wood, cast iron, reinforced concrete, asbestos cement, pre-stressed concrete, nodulair cast iron, steel and various sorts of synthetic materials. These days, some materials are still used, others have disappeared, while new materials are added all the time. Several considerations play a part in the choice of material, but the most important ones are:

- the mechanical strength and firmness
- the durability against corrosion, separated into corrosion from the outside and from the inside
- the protection of the water quality against dissolving heavy metals like cadmium and zinc,

erosion of asbestos fibers, or diffusion of organic compounds originating from soil pollution

- the wall roughness and correlating friction resistance
- the construction costs

For the construction of transport pipes, most often the following are chosen:

synthetic material:	$\emptyset \leq 600$ mm
nodulair cast iron:	300 mm $\leq \emptyset \leq 1,000$ mm
steel:	$\emptyset \geq 800$ mm
pre-stressed concrete:	$\emptyset \leq 1,200$ mm

Subsurface

In densely populated areas, the pipes are constructed under the surface, which, in colder regions, is a requirement to prevent freezing.

In the Netherlands the necessary groundcover is 0.8 in the west and up to 1 or 1.2 m in the east of the country, while in Scandinavian countries even values of 1.5 up to 2.5 can be necessary.

As a matter of fact, considering the deep ploughing of agricultural land, deep placement is often required in the Netherlands as well.

With a high groundwater level, this means considerable costs for drainage of the construction site. In sparsely populated areas without the danger of freezing, pipes can be put above the surface, allowing for leaks to be rapidly observed.

In an unstable subsurface (Figure 10) a special foundation is required for a transport pipe (pile, buoyant body, etc.). Foundations lead to a greater increase in pipe costs.

Table 5   - Remaining pipe capacity with pipe breakage in a double transport system with segmentation

Number of segments	Number of nodes	Remaining capacity (%)
1	0	50
2	1	63
4	3	75
8	7	85

Figure 9   - Construction of a pipe

Figure 10 - Pipe construction in a peat area (second Bergambacht pipe)

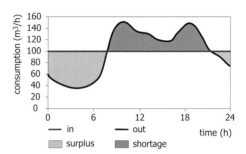

Figure 12 - Storage to overcome difference between consumption (demand) and production (supply)

closed. By reading the water meters in the system, the pipe section in which the leak is located can be found. The right location has to be found by visual inspection, after which repair can take place.

4. Storage

4.1 Required volume

General storage formula
Storage reservoirs level the fluctuations of demand. During large demands the reservoir makes up the difference between demand and supply (Figure 12).

The general formula for a reservoir is:

In = Out - ΔStorage

in which:

Out	= outgoing discharge	(m^3/s)
In	= entering discharge	(m^3/s)
ΔStorage	= increase of storage	(m^3/s)

The increase in storage is the increase of volume in the storage per unit of time.

Accessories
Pipe systems are provided with various accessories, such as flow meters, valves for segmentation, drain and flush appliances for maintenance, manholes for personnel entrance, ventilation facilities to prevent air accumulation, and facilities for cathodic protection of steel pipes.

Pipe leaks are expensive due to water loss and due to the damage that can be done by the outflowing water to property of third parties.
Directly after construction, the takeover-test takes place and the leakage under full operation pressure shall not be larger than about 1/2,000 of the pipe volume per 24 hours.
During operation, the discharge at the beginning and at the end of the pipe is continuously measured (Figure 11) and the difference calculated. If this difference is larger than 1 to 5 m^3 per 15 minutes, then an alarm goes off and all valves are

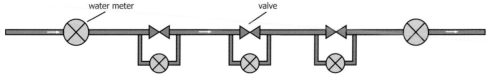

Figure 11 - Pipe leakage monitoring for a transport main

The storage formula is also often used for a fixed time period (e.g., hour or day); the formula is transferred into a pure volume balance. This is the basis for the balance-method.

Balance method

Table 6 shows the calculation for the volume of the storage using the balance method for the consumption pattern on a normal day.

The consumption pattern during 24 hours is the outgoing flow, the production is the entering flow. The production is constant and is assumed equal to the daily demand (2,400 m³). For every hour, the increase in storage can be calculated.

The required storage can be determined by totaling the storage decrease from the moment the outflow equals the inflow (hour 8) until the inflow equals the outflow again (hour 22). During this period the total outflow of the storage was 430 m³, or 18% of the daily consumption.

In practice, on extreme days, higher peak consumption will occur with a relatively larger demand for storage. Therefore, most often storage of 25% of the maximum day's consumption is assumed, that is, 6 hours production time. With a maximum day peak factor of 1.41 the required storage equals

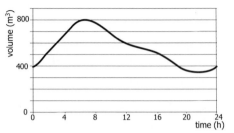

Figure 13 - Fluctuation of the water volume in a storage reservoir

850 m³ (1.41·0.25·2,400). Then, the available storage on the average day is 35% (1.41·25%).

Management of the storage reservoir should be such that the reservoir will never completely fill up (overflow), and certainly not completely empty (shortage of supply). Such situations can only be avoided in small storages by adjusting or turning off the production, as far as this is possible. Fluctuations in the production, however, usually lead to poorer water quality. Therefore, it can be said that a large-sized storage is not an unnecessary luxury.

Figure 13 shows the development in the volume of the storage. The volume in the storage reservoir fluctuates around 50%, for a maximum stability of production. The minimum storage volume is present in the evening, the maximum storage volume in the early morning. The storage reservoir fills at night and empties during the day and evening.

The used storage shown in Figure 12 equals the "area above the production line," and the refilling of the reservoir, the "area below the production line." The surfaces are equal with a "closed balance."

Summation method

The previous method is less suitable for computer calculations, because the moment at which outflow equals inflow is used. In the summation method, the sum increase depicted in Table 6 is outlined in time, together with the summation of the production, as illustrated in Figure 14, for the same consumption pattern as in Figure 12.

The required storage can be calculated from the largest difference between both parameters. In

Table 6 - Water consumption (out) and water production (in) for a storage reservoir

Period	Out (m³)	In (m³)	Increase (m³)	Sum increase (m³)
1	60	100	40	
2	45	100	55	
3	40	100	60	
4	35	100	65	
5	35	100	65	
6	40	100	60	
7	50	100	50	
8	100	100	0	0
9	135	100	-35	-35
10	150	100	-50	-85
11	145	100	-45	-130
12	135	100	-35	-165
13	130	100	-30	-195
14	130	100	-30	-225
15	120	100	-20	-245
16	115	100	-15	-260
17	120	100	-20	-280
18	140	100	-40	-320
19	150	100	-50	-370
20	140	100	-40	-410
21	120	100	-20	-430
22	100	100	0	-430
23	90	100	10	-420
24	75	100	25	-395
Total	2,400	2,400		

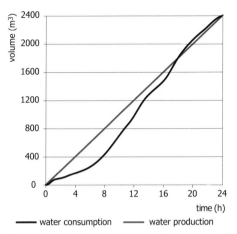

— water consumption   — water production

Figure 14 - Example of a calculation of the storage volume based on the summation method

Figure 14 this is -395 m³ at 8.00h and 35 m³ at 21.00h. The largest difference is, therefore, 430 m³.

Minimum storage
Besides the required storage for levelling, also a minimum storage volume is used for unexpected operation disturbances.

The interim period is based on the response time of the disturbance that has to be determined. Typical disturbances are caused by failures of electricity and, because of that, cause a complete disturbance of the treatment process. Also, a failure in the process operation can result in such process disturbances. Critical processes are flocculation (sedimentation of flocs when flocculators fail) and floc blanket sedimentation (sedimentation of the floc blanket). For these processes it takes some time before sufficient treatment results are achieved again, and such process disturbances cannot always be compensated in trailing treatment processes.

For process disturbances it takes, for example, an hour at minimum before an unmanned installation is back in operation, by hand, after a failure. The minimum storage must deliver the production losses during the disturbance.

4.2   Design aspects

Drinking water reservoirs
Storage reservoirs for drinking water have to comply with a large number of requirements because of the quality aspects of drinking water. First of all, the reservoirs have to be well sealed, not only to protect from weather influences, but also from humans, animals and insects. However, complete hermetical sealing is not possible because a reservoir has to "breathe." While a reservoir is filling, air has to leave, and during emptying, air will have to enter. Therefore, filtration of this air is necessary.

Drinking water should not remain in a reservoir for too long, because the quality could decline due to bacteriological growth.

Therefore, a drinking water reservoir should have good circulation, and dead corners should be avoided. Because of bacteriological growth, small amounts of "dead water" can lead to undesirable amounts of "life" in drinking water.

In practice large reservoirs will never be completely water tight. Due to the settlling and aging of the construction material, small cracks are unavoidable. Anticipating such a "leakage," drinking water reservoirs are situated in such a way that the lowest water level in the reservoir is above the highest groundwater level. This will prevent "contaminated groundwater" from entering the drinking water reservoir.

Drinking water reservoirs are equipped with an emergency overflow that prevents the water from touching the roof of the reservoir. Its purposes are twofold: to prevent the decline of the water quality, and to avoid damage to the roof construction due to unexpected upward forces.

Drinking water reservoirs may not completely empty during the operation period, because sediment will resuspend from the bottom. In practice, a minimum water level of circa 0.5 m is used.

Due to the requirements for the maximum and minimum water levels, the net available volume of a reservoir is considerably smaller than the gross construction volume for low reservoirs.

Figure 15 - Drinking water reservoir in maintenance

A reservoir has to be inspected and cleaned regularly (Figure 15), and an adequate access for humans and material is also necessary. After cleaning a reservoir, the rinse water has to be drained well. The reservoir bottom is constructed at a slope, possibly equipped with collection gullies. After maintenance and inspection, the reservoirs have to be thoroughly disinfected. Over several days, water with a high chloride content is stored in the reservoir. It is subsequently rinsed out, and the water is checked to determine whether it is bacteriologically reliable again.

Supplemental reservoirs

Supplemental reservoirs are special features of drinking water reservoirs. These reservoirs are located in the middle or at the boundary of a distribution area. They are filled during the night from the distribution network, and during the day the water is used for extra supply. During the filling of the reservoir, the distribution pressure is reduced through heavy regulation valves or very small filling pipes. During the day distribution pumps supply the uptaken water back to the network to supplement the more-or-less constant drinking water flow originating from a production or distribution location.

Supplemental reservoirs make sure that the distribution network between the production location and the nearby demand center is evenly loaded. On the other hand, the supplemental reservoirs

cause a to-and-fro flow pattern in the distribution network, with a possible decline in quality.

These reservoirs are designed for a demand center (small city or village) that is located a great distance from the rest of the distribution area.

Because of the relatively high costs for management and maintenance, supplemental reservoirs are built less and less. More often the choice is made for extra pipes in the distribution network, for which the security of supply benefits.

High reservoirs

In hilly areas high reservoirs are sometimes employed. These are reservoirs for the levelling of production, which can operate as very large water towers because of their high location. The reservoirs are built on top of a hill, and it is therefore less expensive to contain large volumes. The reservoirs are fed through the distribution network.

5. Distribution

5.1 Design

Branched versus looped

The distribution systems transport water from the distribution pumps to the consumers. From the distribution pumps, large pipes run to the differ-

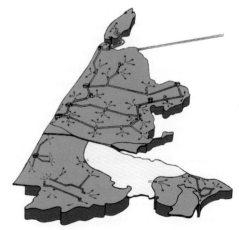

Figure 16 - Main elements of distribution in Noord-Holland (PWN)

ent consumption centers in the distribution area (Figure 16). Nearing the dead-ends of the distribution area, these pipes become smaller and smaller because fewer consumers have to be supplied.

The nature of a distribution area is a branched system (single pipe becoming smaller); however, a branched system is vulnerable. During a disturbance (pipe fracture, changes, maintenance, etc.), the customers will receive no water. Therefore, because of security of supply, there will need to be an alternative route from which an area can be supplied with drinking water. Such a distribution network is called a looped system.

Calculations of distribution pipes

Calculations of distribution pipes are complex because of their looped structure, so computer programs are used. These programs use network algorithms in which pipes are schematized to one-dimensional connections and the demand is assumed to be concentrated in a node of pipes.

The pipe characteristics are input for each pipe (diameter, length, local loss coefficient, friction coefficient, etc.). For every node the altitude and demand are established.

Pipe calculations also determine the pressure in the nodes for a chosen demand moment using the peak factor. By calculating with different peak factors, a representation is derived for the different operational situations in the network.

When the outcomes are undesirable, the calculations are repeated with adjusted configurations. Finally, a suitable pipe configuration is chosen (based on costs, residence time of the water in the network, avoiding to-and-fro water flows in the network, etc.).

The principle of such a computer calculation can be shown using a simple pipe network configuration in a residential district, as illustrated in Figure 17. The inhabitants live near nodes A through F, the district is fed from node G.

For every node, the number of connected inhabitants is given. A consumption of 20 l/p/h on a maximum hour of a maximum day is assumed.

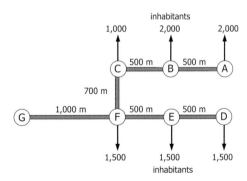

Figure 17 - Branched distribution network in a residential area with node loading in number of inhabitants

With this, the load for every pipe section with inhabitants can be determined (1,000 inhabitants consume 5.56 l/s), as well as the pressure drop for the considered pipe. To transform a branched pipe network to a looped network, pipes are constructed between A and D, and between G and C, which results in a smaller pressure drop in the network.

To decrease the pressure drop further, extra pipes can be constructed in the residence district (e.g., between E and B or between B and F). For all options, cost calculations are made for an optimal decision.

Security of supply

Drinking water production plants and distribution networks are designed in such a way that a minimum supply capacity is available even with serious disturbances. A criterion for this supply capacity could be that, only on a limited number of days per year (or hours per year), the complete demand cannot be met. In Figure 18 it can be seen that for the concerned distribution area, a peak factor of 1.1 for 20% of the days is exceeded (73 days per year). Such a peak factor requires a minimum remaining capacity of 78% of the maximum demand in the concerned year (1.1/1.41). The Dutch drinking water companies generally work with the view that, when a critical part of the drinking water infrastructure fails, no less than 75% of the maximum day should be able to be supplied.

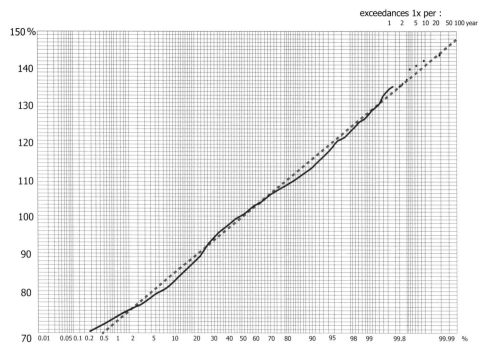

Figure 18 - Determination of design peak factor based on statistical data

Because of the available remaining capacity in a distribution network, for example the increase in demand, the real available remaining capacity is actually higher.

For security of supply, analyses can also be conducted concerning the amount of water that can still be delivered on a maximum day (calculated once per 10 years). It is assumed that with a pressure below 20 m the supply decreases per consumption point.

5.2 Pressure

Minimum and maximum pressures

The Dutch Water Supply Act mandates the following as a requirement for a distribution network:
"The owner of a water supply company should take care that the supply of decent tap water is guaranteed to the consumers in his distribution area in such amounts and with such a pressure as the interest in public health requires." This requirement is not defined further.

The Dutch drinking water companies have made this a concrete requirement for a minimum pressure at the tap, which also, implicitly, means at a sufficient amount.

The recommendation of VEWIN 1995 claims:
"The effective pressure in all consumers' taps, up to a height of 10 m above surface level, should be at minimum 100 kPa."

For the design of a distribution system, a minimum pressure in the streets of circa 25 mwc above surface level can be used, meaning an available pressure drop of circa 5 mwc between the street and the tap.

In flat, urban areas this minimum pressure is relatively simple to realize because the distances are not very large and there are no height differences. With a gradient of 2 m/km and a maximum distance of 5 km, the maximum pressure near the distribution pumps will be 35 mwc above surface level (25 + 5 · 2). During low demand there is almost no gradient and the pressure is almost 25 mwc everywhere. Near the distribution pumps the

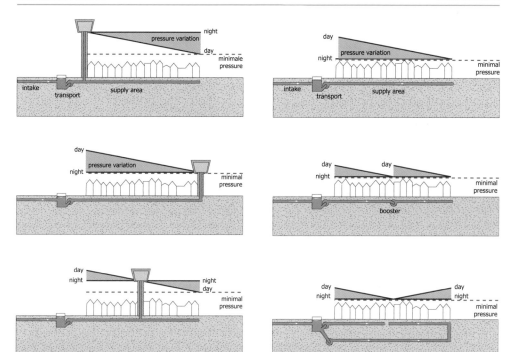

Figure 19 - Limitation of pressure fluctuation in a distribution network

pressure fluctuation is, therefore, 10 mwc (35 - 25), considered a very acceptable fluctuation.

In a flat, rural area the maximum pressure near the distribution pumps is much higher. With the same gradient and a distribution distance of 25 km, the maximum pressure is 75 mwc (25 + 25 · 2), and the maximum pressure fluctuation is 50 mwc (75 - 25). Not only are the rural consumers near the distribution pumps regularly confronted with very high pressures, but the differences over 24 hours will be considerable. This will make the consumption of water unsatisfactory, and the regulation valves in the sanitary installations heavily loaded.

Figure 19 shows that with a booster, or adjusted pipe configurations, the pressure fluctuations can be reduced.

Pressure zones

In hilly areas high pressures will occur at the lowest elevations.

Therefore, in areas with variable topography, pressure zones are used. These zones are classified based on their own height. Each zone has a specific pressure.

Figure 20 illustrates that pressure zones can also be attractive because of energy savings.

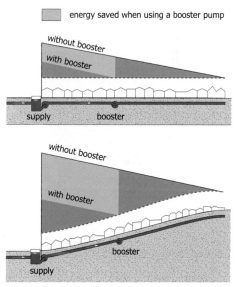

Figure 20 - Pressure zones with boosters and energy saving for different sloping terrains

Distribution pumps

Distribution pumps (Figure 21) supply the desired water pressure in the distribution network. In principle, the pumps make sure that, at dead-ends of the distribution network, a minimum desired pressure is maintained. A higher pressure means unnecessary energy losses.

The required pressure at the distribution pumps is determined using the pipe characteristics of a distribution network. This is the quadratic relationship between pressure and discharge, as a result of flow resistance, as shown in Figure 22. H_{min} is the minimum desired pressure (which is equal in the network to $Q = 0$, so the same applies at the distribution pumps as at the dead-ends) and H_s is the flow resistance.

The lowest pressure is often 25 mwc, the highest pressure can be 65 mwc for rural areas.

The discharge range of the distribution pumps is very large. The smallest discharge has a peak factor of circa 0.1 (a day factor of 0.7 and an hour factor at night of 0.15); the largest discharge has a peak factor of circa 3.0 (a day factor of 1.5 and an hour

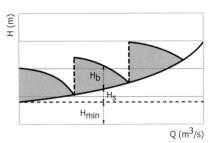

Figure 22 - Pipe characteristics of a distribution system and Q-H curves for distribution pumps

factor during garden watering of 2.0). This results in a relationship between the minimum discharge and the maximum discharge at a factor of 30.

The combination of discharge reach and pressure reach makes the application of more distribution pumps necessary. The number of pumps is initially determined by the maximum working area of the different pumps and is further determined by an optimization, in which the extra investment costs for more pumps is weighed against the savings in energy costs. This is illustrated in Figure 22, in which H_b is the unnecessary consumed energy at a certain water demand and with the pumps running a fixed rotation speed (fixed Q-H curve). With a decrease in the number of revolutions, a lower Q-H line is obtained with a lower distribution pressure and lower energy costs.

In practice, often 4 to 6 distribution pumps are employed (Figure 23) including a separate night pump, because there are many hours during which a relatively small discharge has to be pumped with a low pumping height (every 24 hours, about 7 hour).

Figure 21 - Distribution pumps with noise reduction

Figure 23 - Distribution pumping station

The total installed pumping capacity should supply the maximum discharge, for which the highest pressure is also needed. Quite significant, however, is that this total pumping capacity will almost never be needed.

Water towers

Water towers were used in the past to create an even pressure in the distribution network. At a sudden increase in demand, extra water comes from the water tower, and at sudden decrease, the remainder goes to the tower. The water tower also functions to limit pressure waves as a result of water hammer.

Nowadays, the function of a water tower has been replaced by speed-regulated pumping installations with pressure vessels supplied with sufficient spare pumps and fast-starting emergency power facilities.

Water towers only supplied the water shortfall between demand and supply. The in- and outflow of a water tower flows through the same pipe, which has a limited diameter. Most water towers had a height of 30 to 45 m and had a variation in water levels between 5 to 10 m.

The diameter of the water reservoir in the tower depended on the desired volume; this is why water towers differ more in thickness than in height.

The volume of most water towers varies between 200 and 800 m³, and a 10 - 30 minute failure of the distribution pumps during the day could be covered and occasional peaks could be taken care of, like during firefighting and toilet flushing during half-time of TV soccer games.

5.3   Facilities

Fire extinguishing facilities

Drinking water networks are also often used for firefighting in urban areas. Fire hydrants are located at regular intervals in the pipe network. They have a very high water consumption (25 l/s = 90 m³/h), which requires that the drinking water network pipes have a much larger diameter than necessary for the supply of drinking water. Due to the negative aspects (long residence time of drinking water in

the pipe, danger of contamination, etc.), the use of the drinking water network for firefighting is more and more often a subject of discussion.

Accessories

Distribution networks have a large number of accessories, like valves, connections, service-connections, flushing facilities, fire hydrants, etc. The valves in the network are needed to limit the area of influence during a disturbance or maintenance.

In pipes, sedimentation of dirt particles can occur. To remove these, the pipe network is regularly flushed and high flow velocities carry the dirt along.

Service connections

As a part of the distribution network, every street with buildings has a distribution pipe. The diameter of these pipes varies mostly between 50 and 150 mm.

Houses are connected to these pipes through so-called "service connections." These connections consist, in general, of a hot tap from the distribution pipe and a pipe that connects the distribution pipe to the drinking water installation, including the water meter and all the other installed equipment, like the service tap, main tap, non-return valve, flow limiter, etc. A standard house connection (single-family dwelling) has a diameter of 20 mm, and a water meter with a capacity of 1.5 m³/h. Installing a service connection on a pipe under pressure is an often-occurring activity within a drinking water company (Figure 24).

Figure 24 - In the world championship "pipe fitting" several methods for pipe connection are used, all originating from different national regulations

Emergency drinking water supply

In our modern society the social interest in drinking water supply is so great that failure to supply has become unacceptable. As discussed before, demands on the quality of the infrastructure and reliability are high. The design must ensure the public that the drinking water supply can continue 24 hours a day and 365 days a year, as well as during the failure of critical parts, such as electricity, part of the production plant, or a large transport pipe.

In addition to this, it is acknowledged that disasters can occur causing a complete facility failure. This could happen during war time or terrorist attacks.

For these extreme situations an emergency drinking water supply is needed. For this drinking water supply, drinking water companies have prepared facilities which can supply the population with a minimum of 3 liters per person per day using water boats, water trucks, mobile treatment installations, mobile pipes and mobile taps. To access the emergency supply, water equipment is available and practice scenarios are role-played (Figure 25). As a matter of fact, the installations are sometimes used by the Dutch army during peace time operations abroad.

Figure 25 - Children practicing with the emergency drinking water supply in Rotterdam

Based on the government's and the drinking water companies' policies and practices, these emergency facilities have never been needed in the Netherlands. Also, extensive measures are taken for the security of the drinking water infrastructure against terrorist attacks.

6. Drinking water installations

Since the Dutch Water Supply Act 2000 came into operation, the responsibility of a water supply company for the supply of drinking water no longer stops at the water meter or at the tap at the end of the service connection.

It is true that the property of both the technical infrastructure and the water ends, but the water supply company must also maintain the drinking water installation in such a state that the water quality is good up through the tap, and the hot water facilities are free of problems, like Legionella.

This responsibility is carried out by obligating the consumers to construct their drinking water installation to conform to NEN1006 (General regulations for drinking water installations (AVWI-2002). This standard roughly includes the requirements for the complete drinking water installation and the background. Table 7 shows the division of NEN1006. The general standard is further described in the very detailed VEWIN Werkbladen 2004. The calculation methods are included, as well as elaborated examples, concrete specifications, etc. The VEWIN Werkbladen are numbered to conform to the accompanying section in NEN1006.

Collective pipe network

Most drinking water installations involve a single-family dwelling. The supply point in the house (directly after the water meter) is the property of the water supply company.

In apartment buildings a collective pipe network runs from a central supply point to the supply points in the apartments. Such a collective pipe network is often designed with a pressure installation consisting of pumps, a water hammer vessel and the accompanying operation installation. These installations are very advanced, so now

Table 7   - Contents NEN1006:2002

Part	Title	General content
1	Objective and basics	Additional regulations, terms and definitions
2	General technical regulations	Pressures, materials, testing, safety, grounding
3	Operational regulations	Division into groups, disconnection and connection possibilities, pipes, connection of appliances
4	Additional regulations for special supplies	Reservoirs, pressure increase installations, hot water installations, firefighting installations, water treatment, secondary water installations
A	Explanation (informative)	Legislative framework, explanation

there are no drinking water reservoirs constructed on top of apartments and high buildings.

Collective pipe networks are also at:
- offices, schools, hospitals, hotels, etc.
- camping sites
- large companies, industrial complexes, etc.

Large installations can be present, consisting of storage reservoirs, pumping installations, pipes, etc. In a number of cases also water treatment installations are present to make the drinking water suitable for a specific application, like desalination for steam kettles, softening for hot flush water, etc.

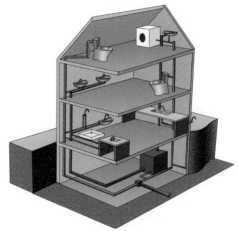

Figure 26 - Drinking water installation with cold and hot water

Further reading

- Introduction to urban water distribution, N. Trifunovic, Unesco-IHE (2006)
- Principles and practices of water supply operations: Water transmission and distribution, AWWA (2003)
- Watertorens in Nederland, H. van der Veen, 010 (1994)
- Stromingsweerstanden in leidingen, L. Huisman, Kiwa (1969)

- www.vewin.nl
- www.kiwa.nl
- www.kvwn.nl
- www.minvrom.nl
- www.watertorens.nl
- www.eber.se

Questions and applications

Transport

1. Determine for a transport pipe:
   a. the velocity in the pipe
   b. the friction factor
   c. the friction losses
   d. the gradient of the pipe
   using the following data:
   discharge = 12,500 m³/h = 3.47 m³/s
   transport distance = 25 km = 25,000 m
   pipe diameter = 1,500 mm = 1.5 m
   wall roughness = 1.0 mm = 1.0 10⁻³ m

2. Calculate the local losses with the information below. Use for this calculation estimations for the coefficients of the losses at bends, valves, non-return valves and in- and outflow.
   discharge = 12,500 m³/h = 3.47 m³/s
   transport distance = 25 km
   pipe diameter = 1,500 mm
   number of bends = 35
   number of valves = 23
   non-return valve = 1
   in- and outflow = 1

3. Calculate for a transport pipe the:
   a. required power
   b. energy consumption
   c. pumped amounts
   d. specific consumption
   e. energy costs
   f. specific costs
   Use the following data:
   discharge = 12,500 m³/h = 3.47 m³/s
   pumping height = 58.7 + 5.5 = 64.2 m
   efficiency = 0.75 · 0.9 = 0.68
   density of water = 1,000 kg/m³
   operation time = 365 days per year
   energy costs = € 0.08/kWh

Storage

1. A water supply company produces 150 m³ per hour. The water consumption is given in the table below. Determine with the balance method and the summation method the required volume of the storage reservoir.

Time	Consumption	Time	Consumption	Time	Consumption
1	90	9	205	17	180
2	65	10	225	18	210
3	60	11	215	19	225
4	50	12	205	20	210
5	55	13	195	21	180
6	60	14	195	22	150
7	75	15	180	23	135
8	150	16	170	24	115

Distribution

1. Define the difference between a branched and a looped distribution system.

2. Indicate which design aspects are of importance for distribution systems.

Applications

1. Design a new infiltration transport system for the route from Brakel to Bergambacht for a discharge of 74 million m³/year.
   Due to supply requirements/rules/demands (reliability), 2 pipes with the same diameter will be constructed.
   The friction losses for one pipe for the route of 30 km are 160 mwc when using a pipe with 1,000 mm diameter.
   Calculate the optimal diameter (rounded to 100 mm) and the accompanying friction losses. Local losses do not have to be taken into account for these calculations.

Answers

Transport

1. a. velocity in the pipe =

$$\frac{3.47}{0.25 \cdot \pi \cdot 1.5^2} = 1.96 \text{ m/s}$$

   b. $Re = \dfrac{v \cdot d}{\nu} = \dfrac{1.96 \cdot 1.5}{1.0 \cdot 10^{-6}} = 2.95 \cdot 10^6$

$$\frac{1}{\sqrt{\lambda}} = -2\log\left(\frac{k}{3.7 \cdot D} + \frac{2.51}{Re\sqrt{\lambda}}\right)$$

   iterative: $\lambda = 0.0180$
   (without Re term: $\lambda = 0.0178$)

   c. $\Delta H_F = \lambda \cdot \dfrac{L}{D} \cdot \dfrac{v^2}{2 \cdot g} =$

$$0.0180 \cdot \frac{25,000}{1.5} \cdot \frac{1.96^2}{2 \cdot 9.81} = 58.7 \text{ m}$$

   d. gradient = $\Delta H / L = 58.7 / 25 = 2.3$ m/km

2. number of bends   = 35   ($\xi = 0.5$ per bend)
   number of valves   = 23   ($\xi = 0.3$ per valve)
   non-return valve   = 1   ($\xi = 2.5$)
   in- and outflow   = 1   ($\xi = 1.5$ in total)

   velocity in the pipe =
   $$\frac{12,500/3,600}{0.25 \cdot \pi \cdot 1.5^2} = 1.96 \text{ m/s}$$

   $\Delta H_L = ((35 \cdot 0.5) + (23 \cdot 0.3) + 2.5 + 1.5) \cdot$
   $$\frac{1.96^2}{2 \cdot 9.81} = 28.4 \cdot \frac{1.96^2}{2 \cdot 9.81} = 5.5 \text{ m}$$

3. a. required power =
      $3.47 \cdot 64.2 \cdot 1,000 \cdot 9.81/0.68 = 3,210$ kW
   b. energy consumption =
      $3,210 \cdot 365 \cdot 24 = 28.1$ million kWh/y
   c. pumped amounts =
      $12,500 \cdot 365 \cdot 24 = 109.5$ million m³/y
   d. specific consumption =
      $28.1 / 109.5 = 0.26$ kWh per m³
   e. energy costs =
      $28.1 \cdot € 0.08 = € 2.25$ million per year
   f. specific costs =
      $0.26 \cdot € 0.08 = € 0.021$ per m³

Storage

1. Calculation with the table below

	Out	In	Balance method		Summation method		
			Increase	Decrease	Sum-out	Sum-in	Sum shortage
1	90	150	60		90	150	60
2	65	150	85		155	300	145
3	60	150	90		215	450	235
4	50	150	100		265	600	335
5	55	150	95		320	750	430
6	60	150	90		380	900	520
7	75	150	75		455	1,050	595
8	150	150	0	0	605	1,200	595
9	205	150	-55	-55	810	1,350	540
10	225	150	-75	-130	1,035	1,500	465
11	215	150	-65	-195	1,250	1,650	400
12	205	150	-55	-250	1,455	1,800	345
13	195	150	-45	-295	1,650	1,950	300
14	195	150	-45	-340	1,845	2,100	255
15	180	150	-30	-370	2,025	2,250	225
16	170	150	-20	-390	2,195	2,400	205
17	180	150	-30	-420	2,375	2,550	175
18	210	150	-60	-480	2,585	2,700	115
19	225	150	-75	-555	2,810	2,850	40
20	210	150	-60	-615	3,020	3,000	-20
21	180	150	-30	-645	3,200	3,150	-50
22	150	150	0	-645	3,350	3,300	-50
23	135	150	15		3,485	3,450	-35
24	115	150	35		3,600	3,600	0
total	3,600	3,600	0				

Balance method:
Required storage is 645 m³ (maximum shortage)

Summation method:
Required storage is 595 - (-50) = 645 m³ (difference extremes sum-shortage)

Distribution

1. In a branched distribution system there is no alternative route near the ends of the network, in a looped system there is.

2. - Minimum and maximum pressure
   - Pressure zones
   - Fire extinguisher facilities
   - Accessories
   - Distribution pumps

Applications

1. 2 pipes with 74 million m³/year, so for one pipe, 37 million m³/year

The optimal velocity in a transport pipe is: 0.88 m/s

The discharge through the pipe is:

$Q = 37{,}000{,}000/365/24/60/60 = 1.173$ m³/s

Then the cross-section of the pipe is:

$A = 1.173/0.88 = 1.333$ m²

The optimal diameter is:

$D = \sqrt{(1.333/(0.25 \cdot \pi))} = 1.3029$ m = 1,300 mm.

For friction losses use:

$$\Delta H_F = \lambda \cdot (8 \cdot L \cdot Q^2)/(g \cdot \pi^2 \cdot D^5)$$

That is:

$$\Delta H_F = \alpha \cdot Q^2/D^5$$

At a discharge of 1.173 m³/s and a diameter of 1,000 m the friction losses are 160 mwc thus:

$$\alpha = 160/(1.173^2/1.0^5) = 116.285$$

At an optimal diameter of 1,300 mm, then the friction losses are:

$$\Delta H_F = 116.285 \cdot (1.173^2/1.3^5) = 43 \text{ m}.$$

ADDENDUM

Drinking water and the Netherlands

Drinking water and Delft

Acknowledgement

Register

Drinking water and the Netherlands

Student questions

All our foreign students are putting the same question on the table:
"How do we benefit from studying the Dutch water supply?"
We are used to giving them the following answer:
"The Netherlands has developed the most highly respected drinking water infrastructure in the world, so you not only learn the most sophisticated and modern techniques, but also you learn from 150 years of experiences, from the successes and, especially, from the failures on the road to that high ranking."

150 years of history
Focus on public health
100% coverage
Regional supply areas
Private companies
Publicly owned
Cooperation in research

Environmental watchdog
Protected sources
Safe groundwater
Artificial groundwater
Multiple barriers

No chlorine
No hard water
No fluoride
No pesticides
No home filters
No bottled water
No leakage
No wasting water

Most often, they come up with the second question:
"Can you give us, in a few words, what makes this infrastructure so special and worthwhile to study?"
For this we typically come up with the following explanation:
"Between 1853 and 1970 everyone in the Netherlands was connected to a piped water supply system.
"Public health was the leading focus since the early 1900s. It was the motivating factor for establishing public water systems in the country, and for connecting even the most remote houses to the public water system. The concern for public health still dominates the Dutch drinking water culture which is reflected in the technical, institutional and legal policies and regulations.
"With the Water Supply Act of 1957, the many small water supply companies were consolidated into regional public companies. Now, we have 11 drinking water companies, which are fully publicly owned, and the focus is still on public health.
"Nearly the entire present situation can be understood from this focus on public health and the ongoing concern for high quality drinking water. What we can applaud is the extensive cooperation in research, the use of safe groundwater when available, the use of artificial groundwater, the use of surface water with "multiple barriers," water treatment without chlorine, the supply of softened water, the very low leakage in the distribution system, etc.
"The high quality standard of the Dutch public tap water has resulted in a few remarkable developments. Examples of these are the very low sales of bottled water, the effectiveness of water-savings programs (in a country which abounds in water), and the ban on fluoride. All this shows the Dutch citizens' appreciation for their tap water."

This answer makes the students interested in knowing more. Modern students do not blindly accept what their professors tells them, so their next query is:
"Can you show me that all these statements hold true, with facts and figures?"
That is when we take our books and reports and show them the following:

Full coverage took 100 years ...

Piped drinking water in the Netherlands started in 1853 when the Amsterdam water supply system came into operation.

Between 1874 (now in Rotterdam and The Hague) and 1920, piped drinking water became available in all Dutch cities and towns, via municipalities or private water supply companies. By that time some 48% of the population lived in houses connected to a piped drinking water system.

Period	Focus
1853-1920	Cities and towns
1921-1950	Villages
1951-1970	Remote area's

Introduction of piped water systems

before 1899
before 1924
before 1949
before 1970

Coverage of piped water (VEWIN)

Between 1920 (in North Holland) and 1950, regional water companies were established, which provided drinking water to the villages. By that time some 82% of the total population had a house connection.

Between 1950 and 1970, these regional water companies were financially supported by the central government to help cover the cost to connect the houses in remote areas, thus bringing the house connection coverage to 99%.

It should be noted that the Dutch population increased from 3.1 million in 1853 to 13.0 million in 1970. This means that most house connections were made in newly built residential areas.

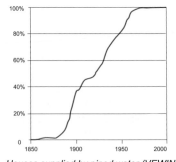

Houses supplied by piped water (VEWIN)

At present all houses are connected, providing drinking water to 16.3 million inhabitants.

... and merging into regional companies took 50 years

The water supply for the cities and towns was locally developed by separate private and municipal companies. In 1910 there were 90 different drinking water companies, about 55% were private and about 45% municipal.

The number of drinking water companies was at its peak in 1938, when 228 (mostly municipal) water companies were active.

In 1957 the Water Supply Act was accepted by the Dutch parliament. One of its major goals was to strengthen the water supply sector by merging the companies into provincial public drinking water companies.

Under this law, the number of water supply companies has decreased to 11 in 2006.

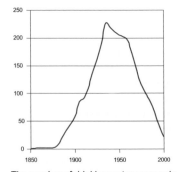

The number of drinking water companies. First locally and small, afterwards merging into a few large companies (VEWIN)

Public health as driving force ...

In a "Report to the King" (1868), it was concluded that a piped water supply was essential for improving public health. It further stated that the central government should enforce the development of municipal and private water supply companies, and should supervise the drinking water quality.

Defeating Cholera required a water supply in the urban areas. To defeat Typhoid, the rural areas also had to be provided with safe drinking water.

Since 1999, Legionellosis has been recognized as an important public health issue related to water systems with elevated temperatures.

During the last 50 years, the environment has become more polluted, requiring additional water quality regulations, as well as more advanced treatment techniques.

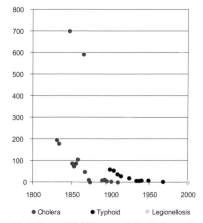

● Cholera   ● Typhoid   ● Legionellosis

Mortality per 100,000 person in the Netherlands by drinking water related diseases (RIVM)

Yearly, the National Institute for Public Health and the Environment ("Rijksinstituut voor Volksgezondheid en Milieuhygiëne – RIVM") reports to the Dutch government on drinking water quality in the Netherlands.

... for publicly owned private companies ...

All but two drinking water companies in the Netherlands are publicly owned private companies. These companies are managed quite autonomously according to business principles, but are controlled by their public shareholders. Contrary to private companies, their shares can only be owned by municipalities and/or provinces ("public companies").

The companies are full-cost recovering without any municipal or governmental subsidies.

The companies operate on a "not for profit" basis, without paying dividends to their shareholders.

The city of Amsterdam's water is supplied by a municipal water company, which functions in a more or less similar way.

The village of Doorn is supplied by a private company.

As part of the European doctrine on privatization, the ownership of drinking water companies was discussed in the late nineties.

In 1999 the Dutch government decided that water services would remain in public hands in view of the important role of the drinking water companies in public health and the environment.

From 225 in 1938 down to 11 water companies in 2006, and still merging (TU Delft)

... with joined efforts in research and public education ...

The shared focus on public health and the absence of commercial competition was, and is, a sound basis for intensive cooperation between the water companies. Moreover, such collaboration is in line with the century-old Dutch tradition of the joined struggle against the water from the sea.

Additionally, the short travel distances in the Netherlands were and are a boon to information exchanges.

In 1899 the Royal Association of Drinking Water Supply in the Netherlands (KVWN) was founded as a multi-disciplinary body of people. It is the oldest association in the field of drinking water supply in the Netherlands, and is still noticeably active (1,400 members).

The KVWN was the birthplace of organizations such as VEWIN, Kiwa, Wateropleidingen, Aqua for All and others.

Koninklijke Vereniging voor Waterleidingbelangen in Nederland

National Institute for Public Health and the Environment

The Netherlands Ministry of Housing, Spatial Planning and the Environment (VROM) is responsible for the Dutch drinking water supply.

VROM uses the National Institute for Public Health and the Environment (RIVM) for its research on health issues, as well as for (independent) drinking water quality control.

VROM and RIVM are working in close cooperation with the drinking water sector.

The Association of Dutch Water Companies (VEWIN) is the association for all drinking water companies in the Netherlands (except the private company of Doorn).

VEWIN is the voice of the water companies, both to the public as well as to the Dutch and European governments. VEWIN employs almost 30 people and has a yearly budget of over € 5 million.

Partner for progress

The water supply companies of the Netherlands founded Kiwa, for quality control of all equipment related to drinking water (pipes, meters, etc.).

In addition, Kiwa Water Research carries out the joint research program as defined by the water companies (€ 6 million per year). In this research, Kiwa works with TU Delft, as well as with international partners including Unesco-IHE, AWWARF, UKWIR, TZW, CRC, Veolia and Ondeo.

... and open information to the public

The Dutch drinking water companies maintain open communication with the public.

All water companies publish annual reports and include technical and financial information. The Waterleidingstatistiek gives the yearly statistics of the water companies (since 1902). RIVM reports yearly on the drinking water quality (since 1992).

The efficiency of the drinking water companies is publicly evaluated with the VEWIN benchmark (every 3 years).

Safe groundwater when available ...

Groundwater is the preferred source for the production of drinking water in the Netherlands.

Groundwater in the Netherlands is free of pathogenic organisms, and therefore usable without disinfection. Moreover, it has a consistent good quality and a constant pleasant temperature.

Groundwater in the Netherlands is abstracted within restricted areas, where land use is regulated. Land in the immediate neighborhood of the abstraction wells is owned by the water companies.

Water from outside the restricted areas will take at least 25-50 years to arrive at the abstraction wells.

These large areas (in total some 1,500 km², 4.4% of the land area in the Netherlands) allow adequate protection and a very long response time in case of a groundwater contamination.

- phreatic groundwater
- confined groundwater
- riverbank water
- infiltrated water
- surface water via storage

At more than 30-40 km from the sea, fresh groundwater is available for drinking water production (RIVM 2004)

Source	Number of locations	Abstraction (million m³)
Groundwater (natural)	192	709
Artificial groundwater (riverbank filtration)	12	61
Artificial groundwater (dune infiltration)	7	214
Surface water (reservoirs)	7	293
Total	218	1,277

Different sources for drinking water production in the Netherlands in 2004 (VEWIN/RIVM 2004)

... or artificial groundwater ...

The available quantity of groundwater is insufficient for the total drinking water needed. Therefore, availability is increased by infiltrating surface water into aquifers along the North Sea coast and major rivers. In this way, surface water is converted into "artificial groundwater," yielding the above mentioned benefits of groundwater (safe, constant, and reliable).

Some 20% of the Dutch drinking water comes from artificial groundwater abstracted in the dunes.

The infiltration of pretreated surface

Infiltration ponds in the dunes along the North Sea coast at The Hague

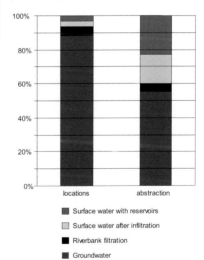

Legend:
- Surface water with reservoirs
- Surface water after infiltration
- Riverbank filtration
- Groundwater

Nearly 80% of the Dutch drinking water comes from groundwater (and artificial groundwater) (VEWIN/RIVM 2004)

water in unconfined aquifers is unique in the world. This system enables more than a 10-fold capacity in the same abstraction area compared to natural groundwater. It provides a natural filter for pathogenic bacteria and viruses, a constant water quality and temperature, and a large storage reservoir to overcome pollution waves in the river.

To a smaller extent, use is made of artificial ground-water along the rivers (riverbank filtration). This system is more widely used in Germany where coarser aquifers are found.

The modern variant is reservoir bank filtration. This combines the simplicity of riverbank filtration with the reservoir advantage of interrupting the intake during contamination waves.

Reservoirbank filtration along a former gravel pit near the Meuse (WML 2004)

... and surface water with "multiple barriers" ...

Around 25% of the drinking water in the Netherlands is produced directly from surface water.

Over the years these systems have had to be transformed from simple treatment systems into more complex schemes in order to cope with the increased pollution of the rivers.

Presently, the rivers Rhine and Meuse have extensive "early warning" systems.

During contamination waves, the intake in the reservoirs is interrupted.

Source protection
Enforcing environmental protection laws in Europe
Early warning along Rhine and Meuse
Large reservoirs to overcome contamination waves

$\downarrow$

Reliable treatment
Self-purification in reservoirs
Double filtration systems
Absorption and oxidation processes
Safe water even during a failure

Multiple barriers in drinking water production from surface water

Three water reservoirs in Biesbosch National Park

The most important reservoir system in the Netherlands is located in the Biesbosch National Park. The three large reservoirs provide for a residence time of several months, and storage for over a month to overcome intake interruptions.

This system provides the source for safe drinking water for over 1.5 million people in Rotterdam and surrounding regions.

... with extended treatment schemes

The treatment of surface water in the Netherlands always includes double filtration systems (dual media filtration and granular activated carbon filtration).

The water is disinfected by ozone, hydrogen peroxide and/or UV-radiation.

The Dutch drinking water is free from pesticides and low in organic material.

The treatment is so extensive that the water is biologically stable. Therefore no chlorine is needed for the distribution.

UV for disinfection at Andijk (PWN 2005)

Safe water without chlorine ...

Chlorine is not used anymore in the Netherlands for disinfection of drinking water. Worldwide, it is still the most used disinfectant by far. In 1974 Jan Rook, a chemist at Rotterdam water supply, discovered that chlorination leads to the formation of trihalomethanes, which have negative health effects.

Immediately after this discovery, the use of chlorine was reduced to the minimum. Existing treatment plants have been modified and, since 2005, chlorine is no longer used for disinfection by any treatment plant.

Alternatively, other disinfection methods have been developed and improved, such as dissolved ozone and UV/H_2O_2-systems.

Chlorine is longer used for disinfection of drinking water in the Netherlands

In order to prevent bacteriological activity in the distribution system, the Dutch water companies produce drinking water with very low content of assimilable organic carbon (AOC), and they operate the distribution systems at minimum residence times.

There has not been any outbreak of illness in the Netherlands related to drinking water since 1950.

... with a very low hardness ...

The Netherlands is (still) the only country in the world where the drinking water quality requirements ask for the supply of soft water (upper limit 2.5 mmol/l or 250 ppm as $CaCO_3$). This ensures water softening at many production locations.

This requirement is based on the obvious advantages of low hardness for public health and the environment, combined with comfort and economics for the consumers.

Some 50% of the drinking water is softened, either by crystallization in pellet reactors or reservoirs, by membrane filtration or by blending hard water with soft water from another location.

▲ ●   < 1 mmol/l
●   1.0 - 2.5 mmol/l
●   > 2.5 mmol/l

Softening is also planned for the few remaining locations with a total hardness above 2.5 mmol/l (RIVM 2004)).

Public health	The environment	Comfort	Economics
Less lead, copper and zinc No risky home filters	Less phosphate Less household waste water Less metals in waste sludge	Better soap while showering Better taste Better appearance (tea) Less scaling in hot water	Savings on washing powder Savings on home-filters Savings on scaling Overall lower costs

The benefits of soft drinking water are recognized in the Dutch drinking water regulations

... and without fluoride ...

Around 1960 the Dutch water supply companies investigated the possibility of dosing fluoride in the drinking water, in order to improve dental health. Many North American and Australian municipalities fluoridate their water supplies. They cite the effectiveness of this practice in reducing tooth decay, believe in the safety of fluoridation, and enjoy its low cost as well. As of 2000, around two-thirds of U.S. citizens have access to fluoridated drinking water. This fluoridation does not have the full acceptance of the general public.

The Dutch public disapproved the dosing of fluoride in drinking water in 1974. Most European countries also rejected fluoridation.
The main reason for opposition against the fluoridation of drinking water was that it was seen as "medicine" being put in the drinking water by the government.

Dutch people rejected the use of fluoride in drinking water

Caries is prevented in the Netherlands by the use of toothpaste containing fluoride and well developed dental care, which is fully sponsored for children.

... prevents the use of home filter ...

Home filters are more or less standard practice in kitchens and houses in North America and Australia.

Because of the very good quality of the Dutch drinking water, home filters are nearly completely absent in the Netherlands.
The use of home filters is considered uneconomical for consumers, and also has drawbacks on public health and the environment.

For the Dutch drinking water industry, home filters are thought to be a solution for insufficient treatment or in cases where supplying safe drinking water is technically and economically not feasible.

Dutch people drink water straight from the tap

... and results in a very low use of bottled water

Bottled water is used to a large extent in other European countries, in the United States and in Australia.

The public's awareness of the good quality of drinking water in the Netherlands can also been seen in the very low consumption of bottled water.
Bottled water is considered expensive and unfriendly for the environment.

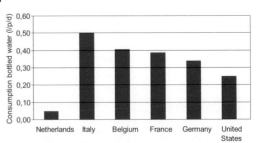

Consumption of bottled water (Bottled water reporter 2005/ VEWIN 2006)

No leakage ...

The leakage in the distribution system of the Dutch water supply companies is very low.

In part, this is achieved by the use of high quality materials (Kiwa certificated) and careful supervision during construction and repair. Also, prompt response to any reported incident, and timely replacement of old mains contributes to this figure.

In the fully metered Dutch drinking water systems, the non-revenue water is measured as 4.6% of the input.

From this figure, the leakage, or "real losses" as reported in many other counties is estimated as some 2.5%, as part of the non-revenue water is used for flushing the distribution mains and for fire-fighting.

Illegal tapping is nearly absent.

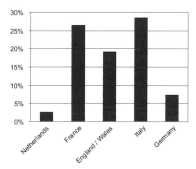

Lowest leakage in the world (DGW 2006, VEWIN 2004).

... reliable supply systems ...

The Dutch water supply companies aim at an uninterrupted supply for their customers, 24 hours a day, 7 days a week. In practice, this goal can not completely be reached, partly because of planned maintenance in the distribution system (flushing a.o.) and partly due to unplanned breakdowns.

The mean uptime of the Dutch water supply companies is 99.9932%. This means that in a year, each connection is without adequate supply for 36 minutes per year (substandard supply minutes), on average.

Some 40% of these interruptions are planned, for which the customers have been informed in advance.

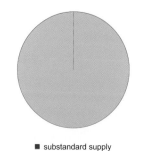

■ substandard supply
▨ normal supply

Drinking water supply with 99,9932% uptime (TU Delft 2005)

... and impressive water savings

Households consume some 65% of the total production of the Dutch water supply companies.

In 1970 this consumption amounted to 117 l/p/d (liters per person per day). Due to the increasing use of water-consuming appliances in houses, it was predicted that this consumption would increase to over 200 l/p/d, in the year 2000.

The increase in water consumption was stopped, and it actually decreased, due to the introduction of water-saving equipment, supported by extended public information programs. Important new developments are water-saving toilets, washing machines, dishwashers and showers.

At present, the actual water consumption (124 l/p/d) is nearly the same as it was in 1970, and still decreasing, after reaching its top (140 l/p/d) in 1990.

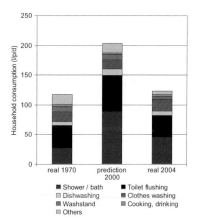

■ Shower / bath   ■ Toilet flushing
▨ Dishwashing   ■ Clothes washing
■ Washstand   ▨ Cooking, drinking
▨ Others

Water saving in households (Vakantiecursus 1973, VEWIN 2004)

International activities of Dutch drinking water sector

The remarkable drinking water standard in the Netherlands has drawn the attention of many foreign countries.

This attention is enhanced by the extensive involvement of the Dutch drinking water sector in international institutes like WHO (RIVM), UNESCO (IHE), UNICEF (IRC) and Worldbank (BNWP), as well as its very active contribution at international research and scientific congresses (Kiwa, TU Delft).

A large part of Dutch international activities on drinking water is included in their foreign aid program. During its Presidency of the European Union, the Netherlands urged the other countries of Western Europe to raise their spending on development aid to the 0.7 percent level of its gross national product, as is done by the Dutch. Britain, France, Germany and Spain, who are now at about 0.4 percent, have adopted an accelerated timetable for reaching 0.7 percent. This means that by 2010, there will be about 42 billion euros more to spend on development aid, including drinking water facilities.

The Netherlands is the only country in the world to have drawn up output targets for water and sanitation. In the past year, contracts have been signed which will provide safe drinking water for 5.5 million people and sanitary services for 0.9 million.

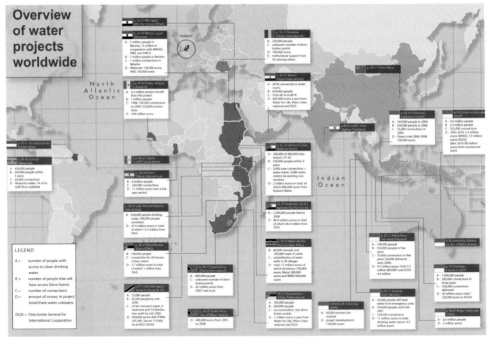

Drinking water projects within the Dutch foreign aid program (VEWIN 2006)

The Dutch drinking water sector is also involved in commercial activities. For years, Dutch consulting engineers have been involved in drinking water projects around the world. Also contractors, as well as equipment and process suppliers, continue to be internationally active. Often, these private companies cooperate with Dutch drinking water companies and research institutes.

The Netherlands Water Partnership is worldwide promoter of the Dutch expertise as it relates to water in the Dutch private and public sectors.

Crown Prince Willem Alexander of the Netherlands is a great ambassador for the Dutch water sector. His job is surely made easier by the strong water sector in his homeland.

Drinking water and Delft

Delft

The city of Delft is the water knowledge city of the Netherlands.

Delft University of Technology (TU Delft) and UNESCO-IHE are technical universities with outstanding reputations and both attract national and international students.

Other internationally well-known water institutes in Delft are WL|Delft Hydraulics, GeoDelft and UNICEF-IRC.

TU Delft

In 1937 the "Faculteit Weg- en Waterbouwkunde der Technische Hogeschool te Delft" (or "Faculty Road and Water Engineering of the Technical University of Delft") started with education about the public drinking water service. The future engineers were educated in the fundamentals of the infrastructure for a drinking water service, under the guidance of Mr. Krul, who was the director of the Dutch Governmental Institute for Drinking Water. In 1947, he became the first professor of drinking water in the Netherlands. At that time the domain was considered more like "art" than "science."

The 1st lecture (1937)

Prof. Krul   Prof. Huisman
(1947-1964)   (1964-1984)

Over the years our understanding and explanations have improved.

Professor Huisman developed the scientific base for drinking water supply and his lecture notes on artificial recharge, sedimentation, rapid sand filtration, and slow sand filtration became international classics, and are still used today.

Huisman's successor in 1984 was Professor Kop, who introduced the environmental aspects of drinking water supply into the curriculum.

Since 1990, the chair of drinking water education has been Professor van Dijk, who modernized the curriculum and has focused on the development of advanced technology to achieve the goal of high quality drinking water.

Moreover, he has developed a close collaboration between TU Delft and the Dutch water industry, including Kiwa, the research institute of the Dutch water companies.

Inauguration of Prof. van Dijk

401

Education

TU Delft offers several possibilities to study water-related topics.

Within the BSc program on civil engineering, students are introduced into hydrology and water management.

In the MSc program, students can choose specialized pro-

The faculty of Civil Engineering and Geosciences

grams in hydrology, water management and sanitary engineering. Within sanitary engineering several courses on drinking water infrastructure are taught, including treatment processes, practical applications and design exercises.

Field experiments in Luxembourg

Students include Dutch and international BSc-graduates, but also BEng-graduates and "mid-careers," who are already working at water companies and follow a part-time, intensive course.

The courses are given by academics working at the university and at Kiwa and sometimes by special guest lecturers, like the Dutch Crown Prince Willem-Alexander.

Crown Prince Willem-Alexander during a guest lecture at TU Delft

Students in front of a lecture hall

Laboratory course

Excursion to the infiltration in the dunes

Celebrating the completion of design course

402

Research

The primary focus of the research of TU Delft on drinking water lies on providing high quality drinking water. Challenges for research are:

- optimizing existing infrastructure (through modeling and improved operation)
- developing new technologies (such as membrane filtration, UV-disinfection) to improve water quality and to deal with emerging threats such as Legionella and endocrine disrupting compounds (EDCs)
- developing an integrated approach for the design and operation of the urban water cycle (drinking water, sewerage, wastewater treatment) as a whole, rather than the individual elements.

In March 2006 there were 12 on-going PhD projects on drinking water supply.

The PhD projects are defined in close cooperation with partners from the water sector. All projects are funded by these partners, which ensures that the projects are well-prepared and supported. Experimental research is carried out at drinking water treatment plants and sometimes the results are immediate adopted by the water companies. This provides a highly stimulating environment for the PhD students.

Laboratory research

Pilot plant research

Our researchers regularly organize workshops, congresses and colloquia. The results of the research are published in scientific journals and presented at scientific congresses, and also in Dutch journals.

The research is primarily focused on the Dutch water sector and attuned to the research program of Kiwa, but is carried out in an international framework and in cooperation with foreign universities. The drinking water research group is actively involved in several European research projects. A special project that is being conducted in close collaboration with Kiwa Water Research and UNESCO-IHE is called "Quality for the 21st century." In this project attention is given to:

- identifying new emerging substances (pesticides, pharmaceuticals) in the source waters, and the treatment processes to remove these substances
- defining the biological stability of water to prevent quality deterioration (a.o. Legionella) in the distribution system and in home installations
- maintaining drinking water quality in the distribution system

PhD graduation of Jasper Verberk (2005)

Vakantiecursus

Every year TU Delft organizes a symposium for the Dutch water world.

This symposium is called "Vakantiecursus," which in English would mean something like "Holiday course." This name originates from the early days in 1948 when Professor Krul thought that it was a waste of money not to use the lecture halls during the holiday period, so he organized a course for the alumni of the university, and engineers, scientists and managers of water companies to keep them updated with the latest developments in the field of drinking water.

Full lecture hall (annually, from 1948)

In the corridors and New Year's reception

The content of the Vakantiecursus has changed somewhat over the years: from exchanging technical experiences in drinking water, to science, the environment, policy and management.

Over the years it has developed into the leading Dutch congress on drinking water.

Because the Vakantiecursus is scheduled for the second Friday of the new year, it also serves as a New Year's party for the Dutch water world. This provides an opportunity to review the highs and lows of the year gone by, noting that we will learn from our missteps and build on our progress in the year to come.

Biannual Gijs Oskam Award for best MSc-thesis

Prof. van Dijk during his annual "state of the union"

Every year over 400 water professionals take part in the Vakantiecursus to listen to presentations by national and international experts, such as Don Bursill (CRC WQ&T, Australia), Wolfgang Kuhn (TZW, Germany), Jim Manwaring (AWWARF, USA) and Fred Hauchmann (EPA, USA).

Fast coffee served by students

Learning and laughing combined

Acknowledgement

Background

The introduction of the Bachelor/Master structure in 2002 to synchronize the educational structures within all European universities has forced the Faculty of Civil Engineering of TU Delft to modify its curriculum. The Bachelor's basic course is designed to give a broad overview. Since drinking water practices vary greatly, even within western countries, the faculty decided to use the Dutch experiences as an example. Understanding this well-developed and successful framework makes it easier for students to study situations found in other countries and cultures.

Additionally, it was decided to provide the students with the theoretical principles of modern drinking water supply and also show them the designed solutions in actual practice.

Support

The compiling of these course modules was preceded by a long history of involvement of many people, which also parallels the history of the drinking water education program at TU Delft.

The experiences and perspectives of the Dutch drinking water sector have been extensively used for the preparation of this book. VEWIN, Kiwa and the Dutch drinking water companies have generously provided pictures and other illustrative materials. Material from DHV-projects has also been used.

In particular, we would like to thank the following companies for their enthusiastic cooperation and readiness to make photographic illustrations available:

- Waterbedrijf Groningen
- Waterleidingmaatschappij Drenthe
- Vitens
- PWN Waterleidingbedrijf Noord-Holland
- Waternet (Amsterdam Water)
- Duinwaterbedrijf Zuid-Holland
- Oasen
- Evides
- Brabant Water
- Waterleiding Maatschappij Limburg
- VEWIN
- Kiwa
- DHV

The Dutch water companies assisted in information and photos

The authors would like to show their gratitude for this uplifting cooperation and advise their readers that the property rights to these pictures lie with the relevant companies. A special word of thanks is due to Kiwa and in particular Ron van Megen for support with the publishing of this manuscript.

This book was originally published in the Dutch language. The overwhelming response from readers has not only resulted in a second, extended edition, but has also led to the publication of this English language text.

We received valuable comments from the following people:

- M. den Blanken (PWN)
- C. Bruggink (Hydron)
- R. Campen (DHV)
- M. Gast (Waternet)
- P. Hesselink (Kiwa)
- J.P. van der Hoek (Waternet)
- K. Hoogsteen (WMD)
- Th. van den Hoven (Kiwa)

- E. Hulshof (WML)
- P. Jonker (DZH)
- P. Kamp (PWN)
- J. Koelink (WGroningen)
- J. Kop (TU Delft)
- H. de Kraa (Evides)
- H. van Lieverloo (Kiwa)
- R. van Megen (Kiwa)

- P. Mense (Oasen)
- M. Mons (Kiwa)
- W. van Paassen (Brabant Water)
- T. Schmitz (VEWIN)
- R. Schuurmans (Waternet)
- G. Vogelesang (Evides)
- F. van der Willigen (WML)
- J. van Winkelen (Vitens)

Production team

With texts, pictures and illustrations there was still no book. Without Adele Sanders (English translation and editing) and Eefje Ooms (layout and composing), we would never have succeeded in processing all these pieces into a professional product.

For the technical realization of the manuscript, we want to thank all the staff and students who helped with its preparation, in particular Michiel van der Meulen (composing), Bertus van Woerden (illustrations), Simon Frans de Vries (illustrations), Paul Korthagen (layout and software support), and Martijn Klootwijk (material collection).

Authors

Peter de Moel (1954) has been working in the drinking water sector since 1979. Within Kiwa Water Research (1979-1980), he published on water chemistry, on coagulation, and on dewatering of drinking water sludge.

Within DHV (1980-2000), he designed water supply facilities for all drinking water companies in the Netherlands, and for organizations in over 20 countries, world-wide. His patents (membrane filtration) are applied in full scale installations.

Since 2000, he works in his own consulting firm and is a part-time lecturer at TU Delft.

Peter de Moel

Jasper Verberk (1970) started working at TU Delft as a lecturer and researcher in 1996.

In 2005 he finished his PhD research on the application of air in membrane filtration.

Presently, he is assistant professor at TU Delft and has a 1.5 year research assignment at the Cooperative Research Centre for Water Quality and Treatment in Adelaide, Australia.

Jasper Verberk

Hans van Dijk (1954) is a water-quality expert with life-long experience in the field of drinking water supply. Since 1990 he has been the lead professor in drinking water supply at TU Delft. In 1991, he was awarded the IWA Maarten Schalenkamp Award for his work on the development of pellet reactors for the softening of drinking water.

Since 2001 Hans van Dijk is also the scientific director for Kiwa Water Research. Presently, Professor van Dijk is chairman of the Department of Water Management at TU Delft, member of the board of the Global Water Research Coalition, chairman of the Dutch Water Tower Foundation and member of the board of Aqua for All.

Hans van Dijk

Register

A

B

C